Transcending Trauma

ROUTLEDGE PSYCHOSOCIAL STRESS SERIES
Charles R. Figley, Ph.D., Series Editor

Editorial Board

Transcending Trauma

Survival, Resilience, and Clinical Implications in Survivor Families

Bea Hollander-Goldfein

Nancy Isserman

Jennifer Goldenberg

Routledge
Taylor & Francis Group
New York   London

This book is part of the Psychosocial Stress Series, edited by Charles R. Figley.

Routledge
Taylor & Francis Group
711 Third Avenue
New York, NY 10017

Routledge
Taylor & Francis Group
27 Church Road
Hove, East Sussex BN3 2FA

© 2012 by Taylor & Francis Group, LLC
Routledge is an imprint of Taylor & Francis Group, an Informa business

Printed in the United States of America on acid-free paper
Version Date: 2011902

International Standard Book Number: 978-0-415-88286-6 (Hardback)

Library of Congress Cataloging-in-Publication Data

Hollander-Goldfein, Bea, 1951-
Transcending trauma : survival, resilience and clinical implications in survivor families / Bea Hollander-Goldfein, Nancy Isserman, and Jennifer Goldenberg.
p. ; cm. -- (Routledge psychosocial stress series ; 40)
Includes bibliographical references and index.
Summary: "The Transcending Trauma Project (TTP), begun in 1991, is a large qualitative research endeavor based on 275 comprehensive life interviews of survivors of the Nazi Holocaust, their children, and their grandchildren. Using this research as a base, Transcending Trauma presents an integrated model of coping and adaptation after trauma that incorporates the best of recent work in the field with the expanded insights offered by Holocaust survivors. In the book's vignettes, interview transcripts, and audio excerpts, survivors of a broad range of traumas will recognize their own challenges, and mental health professionals will gain invaluable insight into the dominant themes of Holocaust survivors' experiences and of trauma survivors' experiences more generally. The study of lives conducted by TTP has illuminated universal aspects of the recovery from trauma, and Transcending Trauma makes a vital contribution to our understanding of how survivors find meaning after traumatic events"--Provided by publisher.
ISBN 978-0-415-88286-6 (hardback : alk. paper)
1. Holocaust survivors--Psychology. 2. Holocaust survivors—Mental health. 3. Victims--Psychology. 4. Psychic trauma. I. Isserman, Nancy, 1951- II. Goldenberg, Jennifer E. III. Title. IV. Series: Routledge psychosocial stress series ; 40.
[DNLM: 1. Holocaust--psychology. 2. Survivors--psychology. 3. Crime Victims--psychology. 4. Family Relations. 5. Qualitative Research. 6. Resilience, Psychological. WM 167]

RC451.4.H62H64 2011
940.53'180922--dc23
2011018667

Visit the Taylor & Francis Web site at
http://www.taylorandfrancis.com

and the Routledge Web site at
http://www.routledgementalhealth.com

Contents

Series Editor's Foreword

We welcome *Transcending Trauma* as the latest addition to the Psychosocial Stress book series. The first book in the series, *Stress Disorders Among Vietnam Veterans*, charted new territory in attracting and guiding researchers and practitioners about a special population. *Transcending Trauma* follows closely in its footsteps.

The challenge with bringing attention to a neglected group of traumatized people is overemphasis on their problems. News accounts, personal experiences represented in news articles and art, and scholarly research often focus on the negative consequences to emphasize the need for services and research attention. Once, for example, we assumed that everyone who endured child trauma, combat, a major disaster, or terrorist attack would have behavioral health problems, and this did help attract increased attention to trauma's effects. However, what emerged was the impression that everyone touched by trauma was unable to function. Now, in the second decade of the 21st century, in part due to the pioneering work in positive psychology, we recognize that not everyone exposed to trauma becomes traumatized, and not all traumatized people remain so forever. Indeed, what we now understand is that there is first a traumatic stress injury (cf. Figley & Nash, 2007) that may or may not lead to depression, posttraumatic stress disorder (PTSD), or some other anxiety disorder.

Transcending Trauma changes the paradigm through which we view Holocaust survivors and their families. The Transcending Trauma Project (TTP) focuses on the protective factors that enabled Holocaust survivors to remain resilient and even thriving despite all the horror they endured. Building on the insights from the TTP, this book brings new understanding and appreciation of the long-term and systemic impacts of trauma—specifically being the target of genocide. Throughout these pages, the survivors interviewed share their stories of horror, fear, sadness, and so many other emotions experienced at the time of their internment and the experiences before and after. Survivor family members' interviews complement and extend what has been learned about the survivors, making an important contribution not only to this project but also to the field in general.

As a result of this effort to understand the mutual impact of family on survivors and vice versa, there is a new and exciting attention to the intergenerational impact of trauma and the emergence of resilience, hope, and thriving. Moreover, the authors were able to identify and provide an extended discussion of the clinical implications of the findings to understanding and helping not only the survivors of genocide and their families but also all traumatized clients. The book also helps to illuminate the process of recovery in survivors and their family members through generous quotations and case studies.

The authors from the beginning were guided by the following hypothesis: *Many Holocaust survivors and their children are high functioning, have adapted to the long-term impacts of their traumatic experiences, and have been able to create new families and productive lives.* The natural question, then, is: How did they do this? What were their prewar lives like, and how did their prewar attitudes inform their ability to cope with trauma? What kinds of stumbling blocks and stepping stones affected their posttrauma adjustments?

Among the important innovations offered in *Transcending Trauma* is the discussion of a paradigm for divided families, based on numerous interviews about the parent–child relationship and detailed study of family functioning among survivor families. Importantly, *Transcending Trauma* also focuses on the intergenerational transmission of trauma and resilience of survivors' children. These children not only heard about their parents' ordeal but also learned a great deal about the strength and courage required to survive and thrive after trauma. This "transformative narrative" had a profound impact on survivors' children, and their exposure to their parents' stories has had multiple and complex consequences.

Transcending Trauma changes the way we think about Holocaust survivors—and, indeed, about the human ability to cope with all manner of traumatic experience. It challenges the simplistic ways of viewing the traumatized as troubled and helpless and helps us understand Holocaust survivors and their families in their transformation toward resilience and thriving. This is a welcome shift, and Drs. Hollander-Goldfein, Isserman, and Goldenberg deserve considerable credit for proving that it has taken place.

Charles R. Figley, PhD
Series Editor
New Orleans

References

Figley, C. R., & Nash, W. P. (Eds.) (2007). *Combat Stress Injury, Theory, Research, and Management.* New York: Routledge Psychosocial Stress Book Series.

Preface and Acknowledgments

No matter what you tell, and no matter how much you tell, you're not telling everything. And there is not one person in the whole world that can put himself in the situation what I was in—what we were in—in the concentration camp.

Survivor

Over 20 years ago, a small group of therapists and social scientists came together to study the impact of the trauma of the Holocaust on survivors. They had reviewed the published literature at that time, which overwhelmingly characterized survivors as victims and damaged individuals who passed on their problems to their children, creating, the research stated, poorly functioning families as a result. Yet, these therapists and social scientists surveyed the world they lived in and saw that this view of survivors was not what they had experienced. In their personal lives, survivors worked, married, and raised children; coped with the aftermath of the war; and rebuilt their lives in often positive and successful ways. As we ask many times throughout this book, how and why did these survivors exhibit resilience and posttraumatic growth after undergoing extreme trauma, including the destruction of their families, communities, and the worlds in which they spent their formative years?

This book is our means of exploring the answers to this question. Yet, we need to note that the Transcending Trauma Project (TTP) has had a profound impact on our own lives as well. We have reflected on how we have absorbed the stories, so often traumatic and full of grief and loss, and the impact they have had on all of us. Over the years, we have developed our own means for absorbing the powerful narratives that we have heard.

We are grateful for the TTP research team, who provided support in the earlier years of the project when frequently the stories from the survivors and their families were almost too painful to hear. All of us developed our own ways of coping with, listening to, and bearing witness to the experiences shared with us. One team member created a ritual after particularly painful interviews; she returned home and lit a memorial candle in remembrance of all those killed in the Holocaust. This simple act helped her to move beyond the pain of witnessing the stories and to return to her everyday life as a wife and mother of young children. Others sought support from team meetings with the other TTP researchers, taking comfort from the healing words of their colleagues.

The words of the survivors have changed all of us on the TTP team and others who engage in research on survivors. As one researcher noted about another group of survivors who faced genocide:

> The Cambodian survivors' stories evoke not only pain and horror in the hearer, but also a compassion that links the speaker to the listener in a bond that is powerful and also inclusive. ... Those of us who are privileged to sit with them can sometimes hear their cry. ... In this cry and hearing a more hopeful vision of our self and our species seems to emerge. (Gerber, 1996, pp. 304–305)

Through our work we have come to admire the people we interviewed who came to a new country after experiencing unbelievable tragedies. Our roles as interviewers and analysts of their stories will, we hope, serve to bear witness to the trauma and losses suffered as well as to the resiliency in rebuilding their lives. In doing so, we have been changed by the narratives that have been told to us by survivors, often struggling to express in words what happened to them and how they felt and still feel even after all these years. We have listened to their stories and those of their family members, read them many times in the transcriptions of the taped interviews, analyzed them, and made them part of our lives. As one of us noted in an earlier article on the impact of the narratives on the interviewer, "They change us, drive us, inspire us—every day. They give a voice to the silenced and will not be still. Neither will they let us be still. They challenge us all to do justice to them, and to do justice—and live justly—in an unjust world" (Goldenberg, 2002, p. 216).

A project of this size, depth, and length involved many individuals who contributed to the birth of this book. First and foremost, we owe a debt of gratitude and thanks to the TTP research team, past and present members, most of whom volunteered their time and labor for years because they felt committed to the need to explore and explain the resilient nature of the survivors and their families. Their friendship and support through the years have enriched our lives. Key members of the team that we want to acknowledge include Nina Albert, Sherry Bowen, Norman Garfield, Mina Gobler, Lyn Groome, Hannah Kliger, Judy Levin, Julie Levitt, Gail Morgenstern, Freema Nichols, Emilie Passow, Mindelle Pierce, Judy Rader, Lucy S. Raizman, Claire Reichlin, Peggy Roth, Juliet Spitzer, Carol Targum, Leila Verman, Neal Welsh, and Ann Weiss. Special thanks go to Judy Levin, who provided careful, close, and insightful readings of the chapters and contributed in significant ways to the analysis of the coping and family chapters of the book. Most important, she helped to keep us on track, particularly in the last stages of the book preparation. We are also deeply thankful to Phil Wachs and Juliet Spitzer, who supported the project in so many ways over the years, and to Dennis Alter, who along with Phil Wachs gave us the opportunity to start this project. Words are inadequate to express how we feel about Phil and Juliet—without them this book would never have happened.

We are appreciative of the support of our families from the beginning, especially our husbands and significant others. We started this project with babies and young children who have, in the intervening years, grown up with us and with the project as an ever-present part of their lives. We are thankful for the encouragement and understanding they have given us.

Finally, we thank the many survivors and their families who gave their time and thought to answering our questions in many hours of interviews. This book is a tribute to your courage and resilience after the horrors of the war years. We are grateful that you have shared your lives with us so that others may learn from your stories how to cope and rebuild after extreme trauma.

Bea Hollander-Goldfein, Nancy Isserman, and Jennifer Goldenberg

References

Gerber, L. (1996). We must hear each other's cry: Lessons from Pol Pot survivors. In C.B. Strozier & M. Flynn (eds.), *Genocide, War and Human Survival*. Lanham, MD, England: Rowman & Littlefield Publishers, Inc., 297–305.

Goldenberg, J. (2002) The impact on the interviewer of Holocaust survivor narratives: Vicarious traumatization or transformation? *Traumatology*, 8(4), 215–231.

Acknowledgments

The Transcending Trauma Project would like to thank its funders for their support.

Funders:

Dennis and Gisela Alter; Charles and Sally Bedzow; Peter Buttenweiser and Terry Marek; Wayne and Helen Diamond; Bea Hollander-Goldfein and Ephraim Goldfein; Henzel Family Foundation; Jack and Ellen Hollander; Julie Levitt; The Arthur and Gail Morgenstern Foundation; Ira and Mindelle Pierce; Allan and Barbara Russkamm Philanthropic Fund; Daniel and Jamie Schwartz; Michael and Constance Solomon; Spitzer-Wachs Foundation; Susquehanna Foundation; Steven and Carol Targum; Michael Weinberg

Donors:

Nina and Billy Albert; Joel and Elaine Gershman Foundation; David Glimcher; Robert Glimcher; Joel Golden; Harold and Marla Kaufman z"l; Allan and Loretta Kiron; Edith Klausner; Phyllis and Theodore Kosloff; Judy and Howard Levin; Geoffrey and Roberta Levy; Millennium Management and Employees Foundation; Suri Rabinovici; Lucy and David Raizman; Monica Rasch; Schwartz Family Foundation; Kenneth Sherrill; Steven Sherrill; The Louis and Bessie Stein Foundation Fund; Mark Taylor and Ilene Wasserman; Arn and Nancy Tellem; The Wilf Family Foundation; Whorton Family (Simmons Foods); Mrs. Sybille Zeldin; Zeldin Family Foundation; Diane and David Zwillenberg.

About the Authors and Contributors

Authors

Bea Hollander-Goldfein, PhD, licensed psychologist and LMFT. Since 1991, Bea Hollander-Goldfein has been the director of the Transcending Trauma Project at the Council for Relationships, a nonprofit outpatient therapy center and postgraduate training center, which is the Division of Couple and Family Studies, Department of Psychiatry and Human Behavior, Jefferson Medical College, Philadelphia, Pennsylvania. Dr. Hollander-Goldfein is the director of the Post Graduate Certificate Program in Marriage and Family Therapy accredited by the AAMFT (American Association for Marriage and Family Therapy), the director of research, and the director of Supervision at the Council for Relationships. She is an instructor and supervisor in the Post Graduate Training Program and a clinical assistant professor at Jefferson Medical College. In addition, she is a senior staff clinician and licensed clinical psychologist specializing in marriage and family therapy. She received her doctorate in psychology from Teachers College, Columbia University, and subsequently she expanded her training to include certification and licensure in marriage and family therapy. Systemic theory has guided her clinical practice and research activities for 30 years. She has presented broadly on the topic of trauma and the importance of an integrated model of coping and adaptation. She has also published in the fields of marriage and family therapy and trauma studies.

Nancy Isserman, PhD, senior research fellow, Council for Relationships. Since 1993, Dr. Isserman has been the codirector of the Transcending Trauma Project, a qualitative research project of 275 Holocaust survivors and three-generation family members on resilience and coping after the war. She also directs the research for Council for Relationship's Center for the Advancement of Relationship Education, where she was the research coordinator of the Philadelphia Healthy Marriage Project, a three-year Community Development Service Grant, to develop a curriculum based on research for the Mayor's Office of Community Services' Fatherhood Initiative Program. Dr. Isserman is also affiliated with the Feinstein Center for American Jewish History, Temple University. She has published reports, articles, and book reviews and edited books on topics relating to the contemporary Jewish experience and healthy marriage/relationships in low-income minority populations and on tolerance in survivors. Dr. Isserman received her PhD from the Graduate Center, City University of New York. Her dissertation, "I Harbor No Hate: Tolerance and Intolerance in Holocaust Survivors," received the 2004–2005 Braham Dissertation Award. She is working on a book examining the issue of forgiveness versus tolerance in three generations of Holocaust survivors.

Jennifer Goldenberg, PhD, LCSW, is a licensed clinical social worker in private practice in Bangor, Maine, specializing in adult female survivors of childhood sexual and physical abuse. She is a senior researcher for the Transcending Trauma Project, having worked with the project since 1991. She teaches human behavior and trauma theory, assessment, and treatment at the School of Social Work, University of Maine. Dr. Goldenberg received her PhD from Bryn Mawr Graduate School of Social Work and Social Research. Her research focuses on the development of resilience theory, and vicarious trauma in clinical workers. She is currently working on a book comparing the long-term differential developmental impacts of genocide on adolescent and child survivors and their coping responses.

Contributors

Sheryl Perlmutter Bowen, PhD, is an associate professor of communication at Villanova University and a research associate on the Transcending Trauma team. She focuses on interpersonal communication, particularly on how identity (e.g., race, class, gender, and religious or ethnic background) is constructed through interaction and how our perceived identities influence how we communicate. Bowen's interest in the Holocaust centers on how individuals talk about their experiences and how hearers interpret those stories. Bowen holds a PhD in communication from the University of Massachusetts and previously did research on HIV/AIDS education and prevention for college students and urban African American youth. At Villanova, she teaches courses on communication and gender, team building, leadership, and small groups, conflict, and health, and has served as director of the Gender and Women's Studies Program.

Hannah Kliger, PhD, is senior adviser to the chancellor and professor of communication and Jewish studies at Pennsylvania State University, Abington College, where she has also been associate dean for Academic Affairs. Dr. Kliger also served as associate dean for Graduate Studies and senior research investigator at the University of Pennsylvania's Annenberg School for Communication and as associate dean for education at MCP Hahnemann University (now Drexel) School of Public Health. From 1985 until 1997, she was a faculty member at the University of Massachusetts, Amherst. A graduate of Barnard College, Dr. Kliger earned her doctorate in communication from the University of Pennsylvania and received her master's degree in clinical social work from Bryn Mawr Graduate School of Social Work and Social Research. Dr. Kliger's publications focus on the communicative practices and communal organizations of minority groups. In addition to her book on ethnic voluntary associations of Jewish immigrants (Indiana University Press, 1992), she has authored numerous articles on communication and culture in immigrant communities. Her current research as a Transcending Trauma Project research associate is with the project at the Council for Relationships, where she also maintains a part-time practice.

Emilie S. Passow, PhD, graduated from the City College of New York magna cum laude with honors as a member of Phi Beta Kappa and a Woodrow Wilson Fellow. Dr. Passow received her master's degree and doctorate in English literature, with honors, from Columbia University. Dr. Passow has taught a wide range of courses in English and American Jewish Literature, medical humanities, biblical narrative, Holocaust testimonies, and Jewish studies in colleges and universities throughout the Philadelphia area, including Haverford, Swarthmore, the University of Pennsylvania, and Thomas Jefferson University. In addition to her position as research associate in the Transcending Trauma Project, Dr. Passow is an associate teaching professor in the Department of English and Philosophy and the Judaic Studies Program at Drexel University, where she also is director of the new Certificate Program in Medical Humanities, sponsored by the College of Arts and Sciences and the Department of English and Philosophy. Dr. Passow lectures widely on the topics she teaches and writes about. She lives in Bala Cynwyd, Pennsylvania.

Lucy S. Raizman, MSW, LCSW, LMFT, is a senior staff therapist working with individuals, couples, and families. She is a licensed clinical social worker and marriage and family therapist, an AAMFT-approved supervisor, and a research associate and interviewer for the Transcending Trauma Project since 1992. She received her MSW from the University of Pittsburgh and completed her postgraduate training at the Council for

Relationships. Areas of professional interest and expertise include certification in attachment-based emotionally focused couple therapy and in sex therapy. She integrates in a mind-body-oriented approach her specialized training and experience in EMDR (eye movement desensitization and reprocessing) and SE (somatic experiencing) for helping individuals recover from trauma and attachment injuries. She also supervises, teaches, trains, and presents on couples and trauma-related therapies.

Juliet I. Spitzer, MSEd (http://www.julietspitzer.com), is director of Inter-Cultural Exchange at the International Center for Contemporary Education, promoting the peaceful management of conflict through cultural understanding and tolerance for religious, ethnic, and racial differences. She is also a research associate and past interviewer for the Transcending Trauma team. She is on the faculty of the Florence Melton Adult Mini-Schools and the Delaware Valley Learning Institute, teaching on a variety of topics in Judaism. Juliet is an international award-winning singer/songwriter and recording artist and the guest cantor at Congregation Beth Israel in Media, Pennsylvania.

PART I

The Transcending Trauma Project

CHAPTER 1

Introduction

The Transcending Trauma Project

JENNIFER GOLDENBERG, NANCY ISSERMAN,
and BEA HOLLANDER-GOLDFEIN

The Transcending Trauma Project (TTP) is a research project dedicated to identifying the coping strategies that have enabled Holocaust survivors to love and to work in the aftermath of the horror they endured. This book, however, is not solely devoted to the Holocaust, although that has been the ostensible focus of our work over many years. In our analysis of survivor interviews,[1] and of the interviews of their family members, we concentrated on understanding the long-term impacts of trauma—specifically genocide. Survivors taught us much about what it was like for them to travel to the abyss and back. Their family members' interviews contributed greatly to our understanding of the process of recovery and the intergenerational impacts of both trauma and resilience.

As we conducted this research into a difficult and painful chapter of our history, we realized that our findings had clinical implications well beyond survivors of genocide—that they could be applied to our own work as mental health professionals with our own traumatized clients. The TTP interviews illuminate the process of recovery in survivors' and their family members' own words. Their strengths and struggles inspire us and motivate us to continue to work to heal suffering and fight injustice—whether it is domestic violence and sexual abuse within individual homes inside our own borders or ongoing ethnic conflicts and genocides in far-flung regions of the globe.

In 1986, the Marriage Council of Philadelphia (now Council for Relationships) convened the first conference on Holocaust survivors that was sponsored by a mental health agency rather than a Jewish or Holocaust organization. Titled "Shattered Promises and Broken Dreams," the conference drew several attendees who were both children of survivors (COS) and mental health practitioners. They realized that the image of the survivor as portrayed in the existing research literature was that of a mostly damaged, traumatized individual, and that the damage had been purported to have been visited on the second generation (COSs or 2Gs). This image in the literature provided neither an accurate representation of their own family members nor of the dynamics of other survivor families within their communities. Damage and negative impacts surely existed. But, what about the resilient aspects of these survivors?

The conference in Philadelphia motivated these COSs, in addition to other mental health professionals and those from related fields, to create a study group to examine the existing literature on Holocaust survivors and their families in more depth. The group confirmed that research prior to the late 1980s had focused almost exclusively on the negative impacts of the Holocaust on survivors, without examining the adaptive, more resilient long-term functioning of these individuals or focusing on the processes of coping, adaptation, and resilience after such extreme trauma as genocide.

Their work led to the development in 1990 of a pilot project that conducted interviews with survivors and their children ($N = 10$). The working hypothesis of the pilot project reflected the original hunch of the study group members: that many Holocaust survivors and their children are high functioning, have adapted to the long-term impacts of their traumatic experiences, and have been able to create new families and productive lives.

After reviewing the results of the pilot study interviews, the group formed the nucleus of a research team comprised of mental health practitioners and researchers from other social science disciplines, such as anthropology, communications, and political science. The team, which called itself the Transcending Trauma Project (TTP), was committed to exploring the gaps they found between how the survivors were portrayed in the trauma and Holocaust studies literatures and the more resilient aspects of survivors' lives as they knew them. The TTP team sought to provide a more complete and balanced, in-depth understanding of survivors and their families: how they coped and adapted after liberation; how they rebuilt their lives and families in a new environment; and how the survivors and their family members themselves understood the process of their long-term adaptation after the Holocaust.

Over several decades, the field of traumatic stress studies has progressed from the almost-exclusive focus on the negative sequelae of traumatic experiences to a multidimensional understanding of the impact of trauma on its victims. With the introduction in 1980 of the diagnosis posttraumatic stress disorder (PTSD), society finally came to terms with the phenomenological reality of the suffering of individuals exposed to extreme life circumstances. This marked a paradigm shift in the field and promoted the investigation of the full range of responses to trauma, including both the negative impacts and the capacity to recover, heal, and rebuild after devastating events. The ongoing work of the TTP has coincided with this shift in focus. In Part 1, we establish the foundation for the TTP through a review of the literatures on Holocaust and trauma studies and provide an explanation of the qualitative methodology we used. Chapter 2, "Resilience After Prolonged Trauma: An Integrated Framework," by Jennifer Goldenberg and Bea Hollander-Goldfein, explores the relevant literature to date and places the research of the TTP within the context of the large bodies of literature that address traumatic stress, coping, adaptation and understanding of resilience.

The grounded theory approach of our qualitative research project prioritized the phenomenological investigation of extreme trauma and its long-term impacts, including the intergenerational transmission of both trauma and resilience. What is, we believe, a contribution to the field is our analysis of survivors' accounts of their prewar and postwar lives and the connections between the two in posttraumatic coping and adaptation. We examined the war years in our analysis, of course—the years of prolonged suffering and multiple losses. However, we recognized that survivors were not tabulae rasae going into the Holocaust; rather, we saw them—as indeed they saw themselves—as people who had lives before the war, children, adolescents, and young adults who had significant attachment figures: relationships with adults who imparted meaningful values they had assimilated. They also carried into the war individual strengths that helped shape them and helped them cope with the long-term impacts of what they endured. Similarly, for those of us who are mental health professionals working with clients who have endured traumatic events, there is a need to recognize that many of these individuals had positive relationships with a caring adult before the trauma, as well as values and strengths developed early on that serve them well in the process of recovery. The clinical implications of linking Holocaust survivors' prewar lives with postwar coping strategies are, we hope, demonstrated in the clinical applications and case studies that are presented throughout this volume.

Also, the inclusion of survivors' family members to this qualitative inquiry added a crucial component to the data we analyzed. By interviewing survivors' spouses, children, and grandchildren, we were better able to understand the intergenerational transmission of the impacts of trauma—both positive and negative. Family members provided "other pieces of the puzzle" to help us more fully comprehend the survivor's experience, as well as "the experience of the survivor" in the eyes of his or her family members.

Our large qualitative data set consists of 275 comprehensive life interviews of survivors of the Nazi Holocaust, their spouses, children, and grandchildren, representing 50 intergenerational survivor families. In Chapter 3, "Making the Unmanageable Manageable: Innovative Tools for Analyzing a Large Qualitative Dataset," Nancy Isserman provides an in-depth discussion of the acquisition of the sample and the process by which these interviews were analyzed and then compared within and across families to identify themes and patterns. Meaningful patterns of functioning in individuals and families revealed multidimensional processes of coping and resilience. The methodology required creative approaches designed specifically for the qualitative analysis of this large dataset that would reveal a continuum of psychological processes related to the impact and recovery of trauma.

Three instruments—the semistructured interview guide, the protocol of analysis, and the synopsis—made it possible to assess the large number of variables found within the expansive life histories. Two processes, the analysis triad and charting, focused the analysis and provided a means by which the researchers could track patterns of emotional, cognitive, and behavioral phenomena. By employing these instruments and processes, the TTP compared data within individual interviews and within the intergenerational families to focus on the study of coping and adaptation after extreme trauma.

Part 2 focuses on the survivors. The chapters in this section explore their prewar lives and provide an examination of the factors that helped or hindered their postwar adjustments.

In Chapter 4, "'The Biggest Star Is Your Mother': Prewar Coping Strategies of 18 Adolescent Survivors," Jennifer Goldenberg discusses the many prewar risk and protective factors revealed in the interviews of survivors who were adolescents during the Holocaust years. These include secure attachments with at least one caring adult in their environments and strong ethical and moral values that they were able to draw on for coping after the war. They also contain messages from parents about the importance of human dignity and integrity and, for those survivors who were raised in religious homes, the importance of faith and Jewish ritual practice. In fact, stories of faith were often embedded in secure attachment relationships. Stories of strength—narratives regarding adolescents' prewar courage or self-efficacy—were also able to be drawn on after the war as coping strategies. Goldenberg's analysis revealed that prewar

losses of major attachment figures and the larger environment of pervasive and brutal anti-Semitism may have provided "stress inoculation"
(Meichenbaum, 2009) for some survivors that helped them through the
war years.

These findings speak to the challenges of all individuals who have suffered trauma and loss—whether in wars, natural disasters, or at the hands
of perpetrators within their own families. The reconstruction of a life after
trauma may be aided by invoking memories of lost loved ones, by calling
on the values and positive messages that were imparted to them, and by
remembering their own strength, courage, and self-efficacy.

In Chapter 5, "The Hows and Whys of Survival: Causal Attributions
and the Search for Meaning," Jennifer Goldenberg found that survivors
commonly give multiple attributions for survival, sometimes choosing different attributions for each "moment of crisis" and often mixing
internal and external attributions. The interviews identified such external attributions as the help of others, luck, fate, and God. These external
attributions were somewhat more common than internal attributions,
suggesting that external attributions may have been more adaptive for
survivors in coping with survivor guilt—surviving when so many of their
family members did not.

In addition, Goldenberg found that some survivors were eventually able
to find meaning in their own survival during the postwar years, whether
it was to rebuild the Jewish people by starting families of their own or to
remember the dead by telling about what happened. The meaning they
found played an adaptive role in their postwar coping. Yet, Goldenberg
stresses that there is strength to be found in the search for meaning after
trauma—whether or not that meaning is ever found. For those of us who
are mental health professionals, we often enter the story of our clients' lives
when they are still struggling for meaning. We would do well to remember that the search for meaning after trauma is indeed a process, and that
not everyone will find meaning in it. Still, while they may not find the
"why" of their own survival, perhaps we can help them find strength in
the "how."

In Chapter 6, "'If Somebody Throws a Rock on You, You Throw Back
Bread': The Impact of Family Dynamics on Tolerance and Intolerance in
Survivors of Genocide," Nancy Isserman explores the ways in which the
quality of family relationships were found to be influential in creating tolerance in survivors toward both perpetrators and other groups in society.
The instrument that she used for her analysis was the TTP's quality of
family dynamics paradigm, a five-factor continuum of behavior between
the caregivers and the child that described the nature of the caregiver–
child relationship. This five-factor rating grew out of the grounded theory
work of the TTP. The paradigm (Hollander-Goldfein & Isserman, 1999)

described five sets of patterns of interaction/attachment between the parent/caregiver and the child that directly influenced political beliefs in adulthood. The five factors are closeness-distance, empathy-self-centeredness, validation-criticalness, expressive of positive emotion-expressive of negative emotion, and open communication–closed communication. When the relationships between the survivor and the family of origin members clustered on the negative end of the paradigm—evidencing distant, critical, self-centered, or negative ties between the survivors and their parents—intolerant attitudes predominated in the survivors. When the relationships between the survivors and their families of origin clustered on the positive end of the paradigm—demonstrated by close, validating, empathic, and positively expressed emotions—psychological security needs were met, and attitudes of tolerance predominated in the survivors.

Isserman found many reasons provided by survivors to justify their tolerant or intolerant attitudes, but the connection to positive and negative family relationships was an unexpected finding that adds a new dimension to the study of attitude formation and group relations. Finally, Isserman found that some tolerant survivors reported receiving messages from close family members—often parents, but sometimes a sibling or grandparent—that functioned as a guide for their future tolerant attitudes.

In Chapter 7, "A Minyan of Trees: The Role of Faith and Ritual in Postwar Coping and Its Relevance to Working With Trauma Survivors," Jennifer Goldenberg indicates that faith or ritual practice became important long-term strategies used by the majority of the TTP survivor respondents to cope with the massive losses suffered in the war. Descriptions of faith and ritual practice were often embedded within the narratives of important attachment relationships, demonstrating again the importance of the analysis of attachment relationships for providing an understanding of the survivor. Using faith as a coping strategy appeared to be related to the quality of family relationships in childhood before the war. Goldenberg found that most of those survivors who had close, warm family attachments before the war were more likely to retain their prewar beliefs or Jewish ritual practices afterward. Those survivors who reported troubled relationships in their families of origin did not exhibit loyalty to retaining the beliefs or practices of their families of origin, and often rejected them, while still retaining their Jewish identity and connection to Jewish community and tradition. The clinical implications of Goldenberg's findings are explored in case studies. Faith is rarely static in the face of adversity; it is strengthened, changed, or abandoned. Helping survivors of faith understand how their belief systems have been affected by their experiences is an important part of reintegration and healing often ignored by mental health practitioners.

Part 3 is composed of two related chapters by Bea Hollander-Goldfein, Nancy Isserman, and Lucy Raizman that focus on the second generation. In Chapter 8, "Parenting in Survivor Families: Critical Factors in Determining Family Patterns," the authors examine the parent-child dyad as a tool for better understanding the quality of family dynamics in the survivor's nuclear family.

This focus on the parent-child relationship led the authors to categorize the family levels of functioning into groups of positive, negative, and mixed families. The observed trends pointed to families in which both survivor parents functioned well and raised their children in an essentially positive family environment; families in which both parents were distressed, and the children experienced the symptoms of dysfunctional parenting; and families in which both parents engaged with the children in both positive and negative ways, resulting in mixed characteristics in adulthood.

Two critical elements of determining which pattern the family followed related to the distinction between self and other on the part of the survivor parent and the degree of marital strife within the post-war family. The absence of marital strife characterized the positive family pattern, while the more conflicted marriages dominated the negative family pattern. However, the parents who were able to put their children's needs first and somehow hold back on their own needs could provide the nurture and sustenance that the children needed to develop in healthy ways while acknowledging their parents' difficulties. In mixed families, this ability on the part of the parents was inconsistent, while the negative families suffered most from the parents' anger and depression.

In Chapter 9, "'Like a Bridge Over Troubled Waters': Divergent Parenting and the Mediating Influence of Positive Parental Attachment," the same authors discuss the impact of a mediating parent on the child of a survivor. In a small number of families, there was one parent who succeeded in mediating the negative impact of the emotionally distressed parent to such an extent that the children felt that they were able to live normal adulthoods because of the extraordinary positive relationship with the mediating parent.

In each of the four families whose vignettes are provided in this chapter in which the mediating pattern was found, there was a clear emotionally distressed parent, but the nondistressed parent was described in exclusively positive terms, effective in compensating for the negative parenting of the emotionally distressed parent. When compared to the negative and mixed family groups, there were proportionally less severely distressed marriages among these parents and less targeting of the child by the distressed parent. The descriptions by the children of the healthier parent were so consistently positive and so clearly described as effective in mediating the impact of the impaired parent that this pattern could serve as a potential model for other families with similar dynamics. The positive descriptions of the healthier parents clearly point to the powerful role they played as mediators of the negative family dynamics. The therapist thus needs to be aware that the parental impact on children varies, and that children are able to distinguish the differing effects. Exploring separately the nature of each of the parental interactions within the family could give the therapist the information needed to help the healthier parent mediate more effectively.

The final unit of this volume is concerned with several themes of intergenerational transmission of trauma and resilience to the children of survivors. In Chapter 10, "'The Elephant in the Room': Survivors' Holocaust Communication With Their Children," Sheryl Perlmutter Bowen, Juliet I. Spitzer, and Emilie S. Passow examine in detail the impact of the survivors' stories on the second generation. They found that communication patterns in Holocaust survivor families were more complex than the standard dichotomy between the impact of survivors who "talked about the war" compared to those who "didn't talk about the war."

In analyzing the various communication patterns found in survivor narratives, the authors noted the importance of motives. By documenting a continuum of motives for sharing traumatic experiences, the complexity of meaning and the variety of functions attributed to communication were brought into clearer focus. Perlmutter Bowen, Spitzer, and Passow's findings demonstrate that the impact of trauma narratives on a child of survivors was based not only on what was said, but also on how it was said, including the nonverbal messages that accompanied the spoken words.

Understanding the communication patterns in families provides insight into the systemic aftershocks of trauma. How members of families talk or are silent about traumatic experiences is important to understand in terms of the impact it has on intergenerational transmission of both trauma and resilience. How do survivors communicate about personal vulnerability? How open are they to questioning? To what extent do they hold secrets or regard the discussion of the trauma as taboo? Communication also reflects the mission of the speaker and what role the listener is to have in the verbal or nonverbal interchange. Perlmutter Bowen, Spitzer, and Passow found that the motives of the trauma survivor in sharing his or her story have a role in the recovery process of the survivor.

Similarly, survivors of other traumatic events face the challenge of communication for the rest of their lives. What do they want others to know? What are the embedded messages about values, role models, bearing witness, continuity, and meaning? The process of rebuilding and meaning reconstruction following traumatic events is a process that is central to family life. We feel that these questions are relevant to all individuals and families who have experienced interpersonal trauma, including veterans of wars, victims of ethnic conflict and other genocides, as well as survivors of abuse and domestic violence within their own families.

In Chapter 11, "Holocaust Narratives and Their Impact on Adult Children of Survivors," Hannah Kliger and Bea Hollander-Goldfein provide an essay on the experience of listening to survivor parents in which they describe how the listening has multiple consequences. In their reading of the interviews, they observed that the children heard not only what the parent went through but also who the parent was. When a particular attribute of a survivor parent was clear and emotionally compelling, this attribute became an organizing value system in the developing identity of the child. The authors label this "the transformative narrative." In this narrative, certain events that the survivor tells become integrated within the child of survivor as core values that involve highly personal, moral choices. The story therefore assumed its place as a guiding principle for the child of the survivor's own standard of behavior. Thus, these transformative or pivotal narratives, verbally communicated or nonverbally conveyed, played a role in identity formation of the child of the survivor.

In Chapter 12, the last chapter, "A Systemic Perspective of Coping and Adaptation: The Inextricable Connection Between Individual and Family," Bea Hollander-Goldfein presents an integrated model of coping and adaptation after trauma incorporating current knowledge in the field with expanded insights informed by the TTP research. The survivor model in Table 12.1, "Survivors' Foundation of Psychosocial Development Before the Trauma," is a developmental view of the individual survivor that tracks development from birth to adulthood and pays special attention to coping, adaptation, and recovery from adversity and extreme trauma. Important components of the model include an understanding of how survivors differ from each other—how relative strengths and weaknesses coexist, how prewar upbringing has differentially affected postwar adaptation, how resilience takes various forms, and how survivors influenced the psychological development of their children. In future research, the model may serve as a template to analyze the processes that enable certain individuals to be psychologically healthy and achieve successful lives, while other individuals are not.

In this book, the names of the survivors and their children have been changed, with the exception of the respondents whose interviews are included in the CD at the back of the book. The CD contains seven interviews from the project, consisting of one three-generation family, one mother–daughter pair, and one survivor. All are mentioned in this book using their real first names with their written permission. They were chosen as good examples of the 275 interviews that comprise the TTP dataset.

In summary, the conceptually rich descriptions provided by the TTP interviews with survivors and their family members have revealed patterns of coping and dimensions of resilience that help us understand the process of coping after trauma and the ways in which both trauma and resilience are transmitted to the next generation. The findings illuminate stories of how individuals and families cope with devastation and reflect a continuum of variability among survivors and their families in terms of how well they coped. The TTP has gleaned many lessons from these narratives that can offer hope and help for those who have suffered life's adversities, for those seeking the tools to handle life's challenges, and for mental health professionals themselves.

Indeed, the clinical implications of the research of the TTP are, we believe, the heart and soul of this book. If we have learned anything from our collective years of working on this project, it is that resilience can be found within everyone, that it is neither a trait nor an outcome, but rather a process of healing—sometimes over many years.

We are grateful beyond words for the opportunity to have sat with the survivors and their families and, for those of us who are mental health professionals, to be entrusted with our clients' stories of trauma and loss and to hear their words of struggle, strength, and resilience. As one survivor adamantly stated, "No matter what you tell, and no matter how much you tell, you're not telling everything. And there is not one person in the whole world that can put himself in the situation … we were in." No, surely not.

We give our deeply felt thanks to the survivors and their families who told us what they could. This book is our humble attempt to understand.

Note

1. The TTP study defines *Holocaust survivors* as Jewish individuals who lived in Europe and were in danger after 1933 with the rise of Hitler because they resided in countries controlled by Nazi Germany. Even those individuals who emigrated from Europe prior to the start of World War II were considered survivors by this definition. This definition is widely accepted in academic circles, especially in European countries.

References

Hollander-Goldfein, B., & Isserman, N. (1999) Overview of the Transcending Trauma project: Rationale, goals, methodology, and preliminary findings. In David, P. & Goldhar, J. (Eds.). *Selected papers from a time to heal: caring for the aging Holocaust survivor* (pp. 77–89). Toronto: Baycrest Centre for Geriatric Care.

Meichenbaum, D. (1996). Stress inoculation training for coping with stressors. *The Clinical Psychologist, 49,* 4–7.

CHAPTER 2

Resilience After Prolonged Trauma

An Integrated Framework

JENNIFER GOLDENBERG and BEA HOLLANDER-GOLDFEIN

Introduction

This review traces some of the most relevant thematic material from both the theoretical and the empirical literatures that have informed the research on Holocaust survivors and their families of the Transcending Trauma Project (TTP). It focuses on several broad bodies of literature— traumatic stress, coping, and resilience—highlighting the most salient work that has informed our own and that has given the TTP its foundational underpinnings.

As will become clear by the end of this review, our own work is situated within a process-oriented perspective, the most recent phase of research into trauma and its effects, and is focused largely on understanding the underlying and complex processes involved in coping, adaptation, and resilience after the trauma of the Holocaust. Our research findings have, we believe, important clinical implications for mental health professionals who work with survivors of various types of trauma.

The Traumatic Stress Literature: The Early Emphasis on Pathology

There is an extensive literature documenting the experiences of European Jews in the Holocaust (see, for example, Krell and Sherman's exhaustive 1997 bibliography). An early phase of the traumatic stress literature also examined Holocaust survivors and is almost exclusively weighted toward the pathological consequences of the traumatic events of the Nazi genocide (Suedfeld et al., 2005).

It is important to note that the early researchers, many of them survivors themselves, were working in the 1950s, 1960s, and 1970s either as therapists with clinical populations or for the purpose of establishing credibility for survivors in their claims against the German government for war crimes reparations (Glicksman, van Haitsma, Mamber, & Gagnon, 2003; Kahana, Harel, & Kahana, 1988). Consequently, these early investigations after the war laid a foundation that pathologized survivors of the Holocaust, a perspective that has survived unchallenged until fairly recently (Ayalon, 2005; Suedfeld et al., 2005). Survivors have been categorized as victims, not heroes; shattered and damaged, not whole. Investigators studying Holocaust survivors and the impact of the horrors of their stygian journey did not see that journey as contributing, in many cases, to being "stronger at the broken places" (Hemingway, 1929).

The largely pathologizing focus of this early phase of research, coming mostly from descriptive clinical observations, but also from some systematic empirical research, depicted Holocaust survivors as psychically numb, alexythymic, unable to overcome the effects of their severe persecution and massive losses of family, community, and faith, and generally unable to sustain meaningful relationships after the war. Much was made of "survivor syndrome," which, as defined by Niederland (1968) as a result of his clinical observations, includes anxiety, fear, disturbances in cognition and memory, depressive states, psychosomatic symptoms, a lifelong sense of vulnerability, disturbances in identity and body image, nightmares and flashbacks, psychic numbing, and survivor guilt. Eitinger (1964), working with a clinical population of Holocaust survivors and also basing his findings on his early, systematic study of three groups of concentration camp survivors, both Jewish and non-Jewish, coined a similar term for similar symptoms: "concentration camp syndrome" (Eitinger, 1964). Eitinger, Niederland, and others were writing a decade or more before posttraumatic stress disorder (PTSD) was first recognized in the third edition of the *Diagnostic and Statistical Manual of Mental Disorders* (*DSM-III*; American Psychiatric Association [APA], 1980). Through contact with Holocaust researchers, Vietnam veterans' groups began to see veterans' symptoms as "a manifestation of the same psychological disorder as that experienced by survivors of various catastrophic traumas" (Kutchins & Kirk, 1997, p. 112), including survivors of concentration camps.

There were some researchers who challenged the emphasis on the pathology of Holocaust survivors, however, including Sigal and Weinfeld (1989), Harel, Kahana, and Kahana (1988), and Carmil and Breznitz

(1991). But, Robert Jay Lifton's work (Lifton, 1967) provided a broader conceptualization of posttraumatic effects by going beyond assessments of PTSD-like sequelae to the meaning of being a survivor.

A Shift in Emphasis: The Search for Meaning in Survival

Lifton, a psychiatrist coming out of the psychoanalytic tradition, immersed himself in trauma narratives, including those of survivors of human-made wars such as Hiroshima and the Vietnam conflict, and disasters such as the Buffalo Creek flood, many of whom he interviewed himself (Lifton, 1967, 1973, 1988). Through his research, Lifton came to a "psychology of the survivor" (Lifton, 1967, 1988). Despite his emphasis on the pathological sequelae of trauma, Lifton (1967, 1988) added the important dimension of the experience of *being* a survivor to the trauma discussion and the meaning that experience has for the individual who goes through it. He perceived survivors as experiencing a "death imprint," a "radical intrusion of an image-feeling of threat or end to life" (Lifton, 1967, p. 169). This is expressed "as a continuing struggle to master and assimilate the threat" (Lifton, 1988, p. 170), compelling the survivor to a search for meaning that, in time, may lead to healing and recovery.

For Lifton, the Hiroshima survivors' traumatic sequelae are in themselves "neither pathological nor 'normal.' Rather, they are consistent human adaptations to nuclear weapons exposure" (Lifton, 1967, p. 11). He saw these responses as "distinctly universal in nature" (Lifton, 1967, p. 11). Despite cultural differences, "under extreme conditions, universal patterns become especially manifest" (p. 11). Lifton's work brings in a different phase or emphasis to the research on trauma survivors—the shift to an understanding that a search for meaning in the survival of trauma is part of the posttraumatic impact. He did not view this as pathological, but rather adaptive.

Viktor Frankl, in his seminal work, *Man's Search for Meaning* (1959), approached the understanding of the survivor experience from an existential perspective. A psychiatrist and survivor of Auschwitz and other concentration camps, Frankl used his own Holocaust experiences and those of his fellow prisoners to articulate a psychological framework that views the search for meaning as a "primary motivational force in man" (p. 54). The survivor, in Frankl's view, is severely "questioned by life" through his or her traumatic experiences. "Each man is questioned by life; and he can only answer to life by *answering for his own life*; to life he can only respond by being responsible" (p. 172, italics in the original). Being responsible, by giving one's life meaning and purpose, is the key to the resolution of trauma. "Suffering ceases to be suffering in some way at the moment it finds a meaning" (p. 179).

Paraphrasing Nietszche, Frankl (1959) posited that the survivor who "knows the 'why' for his existence … will be able to bear almost any 'how'" (p. 127). He pointed to an inner resilience of survivors, the strength within an individual that can be called on at will. Frankl's work has been criticized for being too judgmental, perhaps, of those who were unable to find meaning in the exigencies of life in the concentration camps. Nevertheless, it is important to note that his theoretical focus on the search for meaning after trauma contributes to the same paradigmatic shift of emphasis from an exclusive focus on pathological sequelae to the recognition of more adaptive, resilient responses to trauma, including this strongly cognitive and affective component.

Cognitive Models of Trauma and Recovery

More recent trauma literature, including that related to adult survivors of child sexual, physical, and emotional abuse and neglect, continues in this phase of understanding trauma and its impact from a less-pathological focus, with an emphasis on the cognitive component of trauma's effects. Following on the work of Lifton and Frankl, it suggests that those who are able to find meaning in their survival are better able to assimilate, cope with, and "move on" from their traumatic experiences. Some of these theorists are basing their work largely on empirical research (Calhoun & Tedeschi, 1999, 2006; McCann & Pearlman, 1990; Rosner & Powell, 2006; Taylor, 1989; Tedeschi & Calhoun, 1995; Tedeschi, Park, & Calhoun, 1998). Others base their theoretical contributions on clinical observations as well as empirical research (Courtois, 2010: Courtois & Ford, 2009; Herman, 1992/1997; Janoff-Bulman, 1992).

According to Janoff-Bulman (1992), we have beliefs, or cognitive schemata, that consist of three fundamental, positive assumptions that most of us hold. The first is the assumption of a *benevolent world*, that people are basically good and are not out to harm us. The second is the assumption of a *meaningful world*, that events that happen to us are meaningful and make sense; they are not random and chaotic. The third assumption is one of *self-worth*, that the self is worthy and certainly not worthy of having bad things happen to it.

Trauma strikes seemingly at random, making the world appear chaotic and without meaning or purpose (Janoff-Bulman, 1992). When individuals are exposed to trauma, their assumptions are shattered. For example, an individual whose assumptive schemata include the view of self as worthy would have that sense of self shattered by a trauma such as rape, so that self-esteem is lowered considerably (Taylor, 1989). Similarly, one's sense of people as basically trustworthy and not out to harm the individual intentionally can be shaken by such an experience.

People become untrustworthy; the self becomes suspicious of others and hypervigilant.

Herman (1992/1997), based on her clinical work with traumatized populations, has formulated three stages of recovery for the trauma survivor: the establishment of safety, remembrance and mourning, and reconnection with ordinary life. Herman's stages of recovery include first a gradual rebuilding of the survivor's sense of control and mastery and the reformulation of at least the *illusion* of safety (Taylor, 1989) about his or her environment. The second stage is remembrance and mourning, which consists of the telling of the trauma story "completely, in depth and detail" (Herman, 1992/1997, p. 175). The reconstruction of the trauma story begins with "a review of the [trauma survivor's] life *before the trauma* [italics added] and the circumstances that led up to the event" (p. 176). By reviewing pretrauma life and relationships, the traumatic event is placed into a meaningful context with which the posttrauma life can be connected.

The process of mourning the losses is a critical part of healing for the survivor as well (Herman, 1992/1997). But, when does mourning end? Danieli, who has worked clinically with many Holocaust survivors and their children, quoted a 74-year-old widow who survived the Holocaust as saying: "Even if it takes one year to mourn each loss, and even if I live to be 107 and mourn all the members of my family, what do I do about the rest of the six million?" (Danieli, as quoted in Herman, 1992/1997, p. 188). But many survivors, frozen by survivor guilt ("Why did I survive when the rest of my family did not?")—are unable to face this part of the recovery process. Entrenched resistance to mourning can freeze such processes (Herman, 1992/1997).

The final stage of recovery—reconnection—is about imagining and creating a future through establishing relationships with others (Herman, 1992/1997). For refugees from other cultures such as Holocaust survivors, this part of the recovery process is particularly difficult, as they are forced to recover in an unfamiliar environment, surrounded by unfamiliar customs, languages, and altered roles (deVries, 1996; Ellis, MacDonald, Lincoln, & Cabral, 2008; Hodes, Jagdev, Chandra, & Cunniff, 2008).

As survivors establish relationships and have children, concern for the next generation—generativity—helps them create meaning and purpose within their personal lives (Suedfeld et al., 2005). Some are also able to find meaning and connection within the wider environmental context of political activism or through an existential recommitment to religious faith—Herman's (1992/1997) concept of "survivor mission" (p. 207), an idea similar to those of Frankl (1959) and Lifton (1967). In Herman's view, "recovery" from trauma may never be complete, but "the best indices of resolution are the survivor's restored capacity to take pleasure in her life and to engage fully in relationships with others" (p. 212).

The process of searching for meaning after undergoing traumatic stress can be considered a way to cope cognitively (Brom & Kleber, 2009). Finding meaning in stressful events can help an individual regain a sense of control, which is an important component of recovery from trauma (Bloom, 1997; Courtois & Ford, 2009; Herman, 1992/1997; Wilson, Friedman, & Lindy, 2001). One study of Holocaust survivors discussed the implications of survivors being able to recall events of strength and resilience as a major source of coping with their traumatic memories (Hass, 1995).

Based largely on their clinical observations, Meichenbaum and Fitzpatrick (1993) used a constructivist narrative approach to survivors, emphasizing that "individuals … respond to *their interpretation of these events* [italics added] and to their perceived implications of these events" (p. 720). It is not the event itself that is traumatic to the individual because that varies from individual to individual. Rather, it is the meaning each individual puts to the specific event that makes it traumatic: "The stories we tell ourselves and others about what happened and why will influence how we cope" (p. 720).

Once the concept of individual variation is acknowledged in the trauma literature—that it is not the event itself that makes it a "big T" or "small t" trauma, but rather an individual's internal *perception* of that event and the meaning he or she puts to it—the focus is then placed on a continuum of posttraumatic responses. This phase of the literature on trauma survivors is focused on the subjective, individual interpretation of trauma and the search for meaning.

The Stress and Coping Literature

The literature on coping with stress emphasizes cognitive appraisal and process. The concept of "stress" is obviously a subjective one. Selye's definition seems one of the best and most succinct: "any demand upon the body, be the effect mental or somatic" (as quoted in Kahana, Kahana, Harel, & Rosner, 1988, p. 56). Aldwin's (2007) definition is more detailed: "That quality of experience, produced through a person-environment transaction, that, through either overarousal or underarousal, results in psychological or physiological distress" (p. 24).

Situations of war, including the Holocaust, contain aspects of extreme stress, according to Kahana, Kahana, Harel, and Rosner (1988). In their review of the literature on Holocaust survivors, they emphasized several aspects of coping under the most inhumane life circumstances, such as those pertaining in the concentration camp. These circumstances included intense states of physical degradation, lack of food, extreme cold, isolation, lack of a conventional social structure, the loss of an anchor in reality, and the lack of ability to predict or anticipate outcomes (Kahana, Kahana,

Harel, & Rosner, 1988). Several survivors of concentration camps, some of them psychologists themselves, have described the concentration camps as the ultimate experiment to test human adaptability (Levi, 1993; Frankl, 1959; Wiesel, 1960).

They have also noted, based on personal experience, several coping strategies used in the camps, including a focus on surviving in the present, an avoidance of danger, optimism, a strong sense of identity and self-esteem, a suppression of emotion, and the will to live (Kahana, Kahana, Harel, & Rosner, 1988). According to the model of coping put forth by Kahana et al., having "the will to live" seems to be a key component of survival. Those who did not have such a will to live, who were in such a state of emotional numbing and denial that they could barely put one foot in front of the other (the so-called musselmen), were the ones who succumbed and died. Those who had a will to live focused on day-to-day survival, held on to a sense of optimism, and had a sense of meaning in their life that kept them focused on living.

The catastrophe processing model of coping by Green, Wilson, and Lindy (1985) takes extreme trauma into consideration and is therefore a useful model for the purposes of the research presented here.

> The processing of the event … takes place within an individual and social context. Thus *whether a person is able to assimilate the trauma gradually and restabilize is dependent on what individual characteristics he or she brings to bear when perceiving, understanding, and dealing with the event. It is also dependent on the social environment in which the event and the working through take place. … This notion implies that different people who are present at the same event will have different outcomes because, not only will their experiences differ, but the individual characteristics they bring to bear upon the psychological processing are different, and this processing may take place in differing recovery environments* (Green et al., 1985, pp. 58–59; italics added)

We can see from this conceptualization that the authors included risk and protective factors—both individual characteristics that are present before the traumatic event and environmental factors after the event. What is especially interesting about Green et al.'s (1985) view is their discussion of what may enable some people to adapt more quickly and successfully than others. Some variables they take into consideration include the nature of the event itself. Human-made traumas are more difficult to recover from than natural disasters like floods or earthquakes and therefore have more profound, long-term effects (Ayalon, 2005; Courtois, 2010; Courtois & Ford, 2009; Green et al., 1985; Horowitz, 1986; Kahana, Kahana, et al., 1988; Lifton, 1967, 1973; Rosner & Powell, 2006).

Green et al. (1985) also suggested that the meaning the person ascribes to an event is related to his or her prior experience, including prior stressful or traumatic events. They suggested that the meaning the individual ascribes to an event can be related to the role of the survivor in that event—whether they acted as passive victims or active agents. In addition, coping mechanisms already in place at the time of the trauma will have an influence on posttraumatic adaptation.

They (Green et al., 1985) discussed the nature of the recovery environment as well; the types of social supports the individual has in place will help or hinder the individual's recovery from the traumatic event. This recovery environment can include what the authors called a "trauma membrane" (Green et al., 1985), a protective wall around survivors of trauma by friends and family that can isolate, suffocate, or support them. The recovery or trauma membrane also includes the larger "macro" social and political context: How are survivors viewed after trauma? For example, Vietnam veterans returning home from their experiences in the war were hardly greeted with acceptance and support (Figley, 1985; Lifton, 1973). Similarly, Holocaust survivors were greeted with a "conspiracy of silence" (Danieli, 1980) on arrival in this country after the war. No one wanted to hear about their experiences in the Holocaust, including American Jewish relatives. When they were asked to relate what happened to them, they were asked with an underlying suspicion that implied they had done something terrible to others to survive. Even psychiatrists and psychologists colluded in this conspiracy of silence, refusing to ask their survivor clients about their experiences, perhaps because they could not bear to hear the traumatic events themselves (Danieli, 1980). Such an unsupportive, even hostile, environment could not be conducive to positive adaptation after the Holocaust.

In the research on extreme stress and coping, Kahana, Kahana, et al. (1988) delineated aspects of extreme stress related to interpersonal violence that are qualitatively different from one-time traumatic events. They posited that during what they called extreme stress,

> the total life experience is disrupted … ; the new environment is extremely hostile and dangerous … ; opportunities to remove or act upon the stressor environment are severely limited; there is no predictable end to the experience; and the pain and suffering associated with the experience appear to be meaningless and without rational explanation. (p. 59)

Lazarus and Folkman (1984), focused on less-extreme stress than that experienced in the Holocaust. In their seminal work, *Stress, Appraisal, and Coping*, they saw the coping process as essentially an appraisal process in which the stressor is appraised by the individual, meaning is assigned to it, and coping mechanisms are brought to bear in response. In Lazarus and Folkman's transactional stress appraisal model, coping was defined as "constantly changing cognitive and behavioral efforts to manage specific external and or/internal demands that are appraised as taxing or exceeding the resources of the person" (p. 141). The definition is "process-oriented rather than trait-oriented, as reflected in the words *constantly changing* and *specific* demands and conflicts" (p. 141).

Lazarus and Folkman (1984) viewed coping as efforts to manage. By using the word *manage*, they were not equating coping with mastery. "Managing can include minimizing, avoiding, tolerating and accepting the stressful conditions, as well as attempts to master the environment" (p. 142). Regarding the process-oriented nature of coping, the authors stated:

> Coping is thus a shifting process in which a person must, at certain times, rely more heavily on one form of coping, say defensive strategies, and at other times on problem-solving strategies, as the state of the person-environment relationship changes. … The dynamics and change that characterize coping as a process are not random; they are a function of continuous appraisals and reappraisals of the shifting person-environment relationship. … Regardless of its source, any shift will lead to a reevaluation of what is happening, its significance, and what can be done. The reappraisal in turn influences subsequent coping efforts. The coping process is thus continuously mediated by cognitive reappraisals. (pp. 142–143)

For example, in Kubler-Ross's (1969) stage model of grieving, there is often first a sense of shock and disbelief, then efforts to deny the death, then frantic activity or struggle, followed by temporary disengagement and depression, and (ideally) ultimate acceptance of the loss. The process of grieving can be seen as a coping process; the person alternates between assimilating the information that a loved one has died and avoiding that fact.

The coping process may be characterized in multiple ways: problem focused, emotion focused, or focused on the seeking and obtaining of social support. The authors pointed out that theirs is not a stage model because the sequence can be, and often is, variable (Lazarus & Folkman, 1984).

Moos and Schaefer (1993), building on the work of Lazarus and Folkman, listed several personal coping resources that individuals draw on in times of stress. These include self-efficacy, optimism, and a sense of coherence. The concept of *self-efficacy*, defined by Bandura (1977) as "the strength of people's convictions in their own effectiveness" (p. 79), posits that individuals with a stronger sense of their own effectiveness will meet challenging situations with a more active and persistent style, whereas "those with lower levels are less active or tend to avoid such situations" (Moos & Schaefer, 1993, p. 239).

Moos and Schaefer (1993) also posited that stressful events can result in an even higher level of functioning than that experienced previously, an idea analogous to posttraumatic growth (PTG):

> People are remarkably resilient in the face of adversity. Individuals often emerge from a crisis with new coping skills, closer relationships with family and friends, broader priorities, and a richer appreciation for life. … Accordingly, investigators need to consider the possibility of a new and better level of adaptation that reflects personal growth rather than a return to the status quo. (p. 251)

Transformational Coping and Posttraumatic Growth

Aldwin's (1994, 2007) work on "transformational coping" forms a bridge between the literature on coping with extreme stress and the relatively new area of PTG or "adversarial growth." Aldwin (1994) noted that there is sufficient empirical evidence in the field to indicate that both positive and negative sequelae can result from undergoing a stressful experience. Indeed, there is a large literature that talks about the individual's ability to find meaning after traumatic experiences and to find positive benefit (Frankl, 1959; Janoff-Bulman, 1992; McCann & Pearlman, 1990; Meichenbaum & Fitzpatrick, 1993; Sommer & Baumeister, 1998; Taylor, 1989; Thompson, 1985). There is, no doubt, an element of self-deception and denial in some of this, as Taylor has pointed out so clearly in her book on "positive illusions" (1989). Such cognitive reframing as "having cancer was the best thing that ever happened to me" or "becoming a quadriplegic was a good thing because it forced me to reprioritize my life" helps make intolerable situations more tolerable (Aldwin, 1994, 2007).

Aldwin (1994) discussed the coping process as sometimes having transformational functions. Looking at the outcome of coping strategies, she cited skill acquisition, self-knowledge, and better relationships as transformational—"that is, encountering and coping with a stressful situation has resulted in a change of some sort. This change may be minor or major, positive or negative, transient or permanent" (p. 242). Aldwin argued further that "stress may be a necessary condition in order for individuals to grow as human beings" (p. 242).

Calhoun and Tedeschi (1999, 2006) gave us the concept of PTG, which they defined as "positive change that the individual experiences as a result of the struggle with the traumatic event" (Calhoun & Tedeschi, 1999, p. 11), a similar idea to Aldwin's "transformational coping." The common elements of PTG include a changed sense of one's relationships, increased compassion and sympathy for others, greater ease at expressing emotions, and positive changes in religious, spiritual, or existential matters (Calhoun & Tedeschi, 1999).

Calhoun and Tedeschi (1999) added the proviso that

> there are some sets of circumstances where even the consideration by outsiders that posttraumatic growth may be possible can be regarded by trauma survivors as naïve or even obscene. It is not our intent to imply that posttraumatic growth is a facile consequence of a bit of stress. Life crises can have many negative psychological consequences that for some people may last the rest of their lives. What we are suggesting is that, in their struggle with difficult life circumstances, some persons discover that they have changed for the better—that they have grown as individual persons. (pp. 16–17)

Despite the disclaimer, Calhoun and Tedeschi still seem to be implying that there is some inherent difference between those people who experience PTG as they define it and those who do not. Some persons may be more likely to experience PTG than others, and this depends on the foundations of the individual's pretrauma personality, including a more complex cognitive style, higher levels of optimism and hope, a greater level of extraversion, and creativity (Calhoun & Tedeschi, 1999). But, this may not be the case for people who have suffered chronic, extreme, and prolonged trauma such as the Holocaust or other genocidal wars. It is not clear whether this is only true for people who have experienced extended traumas or one-time traumatic events.

In their model, Calhoun and Tedeschi (1999) offered a transition from "trauma to triumph." They viewed the response to trauma as a series of stages that, with aid from supportive others, gradually leads to "initial growth" (coping success) and "further growth" ("wisdom"). Trauma is dealt with emotionally, cognitively, and behaviorally at each stage. But, the model only discusses positive, not negative, change, and the researchers use terms like "serenity" and "wisdom," which are problematic. It is perhaps naïve to assume a state of serenity in trauma survivors. In addition, stage models wrongly assume that each individual follows the same set of stages in a more or less linear progression.

According to Tedeschi and Calhoun, individual traits such as optimism, self-efficacy, and locus of control are related to positive outcomes following a traumatic event. According to this model, change does not occur until current coping resources are exhausted and new coping strategies emerge.

In the initial growth stage, or "coping success," new meaning is achieved, and the event is seen in light of it (Tedeschi, Park, & Calhoun, 1998).

As the researchers admitted, there are limitations to this model, the most significant perhaps being that it implies that serenity, wisdom, and PTG are achievable by everyone posttrauma. The model suggests that those who do not reach the pinnacle of "growth" are somehow flawed. This model also deals with a single traumatic event and the growth that comes from it; it is unclear how it can be applied to a lifetime of traumatic events or to chronic traumatic experiences, such as surviving war and genocide.

The idea of PTG or adversarial growth (Calhoun & Tedeschi, 1999, 2006; Linley & Joseph, 2004) has been questioned regarding the validity of its measurement and its potentially sanguine approach to the impact of trauma (Linley & Joseph, 2004; Smith & Cook, 2004). In the case of survivors of extreme, prolonged traumatic events like the Holocaust, the concepts of transformational coping and PTG may not apply.

The Resilience Literature

Thus far, we have seen various shifts in the literature on trauma survivors—from an almost-exclusive emphasis on pathology, to cognitive models of recovery, including the search for meaning, the rebuilding of the assumptive world, and even PTG. All of this theoretical and empirical research points toward, if not directly speaks to, the *process* of recovery. The search for meaning is a process, coping appraisals and reappraisals are processes, the rebuilding of the assumptive world is a process.

Turning now to the extensive and ever-growing literature on resilience of the past 20-odd years, we can see how it has provided us with some important insights into the factors that contribute to individual variations in response to stress and risk. Several rigorous longitudinal studies have revealed a host of risk and protective factors, both internal and external, that, in interaction with each other, appear to help people adapt to a variety of stressful and traumatic events in their lives through the process of resilience. But, how do we understand this process?

Researchers are beginning to shift their lens to understand how adaptation after trauma happens (Layne et al., 2009). Person and environment interact in complex ways, involving both internal and external risk and protective factors that move adaptation and resilience forward. There is empirical support for these psychological and environmental risk and protective factors—particularly protective factors such as an "easy" engaging temperament, optimism, self-efficacy, intelligence, secure attachment, planning ability, and social support (Masten, 2001; Rutter, 1999; Werner & Smith, 1992, 2001).

As social scientists began to shift their lens from the pathological toward the resilient and adaptive, they began to look at what was "right" with children who managed to "spring back" despite high levels of risk in their environments. They began to notice and focus on the many "outliers," children who succeeded despite environments and histories that would be expected to doom them to failure in adult life. For example, the majority of those children who were abused did *not* grow up to be abusers themselves (Anthony & Cohler, 1987; Barton, 2002). These were the "invulnerable" (Anthony & Cohler, 1987) or "resilient" children.

As Kaplan (1999) has discussed in convincing detail, there is a complexity and ambiguity about the construct of resilience, and there is no clear, agreed-on definition of it in the literature. Resilience has been described and measured as a trait, an outcome, or a process, with problematic methodological implications (Kaplan, 1999).

The idea of resilience as inner trait was an early view of resilience most clearly put forth in Anthony and Cohler's (1987) concept of the "invulnerable child." The idea that some children are simply "invulnerable," or are stronger than others in the face of compound, chronic stressors—such as abusive parents or the effects of poverty in the environment—implies that there is an innate tendency in *some* children to be resilient, and that not all children have this capacity. Anthony and Cohler likened these invulnerable children to metal dolls that, when struck by a blow from a hammer, are impervious to it, unlike the other dolls in their metaphor, which either shattered (glass) or were permanently marred (plastic). The idea of invulnerability became criticized as researchers grew more convinced that *all* children are somehow marred or changed by their negative experiences. Invulnerability was a myth, and the word *resilient* became the more accepted term (Kaplan, 1999).

The later conceptualization of resilience as an outcome is also problematic because it is necessarily value laden (Kaplan, 1999; Olsson, Bond, Burns, Vella-Broidrick, & Sawyer, 2003). Masten's popular definition, "successful adaptation despite adversity" (Masten, 1994, 1999) is a case in point. *Successful* is a term with variable definitions, as is *adversity*. One person's idea of success is not another's. One person's conception of adversity is not necessarily the same for someone else. These are post hoc value judgments concerning who is and is not resilient, what is and is not considered a stressor, and what is and is not considered adaptive. They are terms imposed by researchers, ill defined, and highly subjective, that leave out much of the context and the process of adaptation.

Finally, resilience more recently has been conceptualized as a process over time, referred to as "functioning flexibility" or "adaptive coping" (Garmezy, 1993). For example, internal factors such as temperament, intelligence, and an outgoing personality (and therefore the ability to seek outside help when needed) have been identified as protective factors that play a large role in a child's resilience. External protective factors, such as the presence of "one caring adult" in the environment of a child facing multiple risk factors, have been studied as well (Werner & Smith, 2001). These protective factors are believed to mitigate the risks.

The risk factors that have been identified include environmental risks such as alcoholic or depressed parents, lack of social support, poverty and its effects, and racism. The interaction of risk and protective factors, both internal and external, have been studied longitudinally, for example, the long-term study of the children of Kauai, which has now followed a cohort of at-risk children from infancy into midlife (Werner & Smith, 1977, 1982, 1992, 2001).

The view of resilience as an adaptive, complex process operating throughout the life span is becoming more firmly established (Kaplan, 1999). The concepts of cumulative risk (Fraser, Richman, & Galinsky, 1999) and risk chains (Huang, Kosterman, Catalano, Hawkins, & Abbott, 2001) have begun to be studied, assessing levels of risk and tracking the chaining process. Cumulative risk is the idea that there is a certain level or pileup of risk that an individual will eventually be unable to withstand (Rutter, 2000a, 2000b, 2001). Risk chains look at contingencies; they are linkages of distinct risk factors (Fraser, Kirby, & Smokowski, 2004).

One resilience model that could be useful for understanding posttraumatic adaptation of Holocaust survivors is the differential resiliency model (DRM) (Palmer, 1997). Palmer conducted a qualitative study of adult children of alcoholics in an attempt to view them from a nonpathological, nonmedical model framework. In this model, Palmer put resilience on a continuum of coping, consisting of "anomic survival, regenerative resilience, adaptive resilience, and flourishing resilience" (p. 202). It is not a stage model and can easily be applied to a developmental perspective.

Palmer's (1997) definition can be summarized as a process over a lifetime, interrupted by greater or lesser periods of disruption, and the use of greater or lesser competencies in managing life stressors. Palmer's model of a continuum of resilience is useful, especially with respect to the aftermath of an event as monumentally traumatic as the Holocaust, because of the continuum of coping she conceptualizes.

At the lower end of the continuum, Palmer (1997) defined *anomic survival* as experiencing life on the edge. "Energy is directed solely to survival and safety. There is little or no coherence or predictability to life" (pp. 202–203). The next level of resilience, regenerative resilience, is characterized by "the formative development of competence and constructive coping strategies … although crisis and disruption are frequent, and limited repair is achieved. … Exceeding survival and safety needs frees energy for learning and integration" (pp. 202–203).

Adaptive resilience, the next level, is "characterized by sustained periods of stability and balance, some disruption, but reassembly for growth. There is a regular use of competencies and coping strategies. ... Reciprocity [between person and environment] provides continual flow of energy to sustain birth of the philosophical self" (Palmer, 1997, pp. 202–203).

Finally, flourishing resilience consists of "extended periods of stability and balance and sustained growth. There is a sustained use of effective cognitive and behavioral coping strategies ... a sense of coherence in life, and an enduring philosophical self" (Palmer, 1997, pp. 202–203).

These descriptions of varying levels of resilience are useful as a guiding framework, with particular relevance to a traumatic series of events in the lives of Holocaust survivors, who would likely display anomic resilience during much of the war period. One of the strengths of this model lies in its nonjudgmental nature—that is, it does not suggest that without attaining the highest level of flourishing resilience (cf. PTG), one is somehow less adaptive or lacking in some way. Neither does it have the limitations of a stage model; people can easily be seen to move among the various levels of resilience throughout their life span and in response to different stressful and traumatic events.

The categories of resilience Palmer (1997) conceptualized are useful for the purposes of this study. *Anomic survival*, for our purposes here, can be seen as barely hanging on to survive the devastating events that are happening in the moment. There is still a level of resilience implied here, but it is almost an instinctual survival mechanism, often without the help of others, which can be seen as applying during the events of the war years. Such a basic level of "survival resilience" could be maintained and sustained as long as possible. But it is still a form of resilience. It is reminiscent of Garmezy's (1993) idea that there can be resilience at the same time as there is an emotional state of distress, anguish, loss, and fear. Regenerative resilience, adaptive resilience, and flourishing resilience are also useful terms that reflect varying levels of stability, meaning making, and integration. "Flourishing" implies growth and integration, difficult to achieve in a life filled with trauma and loss, perhaps, but still attainable for some.

The study of resilience has been criticized not only for the methodological problems inherent in its varying definitions, conceptualizations, and measurements, but also because the mostly quantitatively driven approaches to the study of resilience have been "top-down" (Ungar, 2004). These analyses ignore the rich, contextual descriptions that can tell us *how* individuals are resilient, or what the *process* of individual adaptation looks like over time, as it is subjectively experienced by individual survivors of trauma. Indeed, in a book on the risk and resilience of traumatized children, resilience was conceptualized as having a largely cognitive component: "the individual's capacity to process traumatic experiences" (Brom & Kleber, 2009, p. 133), which, necessarily, is a process over time. Ungar suggested we gather rich descriptions, suspending bias of what is considered resilient or successful adaptation, in an effort to discover more about context, process, and individual variation in recovery from particular stressors (Ungar, 2004).

Survivors of War Trauma

The following is a discussion of some of the most salient empirical studies addressing the issue of how survivors—specifically survivors of war trauma—recover from their traumatic experiences. As is the case in the present study, these researchers have all used qualitative methodology, albeit with much smaller samples than that of the TTP.

Moskovitz (1983) interviewed 23 middle-aged adults who were children during the Holocaust and who survived both in concentration camps and in hiding. These orphans were raised in a group home in England after the war. A major strength of this study is that it used the survivors' own words to describe how they recovered from trauma. It also generates compelling themes salient for adult survivors of childhood trauma, including survivor guilt; mourning, and loss of memories of the events (especially for the youngest survivors, who cannot trust their memories as accurate). Other impacts of the Holocaust the respondents noted include loss of identity, lost childhoods, crises of faith, and loss of community (cf. Erikson's, 1976, concept of "collective trauma"). The "conspiracy of silence" (Danieli, 1980, 1985) figures prominently in these narratives as well. Shame, problems with intimacy with nonsurvivor spouses, and continuing fear of persecution, are some of the other negative impacts these child survivors describe.

On the more resilient end, Moskovitz (1983) found among her respondents optimism, spiritual involvement, communal involvement, social responsibility, the desire to create families, and a lack of revenge motivation. Moskovitz's study also stresses the importance of the "one caring adult" in the recovering child's life. This is consonant with the resilience literature, particularly the work of Werner and Smith (1992, 2001). Moskovitz's interviews with these child survivors indicate that positive postwar experiences can provide healing. Her study suggests the importance of understanding clearly the impact of positive posttraumatic circumstances: "We learn powerfully from these lives that lifelong emotional disability does not automatically follow early trauma. … Apparently, what happens later matters enormously" (Moskovitz, 1983, p. 237). This is clearly an optimistic view that is based on solid empirical research that emphasizes the importance of posttraumatic circumstances in the recovery from trauma.

Miller's (2000) study of women interned in Auschwitz ($N = 16$) focuses on their coping strategies and adaptation. Following Lazarus and Folkman

(1984) and Lazarus (1991), she categorized her respondents' coping strategies into two types: emotion focused and problem focused. Echoing Frankl's (1959) work, Miller's (2000) results indicate that sustaining hope of being reunited with family or friends and maintaining emotional connection with others provided the major motivation of survival for these women. According to Miller, women's relationships with other women in the camps were the lynchpin of their survival in Auschwitz. However, she provided no convincing evidence to support the implication that this is somehow categorically different from men's coping under similar extreme conditions. Her work is useful in its delineation of coping strategies used by these women *during the war* but did not examine either prewar coping styles or postwar adaptation.

Suedfeld, Krell, Wiebe, and Steel (1997) performed a content analysis of 30 videotaped autobiographical interviews of Holocaust survivors; the authors used a combination of quantitative and qualitative approaches. They divided their sample by sex and by age at the end of the Holocaust (child, adolescent, or adult). They argued that the individual's developmental stage at the time of trauma is an important factor in understanding its impact, particularly how the individual copes in response. Subjects who were older during the war tended to use more problem-oriented coping strategies, those who were adolescents used emotion-focused coping styles, and many children were simply overwhelmed by their traumatic experiences, having few coping skills in place at the time of the Holocaust (Suedfeld et al., 1997).

Some of the statistically significant effects the study found include distancing, problem solving, seeking social support, and compartmentalization. An interesting developmental finding of the study is that those survivors who were children during the war cited what the authors termed "supernatural protection" less than the adolescent or adult groups studied. Perhaps the children did not yet have a fully formed religious belief system, unlike some older survivors, who could call on their faith to help them cope. Faith as a coping mechanism is a little-studied phenomenon; respondents who were adolescents when they were forced into the camps, and therefore at a different level of cognitive development than younger children, would have had some sort of belief system in place—including agnosticism—going into the war. In other words, they were old enough to have established some sort of spiritual beliefs or had concluded (or were in the process of concluding) that the God they had learned about in their childhood did not exist (Goldenberg, 2009, and this volume, Chapter 7).

The Suedfeld et al. study (1997) was a methodologically rigorous one based on interviews that included pre- and post-Holocaust material. However, we are not given clear examples of *how* survivors "have successfully transcended not only the Holocaust but the vicissitudes of post-war recovery, emigration, and the re-creation of their lives" (p. 175). Again, survivors' words are omitted; their explanations of how they rebuilt their lives are synopsized, leading to an incomplete picture of the process of adaptation.

These studies all used qualitative methodology and all study survivors many years after the traumatic events occurred. However, they did not address pretrauma life and relationships or discuss posttraumatic adaptation in sufficient detail to help us understand what strengths and coping skills, risks, and vulnerabilities the survivors may have brought with them into the war or *how* the survivors adapted afterward. What did the process of adaptation look like? How did the survivors themselves describe how they rebuilt their lives after massive trauma and loss? With the exception of Moskovitz's (1983) work, in each of these studies the survivors' own words are referred to infrequently in the written analysis. We are given summary statements and paraphrases when it seems critical to know precisely what words the survivors themselves used to describe their adaptation.

Clinical Applications of This Book

How did survivors of the Holocaust rebuild their lives in the wake of the extreme trauma and massive losses they incurred? This was the broad research question of the TTP, which focused on the coping strategies, adaptation, and resilience of survivors before, during, and after their experiences in Hitler's genocide. The qualitative methodology, employing a semistructured interview format, allowed a window into the actual *processes* of the strategies survivors used over their lifetimes. This book, the result of the analysis of the TTP survivor interviews, relies heavily on the survivors' own words to understand their posttraumatic adaptation.

Why is such a study relevant now? The Holocaust was unfortunately neither the first nor the last genocidal war (Charny, 1999). Survivors of more recent genocides and ethnic conflicts live in our midst and sometimes seek our help (Goldenberg, 2009; Wilson & Drozdek, 2004). What do survivors themselves delineate as the long-term effects of genocidal conflicts and the ways they have developed to cope with those effects? If we better understood some of the long-term impacts of extreme, prolonged trauma, we might be able to provide interventions and help put social policies in place that could not only mitigate the negative effects of these horrific wars but also help foster more positive, long-term adaptations for the survivors.

More than this, however, we believe that our work with the TTP has yielded a deeper understanding of the *process* of recovery after severe trauma that is relevant to all trauma survivors. The qualitative research of the TTP gives us a nuanced perspective on both the long-term impacts of extreme, prolonged trauma and the long-term process of coping, adaptation, and resilience that is valuable for both clinicians and researchers of traumatic stress.

In addition, the words survivors use to articulate what they and their lives were like before the war, their descriptions of how they survived and coped during the war, and most important, their explanations of how they coped and adapted in the wake of the traumatic events they experienced can be useful to clinicians and researchers trying to understand long-term posttraumatic sequelae, methods of coping and adaptation over time, the process of resilience, and how mental health professionals can help in the recovery process itself. Their narratives help us understand what life was like before the extreme trauma of the Holocaust, what and how they endured during the Holocaust, and how they went on to form adult relationships, raise children, and provide for their families in a new country, simultaneously living with their traumatic memories of what happened to them and their loved ones.

Further, the work of the TTP begins to look to the second generation and gives voice to the children of survivors, many of whom are now grandparents. Their narratives about their parents and families help us to understand the generational transmission and the legacies—not only of trauma, but also of resilience—within survivor families. Yet, this book is focused more on the survivors' stories. Even when we analyze the interviews of the children and grandchildren, it is in the context of the impact of the survivors' experiences on their lives. We hope in the coming years to concentrate more of our analysis and writing on the children and grandchildren. We believe, however, that the following chapters provide new perspectives and avenues for trauma and resilience researchers and for mental health professionals to pursue in their work with trauma survivors.

References

Aldwin, C. M. (1994). *Stress, coping, and development: An integrative perspective.* New York: Guilford Press.

Aldwin, C. M. (2007). *Stress, coping, and development: An integrative perspective* (2nd ed.). New York: Guilford Press.

American Psychiatric Association. (1980). *Diagnostic and statistical manual of mental disorders* (3rd ed.). Washington, DC: Author.

Anthony, J., & Cohler, J. (1987). *The invulnerable child.* New York: Guilford Press.

Ayalon, L. (2005). Resilience to trauma in Holocaust survivors. *Journal of Loss and Trauma, 10,* 347–358.

Bandura, A. (1977). *Social learning theory*. Englewood Cliffs, NJ: Prentice-Hall.

Barton, W. H. (2002). Methodological square pegs and theoretical black holes. In R. R. Greene (Ed.), *Resiliency: An integrated approach to practice, policy, and research* (pp. 95–114). Washington, DC: NASW Press.

Bloom, S. (1997). *Creating sanctuary*. New York: Routledge.

Brom, D., & Kleber, R. (2009). Resilience as the capacity for processing traumatic experiences. In D. Brom, R. Pat-Horenczyk, and J. D. Ford (Eds.), *Treating traumatized children: Risk, resilience, and recovery* (pp. 133–149). New York: Routledge.

Calhoun, L. G., & Tedeschi, R. G. (1999). Facilitating posttraumatic growth. Mahwah, NJ: Erlbaum.

Calhoun, L. G., & Tedeschi, R. G. (Eds.). (2006). *Handbook of posttraumatic growth: Research and practice*. Mahwah, NJ: Erlbaum.

Carmil, D., &., Breznitz, S. (1991). Personal trauma and world view—Are extremely stressful experiences related to political attitudes, religious beliefs, and future orientation? *Journal of Traumatic Stress, 4*, 393–405.

Charny, I. W. (Ed.). (1999). *Encyclopedia of genocide* (Vols. 1 and 2). Santa Barbara, CA: ABC-CLIO.

Courtois, C. A. (2010). *Healing the incest wound: Adult survivors in therapy*. New York: Norton.

Courtois, C. A. and Ford, J. D. (Eds.). (2009). *Treating complex traumatic stress disorders: An evidence-based guide*. New York: Guilford Press.

Danieli, Y. (1980). Counter-transference in the treatment and study of Nazi Holocaust survivors and their children. *Victimology, 5*, 355–367.

Danieli, Y. (1985). The treatment and prevention of long-term effects and intergenerational transmission of victimization: A lesson from Holocaust survivors and their children. In C. R. Figley (Ed.), *Trauma and its wake* (pp. 295–313). New York: Brunner/Mazel.

deVries, M. W. (1996). Trauma in cultural perspective. In B. A. van der Kolk, A. C. McFarlane, & L. Weisaeth (Eds.), *Traumatic stress* (pp. 398–416). New York: Guilford Press.

Eitinger, L. (1964). *Concentration camp survivors in Norway and Israel*. Oslo: Universitetsforlaget.

Ellis, B. H., MacDonald, H. Z., Lincoln A. K., & Cabral, H. J. (2008). Mental health of Somali adolescent refugees: The role of trauma, stress, and perceived discrimination. *Journal of Consulting and Clinical Psychology, 76*, 184–193.

Erikson, K.T. (1976). *Everything in its path: Destruction of community in the Buffalo Creek flood*. New York: Simon & Schuster.

Figley, C. R. (1985). *Trauma and its wake: The study and treatment of post-traumatic stress disorder*. New York: Brunner/Mazel.

Frankl, V. (1959). *Man's search for meaning*. New York: Washington Square Press.

Fraser, M. W., Kirby, L. D., & Smokowski, P. R. (2004). Risk and resilience in childhood. In M. W. Fraser (Ed.), *Risk and resilience in childhood: An ecological perspective* (pp. 13–66). Washington, DC: NASW Press.

Fraser, M. W., Richman, J. M., & Galinsky, M. J. (1999). Risk, protection, and resilience: Toward a conceptual framework for social work practice. *Social Work Research, 18*, 163–177.

Garmezy, N. (1993). Vulnerability and resilience. In D. C. Funder, R. D. Parke, C. Tomlinson-Keasey, & K. Widaman (Eds.), *Studying lives through time* (pp. 377–398). Washington, DC: American Psychological Association.

Glicksman, A., van Haitsma, K., Mamberg, M. H., Gagnon, M., &., (2003). Caring for Holocaust survivors: Rethinking the paradigms. *Journal of Jewish Communal Service, 79*(2/3), 148–153.

Goldenberg, J. (2009). "I had no family but I made family." Immediate post-war coping strategies of adolescent survivors of the Holocaust. *Counselling and Psychotherapy Research, 9*(1), 18–26.

Green, B. L., Wilson, J. P., & Lindy, J. D. (1985). Conceptualizing post-traumatic stress disorder: A psychosocial framework. In C. R. Figley (Ed.), *Trauma and its wake: The study and treatment of post-traumatic stress disorder* (pp. 53–69). New York: Brunner/Mazel.

Harel, Z., Kahana B., & Kanana, E. (1988). Psychological well-being among Holocaust survivors in Israel. *Journal of Traumatic Stress Studies, 1* (4), 413–428.

Hass, A. (1995). *The aftermath: Living with the Holocaust.* Cambridge, UK: Cambridge University Press.

Hemingway, E. (1929/1998). *A farewell to arms.* New York: Scribner.

Herman, J. (1992/1997). *Trauma and recovery.* New York: Basic Books.

Hodes, M, Jagdev, D., Chandra, N., &., Cunniff, A. (2008). Risk and resilience for psychological distress amongst unaccompanied asylum seeking adolescents. *The Journal of Child Psychology and Psychiatry, 49,* 723–772.

Horowitz, M. (1986). *Stress response syndromes.* Northvale, NJ: Aronson.

Huang, B., Kosterman, R., Catalano, R. F., Hawkins, J. D., & Abbott, R. D. (2001). Modeling mediation in the etiology of violent behavior in adolescence: A test of the Social Development Model. *Criminology, 39*(1), 75–108.

Janoff-Bulman, R. (1992). *Shattered assumptions.* New York: Free Press.

Kahana, B., Harel, Z., & Kahana, E. (1988). Clinical and gerontological issues facing survivors of the Nazi Holocaust. In P. Marcus & A. Rosenberg (Eds.), *Healing their wounds: Psychotherapy with Holocaust survivors and their families* (pp. 197–211). New York: Praeger.

Kahana, E., Kahana, B., Harel, Z., & Rosner, T. (1988). Coping with extreme trauma. In J. P. Wilson, Z. Harel, & B. Kahana (Eds.), *Human adaptation to extreme stress: From the Holocaust to Vietnam* (pp. 55–79). New York: Plenum Press.

Kaplan, H. B. (1999). Toward an understanding of resilience: A critical review of definitions and models. In M. D. Glantz & J. L. Johnson (Eds.), *Resilience and development: Positive life adaptations* (pp. 17–84). New York: Kluwer Academic/Plenum.

Krell, R., & Sherman, M. I. (1997). *Medical and psychological effects of concentration camps on Holocaust survivors.* New Brunswick, NJ: Transaction.

Kubler-Ross, E. (1969). *On death and dying.* New York: Macmillan.

Kutchins, H., & Kirk, S. A. (1997). *Making us crazy.* New York: Free Press.

Layne, C. M., Beck, C. J., Rimmasch, H., Southwick, J. S., Moreno, M. A., Hobfall, S. E., et al. (2009). Promoting "resilient" posttraumatic adjustment in childhood and beyond: "Unpacking" life events, adjustment trajectories, resources, and interventions. In D. Brom, R. Pat-Horenczyk, & J. D. Ford (Eds.), *Treating traumatized children: Risk, resilience and recovery* (pp. 13–48). New York: Routledge.

Lazarus, R. S. (1991). *Emotion and adaptation.* New York: Oxford University Press.

Lazarus, R. S., & Folkman, S. (1984). *Stress, appraisal, and coping.* New York: Springer.

Levi, P. (1993). *Survival in Auschwitz.* New York: Touchstone Press.

Lifton, R. J. (1967). *Death in life.* New York: Random House.

Lifton, R. J. (1973). *Home from the war.* New York: Simon & Schuster.

Lifton, R. J. (1988). Understanding the traumatized self: Imagery, symbolization, and transformation. In J. P. Wilson, Z. Harel, & B. Kahana (Eds.), *Human adaptation to extreme stress: From the Holocaust to Vietnam* (pp. 7–32). New York: Plenum Press.

Linley, P. A., & Joseph, S. (2004). Positive change following trauma and adversity: A review. *Journal of Traumatic Stress, 17,* 11–22.

Masten, A. S. (1994). Resilience in individual development: Successful adaptation despite risk and adversity. In M. C. Wang & E. W. Gordon (Eds.), *Educational resilience in inner-city America: Challenges and prospects* (pp. 3–26). Hillsdale, NJ: Erlbaum.

Masten, A. S. (1999). Commentary: The promise and perils of resilience research as a guide to preventive intervention. In M. D. Glantz, & J. L. Johnson (Eds.), *Resilience and development: Positive life adaptations* (pp. 251–258). New York: Kluwer Academic/Plenum.

Masten, A. S. (2001). Ordinary magic: Resilience processes in development. *American Psychologist, 56,* 227–238.

McCann, L., & Pearlman, L. A. (1990). Vicarious traumatization: A framework for understanding the psychological effects of working with victims. *Journal of Traumatic Stress, 3,* 131–147.

Meichenbaum D., & Fitzpatrick, D. (1993). A constructivist narrative perspective on stress and coping: Stress inoculation applications. In L. Goldberger & S. Breznitz (Eds.), *Handbook of stress: Theoretical and clinical aspects* (pp. 706–723). New York: Free Press.

Miller, J. E. (2000). *Love carried me home: Women surviving Auschwitz.* Deerfield Beach, FL: Simcha Press.

Moos, R. H., & Schaefer, J. A. (1993). Coping resources and processes: Current concepts and measures. In L. Goldberger & S. Breznitz (Eds.), *Handbook of stress: Theoretical and clinical aspects* (2nd ed., pp. 234–257). New York: Free Press.

Moskovitz, S. (1983). *Love despite hate: Child survivors of the Holocaust and their adult lives.* New York: Schocken Books.

Niederland, W. C. (1968). The psychiatric evaluation of emotional disorders in survivors of Nazi persecution. In H. Krystal (Ed.), *Massive psychic trauma* (pp. 9–11). New York: Basic Books.

Olsson, C. A., Bond, L., Burns, J. M., Vella-Broidrick, D. A., & Sawyer, S. M. (2003). Adolescent resilience: A concept analysis. *Journal of Adolescence, 26,* 1–11.

Palmer, N. (1997). Resilience in adult children of alcoholics: A non-pathological approach to social work practice. *Health and Social Work, 22,* 201–209.

Rosner, R., & Powell, S. (2006). Posttraumatic growth after the war. In L. G. Calhoun & R. G. Tedeschi (Eds.), *Handbook of posttraumatic growth: Research and practice* (pp. 197–213). Mahwah, NJ: Erlbaum.

Rutter, M. (1999). Resilience concepts and findings: Implications for family therapy. *Journal of Family Therapy, 21,* 119–144.

Rutter, M. (2000a). Psychosocial influences: Critiques, findings, and research needs. *Development and Psychopathology, 12,* 375–405.

Rutter, M. (2000b). Resilience reconsidered: Conceptual considerations, empirical findings, and policy implications. In J. P. Shonkoff & S. J. Meisels (Eds.), *Handbook of early childhood intervention* (2nd ed., pp. 651–682). New York: Cambridge University Press.

Rutter, M. (2001). Psychosocial adversity: Risk, resilience, and recovery. In J. M. Richman & M. W. Fraser (Eds.), *The context of youth violence: Resilience, risk, and protection* (pp. 13–43). Westport, CT: Praeger.

Sigal, J. J., &., Weinfeld, M. (1989). *Trauma and rebirth: Intergenerational effects of the Holocaust.* New York: Praeger Press.

Smith, S. G., & Cook, S. L. (2004). Are reports of posttraumatic growth positively biased? *Journal of Traumatic Stress, 17,* 353–358.

Sommer, I. L., & Baumeister, R. F. (1998). The construction of meaning from life events: Empirical studies of personal narratives. In P. T. F. Wong & P. S. Fry (Eds.), *The human quest for meaning: A handbook of psychological research and clinical applications* (pp. 143–161). Mahwah, NJ: Erlbaum.

Suedfeld, P., Krell, R. Wiebe, R. E., & Steel, G. D. (1997). Coping strategies in the narratives of Holocaust survivors. *Journal of Stress and Coping, 10,* 153–179.

Suedfeld, P., Soriano, E., McMurtry, D. L., Paterson, H., Weiszbeck, T. L., & Krell, R. (2005). Erikson's "components of a healthy personality" among Holocaust survivors immediately and 40 years after the war. *International Journal of Aging and Human Development, 60,* 229–248.

Taylor, S. E. (1989). *Positive illusions.* New York: Basic Books.

Tedeschi, R. G., & Calhoun, L. G. (1995). *Trauma and transformation: Growing in the aftermath of suffering.* Thousand Oaks, CA: Sage.

Tedeschi, R. G., Park, C. L., & Calhoun, L. G. (Eds.). (1998). *Posttraumatic growth: Positive changes in the aftermath of crisis.* Mahwah, N. J.: Erlbaum.

Thompson, S. C. (1985). Finding positive meaning in a stressful event and coping. *Basic and Applied Social Psychology, 6,* 279–295.

Ungar, M. (2004). A constructionist discourse on resilience: Multiple contexts, multiple realities among at-risk children and youth. *Youth and Society, 35,* 341–365.

Werner, E. E., & Smith, R. S. (1977). *Kauai's children come of age.* Honolulu: University of Hawaii Press.

Werner, E. E., & Smith, R. S. (1982). *Vulnerable but invincible: A longitudinal study of resilient children and youth.* New York: McGraw Hill.

Werner, E. E., & Smith, R. S. (1992). *Overcoming the odds: High risk children from birth to adulthood.* Ithaca, NY: Cornell University Press.

Werner, E. E., & Smith, R. S. (2001). *Journeys from childhood to midlife: Risk, resilience, and recovery.* Ithaca, NY: Cornell University Press.

Wiesel, E. (1960). *Night.* New York: Avon Books.

Wilson J. P., & Drozdek, B. (Eds.). (2004). *Broken spirits: The treatment of traumatized asylum seekers, refugees, war and torture victims.* New York: Brunner-Routledge.

Wilson, J. P., Friedman, M., & Lindy, J. (Eds.). (2001). *Treating psychological trauma and PTSD.* New York: Guilford Press.

CHAPTER 3

Making the Unmanageable Manageable
Innovative Tools for Analyzing a Large Qualitative Dataset

NANCY ISSERMAN

Introduction

Qualitative research has historically played a secondary role to quantitative research in the study of psychological phenomena. However, over the past decade, it has gained recognition as mental health researchers have sought a deeper understanding of complex human experiences. Their goal has been to understand how individuals describe their experience of life events from the inside out. The views of the interviewees are important as their life experiences have made them experts on the particular problem or situation under study. Qualitative research seeks to explore the continuum of the human experience as it relates to a particular problem, to explore the problem in context, and to explore it as experienced by the individual (Denzin & Lincoln, 2000; Gubrium & Holstein, 2002; Kazdin, 1998; Miles & Huberman, 1994; Padgett, 2004, 1998). The primary task of the research is to explicate the ways that people in particular settings come to understand, account for, take action, and otherwise manage their day-to-day situations (Miles & Huberman, 1994).

Qualitative methodology is used to explore a topic about which little is known (Morse & Richards, 2002; Padgett, 2004). When studying the behavior of individuals, it is essential to study the individual in the context of significant relationships, specifically family relationships (Lindsey, 1998). Qualitative methodology is particularly useful in studying families because of the emphasis on meanings, interpretations, interactions, and subjective experiences of family members (Lindsey, 1998). A qualitative approach offers the best route to understanding the depth of the human experience and the wide diversity of individual differences that exist among people who have experienced the same events (Padgett, 2004).

Increasingly since the 1960s, qualitative research has become more widely accepted as a valid methodology in the social sciences (Madill & Gough, 2008). In fact, there has been phenomenal growth in the use of qualitative research methods. While some disciplines, such as anthropology and sociology, have led the way, even in other fields such as psychology, for which quantitative methodology has long predominated, qualitative research has experienced a rapid increase. In psychology, the interview that focuses on the lived experience is particularly popular (Atkinson, Coffey, & Delamont, 2001; Madill & Gough, 2008). A goal of qualitative research is to learn from the interviewees how they experience the problem to be investigated and the meanings they put on it, to learn about the issue from the perspective of the people who have firsthand knowledge (Morse & Richards, 2002; Polkinghorne, 2007).

The Transcending Trauma Project (TTP) relied on grounded theory methodology to gain an understanding of the qualitative family dynamics of three generations of Holocaust survivor families. Strauss and Corbin (1998) described grounded theory as derived from data systematically gathered and analyzed through the research process. The data are more likely to provide a better, in-depth understanding of a particular phenomenon based on the experiences, perceptions, and interpretations of the individuals who are involved (Strauss & Corbin, 1998). To understand the problem in depth, grounded theory encourages methods of discovery of central themes and analysis of core concerns (Morse & Richards, 2002).

The TTP chose to utilize grounded theory in gathering and analyzing the data from the survivor families. To facilitate this process, the TTP not only analyzed the individual as a single unit but also analyzed the individual within his or her family unit. Interviews gathered data not only for the war years but also about the respondent's life both before and after the war trauma. Qualitative methodology based on grounded theory fosters insights into a survivor's thoughts and memories, cultivating a high degree of introspection and contextualization. "To ignore such criteria is to risk trivializing the survivor's experiences as well as to present only a superficial picture" (Suedfeld, 1996, p. 118).

Due to the labor-intensive methodology that gives qualitative research its scientific rigor, proponents of this approach acknowledge the practicality of small samples. Because grounded theory research is small scale and focused, emphasizing the continuous interplay between analysis and data collection until a theory fitting the data is created (Strauss & Corbin, 1998), we thought that it would work well for gathering the TTP data. However, because our sample was much larger than the typical qualitative research project, we needed to adapt common methodology practices and create others to handle the size and depth of the data.

In grounded theory, data are sought in each category until it is "saturated," and no more new information are found. In practice, saturation is "an elastic category that contracts and expands to suit the researcher's definitions rather than any consensual standard" (Charmaz, 2001, p. 690). In fact, Charmaz (2006) supported the argument put forth by Dey (1999) that what is critical is not the claim of achieving saturation but "theoretical sufficiency" (Charmaz, 2006, p. 114). Grounded theorists produce codes through partial analysis of the data and only "conjecture that the properties of the category are saturated" (Charmaz, 2006, p. 114). One way of addressing the concern that categories are saturated is to reanalyze and recode already-analyzed data using different categories of coding that are smaller in content and more refined than the original category. Through meticulous steps that slowly clarify the variables generated by the qualitative methods, a hypothetical explanation for the relationship among the variables emerges using this inductive approach. Thus, as explained in greater detail in this chapter, the analysis structure of the TTP involved multiple layers of analysis and revisiting of the data conducted by different combinations of research teams to reach theoretical sufficiency.

The interview subjects were Holocaust survivors and their spouses, their children and their spouses, their grandchildren, and accessible extended family members. TTP interviewed survivors and their families who were representative of a cross-section of countries of origin, religious beliefs, political affiliation, and socio-economic backgrounds. The empirical representativeness of the sample is neither important nor a goal of qualitative research (Padgett, 1998). Sampling relied on a combination of strategies: snowballing,[1] convenience,[2] and opportunism.[3]

The respondents provided in-depth psychosocial life histories that included information about prewar years, the war experiences, and postwar years along with an exploration of feelings, thoughts, and behaviors of the individual and of significant family and social relationships.

The TTP in-depth psychosocial life histories are rich, detailed, guided conversations that yielded vivid descriptions. In-depth psychosocial life histories ideally foster multiple visits in participants' homes. By building trust of the respondents for their interviewers over multiple visits, it was possible not only to elicit deeper levels of sharing but also to further probe and clarify the information given in previous visits, thus yielding interviews rich in psychosocial information.

The semistructured interview questions were based on the following broad content areas: family of origin dynamics, war experiences, liberation, immigration, and postwar life. Respondents were encouraged to describe the context of their personal experiences and their relationships with others rather than just report on the historical facts of their war experiences. Thoughts, feelings, and behaviors were elicited through questioning that not only probed for the respondents' internal experience but also contextualized their experience within their significant relationships. Prewar information included such topics as demographics of family of origin, description of relationships, religious identity, family values, and any significant life experiences before the war. War information included experiences of self-preservation, dehumanization, and coping strategies, as well as the psychological thoughts and feelings of the survivor and the survivor's connection to significant others. Postwar information included such topics as mourning the losses, finding other survivors, emigration to the United States, marriage, children, religious identity, faith, memories, strategies for coping and adapting, political attitudes, and the impact of the Holocaust on the individual and family members.

A separate semistructured interview format was developed for each category of interviewee: survivor, nonsurvivor spouse, child of survivors (COS), non-COS spouse, and grandchild of survivors (GOS). Each of these semistructured interviews focused on a slightly different set of questions based on the interviewee's family position vis-à-vis the survivor to gain a more complete picture of the family. The interviews ranged from 1 to 18 hours of tape over multiple sittings. As a result of the trust and comfort that developed between the interviewees and the interviewers, several survivors who had never told their stories before or in as much detail gave the TTP in-depth narratives.

Since databases that rely on qualitative analysis usually contain only a small number of individuals in the sample population, the literature is silent or discouraging on how to work with large qualitative databases (Stanley, 2008). Yet, due to the underexplored nature at that time of the topic of coping and resilience in survivor families, the decision was made early on in the project to interview a larger-than-usual number of survivors and their family members. Consequently, the TTP had to create its own protocols and procedures to manage the large database.

The TTP Analysis Process

The TTP analysis process paralleled the five stages of analysis described in McCracken's work (1988). His five stages represent a progression from more specific to an increasing level of generality. McCracken's process started from the words of the respondents on their own terms, with each useful statement creating an observation and ending with patterns and themes that move from the particular to the general level of analysis.

More recent discussions of grounded theory divide the process by coding (i.e., initial or line-by-line coding), which leads into focused or more directed and conceptual coding, followed by axial coding, which answers the questions of when, where, why, who, how, and what are the consequences (Charmaz, 2006; Strauss & Corbin, 1998). In both of these frameworks, qualitative analysis is inductive, moving from the specific to the general and systematic. The analysis processes created for the TTP complied with this same pattern from specific to general and systematic.

However, the TTP added innovative procedures, consisting of three parts that structured our analysis process. In the first phase of the analysis, we created an instrument called the protocol of analysis for in-depth interviews (the protocol), which permitted us to track the words of the respondents in the transcripts. The protocol asked each researcher to highlight important or descriptive comments, compare comments within the transcript itself, and then compare them to the literature in the relevant fields. The protocol contained over 50 psychosocial categories relating to the prewar, war, and postwar years of the respondents' lives. Table 3.1 summarizes the categories of the protocol.

Table 3.1 Summary Categories of the Protocol of Analysis for In-Depth Interviews

1. Demographic profile of family of origin and nuclear family
2. Descriptions of individuals: self; family; friends; family of origin/nuclear
3. Descriptions of family relationships: family of origin and nuclear family, including marriage/children
4. Dynamics of family of origin and nuclear family
5. General beliefs/attitudes: prewar/postwar
6. Faith/Relationship with God; Jewish identity/intergeneration transmission: prewar/war/postwar
7. Prewar experiences
8. War experiences
   - Brief chronology
   - Preservation and human connection
   - Dehumanization and despair, coping
   - Poignant stories of war
9. Personal explanations for survival
10. Liberation and immigration to the United States
11. Beliefs about the Holocaust
12. Postwar attitudes about groups and politics
13. Looking back: successes and regrets
14. Coping: prewar, war, and postwar
15. Special topics: food, dreams, losses, guilt, etc.
16. Impact of Holocaust on interviewee and family
17. Impressions of interview/interviewee

The researcher/analyst recorded demographic information about the respondents and their families; any descriptions of individuals given in the interview; any descriptions of family relationships and the dynamics of the family of origin; the prewar and war experiences; and the experiences postwar regarding immigration to the United States and creating a new family. Observations in the form of quotations or summary statements were recorded on the protocol. When the coding of the interview data through the protocol was finished, each researcher ended up with a psychosocial profile of each interviewee within his or her family context.

In qualitative research, a key issue is trustworthiness (Altheide & Johnson, 1994; Kazdin, 1998; Padgett, 1998). A trustworthy study (i.e., a valid study) is one that is carried out fairly and ethically and has findings that represent as closely as possible the experiences of the respondents (Padgett, 1998). Threats to credibility and trustworthiness include reactivity, researcher biases, and interviewee biases. Researcher biases may be particularly evident in the analysis phase of a research project. They come through the temptation to filter one's observations and interpretations through a lens clouded by preconceptions and opinions (Goldenberg, 2008; Padgett, 1998).

Padgett (1998) discussed one aspect of minimizing researcher bias: observer triangulation. Observer triangulation uses multiple coders to gain interrater consensus. Triangulation consists of collecting information from a diverse range of individuals and settings, using a variety of methods (Maxwell, 1996). The analysis process of the TTP focused on minimizing researcher bias through the creation of an innovative team process called the triad. The triad consisted of a facilitator, the original interviewer, and a second reader of the interview. Prior to a triad meeting, the facilitator listened to the original tapes, allowing voice intonations and silences to be heard. The facilitator noted key themes to be discussed at meetings based upon the Protocol. The interviewer and the second reader completed the Protocol by reading the transcript and writing the observations in the appropriate categories of the protocol. While the facilitator heard the interviewee's voice just prior to the analysis and the interviewer heard the voice and observed the nonverbal language during the original interview, the second reader lacked both of these sources of data. Thus, each member of the triad came to the meeting with a slightly different orientation to the same material.

Interpretations achieved by consensus lent support to the validity of the interpretive process and fostered validity through intersubjective agreement. By including perspectives that came from conducting the interview, reading the interview, and listening to the interview, the consensus of the team assumed even greater reliability and trustworthiness. In this way, the original interviewer integrated into the analysis observations of the respondents derived from the face-to-face interview encounter. The respondent's tone of voice, affect, and body language contributed to the analysis picture. Often, each triad included a child of survivors and a mental health professional. The addition of a researcher who was also a child of survivors in the beginning of the analysis phase of the project served as a reality check against the assumptions about the total negativity of life in survivor families found in the early literature.

To fulfill the project goal of understanding individuals within their own family units and across family units, the triads analyzed the respondents in the context of their own family groupings. By starting with the analysis of each member of the survivor generation and ending with their grandchildren, the thematic findings for each interview built on the thematic findings from the previous interviews within the family grouping. The movement from the analysis of individual narrative data to the analysis of family data is an additional innovation of the triad process. When all the interviews in a family had each been examined through the triad process, the themes articulated by the triad not only reflected the findings for the individual but also created a psychosocial profile of the family and provided important insights into the intergenerational transmission of both trauma and resilience.

All triad meetings were audiotaped and later transcribed, thus creating a permanent record of the discussions. These transcripts served a threefold purpose: to document the analysis process, to serve as the foundation for the next stage of analysis, and to provide transparency of the analysis process (Padgett, 1998). This documentation left an audit trail that is useful for verification of the process and findings by others, thus providing an innovative method of creating an audit trail through memos. The transcripts of the triad meetings reflected the oral version of memos, providing a verbatim written documentation of the analysis process on each individual and each family. Memos function as the intermediate step between coding and writing and are where the codes are analyzed (Charmaz, 2006). The three-way discussion in the triads examined the coding of each interview, relating the data in the interview to previous patterns seen in the sample, to research findings by others, and to the in vivo codes as defined by the respondents' own words.

In addition, the audit trail came from writing the data onto the protocol, from transcribing the analysis meetings, and from highlighting the significant passages in each transcript. The highlighted passages from the transcript of the triad analysis were then analyzed a second time by a team of two, who created synopses. The synopses reflected the consensus ideas expressed in the analysis transcripts while reducing the 60- to 100-page transcripts to manageable 10- to 15-page summary documents.

The first task of the creators of the synopsis was to validate that the highlighted passage was truly a theme achieved by consensus and corroborated by observations from the interview text. Their second task was to use the highlighted text to create the synopsis, which contained only the consensus themes. The two researchers worked independently on these separate tasks and then blended their work into one document. This served as a double check of the findings by verifying the consensus themes and verifying that the interpretive material was highlighted correctly in the transcription.

The synopsis, the instrument for the second phase of the TTP analysis process, was created to address the challenge of managing both the huge quantity of information generated by a large sample and the lengthy in-depth interviews of each interviewee. Each synopsis recorded the psychosocial profile for each interviewee and, when read together with the synopses that comprise a family grouping, provided the psychosocial profile for the family. The result was the reduction from a 60- to 100-page transcript that distilled the entire interview to a manageable 10- to 15-page summary document that recorded the thematic findings.

While the protocol included over 50 categories, the synopsis summarized the findings into 15–20 categories, less than half that number (see Table 3.2). The summary categories included quotations that presented the thematic findings in the interviewee's own words. The synopses consequently facilitated the identification of relevant themes within and across the family and the individual profiles in the study.

Table 3.2 Phase 2: Synopses Topics

1. First impressions of the interviewee by the triad members
2. Demographics of family of origin, nuclear family
3. Description of individuals
4. Description of key relationships of the interviewee and family members
5. Dynamics of family of origin/nuclear family
6. Prewar/war/postwar faith and general beliefs
7. Prewar experiences
8. Chronology of war experience
9. Self-preservation, dehumanization, coping during the war
10. Explanations for survival
11. Liberation and immigration to the United States
12. Successes/regrets
13. Attitudes about people, groups, and politics
14. Beliefs about the Holocaust
15. Impact of Holocaust on interviewee or family
16. Characteristics of survival

The third phase of the project involved the investigation of more focused topics within the overall analysis through a comparison of individuals and families across the study. Comparing the themes generated by the triad process across the sample fostered the investigation of similarities and differences among individuals and families and the designation of factors that accounted for these patterns. One method of analyzing topics across individuals and across families is "charting."

The process of charting the possibilities that result from the conjunction of two or more variables is called substructing, dimensionalizing, or cross-classifying typologizing (Lofland & Lofland, 1995). Further defined by Lofland and Lofland as "concept charting," it consists of arranging summaries of the findings on a single sheet of paper to more clearly envision the relations among the different factors (Lofland & Lofland, 1995). Charting the findings revealed patterns and themes that carried across the family units in the project. Charting is not a uniquely developed tool of analysis for use by the TTP. However, the TTP utilized charting to reveal new findings that applied to families and individuals across the entire database.

The topics of the charts came from several sources: the literature on that topic; questions that arose from the findings from the TTP analysis of the entire project sample of survivors; and through the grounded theory process that facilitates the identification of new factors and investigative areas to explore as the analysis of the data unfolds. For example, the TTP asked the survivors about their feelings toward the perpetrators of the crimes against them and their families. From this question, an unexpected finding arose: Many survivors expressed political attitudes of tolerance toward the perpetrators. Using grounded theory, the factors influencing tolerance in survivors were then identified from the data (Isserman, 2005) and from the literature of previous studies on tolerance. After coding the interviews and analyzing them, a series of charts consisting of groups of factors was created. These charts revealed patterns of interaction between the factors and the tolerant survivors (see Chapter 6 for an example of a chart).

Table 3.3 is one example. This is a modification of a chart of key sociological factors identified in the literature as influencing tolerance. The chart tracks the differences or similarities in each factor by survivor. The chart led to a new finding on religion and tolerance. It revealed on analysis that no relationship existed between belief in God and intolerance or between ritual practice and intolerance. However, further analysis of the data by factors recorded on this chart led to the new finding that change in belief and change in ritual practice from prewar to postwar years was related to tolerance and intolerance. The chart showed that tolerant survivors changed their beliefs but did not change their practices from pre- to postwar. This pattern became clear through the chart. Other charts focusing

Table 3.3 Example of Charting Tolerant Survivors

	Survivor Name					
	Survivor 1	Survivor 2	Survivor 3	Survivor 4	Survivor 5	Survivor 6
Belief in God prewar	Yes	Yes	No	No	Yes	Yes
Beliefs changed postwar	<u>Yes</u>	<u>Yes</u>	<u>No</u>	<u>Yes</u>	<u>Yes</u>	<u>Yes</u>
Ritual practice prewar	Yes	Yes	No	No	No	Yes
Ritual practice changed postwar	<u>No</u>	<u>No</u>	<u>No</u>	<u>No</u>	<u>No</u>	<u>Yes</u>
Survivor guilt present	No	No	No	No	No	Yes

Note: Findings are <u>underlined</u>.

on intolerant survivors revealed the finding that intolerant survivors did not change their beliefs postwar but did change their ritual practices from prewar to postwar.

Conclusion

In conclusion, the TTP, faced with the unique challenge of doing qualitative research with a large sample of respondents, developed research tools to aid in the analysis of the data. It was important to create processes that minimized researcher bias, maximized objective inquiry, and fostered group consensus of thematic findings. The pioneering instrument, the protocol, made it possible to assess the large number of variables found within the expansive life histories. The two innovative processes, the triad and the synopsis, focused the analysis and provided a means by which the researchers could track patterns of emotional, cognitive, and behavioral phenomena for 275 individuals, patterns of intergenerational family dynamics in 50 families, and patterns of similarities and differences across the sample. Thus, these three tools, created specifically to face the challenges that arose from the large qualitative database, served the project well. They allowed researchers to analyze a dataset containing 275 interviews while tracking many different factors. The tools facilitated the comparison of themes and findings found in individual interviews to other family members and other family units in the dataset. The methods developed for TTP can be adapted to other projects using grounded research with large datasets and qualitative in-depth interviews.

Notes

1. Respondents were identified by asking for referrals after interviewing each survivor. For example, one researcher interviewed a neighbor who was a child of survivors. This contact opened the door to his wife, his brothers and their wives, and other family members. Ultimately using snowball sampling, 19 members of the extended family were interviewed; none of them had ever told their stories to an interviewer before.
2. Interviewees all maintained some connection to a large metropolitan area on the east coast. In only a few instances, interviewers traveled to other parts of the country or Israel to interview survivors.
3. Opportunistic sampling led researchers to follow leads in tracking down interviewees who could offer a particular perspective or experience. One survivor who spent the war in Siberia with her family told the interviewer that her good friend, who spent the war in Siberia with her, lived only a few blocks away. The interviewer contacted this friend who gave her a different perspective on the same events in Siberia.

References

Altheide, D. L., & Johnson, M. (1994). Criteria for assessing interpretive validity for qualitative research. In N. K. Denzin & Y. S. Lincoln (Eds.), *Handbook of qualitative research* (pp. 485–499). Thousand Oaks, CA: Sage.

Atkinson, P., Coffey, A., & Delamont, S. (2001). A debate about our canon. *Qualitative Inquiry, 1,* 1–5.

Charmaz, K. (2001). Qualitative interviewing and grounded theory analysis. In J. F. Gubrium & J. A. Golstein (Eds.), *Handbook of interview research* (pp. 675–694). Thousand Oaks, CA: Sage.

Charmaz, K. (2006). *Constructing grounded theory.* Thousand Oaks, CA: Sage.

Denzin, N. K., & Lincoln, Y. S. (Eds.). (2000). *Handbook of qualitative research* (2nd ed.). Thousand Oaks, CA: Sage.

Dey, I. (1999). *Grounding grounded theory.* San Diego, CA: Academic Press.

Goldenberg, J. (2008*). "The feelings of my family are with me." The posttraumatic coping of adolescent survivors of the Holocaust.* Unpublished doctoral dissertation, Bryn Mawr College, Bryn Mawr, PA.

Gubrium, J. F., & Holstein, J. A. (2002). *Handbook of interview research* (pp. 83–101). Thousand Oaks, CA: Sage.

Isserman, N. (2005). *"I harbor no hate": A study of political tolerance and intolerance.* Unpublished dissertation, Graduate Center, City University of New York, New York, NY.

Kazdin, A. E. (1998). *Research design in clinical psychology.* Boston: Allyn & Bacon.

Kotler-Berkowitz, L., Blass, L. & Neuman, D. (2004). *Nazi victims residing in the United States.* United Jewish Communities Report Series on the National Jewish Population Survey 2000–01, report 2.

Lindsey, E. (1998). The impact of homelessness and shelter life on family relationships. *Family Relations, 47,* 243–252.

Lofland, J., & Lofland, L. H. (1995). *Analyzing social settings: A guide to qualitative observation and analysis.* Belmont, CA: Wadsworth.

Madill, A., & Gough, B. (2008). Qualitative research and its place in psychological science. *Psychological Methods, 13,* 254–271.

Maxwell, J. A. (1996). *Using qualitative research to develop causal explanations.* Boston: Harvard Project on Schooling and Children.

McCracken, G. (1988). *The long interview.* In Qualitative Research Methods Series *13.* Newbury Park, NJ: Sage.

Miles, M. B., & Huberman, A. M. (1994). *Qualitative data analysis.* Thousand Oaks, CA: Sage.

Morse, J. M., & Richards, L. (2002). *Read me first for a user's guide to qualitative methods.* Thousand Oaks, CA: Sage.

Padgett, D. K. (1998). *Qualitative methods in social work research: Challenges and rewards.* Thousand Oaks, CA: Sage.

Padgett, D. K. (Ed.). (2004). *The qualitative research experience.* Belmont, CA: Thomson/Brooks-Cole.

Polkinghorne, D. (2007). Validity issues in narrative research. *Qualitative Inquiry, 13,* 471–486.

Stanley, L. (2008). Madness to the method? Using a narrative methodology to analyze large-scale complex social phenomena. *Qualitative Research, 8,* 435–447.

Strauss, A., & Corbin, J. (1998). *Basics of qualitative research.* Thousand Oaks, CA: Sage.

Suedfeld, P. (1996). Thematic content analyses: Nomothetic methods for using Holocaust survivor narratives in psychological research. *Holocaust and Genocide Studies, 10,* 169.

PART II

The Survivors and the Impact of Prewar
Family Dynamics on Their Postwar Lives

CHAPTER 4

"The Biggest Star Is Your Mother"
Prewar Coping Strategies of 18 Adolescent Survivors

JENNIFER GOLDENBERG

Introduction

Adolescent survivors were far from tabulae rasae going into the war. To understand their postwar adaptation, it is important first to understand their prewar lives, experiences, and coping skills. In fact, the survivors who were between 12 and 18 when the Holocaust interrupted their lives already had a well-stocked arsenal of coping strategies and protective factors in place that helped them survive and rebuild after the war. The Transcending Trauma Project (TTP) interviews provide us with much useful information regarding what I call the "arsenal of self." This tool kit of coping strategies and protective factors included secure attachments and loyalty to parents, siblings, or other caring adults; religious belief systems and moral values learned from parents and grandparents; various forms of social support; a strong sense of group identity; a perceived sense of self-efficacy; and an exposure to traumatic events and losses that served as a source of "stress inoculation" (Meichenbaum, 2009) going into the Holocaust years.

Clinicians can help their traumatized adult clients locate and access their own pretrauma foundational strengths. Recognizing and building on those strengths can help restore a client's "shattered assumptions" (Janoff-Bulman, 1997)—particularly his or her beliefs about self—and aid in healing.

Methodology

This chapter is based on work I conducted for my doctoral dissertation, which focused on the long-term impacts and coping of 18 survivors of the Holocaust (Goldenberg, 2008). It is an analysis of the most complete interviews of survivors in the TTP database who were between the ages of 12 and 18 when the war began. By *complete*, I mean that these interviews contain information on the prewar, war, and postwar periods. I chose adolescent survivors both because they were the largest group in the TTP database and because they were more developed cognitively and emotionally than their child counterparts and therefore would have more memories and stories of prewar life.

There are 14 women and 4 men in the sample. This roughly approximates the gender ratio of the larger TTP database, which is 36% male. My sample includes people from the following countries of origin: Poland (nine), Czechoslovakia (four), Germany (three), and Hungary (two). Most experienced part of the Holocaust in concentration camps; some spent the entire Holocaust in hiding. Many were the sole survivors of their families of origin.

All of these interviews followed a semistructured interview schedule. These are essentially life narratives, and in most cases the respondents told their stories, guided by the interviewers, in chronological sequence: a coherent beginning (prewar life), middle (war), penultimate (immediate postwar), and ultimate (long-term postwar) chapter for each of those lives.

The prewar foundations, the specific war traumas, and the immediate postwar events together became the crucible for postwar coping and adaptation. We therefore need first to understand the prewar foundations of coping strategies to understand how survivors coped and adapted during and after the war.

In beginning my analysis, I made the decision to code the interviews with the women first ($N = 14$), before then coding the men ($N = 4$), in case any issues of gender differences might be discernible. Using NUD*IST 4 qualitative software, I started my coding by looking at self-descriptions, which I soon termed "stories of self." These self-descriptions are grounded in stories, as are many of the other descriptions of significant people and attachments in these interviews. For example, when a survivor was asked to describe her mother, she would tell a story about her kindness, her charity, or her cruelty. When asked to give descriptions of themselves and others, survivors were rarely limited to a few adjectives; their descriptions were almost always grounded in a particular narrative. These narratives are rich in stories of self and contain information regarding coping strategies, the nature of attachments, and risk and protective factors. They give us a window onto the prewar foundations of coping strategies that adolescent survivors took with them to endure the Holocaust.

The information from these interviews regarding prewar lives and foundations of coping fall into five broad categories: descriptions of self; significant attachment figures; Jewish faith and practice; mastery experiences; and childhood trauma. Within these narratives can be found several prewar coping strategies. I discuss the women in the sample first and then the men.

The Women

Descriptions of Self

Questions were asked regarding descriptions of self in the TTP interviews. Typical questions might be: "How would you describe yourself as a child?" Or, "What kind of child were you?" I looked at the replies to find some evidence of temperament, strengths, and coping skills survivors had developed before the war as children—in other words, as part of what I conceived of as an arsenal of self that they took with them into the war. My hypothesis going in was that I might find evidence of strengths and coping, as well as evidence of temperament (i.e., anxious, easygoing, shy) that would help me understand how they coped as adolescents with the war trauma and the years after the war. What I found in these descriptions by the female respondents provided a glimpse, but not enough convincing evidence, to make any conclusive statements. Male respondents were more expansive, as demonstrated separately.

One "outlier" example was provided by one of the youngest women in the sample. Edith was only 10 when her war trauma began and 15 at liberation. She is also the only survivor of her entire family. When asked what she was like as a little girl, Edith responded:

> I don't know. I have nobody to tell me [emphasis added]. … It's very difficult to be objective, you know. To look into yourself.

Aside from the poignancy of this statement of an orphan, Edith's response is indicative of a loss of her sense of herself as a child. What those of us whose parents lived into our adulthood take for granted—the stories of ourselves as children told (often repetitively) into our adult lives, and even sometimes told to our own children—is glaringly absent for Edith, who was young at the start of the war and whose entire family did not survive.

Most of these survivors, however, were able to provide at least some brief descriptions of themselves as children and adolescents.

> I was very tiny for my age. I was running away from whatever I saw. I was listening to everything. I was curious. But if I saw anybody fight, I would be the first to run away from it. And I guess, until today, too. (Cynthia)

> The whole family wanted me all the time. I don't know. Because the other ones were more aggressive. I'm the quieter of them all. (Florence)

> I would always open up my mouth, you know. And talk back. (Gittel)

However, self-descriptions in these interviews became much more pronounced and detailed when the war years and postwar years were addressed. It is unclear whether this is a remarkable finding. It may, in fact, be difficult for many people to describe themselves as children—whether they are survivors or not. Perhaps it is easier to describe oneself when in the midst of a trauma—and how one fought, fled, or froze. Perhaps it is easier still to describe oneself as an adult, compared to self-descriptions of childhood. Narrative and developmental psychologists have spoken of the ways in which we create our own personal myths that continue to evolve and change throughout our lives. These narratives can have a healing power (Angus & McLeod, 2004: McAdams, 1993, 2001; Mishler, 2004; Schafer, 1992; White & Epston, 1990).

In sum, self-descriptions of survivors in childhood and adolescence provided only minimal information. These few clues might give us a glimpse into who they were as children, but only tantalizing leads, not substantive information regarding their coping strategies.

Still, it is worth noting that self-descriptions became far more detailed when describing the war years and immediately after the war. Noteworthy, as well, is the fact that descriptions of significant attachment figures— parents, siblings, and grandparents, most of whom were killed in the Holocaust—were far more complex and detailed than the self-descriptions of prewar childhood and adolescence.

Significant Attachment Figures

With the exception of three of the women, the female respondents described their childhoods—in particular family relationships—in terms that can be described as generally positive. I looked first at how they described their parents.

> My mother was a very good woman. Very, very good woman. She did for everybody. … My mother was very farsighted. She put a lot of confidence in us. (Florence)

Very quiet. Very devoted to her family. Very hard-working. Co-operated. Nothing special to tell. Talked little, discussed little. Something had to be told, she let Father tell it. (Tova)

My father was a very warm, giving person. I never remember that he was saying a loud word to anybody. (Ella)

My father was a very learned man, a very humble man. (Ilana)

A speculation could be made, perhaps, that some of these descriptions are idealizations of the dead, a retrospective look at the past that is somewhat rose tinged and forgiving. This has, in fact, been suggested in the literature regarding Holocaust survivors' accounts (Suedfeld et al., 2005).

The third child was a boy, but he didn't live. And I was the oldest, so he [her father] used to talk to me like I would be a son, not a daughter. And we had a very good relationship. (Cynthia)

She used to tell us stories. She used to sing to us. (Florence)

My father was a very good father. And my mother was an exceptionally good mother. (Gerda)

But three of the women paint a darker picture of their parents.

Either my mother or the maid would sit with me and feed me. I wouldn't eat. And they would feed me with a teaspoon, until I vomited. And then I would be spanked for vomiting. Up until the age of 10. This was the biggest struggle with my mother. (Edith)

My mom hit me more than my father. She didn't like anything that I did whatever. (Charlotte)

Sometimes I was very angry because instead of cooking dinner she was reading a book. … I don't want to lie. My relationship with my mother was not too good. … When I was a little kid, I remember my mother hit me many times. (Ella)

Many of the women described other important attachment figures, such as a beloved aunt or grandmother. For the three women in the sample (Edith, Charlotte, and Ella) who came from what could be described as significantly abusive homes, and for one woman whose mother suffered from mental illness (Eva), these nonparental family members were major protective factors for children trying to escape a troubled childhood. They provided a respite, a warm and loving "holding environment" of recovery from the unhappiness at home (Werner & Smith, 2001). These other attachment figures served as mitigating factors in these adolescents' unhappy childhoods. Eva described this well:

> My mother was unwell, and the loss of baby after baby did not contribute to her mental stability. She always had headaches. … My grandmother, this was the mainstay of my life. … Grandma's house was always full of people with jokes and laughter and singing. And my Grandma had a lot of land. It was a happy house, with singing, with joking, with pushing, with crawling on top. There were trees— cherry trees, plum trees, apple trees. You could sit there and read a book for a day and nobody would see you.

Ella's mother beat her often. She sought out older people for comfort, almost as if she knew she was at risk and was reaching out for the help of one older, caring person in the environment.

> I was very introverted. I would like to run to older people. There was a lady living in the back of our house, a Gentile lady, who was very good to me. I would like to run to her house, and I don't know if I would eat something, or she would give me to drink. She used to make preservatives [sic: preserves], and she would give me that. … She would look out for me.

While these female respondents reported using other adults, grandmothers, or kind neighbors as holding environments where they could get some respite and relief from stressors, another means of coping was their peer group. Peers provided social support, gave advice, and were more comfortable to talk with about certain issues than were parents.

> Sometimes it took a year until she [her mother] realized my body had changed. You knew from school. In school you talked. She couldn't talk about the facts of life. A married woman, her children. She couldn't talk. (Tova)

Parents would also be used for support, but less frequently as the girls got older, and more often in the context of dealing with the pervasive anti-Semitism. Distraction was also used; Tova described going to the movies as a way to relieve her stress. Ella, abused at home, described doing her best to avoid conflict.

Sibling relationships were also described in both positive and realistic terms, with sibling rivalry mentioned as well.

> Well, my sister was 2 years younger than me, and she was the prettier. I had a little complex, you know, because she was very pretty. And my father's side of the family used to say that when the boys would start to come, they would have to hide her under the bed because she's so pretty. (Cynthia)

> I love my sisters. I can't tell you I didn't have a squabble here and there at home, but it doesn't amount to anything. I think I realize what's important; you don't keep harping, and wanting, and be mad about it, and then keep it in your heart and don't forget it. I love them and I guess I'll love them 'til I die, and I know they love me. (Charlotte. She survived Auschwitz with her four younger sisters.)

> My sister was 9 years older than me. … Even when she was married I had to go once a week to sleep with her. We were very close. (Gerda)

The drama and pathos of relationships with siblings is more pronounced when the survivors described their experiences during the war years. This is no doubt due to the fact that so many siblings were killed then. Other siblings survived and served as sources of support as well as burdens to survival when parents had been killed. Some siblings survived under different circumstances than the respondents. In one notable case (Ella), the mother chose to protect one child (Ella's younger sister) over Ella, in a variation of a *Sophie's Choice* (Styron, 1979) scenario. This contributed to a lifelong estrangement between these siblings (and between Ella and her mother).

In sum, with the exception of three of the female survivors in this sample, these adolescents had formed positive, secure attachments with family members before the war, and the three exceptions were able to seek out other, older adults with whom to form secure attachments. They were able to tell many stories regarding these important attachment figures; within these stories can be found the foundations contributing to their posttraumatic adaptation and resilience. Even for the three who described abusive homes, there is evidence that they demonstrated an ability to seek out an older, caring adult for comfort, attachment, and a relief from the stressors of their young lives, a key component of resilience in childhood and adolescence (O'Connell Higgins, 1994; Spencer, 2002; Werner & Smith, 2001).

Family Messages and Values

Messages and values were imparted by parents to their children before the war. Developmentally, these female respondents were old enough to have integrated these messages from parents about life, about what is to be valued in life, about coping with anger, about human dignity and integrity. Lessons were taught and absorbed on a regular basis in many of these families. Ella, from an abusive home, is the single exception; not surprisingly, she did not mention any positive messages from her parents.

The clarity with which most of the survivors related these messages and the ease with which they summoned them seem to indicate that they served as wellsprings of support throughout the difficult years after the war. They were old enough to have heard the messages, understood them, and processed them and could then use them as necessary in times of stress.

> So, my father always used to tell us, if you are upset with something, and you want to tell something to the person you are upset, first you sleep with it, and keep it, and try next morning. That means the next morning you'll feel more relaxed. … And the other thing he would tell us is the word you are letting out is no more yours. You count your words. … *So these are very important things to remember* [emphasis added]. (Gerda)

> My father believed everything was from heaven. [In business, if there was a financial loss] he said, "We had to have this loss. And better this loss than a loss of health." And to this day if I lose money, or if I ruin anything, it never bothers me. … *It's still deep in me* [emphasis added], I have a feeling that it had to happen, and it shouldn't bother me. (Tova)

> At home, as a Jew, I never felt I had to hide, or do anything less, because we were as capable, because we had education, and we tried to help [the Gentiles in their community]. And yet, never looking at the peasant that he didn't have an education, that he was not capable, because he could do other things that we couldn't do. … I remember my dad telling us, school was important because no one can take your education away. They can take everything else away from you. But who you are, what you are, will always be yours. *And during the war, we felt the same way. No matter what the Germans did, we were hoping and praying that we would remain human and not lose our humanity* [emphasis added]. (Hinda)

In sum, perhaps by summoning their parents' lessons, it seems as though these adolescent survivors were also summoning their parents—their voices and values speaking to them after death. These were often the only legacies these female adolescents inherited from their parents, messages they would eventually transmit to the next generation.

Jewish Faith, Practice, and Group Identity

Almost all of the women came from Orthodox Jewish homes, which seemed to be the major form of Judaism practiced at that time, particularly in the smaller towns. The women described the levels of observance in their families.

> Strong Orthodoxy. There was no other way. Most of the women of my town wore sheitels. [Yiddish for wigs; many Orthodox married women cover their hair for reasons of modesty.] (Cynthia)

> Everybody was religious. Not extremely religious, not like you see the Hasidim in New York. My father always had a yarmulke and hat on. My mother had no hair; she wore a sheitel all the time. There was no question about eating unkosher. (Charlotte)

There were more progressive types of Judaism in the larger cities, such as Warsaw, Budapest, or Berlin, somewhat along the lines of contemporary branches of Conservative and Reform Judaism in America.

> We were what you would call here Conservative or Reform. My parents went to synagogue, where of course the men and the women were separated, and my parents had a small department store, which was closed for Shabbas [Yiddish for the Jewish Sabbath, sundown Friday until sundown Saturday]. (Edith)

The subject of Jewish faith and observance weaves throughout these interviews and seems to have played an important role in these adolescents' prewar development, as well as after the war. It was a notable finding that stories of faith were often embedded in important relationships of attachment demonstrating "secure attachment connected to sensitive caregivers" (Granqvist, Mikulincer, & Shaver, 2010, p. 49). Charlotte talked about climbing into bed with her grandmother on cold winter evenings and hearing her say her prayers at bedtime and in the morning.

> That grandmother came in every morning to say Modeh Ani, that morning prayer, with us, with the children. I still say that prayer every morning that she taught me.

Gerda lost her mother at a very young age, before the war. When asked if she had any memories of her, she replied:

> I remember one moment, when she hold me in her lap, sitting next to the window. On Saturday, between day and night, you know at twilight, there is a prayer, "God from Abraham and Yaakov." I don't

remember her face; I remember feeling her hand in my hand. And I remember saying after her. This is the only thing I remember [about her mother], not that somebody told me. This I really remember, and I feel it. This was always with me.

Iliana connected family with synagogue:

My father was the president of the synagogue. And he was sitting in front, you know, with a high hat. ... Oh, my father, did I have a father! Did I have a family. ... And my home away from home was the synagogue. We had our love affairs there. We made our homework there, we learned there. We danced a little there. It was wonderful.

Not all memories of prewar faith and observance were portrayed in such a positive vein, however. Florence, for example, described Orthodox Judaism as oppressive, especially for women.

It was very difficult. We had to live there [Sechel, Hungary, a small town, where everyone was Orthodox], and we [the women] were pushed down. And that's why my mother was always pushing my father to move out, because in the city you could do what you want to do.

As the girls got older, and entered adolescence, a few of them described struggling with questions of faith or ritual observance. This is fairly typical of adolescent development, as cognition becomes more sophisticated, and parental values and beliefs are held up to scrutiny and skepticism (Coles, 1990). Some of these struggles were precipitated as these adolescent girls were becoming involved in Zionist youth groups and thus becoming exposed not only to politics but also to more progressive, secular ideas.

I grew up with a belief in God, of course. Until I came to this movement which started teaching about Darwin. ... And I came back once to my father and I told him a little bit of this new learning ... about Darwin. He had patience. He wasn't a fanatic. So he said, "So tell me. This little bit of dust. Who creates first this little bit of dust? ... Look what happens in the world. Spring on time, and summer on time, and fall comes on time, and the winter. How is it all these things happen?" You know, I really didn't have an answer. I couldn't go and tell him scientific things, because I then didn't know much. (Gerda)

One is reminded of Erikson's (1950) psychosocial crisis of "identity versus role diffusion." In this stage of development, according to Erikson, peer groups provide new ideological perspectives, as well as models of leadership and sources of group identity. For these adolescent survivors, being members of a Zionist group helped them in the formation of a group identity and solidified their individual Jewish identities as well, particularly for the oldest women in the sample, who had reached late adolescence by the beginning of the war (Baumeister & Leary, 1995; Ysseldyk, Matheson, & Anisman, 2010). Zionist youth groups provided new ideas, secular Yiddish culture, music, literature, and even significant shifts in belief systems as some of these adolescent girls began to question their faith before the war. As the girls got older, grew more curious about life and ideas, and social life became more critical at this stage of development, Zionism provided a group where they could belong.

> The whole group [Poalei Zion] went to the mountains, and we had a lot of fun. We had poetry reading, and poetry writing, and singing, and we had lecturers. Writers used to come to us, and it was really very, very worthwhile. I came back, I looked beautiful. My face shined up. (Gerda)

> I started to belong to a Zionist organization, and they had meetings every week, and they had summertime outings. And I was occupied in the store. So I resented it [having to work and not being able to attend meetings]. (Tova)

As life became more difficult and anti-Semitic incidents proliferated, Zionist groups sprung up as an antidote, as an empowering choice. These groups offered social support, a sense of belonging, and a sense of meaning and purpose that mitigated some of the stress of living in that environment (Haslam, O'Brien, Jetten, Vormedal, & Penna, 2005). For some of these adolescent girls, the message was a compelling one. They would become farmers and move to (what was then) Palestine.

> They were talking about going on hachshara [Hebrew for farming; some Zionist youth groups prepared members for farm life in Palestine, but Jews as a whole were not farmers, traditionally], preparing to work on the farm. And then they were even older than I. … And they were talking. And I believed that in my mind, I started doubting that we should wait for Moshiach [Hebrew for the Messiah] to come. … And seeing another solution: buying land and working on a farm. It was never a way for me to leave my family. But young people were going from my town, too, to Israel. (Tova)

The winds of change were coming—even to the smallest towns—before the Holocaust swept these young people up. Modernity was creeping in to the small villages of Eastern Europe. Florence, who expressed strong resentment about the confines of Orthodox Judaism, talked about being literally and figuratively "at the crossroads" between the old ways and the new in her little town:

> If I look back to the town, truthfully, I think it had to come a change … because we were very suppressed. You know, once that religion puts a lock on your neck, you are doomed, and you cannot live only by religion. See, the house I grew up in, it was an open house. We had everybody there. Because we had a business. We lived on the crossroads of the town. … And everybody [Gentiles of all types] had to stop there, you know? [Laughs.] If it was for our benefit, or for our disaster, people still stopped there. (Florence)

In sum, these adolescents were old enough to have integrated the values of their families' religious faith and practice, sources of strength they could take with them into the war, memories of close attachments within the context of Jewish familial and communal faith and practice. Others had joined Zionist groups, which gave them a sense of Jewish identity and pride, role models for leadership and initiative, an antidote to the anti-Semitic climate in the form of social support that mitigated some of the stress, and a dream of a better life in Palestine.

Mastery Experiences at Home and School

Of the 14 women, 6 were only children, and 5 were the oldest in their families. As only children or the oldest child in a family, these survivors seemed to be less protected from "adult information," often treated as small adults and confidantes and given a great deal of responsibility—caring for younger siblings, helping in their parents' businesses before and after school, or finding outside employment at an early age. These responsibilities may well have provided a series of "mastery experiences" (Bandura, 1994) that contributed to a stronger perceived self-efficacy—a protective factor—going into the war. In addition, only children may learn a particular set of coping skills, including the experience of being comfortable alone, that may have helped them later, particularly those who went into hiding and had to spend long periods of time alone.

> I was proud to do that. I was very proud that he [her father] talked to me like that [as if she were the oldest son]. I felt very good about it. (Cynthia)

> Sort of at home, even, I was the provider for my sisters. I was not in school; my job at home was to help my mom and provide for the family.

So I sort of took like the role of providing for my sisters. (Charlotte)
I liked it in the beginning [helping in her parents' store]. I think
many times I resented it. Young children go home and play a little; I
had to be in the store. ... I don't think I ever thought about it in those
terms. I was told to do it, and I did it. I went in the morning, before
I went to school, and I straightened out the textiles. And you had to
close the store at a certain time. (Tova)

Education was highly valued in these families of origin. Most attended
public schools with Gentiles, a few attended religious day schools, and
all of the women received at least some training in Judaism, learning
how to pray from the Hebrew prayer book, for example. Florence, the
respondent who was the strongest in expressing her resentment of the
second-class status of women in Orthodox Judaism, told of her frustration at not being given the same opportunities for religious education as
her brothers.

[Religious] education was very limited. *For the girls, the Jewish language wasn't emphasized. You know, we didn't have to know anything.
See, that's why I'm very angry* [emphasis added]. Because I grew up in
a house, in a family where they were all teachers. My mother's family,
especially, they were teaching everybody Talmud, Tanach [Hebrew
acronym for the first five books of the Bible, plus the Prophets and
other writings], and Chumash [Hebrew for the first five books of the
Bible], and all these things were taught. But the girl didn't have to;
she didn't have to know. This was in our town a lot and in our area a
lot. And I was very upset about it. (Florence)

For the majority of these women, school provided many opportunities
for mastery experiences and self-efficacy (Bandura, 1994). There was pride
in academic achievement in these descriptions of school days and of "what
might have been," had the war not railroaded so many young lives. Most of
these women were not able to complete their educations after the war and
did not go beyond high school. Eva's description is a typical one:

I loved school, every aspect of it. I was popular in school, I became
hooked on science. I couldn't wait for the next week to go into that
lab. I loved it. ... I could stay there day and night and put those tubes
together. The only thing in life that I wanted that much was education. I can never remember wanting anything or anybody as much.

School also provided the opportunity to mingle with Gentile children and
become conversant in languages other than the Yiddish that was often the

mother tongue at home. Particularly for those adolescents who had learned languages other than Yiddish, being fluent in Polish, Ukrainian, Hungarian, Russian, German, or Czech served them well in the war years. Because of the fluidity of populations in Eastern Europe, with shifting boundaries through the years, it was quite common to know many different languages.

> Yes, Yiddish fluent. And I read in Yiddish, and I understand what I'm reading. I speak Czech. Hungarian I speak fluently. Because there were Ukraine [sic], and Polish, and Russian [people in the surrounding area where she grew up], I understand, I would say, 70%. And my English is … [laughs]. (Cynthia)

For those who were in hiding during the war, language fluency was truly a protective factor to bring with them into the Holocaust. Often, parents were the ones who pushed their children to speak languages other than Yiddish, in a conscious and determined attempt to protect them from an increasingly hostile environment. To this end, it was particularly important to speak without a Yiddish accent.

> She [her mother] didn't want us to have an accent, because … the Gentile, we were afraid of him. (Gittel)

> One thing, we picked up languages. My mother was very particular we should speak different languages. (Maya)

> Yiddish was often reserved for private, adult use: My parents spoke Yiddish when they didn't want me to understand what they were speaking about. (Edith)

In sum, both home and school provided these adolescents with mastery experiences: the opportunity to learn responsibility, to be independent, and to familiarize themselves somewhat with the different customs of the Gentiles, as well as providing these young girls with immersion in languages other than Yiddish. All of this would prove helpful during the war. However, school was also the site of many negative experiences, some of them quite traumatic, as anti-Semitism became more virulent throughout the 1930s. Some of these experiences are discussed next.

Childhood Trauma and Stress Inoculation

It was notable that almost all of the female survivors in my sample experienced significant trauma and loss before the war. As mentioned, the environmental stressors were daily and constant, as life among the Gentiles became more precarious and frightening through the 1930s.

> Our neighbors—and when we went to school, the teenagers—used to come at us with stones. And they used to call us names. And you felt the anti-Semitism. This was in the 1930s, and I was quite young. Of course, in the 1940s it got much worse. (Cynthia)

> So this teacher was a real anti-Semite. She called out all the names, and reads mine [an obviously Jewish name]. And she looks at the subject: Polish. Especially in Polish I was very good. Five was like ten then. It was the highest grade. She said, "What? A Jewess with a five in Polish? Not by me! Not by me!" What could I do, a child of not even 13 years old? It hurt me a lot. And we had to write a book report, and she stands in front of the class, and she says, "Listen to what the Jewess writes." And she reads and makes laughing of it. "Such long sentences, just like Jewish beards." Things like that. (Gerda)

> In later years, we couldn't go ice skating; we couldn't go swimming. Because they didn't let Jews go. They had these signs like: "Dogs, Fleas, and Jews not allowed." So we went roller skating. (Ilene)

> I mean, we [Jews living in Germany] did not have it only during the war years, 1939–1945. Each hour was terrible; each minute was terrible. What we have it from 1933 [with the rise of Hitler and the passing of the Nuremberg laws in 1935]. I was 10 years old. And all this trouble in school. It was terrible. Nobody can be as cruel as children. (Iliana)

These vignettes indicate the pervasiveness of the anti-Semitism these children and adolescents experienced for years before the war. It was part of the air they breathed. It came from schoolmates, from former "friends," from neighbors and teachers, from customers in the families' stores, from individual priests in the Catholic Church, and from government sanction. There was no protection from it. Privately and with their Jewish schoolmates, the majority of the survivors were battling with anti-Semitism throughout their childhoods—a painful and humiliating process. The knowledge that they were an unwanted presence, on borrowed time, threatened with death, taunted as "Christ killers," and assaulted— these were the types of serious environmental stressors the adolescents endured long before the war. They had the daily stress of knowing that school was often a gauntlet to be endured, and that even your home was unsafe from anti-Semitic thugs.

Florence's mother needed over 100 stitches in her head after a pogrom [Russian: riot against the Jews] in the 1930s when Romanian paramilitary men invaded their home and other Jewish homes in their neighborhood. Florence witnessed this brutality as a 10-year-old.

> I used to watch her, and I used to want to do something for her, you know, that I could see that she suffered. She had 100 stitches on her. She was in the hospital 6 weeks after that bash up. And people died [after the pogrom]. Maybe 2, 3 days later, they died. We were hiding, in an open space. And my poor mother had to suffer, because they knocked her on the head, on the neck. She was staying there and watching her kids, you know? Not letting go. Another mother would have run out and left the kids there. She was there till the last minute. Everybody was running, but not her. And she got it.

In addition to the dangers of living among the Gentiles, there were other traumatic events and losses within these adolescents' families of origin. Two of the women, Gerda and Iliana, lost their mothers to illness before the war. Eva lost her father before the war, and Gerda, Eva, and Cynthia lost one or more siblings. Eva's mother suffered from severe mental illness and was taken away and hospitalized for long periods of time throughout her childhood. Charlotte, Ella, and Edith were physically and emotionally abused by their mothers.

Eva's father died of tuberculosis when she was 10. He was the mediating parent who provided some happiness and support when her mother was emotionally unavailable—and even frightening at times—due to her mental illness.

> *A part of me died when my father died* [emphasis added]. [Crying.] He always took me in his arms; he cuddled me if I cried. (Eva)

Sibling deaths were also terrible losses. The loss of Gerda's older brother sent her into a year-long depression.

> He died in 1937. It was a terrible tragedy for everybody, and especially for me. I was 16 years old. Because when I grew up, we started to be very close. And I felt that, you know, I have somebody to lean on. And besides, I loved him. He was my brother. And I stopped school for a few months, just going back and forth to the hospital. … So after he died I was really mourning, being sad for months and months. Everybody tried to comfort me.

My mother had six children. Three passed away at home. After she had a little boy, she had a little girl and at 6 weeks she passed away. That third child passed away after 9 months. Don't forget in those days there weren't medicines like today. So three of us [the surviving children] went to concentration camp. (Cynthia)

I was told that she had all together five children. I mean, I cannot say that's what I spoke to my mother about, because my mother was killed when I was 16 or 17. So I wasn't grown up enough to talk to my mother about things like that. ... But I played with the baby, and then all of a sudden Grandma took me away, and I came back home after being a month with Grandma, and the baby wasn't there anymore. (Eva)

When asked what her earliest childhood memory is, Cynthia did not hesitate:

Well, it's of my brother. I can't remember his face, but I remember the morning he died. He was 9 months old. (Cynthia)

How did they cope with these losses as children? Gerda mentioned praying to her mother throughout her childhood.

Since I begin to be a little bit independent, I would walk to the cemetery. So it's very, very dear for me. You know, it helped. It helps me. As a child I remember, you know, a child has a bellyache. So I would say, "Mama, Mama, Mama, Mama." And I believed that it helped. All right, this is many years [ago].

Being motherless also forced her to feel responsible for herself at a younger age than most children would:

As I started to grow up, I feel responsible for myself, first of all. I had to be a mensch [Yiddish for decent human being], I had to be responsible.

At age 3, Iliana also lost her mother. When having difficulty dealing with the anti-Semitism at school, she would cry to her father, and he would tell her to look up in the sky and talk to her mother.

"Well," he said, "look up, and the biggest star is your mother." Somehow I still look up. It helped. ... I was always very happy, I mean, I was content when I told my mother everything. ... And we

visited the grave very often because I felt always very good when I
went to the grave. And I told my mother everything what happened
to me. You have to talk to someone.

Praying to parents was an important way for adolescent survivors to
cope with their losses (see Chapter 6). For some, like Gerda and Iliana who
lost their mothers before the war, this coping strategy was already in place
before the Holocaust years.

In sum, one can speculate that these prewar losses of major attachment
figures and the larger environment of pervasive and brutal anti-Semitism
provided some sort of stress inoculation (Meichenbaum, 2009) for these
children and adolescents. Having been exposed, often on a daily basis, to a
hostile environment in which they had to find ways to cope, as well as having been exposed—many of them—to traumatic loss, may have prepared
some of these children and adolescents for the horrors to come.

Summary: The Prewar Coping of Female Adolescent Survivors

The female survivors in my sample mentioned several coping strategies
they used before the war. As we have seen, we can speculate from self-
descriptions, from descriptions of attachment relationships, from the ways
the survivors described the importance of faith and practice, their inclusion in Zionist groups, their educational experiences, and the stress inoculation they received from childhood trauma before the war that many of
the survivors had developed a tool kit to take with them into the war years.
For most of the women, this kit included secure attachments; enduring
values and spiritual beliefs; identity and pride in group membership; mastery experiences and a perceived sense of self-efficacy; and an exposure
to a stressful environment and losses that may have given them a type
of stress inoculation from their experiences with adversity before Hitler's
onslaught.

The Men

Descriptions of Self

Interestingly, the self-descriptions found in the males' interviews were
more expansive than those of the females and mostly portray the competence and self-efficacy these adolescents had developed before the war.
Tom, when asked if he was the "spokesman of the family" answered:

No, I was probably more of a respect because I accomplished more
than the others. Like my uncle, I used to work with him in the same
store. They were selling bicycles and sewing machines, motorcycles

and everything. And I had a little motorcycle to ride around. I was a big shot over there. … It was not easy, but I was happy. It was a busy day, and I was accomplishing. I was very good. I was producing in that shop. In the first year, I did twice as much work as the people who worked there for 15 years. For some reason I was very handy, and I caught up with everything very fast, and I was capable, and that's why I was doing very good.

A lot of times the children had to go out and look on their own, and contribute to the way of living, and it was not easy. I remember like today, at 14 years old I didn't know how I could contribute all of the sudden to go out and get a job. … And it was really a challenge for us. … There was no money involved; sometimes he [the farmer he worked for] gave us a little food, and I enjoyed that.

Cedric described his competency and capabilities before the war in several examples. He was an excellent student, with a photographic memory. He was also a highly competent worker at an early age and was not afraid to speak out in the family.

Everything that I wrote down, in the morning when I woke up, I was still in bed, I could see that blackboard and read every word. That was a gift, and to me I was one of the two students that could keep up with math.

I spent my youth in the shop. I was 7, 8, 9 years old, I was sewing on the machine. I was fixing galoshes in the winter and so on. Zippers, let's say, on the boots when they broke. That was my speciality [sic]. I always made a few extra zlotys. In other words, I was very handy. No matter what came up, I was very handy.

I was like the rebel in the family. My brother was three and a half years older than I, but he never argues anything. I was more outspoken. … I was more aggressive. We used to fight, you know, like children. I was the one who sometimes provoked it. I'll admit it. But that was in me. And I always said to myself: I can do it. That was my attitude. … My mother, she didn't learn that much and so on, but she said: "You can do it. You can do it." And I had a little encouragement, and I always was advancing. … I had courage, and I believed in my ability, also. I believed that I can do it. Under the hardest times, I believed that I can do it.

Roman had only one description of himself prewar. He told the story of his mother's watch:

She used to wear it on Yontif [the Jewish holidays]. I found it. And when she went away someplace, I took it apart, and I put it together, and it never worked again. She never knew who did it, and I never told her that, and since then it went all to pot anyhow. But … I guess curiosity, and I am very interested in mechanical things. My dream used to be a mechanical engineer. … So you see, I am curious, and I'm not afraid to try.

Zelig told a story in which he was a leader among his Jewish school-mates in fighting back when the Polish students were tormenting them on a daily basis.

I never learned Polish because I never liked it. And the Polish boys used to have fights with us every morning when we came into school. *And there was nothing we could do, and there was nothing our parents could do to help us. They knew we were coming home beat up and everything, but there was nothing they could do to stop it* [emphasis added]. … As soon as we came in, they would beat us over the heads with something, not clubs, but something so that you could feel it. One time I said to the boys, "We have to do something about it." So we took short clubs, and we put them under the sleeves. I mean, when you go through hell, you think of things, you know? You get some education.

Roman told a remarkably similar story:

Anti-Semitism in our town was rampant. … Kids used to beat me up because I never was a tall person. *I came home to my mother crying. She says, "I don't understand. Everything happens to you. I walk on the street, nobody beats me up* [emphasis added]." Well, there's nothing I can say, but I came up with an idea, … I zeroed in on the bully, on the chief bully that used to control the bunch. I waited for him behind his house, and I jumped him. I learned how to play, you know, I learned how to fight the dirty way. I made sure I don't hurt him so I should kill him, but I beat the holy hell out of him, and I explained to him that next time you touch me I'm going to kill you. I didn't mean it, but you know, bluffing is the name of the game. It got to be a situation where I used to bring the Jewish kids from one side of town to the other side without anybody bothering us. It was like a little one-man mafia, and it worked.

In both of these descriptions, the ineffectual role of parents in helping their children deal with daily anti-Semitic assaults is notable. The boys had to find ways to cope with and manage that stress largely on their own. Surely, at least for these two men, these childhood and adolescent experiences of dealing with a hostile environment taught them to fight back and perhaps served as a form of stress inoculation for the war years. They were taught by their parents' unhelpful responses that they had to adapt and survive on the street, even before the Holocaust. Forced to adapt in a hostile environment, they became more confident and empowered as they were successful in fighting off the "chief bullies" of their childhood. Their perceived self-efficacy was enhanced by these true mastery experiences. Furthermore, they were clearly not going into the war years with a naïve view of the hatred surrounding them in their environment. They were already well aware of how the Gentile world perceived them.

In addition, there is pride evident in these stories of self—a portrayal of themselves as boys who will fight back, as leaders. The stories almost have a heroic quality to them. These stories of strength, as I have categorized them, are even more prominent in both the female and male respondents' stories of the war years and postwar years (Goldenberg, 2008).

Like the female respondents, these male adolescents were also expected to work at an early age—either helping in the family business or finding work on their own. Tom spoke with some frustration about these early expectations:

> The only criticism the children got, like I got in the beginning: "Look, you can't get a job for yourself, and you can't do anything on your own." So this boy over there, he is doing great, and you are sitting home, and you that's why, you know, sometimes I got frustrated, because what can you do if you are not guided by a parent what to start, and you go out on your own and finding something. The parent themselves is not capable to make a right living; how can I do? And there was no schooling anymore. In Krakow, I got schooling. I had to pay for it, but I'm glad I was able to get some. And … mechanically I got very capable. I was capable to catch up to the schooling, whatever they gave us. And it helped me in my way to pick up the job what I was doing. And a matter of fact, I was better maybe than the other ones who were working over there.

In sum, the general picture these male respondents gave is that of growing competence and capability, born out of necessity in a hostile environment. They painted a picture of parents who were either unwilling or unable to help them with their difficulties and moreover had traditional expectations of them that may have been too high for young male adolescents to achieve.

Significant Attachment Figures

In most instances, the interviewer asked the questions: "Can you describe your relationships with your parents?" Or, "Can you describe your parents?" But the descriptions, at least of the male respondents' relationships with their mothers, are not as full as they were in the female respondents' interviews. Instead, they were circumspect and tantalizingly sketchy.

> My mother passed away when I was about 13, and it was the most tragic thing happened at that time. I remember I came from the cemetery home, sat on that bench, and I realized: This is it. We are going to be by ourselves. But after 2 years, my father remarried, and then I left the house altogether, and I went to Krakow. (Tom)

We can speculate from these words that Tom was close with his mother, and his words are similar to Eva's when describing how she felt after the death of her father. When asked what his relationship with his mother was like, he responded with a series of compassionate vignettes of how he and his siblings would help her with her work.

> When she was washing her wash, it was a heavy job for her, and we used to bring water from the river. … Sometimes she let us cut those cookies with those cookie cutters, or something, [I was] a helper, and it was a tough life for a mother. I think the mother was working much harder than the father. And they were taking everything as granted, you know, this had to be that way, and this is how it was. (Tom)

In contrast to Tom's description, Zelig briefly remarked and did not elaborate further about his mother's relationship with him:

> My mother would be showing more affection than my father.

However, the males were far more expansive when discussing their relationships with their fathers. This could simply be due to gender differences; boys spent more time with their fathers, girls with their mothers, or were more influenced by them, or modeled themselves after them, for good or ill.

> To me they were both the same. I felt I was afraid of my father, and if I would do something wrong, I would get it. … This was his way of keeping you straight. And I learned, and I never disagreed. *But I never hated him for this, no, and today I don't disagree with it. And this is the way I raised my children, maybe because of this. Because I used to beat up [my son] with a strap because this is what I knew. And thank God he did what he did, because if he didn't do what he did, maybe I wouldn't be here, and maybe I wouldn't be what I am* [emphasis added]. (Zelig)

This is a seemingly forgiving portrait of what appears to be an abusive relationship. Not only does Zelig seem to have forgiven the abuse he suffered at his father's hand, but he attributed being "what he is" to his father's method of punishment and continued this form of discipline with his own son.

Tom, who, as we saw, lost his mother at 13, grew up in severe poverty. He moved out of his home with his older brother as a young adolescent after his father remarried, to live with an uncle in Krakow, a larger city. His stepmother was, apparently, less than kind to them. Like Zelig, Tom also seemed forgiving of his father's limitations.

> He [his father] was in Krakow a few times, too, and he saw our [his brother's and his] way of living, and maybe he didn't like it as much [because it wasn't as religious as his], but he didn't say anything. He had respect for me that I exist, and he was maybe glad in a way that I left the house and I went somewhere where I could do more for myself than over there in that little village. I would have probably landed in the same situation and be the same as he was, which he had a very hard life, and I had an easier life and I made more than he did. He had some kind of respect for me, and our relations were very good. *He probably felt a little bit guilty that his second wife was not treating us the same as our mother did*, and he felt a little guilty, *and it maybe hurt him in some way, but he couldn't do too much about it. There was no way he could just turn her around to be the same as our mother*, and this was the life why we actually disappeared [because the stepmother was abusive]. And then he had a child with her, and that child was treated much differently than the children of his. And it probably hurt him, too, *but he couldn't do too much about it, either* [emphases added]. So we were all grown children [Tom was 15], and we were almost like on our own. (Tom)

Tom portrayed his father in a sympathetic light—as having led a hard life, yet being able, at the same time, to respect his sons' choice of a different lifestyle, even wanting a different lifestyle for them. Ineffectual in the relationship with his new wife, and portrayed as having no choice between taking her side over his children's from his first marriage, he is still viewed as being able to respect and care about his sons, and as being relieved to see that they had an opportunity elsewhere for a better life than his.

This raises a speculative question regarding these retrospective accounts of survivors who lost their parents as adolescents or even younger. It is doubtful, perhaps, that Tom felt as forgiving of his situation and of his parents' limitations at the time those events occurred as he did when he looked back from the distance of 50 years. This may not be a function of surviving extreme trauma and loss—in other words, these may not be examples of loyalty to and idealization of the dead or a form of "survivor guilt." Rather, one could speculate that it reflects a tendency of many of us to soften, mitigate, or even forgive parents' mistakes or outright abuse over time.

In sum, the males' descriptions of their attachments to their mothers were much less well developed than their female counterparts, perhaps due to gender differences. Their descriptions of their fathers were fuller, and at least for two of the men, were forgiving in their retrospective understanding of difficult relationships.

Jewish Faith, Practice, and Group Identity

When asked what his memories were like of his family's celebration of the Sabbath and Jewish holidays, Zelig replied:

> Very, strong, very strong. ... Everybody went to synagogue. Every Shabbat was like a holiday. ... There were poor people coming into the house to ask for donations, so my father used to pick them up in from the synagogue and bring them into the house for meals on Friday night and Saturday.

According to Tom,

> They were pretty religious. There was only one type of religion in the Jewish family. ... Everyone was preparing the same way for the Shabbat, everyone was going to the same prayers. And weddings or circumcisions, all the Jewish traditions were conformed.

Like the female respondents, the males were also becoming involved in Zionist youth groups, motivated by the virulent anti-Semitism surrounding them. They were also being influenced by the winds of change.

> I joined the Zionist organization, which is today the Likud, the right wing of the Zionist organization. I was 8 years old, and my father wasn't active, but he leaned to that organization. When I joined the Betar, I saw the anti-Semitism was so great in Poland that we had no future there. I did not want to be a shoemaker [like his father], but I realized that going to Palestine in those days you needed some kind of craft, for you had to build the country. (Cedric)

> I belonged myself into a youth group which were also leftist. My brother and mostly all the youth were pro-Israel. They had the Israeli like *Ha-poalei* Zion [Hebrew for workers of Zion]. I don't even remember the names what we would call those organizations. Some

people went to different countries, but this was before the war broke out. (Tom)

Tom also described himself as rebelling before the war, particularly once he had moved out of his father's house, away from his small village, to his uncle's house in the city of Krakow.

> [The observance of Shabbat] was a routine, and personally, I was the first one what I was more or less like a rebel, where I took off my hat, and I was walking outside and inside without a hat [observant Jewish men always have their head covered, either with a yarmulke or *kippah*, Yiddish and Hebrew, respectively, for "skullcap," a hat, or both]. And maybe when I was 16 years old I had plans in Krakow with the others, and they went about the same way. They didn't wear any hats, and I was proud ... that I could do the same thing. When I came home to my father, I wouldn't dare to go without a hat. But in Krakow itself, it was more progressive over there, more assimilated than the other little towns. I wouldn't dare to go out in that small town where my father used to live later on without the hat and everything. It had to be the regular Jewish way.

In sum, like some of the female respondents, these descriptions show adolescent boys beginning to think for themselves, to question their parents' ways of religious observance, and to become involved in political Zionist organizations as an empowering response to anti-Semitism and a path toward group identity.

Mastery Experiences at Home and School

Many of the mastery experiences at home have already been described. Like many of the female respondents, the males ended their descriptions of school life on a dark note, as their lives were totally disrupted by the war:

> Well, there was a nice Jewish population in my little town. There were quite a few Jews, and we were always together, and I had a nice life. I really enjoyed it. We were just like one family, all the families. We were very close, and I had a lot of friends. We used to go fishing together, all kinds of games, *until the bad days came in and everything was finished* [emphasis added]. (Zelig)

> I had 7 years, then I had 2 years in night school [a vocational school] still in Poland. ... I could have gone to gymnasium [in Europe, a preparatory high school for university that only the best students could

attend], I was a good student ... but I went to a mechanic shop, and I was working there for a year and a half as an apprentice *until the war broke out* [emphasis added]. (Cedric)

Well, I had 6 years of grade school, 1 year of gymnasium, and umpteen years of cheder [religious school for boys, learning Bible and Talmud], which was kind of an important thing. I had quite a few years of violin; as a matter of fact, I played in our little local symphony. ... *This all came to a hold in 1939. But I lived between 1925 and '39, and there was quite a bit of water coming down the river* [emphasis added]. (Roman)

In sum, like the female respondents, there is a poignant quality to these male survivors' descriptions of how their education was disrupted, but clues, as well, to academic mastery, which could provide these boys with a strong sense of self-efficacy. But more important, perhaps, Roman made a critical observation in the last quotation, reminding us that survivors had a life *before* Hitler and the Nazis took it away from him during his adolescence. He reminded us that his early, formative years were critical ones. "I lived between 1925 and '39, and there was quite a bit of water coming down the river."

Childhood Trauma and Stress Inoculation

Like the female adolescents, some of the males also suffered significant prewar trauma and loss. As we have already noted, Tom lost his mother when he was 13. We have already seen Zelig's and Roman's descriptions of the daily beatings they received at the hands of their Gentile classmates. These boys' experiences with anti-Semitism were much more physically brutal than the girls'. In addition, they had no one to comfort or help them.

I was the only Jew in school, and especially at Easter, when they were teaching that the Jewish people crucified Christ, and there was very unpleasant results that sometimes I got beaten up and everything else. So thanks God we have over here a separation of school and state [sic]. ... *We lived with it, and we lived with a certain fear. And that fear was so common and so overwhelming that we didn't just speak about it and not talk about it* [emphasis added]. ... The only problems we had were that we had a harder life because we were Jews, and we were always pointed out and really persecuted, throwing stones at us and not giving us that same chance to live as other people lived. That's the only problems we really had. (Tom)

Summary: The Prewar Coping of Male Adolescent Survivors

What were some of the coping strategies the male respondents had in place before the war? As we have already seen, the boys had learned how to fight back. All of them described themselves as self-efficacious, with a strong belief in their ability that they "could do it"—whatever the "it" was. Unlike the female respondents, however, they did not give any examples of "recovery" or holding environments—of grandparents or older people who were caring and helpful and provided a safe respite from daily stress. The male respondents described themselves as largely coping on their own or even acting as the leader among friends. Their parents were regarded as generally ineffectual and expected them to act as small adults in the hostile environment of anti-Semitism.

What is remarkable about all four of these interviews is that, like almost all of the female respondents, each of the men described himself as competent, capable, willing to take risks, with leadership abilities and a fighting spirit. Their perceived sense of self-efficacy came through in the stories they told of themselves as children and adolescents. This belief in themselves and their own abilities must have been a strong coping skill to take with them into the Holocaust. In addition, the skills they had learned at vocational trades, whether by working in a father's shoe store or by working in an uncle's mechanics shop, would also serve them well in the war years.

Also like the female respondents, the male respondents were old enough to have learned lessons and values from parents, lessons that they assimilated and used after the war to cope. Roman described one of these:

> My parents told me that first of all, you have to learn. You have to learn. When you are young, you are supposed to associate with older people so that you should learn from them. When you get older, you are supposed to associate with younger people so that you keep yourself on the ball.

The biggest lesson, however, seemed to be that they were expected to be on their own and to cope without relying on their parents. All four of the male respondents expressed learning this lesson—albeit in unpleasant ways—before the war.

Summary of Prewar Coping Strategies

There were several prewar foundations—protective factors and coping strategies—in place for these adolescents going into the war. Most of them described themselves in positive terms. They told stories of strength, which demonstrated a sense of themselves as competent individuals who had faced some fairly stressful experiences and coped with them, sometimes on a daily basis. They described themselves, on the whole, as good students, intelligent and capable, and many of them knew several languages. Many, due to birth order, gender, or status as an only child, had learned a host of skills and responsibilities that younger children may not have had. The female respondents described themselves as children and adolescents in a variety of realistic ways. They were not expansive in their self-descriptions, but they were able to provide us with at least some glimpse of their personalities before the war. If the adjectives themselves are not apparent, the descriptions of themselves within a relationship with significant attachment figures provide more evidence of what these adolescents were like: the devotion of Gerda to her brother as she skipped school to visit him every day in the hospital; the passion of Florence at what she saw as the injustice of how she and her sisters were treated in relation to her brothers; the resourcefulness of Ella, who sought out older women to escape from her unhappy home; the passion for learning and intellectual curiosity of Eva as she described herself in school, before her education was so quickly and cruelly cut off from her.

The men were far more expansive in their self-descriptions, and all four described themselves as having strong perceived self-efficacy going into the war. They presented a picture of competence, resourcefulness, and leadership among their peers. Developmentally, these adolescents were becoming more sophisticated cognitively and confident enough to question some of the belief systems and religious practices of their childhood, while at the same time assimilating and holding on to the important values and messages their parents instilled in them.

The survivors gave many positive descriptions of Jewish life: Sitting around the Shabbas table, celebrating holidays with family and friends, going to synagogue, giving *tzedakah* (Hebrew for charity), learning Jewish prayers and observances—all within the context of close attachments. Some of them described questioning that faith or rebelling against the limitations strict Orthodoxy placed on its adherents, even before the war. This was the case particularly in the older adolescents, as they became exposed to outside, alternative influences such as Zionist youth groups.

Still, amid the sparks of rebellion, these adolescents appear not to have rejected their parents' values. Quite to the contrary, as they continued to develop emotionally and cognitively before the war, they were able to assimilate the teachings of their parents, and their value systems, and cull what they could from what they had been given. It is clear from these descriptions of prewar life that all of them had retained many of the value lessons their parents had given them, lessons that younger children may not have been able either to comprehend or to hold on to. The two notable exceptions are Ella and Eva, both of whom rejected a Jewish lifestyle and values after the war (Goldenberg, 2008).

The majority of the respondents had at least one caring parent or adult in their environment as a means of social support. Even when there was abuse in the home, there seemed to be evidence of some mitigating factor, such as the love of the other parent or time away with loving grandmothers, and the respondents from abusive homes described their resourcefulness in seeking out these alternative attachment figures. The respondents were all old enough to form significant attachments before the war, and the descriptions by the females in particular of these relationships were rich and detailed. The men were more circumspect.

The main gender difference found is in the female respondents' descriptions of what could be called holding environments or recovery environments—a grandmother's house, a friendly older neighbor's house—that provided a respite from daily stressors. These adults may have provided the "one caring adult in a child's environment" (Werner & Smith, 2001) that helped these adolescents become resilient. The males did not describe these sorts of relationships. The general picture one gets for the adolescent boys is that they often had only themselves to rely on, which could have been a gender expectation. Another possibility is that they were not as willing or as skilled as the females to reach out for the social support they needed from older adults other than parents. A third speculation would be that, at least in Tom's case, leaving home to live with an uncle and older brother provided the respite he needed. Perhaps siblings and other relatives were indeed sources of comfort and support for the males, but they were not spoken of in those terms when the survivors related stories of prewar life. In sum, there were many protective factors in varying degrees in these adolescents' lives before the war: caring adults, various forms of social support, intelligence and social skills, religious belief systems, family values, and a developed sense of right and wrong.

To summarize the risk factors facing these young people before the war, a major common denominator seems to have been the fact that all of them were forced to swim in a sea of anti-Semitism throughout their childhood and adolescence, long before the war years. These were hostile waters that provided many tough life lessons for these adolescents: The Gentiles do not want you; you have to find your own ways to protect yourself and adapt to their hostilities; you have only yourself to rely on—not parents, not figures of authority. This last lesson was particularly strong and brutal for the males.

As we have seen, some of these males and females lost significant attachment figures before the war. Some were from abusive homes, and one was from a home of fairly extreme poverty. But, the majority were from solidly middle-class environments and did not describe an abusive household. The anti-Semitic milieu and the traumatic events and losses of childhood and adolescence may have provided them with some sort of stress inoculation

(Meichenbaum, 2009) going into the war. Understanding prewar foundations of strength and coping, of the interaction of risk and protective factors in adolescence (Compas & Reeslund, 2009), will help us understand post traumatic adaptation.

What can we learn from the prewar coping strategies that these survivors of the Holocaust portrayed that can be applied to our work with other adult survivors of trauma? The clinical example of Danielle demonstrates the importance of the clinician's role in helping clients access their pre-trauma strengths as resources for healing.

Clinical Application: Danielle

Danielle is a single woman in her late 40s. She came into treatment with a history of physical, sexual, and emotional abuse and neglect. She has the diagnoses of posttraumatic stress disorder (PTSD), panic disorder, and borderline personality disorder. She is on methadone maintenance treatment and is a recovering alcoholic and long-time user of cannabis. She has a history of hospitalizations for suicidal ideation and gestures and has a history of cutting and other forms of self-injury.

Sexually abused for years by an older brother and physically and emotionally abused by her alcoholic parents, Danielle dropped out of high school at 16 and soon became pregnant with her first child. The father of her child was not interested in becoming involved, and Danielle's daughter was raised in foster care. Only recently has Danielle become reconnected with her daughter, who is now in her late teens.

Danielle has a history of relationships with abusive and drug-addicted men. Over the years, she has "lost herself" and become more and more downtrodden, with nonexistent self-esteem and a core belief that she does not deserve anything better than a life of abuse.

Danielle never learned coping strategies other than drugs, alcohol, and cutting. However, when her clinician tried to teach her visualization and meditation techniques to learn to self-soothe, Danielle was able to access one positive adolescent memory: riding on her horse through the fields near her house and through the shallow waters of a lake. In this visualization, Danielle remembered herself vividly as a spunky teenager, with long hair streaming down her back, angry, independent, and strong. She could recall vividly the feel of her horse's body under her and the way the wind went through her hair and the horse's mane as they galloped through the fields. "I never used a saddle," she told her clinician proudly, with a smile on her face. "That horse and I were like joined at the hip when we were riding together. I never rode with anyone else. Just by myself. It was awesome." She got teary-eyed recalling the memory. "That horse was my best friend, and I was just different when I was riding."

Further explorations of how she was "different" as an adolescent riding her horse helped Danielle to access a part of her she had forgotten about. She recalled more stories of how she would stand up to her abusive father, how she told her brother "no more sexual abuse," and how she was a "tomboy and a bit of a hell-raiser" when she was a teenager. She was able to access several significant stories of strength that, with her therapist's guidance, she could use as resources when she would have the urge to use, cut, or feel like she were "climbing out of her skin."

"I want to get back to that old Danielle," she told her therapist. "I know she's still there inside me, but I just forgot about her!" She is learning in therapy to redirect her anger away from herself and toward those who injured her in the past and in her present life. She uses her visualization of herself and her horse several times per day, has not cut in the past 3 months, and is learning to say no to her abusive boyfriend. As she reclaims her more resilient, assertive, and independent self, she is visibly relaxing into her life, has expressed the desire to wean herself from methadone, and has cut back significantly on cannabis. She is also considering volunteering at a camp that uses animals—including horses—as therapy for disabled and mentally ill children.

Clinical Application: Alicia

Alicia is 36 years old, single, and a social worker. When she was 18 years old, she was hit by a stray bullet in a freak accident while she was at a restaurant. She was given a 50% chance of survival. Her words describe her pretrauma stress inoculation, a developed sense of independence, and leadership and a strong sense of self-efficacy that she had developed prior to the shooting.

> In my story, which is very unusual, it's very easy to just talk about the shooting, because it's so big, and it captures a lot of people's attention, but in fact, the way I was able to get through the shooting has everything to do with my family prior to the shooting, which is a lot of previous trauma that was very hidden. And it's very complicated, because it has to do with an adult parent having mental illness and not being emotionally available. I developed strong leadership in order to survive.
>
> I was very extroverted. Vice-president of my high school, varsity for years, made all A's. … There was a lot of accomplishments, a lot of positive activity. But at home, fighting, screaming parents, one parent of whom was severely mentally ill. But when he was functional, he was very loving, very brilliant and creative, heart was in the right place. But I had to step up. I took everything on, because my mother acted emotionally helpless a lot of the time. I ended up taking care of her while she took care of him.

After the shooting, Alicia returned to college, "determined to overcome," but she suffered from PTSD. Her assumptions about the world were shattered (Janoff-Bulman, 1997); it had become a dangerous, unpredictable place. Bad things could happen "anywhere, anytime. Your life could go in a nanosecond."

Now 18 years posttrauma, she has chosen a meaningful profession, she has put up some boundaries with her parents to cut down on her codependency, she meditates, she has been in therapy on and off for many years, and she walks and tries to be in nature as a way to self-soothe. When asked what part of her adolescent, pretrauma self helps her now as an adult, she talks about reclaiming her adolescent athleticism:

> I played sports as a teen, and I have this theory that moving your body can help you. So 4 years after I was shot, I ran a marathon as a way to reclaim my body. Some stranger invaded my body and suddenly I can't eat or go to the bathroom normally, and at 36 I live with chronic pain and difficulty digesting. It taps into

my complete helplessness. Running a marathon, you really have to be in your body to do it. It's a glorious achievement. It's the triumph over evil, over the rage. It's revenge. My uncle said once, "The best revenge is to live a good life." And yet it's so hard sometimes.

I know from growing up in my family, I've certainly learned to get back up after you fall and keep going. I think that when you grow up in a traumatic family, there's a priority of suffering. You have to figure out which thing to pay attention to. You have limited energy. It's not just about having the coping mechanisms, but it's about being smart about how to apply them.

Conclusion

Studying the narratives of adolescent survivors of the Holocaust, and the stories they told of their prewar selves and attachments, emphasizes the fact that many people have lives and foundations of strength and coping *before* traumatic events happen to them, something that clinicians often overlook. For those adult survivors of trauma who were in the developmental stage of adolescence before their traumatic event (or events), as clinicians we need to understand that they had reached a stage of cognitive development at which they could take in and assimilate the values and messages of their primary attachment figure; form attachments with peers that provided self and group identity; develop a sense of self and experience various forms of mastery experiences that helped them develop a sense of self-efficacy. When trauma shatters assumptions about self, other, and world, people can revisit their pretrauma strengths and reclaim them to heal. Like Danielle on her horse or Alicia running her marathon, adult survivors of adolescent trauma can rebuild their shattered assumptions about self and other. They can remember, like Roman, that they had a life before the trauma, and strong, competent selves, and reclaim aspects of their adolescent selves to aid in healing.

As adult survivors of trauma, it seems important to reconnect with their adolescent selves—associate themselves with their youth—to remember and reclaim some of those highly useful strengths and strategies that worked for them in the past.

References

Angus, L. E., & McLeod, J. (2004). Toward an integrative framework for understanding the role of narrative in psychotherapy process. In L. E. Angus & J. McLeod (Eds.), *The handbook of narrative and psychotherapy: Practice, theory and research* (pp. 367–374). London: Sage.

Bandura, A. (1994). Self-efficacy. In V. S. Ramachaudran (Ed.), *Encyclopedia of human behavior, 4* (pp. 71–81). New York: Academic Press.

Baumeister, R. F., & Leary, M. R. (1995). The need to belong: Desire for interpersonal attachments as a fundamental human motivation. *Psychological Bulletin, 117*, 497–529.

Coles, R. (1990). *The spiritual life of children.* Boston: Houghton Mifflin.

Compas, B. E., & Reeslund, K. L. (2009). Processes of risk and resilience in adolescence. In R. M. Lerner & L. Steinberg (Eds.), *Handbook of adolescent psychology, Vol. 1: Individual bases of adolescent development* (3rd ed., pp. 561–588). Hoboken, NJ: Wiley.

Erikson, E. H. (1950). *Childhood and society.* New York: Norton.

Goldenberg, J. (2008). *"The feelings of my family are with me": The posttraumatic coping of adolescent survivors of the Holocaust.* Unpublished doctoral dissertation, Bryn Mawr College, Bryn Mawr, PA.

Granqvist, P., Mikulincer, M., & Shaver P. R. (2010). Religion as attachment: Normative processes and individual differences. *Personality and Social Psychology Review, 14*, 49–59.

Haslam, S. A., O'Brien, A., Jetten, J., Vormedal, K., & Penna, S. (2005). Taking the strain: Social identity, social support and the experience of stress. *British Journal of Social Psychology, 44*, 55–370.

Janoff-Bulman, R. (1997). *Shattered assumptions.* New York: Free Press.

McAdams, D. P. (1993). *The stories we live by.* New York: Guilford Press.

McAdams, D. P. (2001). The psychology of life stories. *Review of General Psychology, 5*, 100–122.

Meichenbaum, D. (2009). Stress inoculation training. In W. T. O'Donohue & J. E. Fisher (Eds.), *General principles and empirically supported techniques of cognitive behavior therapy* (pp. 627–630). Hoboken, NJ: Wiley.

Mishler, E. (2004). Stories of the self: Restorying lives, revising identities. *Research in Human Development, 1*, 101–121.

O'Connell Higgins, G. (1994). *Resilient adults: Overcoming a cruel past.* San Francisco: Jossey-Bass.

Schafer, R. (1992). *Retelling a life: Narration and dialogue in psychoanalysis.* New York: Basic Books.

Spencer, R. A. (2002). Hanging out and growing strong: A qualitative study of relationships with adults that foster resilience in adolescence. *Dissertation Abstracts International: Section B: The Sciences and Engineering, 63* (6-B) pp. 30-46.

Styron, W. (1979). *Sophie's choice.* New York: Vintage Books.

Suedfeld, P., Soriano, E., McMurtry, D. L., Paterson, H., Weiszbeck, T. L., & Krell, R. (2005). Erikson's "components of a healthy personality" among Holocaust survivors immediately and 40 years after the war. *International Journal of Aging and Human Development, 60*, 229–248.

Werner, E. E., & Smith, R. S. (2001). *Journeys from childhood to midlife: Risk, resilience, and recovery.* Ithaca, NY: Cornell University Press.

White, M., & Epston, D. (1990). *Narrative means to therapeutic ends.* New York: Norton.

Ysseldyk, R., Matheson, K., & Anisman, H. (2010). Religiosity as identity: Toward an understanding of religion from a social identity perspective. *Personality and Social Psychology Review, 14*, 60–71.

CHAPTER 5

The Hows and Whys of Survival

Causal Attributions and the Search for Meaning

JENNIFER GOLDENBERG

Introduction

The causal attributions survivors make to explain how they survived the Holocaust can tell us much about the way people adapt after extremely traumatic events. The process of searching for an explanation for survival—and the search for meaning in that survival—weaves throughout the narratives of the Transcending Trauma Project (TTP). Attributions for survival and meanings found in survival may provide some comfort for those who have lost many of their loved ones to genocide, as well as play an important role in regaining a sense of control and safety, two critical components of recovery from trauma (Herman, 1997).

This chapter explores both the "hows" and the "whys" of survival. It focuses on the causal attributions offered by our TTP respondents, as well as on the meanings they have found to explain why they lived when those they loved did not survive. The attributions given are both internal and external. As will be demonstrated, external attributions—such as the help of others, luck, fate, and God—are somewhat more common than internal attributions. It may be that, for some survivors, external attributions are psychologically "safer" and therefore more adaptive strategies for coping with the trauma of multiple losses over time (Finkelstein & Levy, 2006; Specht, Egloff, & Schmukle, 2011). In contrast, internal attributions (e.g., various individual characteristics such as intelligence, courage, or quick thinking) give the survivor some sort of "credit" for surviving the war and may, in fact, be less adaptive.

In addition, some survivors were eventually able to find meaning in their own survival during the postwar years, and the meaning they found played an adaptive role in their postwar coping. Some of the examples of meaning making found in these narratives include surviving to tell the story to future generations so that genocide will not happen again and continuing the chain of the Jewish people and their traditions. Case study examples—those of a survivor of a near-fatal car accident and of a soldier from the Vietnam War—demonstrate how survivors of other traumatic, near-death experiences explain their own survival and have come to some meaning over time. A case study of a client struggling to find meaning after a childhood of physical and sexual abuse demonstrates the ongoing and sometimes agonizing search for meaning that can be witnessed in a therapeutic setting.

Clinicians should be aware of the importance of causal attributions and the ongoing search for both explanations for survival and meaning in survival by their clients who have suffered various forms of trauma. They should be aware that these searches can sometimes take years and even be lifelong (Ayalon, Perry, Arean, & Horowitz, 2007). In addition, as survivors of trauma age, they face the psychosocial conflict of ego integrity versus despair (Erikson, 1966; Suedfeld et al., 2005) and conduct a retrospective or life review to integrate and make sense of their experiences (Butler, 1963). For some, no meaning may ever be found, but we should recognize that there is strength to be found in the search itself.

Causal Attributions

> I survived because I was young, and healthy, and strong, and could run fast. Because they used to come in the woods with the machine guns and you started running. If you were lucky, the bullet didn't hit you. ... I can't say that I was singled out [for survival]. I don't feel that. I was lucky. And most of the survivors, [if] you ask them how did you survive, unless they are really the frummest [most religious], they will tell you they were lucky. (Edith, survivor)

What causal attributions do Jewish survivors of the Holocaust make to explain how they survived the Nazis' and other perpetrators' systematic torture and annihilation of European Jewry? Exploring survival statements—*how* an individual survived (i.e., in what manner or way, by what means)—raises many questions that have only recently begun to be addressed by the psychological or Holocaust literature (Finkelstein & Levy, 2006; Schiff, 2005; Schiff & Cohler, 2001; Suedfeld, 2003). What can such causal attributions tell us about the way people process traumatic events? More than half a century after World War II, what sense has been made of the senseless by those who have experienced the Holocaust firsthand? With many of the survivors now at the end of their lives, how do they look back on their experiences for understanding or resolution?

Attribution theory emphasizes beliefs and the interpretation of experience (Weiner, 1986). The attribution process is often driven by a negative event or an event of great significance.

> When one encounters a sudden threat or change in one's environment, one will initiate a causal search in an effort to understand the reasons for that threat or change. Attributional search is thought to be initiated so as to understand, predict, and control threat, and hence may be especially functional early on in the adjustment process. (Taylor, Lichtman, & Wood, 1984, p. 490)

The process of attributional search, then, can help an individual regain a sense of control, which is an important component of recovery from trauma (Bloom, 1997; Courtois & Ford, 2009; Herman, 1997; Wilson, Friedman, & Lindy, 2001). Attributions function to reduce uncertainty "to a set of explanations or meanings for why things happen as they do ... as well as ... the tools to handle specific events" (Miner & McKnight, 1999, p. 274).

Attributional or explanatory style refers to the ways in which people explain negative events. It has been conceptualized as falling along three dimensions: internal, stable, and global (Seligman, Abramson, Semmel, & von Baeyer, 1979). For example, researchers found that people who are depressed attribute negative events to internal causes (or self-blame), they view situations as unlikely to get better (stable) and see internal causes as affecting multiple domains in their lives (global) (Seligman et al., 1979). Peterson, Seligman, and Vaillant (1988) found that such negative internal attributions are associated with negative health outcomes. Both Suedfeld (2003) and Orenstein (1999) found that the majority of survivors in their samples made more external attributions for the trauma of the Holocaust than internal attributions.

Attributions survivors make in our interviews were both internal and external, and these dimensions are the ones pursued in this study. Internal attributions include factors like intelligence and skill, facility with languages that could enable one's survival, and having agency, or being "an intentional doer selecting, constructing, and regulating one's own activity to realize certain outcomes" (Bandura, 1999, p. 154). Decision-making abilities and perseverance are internal attributions survivors cite that can be placed under the larger category of agency. Perceived self-efficacy (PSE), or a belief in oneself and one's ability to effect change, is a related concept (Bandura, 2004).

External attributions include factors unrelated to, or outside, the survivor's psychological makeup, behavior, or control, such as the help of others (although this can be seen as actively or passively solicited by a survivor); God; fate; luck; miracles; and random circumstance or chance (Specht et al., 2011). Included within the matrix of external attributions are personal characteristics that do not imply internal control, that just "are," such as physical appearance, youth, the ability to "pass" as a Gentile, or good health (Suedfeld, 2003).

In addition, the survivors of our study commonly give multiple attributions for survival, sometimes choosing different attributions for each "moment of crisis" (Schiff, 1997, p. 84), both internal and external. As the excerpt from Edith's interview in the opening quotation clearly shows, she provided multiple attributions of youth, general good health, the ability to run fast, and luck. A few survivors were consistent in their attributions—consistently crediting God, for example, or consistently crediting their own agency—in multiple "moments of crisis." However, these are in the minority.

Suedfeld (2003) found external attributions to be more common than internal ones in survivor interviews, and the present study has as well. What could account for these findings? In contrast, for those survivors who offered internal attributions, and were therefore able to give themselves at least partial credit for surviving the Holocaust and a sense of agency in the war, what makes that possible for them? What do these different causal attributions tell us about both groups and about how well they have been able to adapt after the Holocaust?

A major methodological point must be noted at the outset: The "hows" and the "whys" of survival statements have been conflated in the handful of studies that have researched the topic of causal attributions of Holocaust survivors. Eitinger, a Holocaust survivor himself, conducted an early study (1964) asking his respondents: "Why did you survive?" He received responses that were really answers to the question: "How did you survive?" However, Eitinger was not looking for an answer to the "why" question of existential meaning and purpose. Conducting his own study a decade later, Matussek (1975) also asked his survivor respondents: "Why did you survive?" and received responses to the question: "How did you survive?"

Schiff, in his doctoral dissertation (1997), used the interrogative words *how* and *why* interchangeably when both posing and analyzing questions about survival to his respondent, that is, inconsistently asking, "How did you survive?" and "Why did you survive?" and then analyzing the responses by conflating the two, as if means and meaning were one and the same. This can lead, of course, to ambiguous responses, as well as ambiguous results, as Suedfeld (2003) also aptly noted and corrected in his own study. "How?" and "Why?" are two separate questions and should not be confused and conflated. The means and the meaning are not the same. However, they may be inextricably linked.

Earlier studies also had broader and ill-defined categories. In Schiff's (1997) study, for example, the broader categories may have been due to the small size ($N = 20$) of his sample. Eitinger (1964) was working with a much larger sample size ($N = 158$), yet he still collapsed many categories into single, large groups, which consequently caused the loss of meaning. For example, his category "mere chance" includes "all those who gave this answer directly or indirectly, i.e., those who talked about 'fate,' or 'destiny,' and so on, but who had no concrete information to offer beyond this" (p. 79). However, *fate* and *destiny* are understood by many survivors to be very different from *mere chance*, or what I call *random circumstance*; such words imply some sort of outside "force" or predetermination that mere chance does not.

In Eitinger's (1964) study, such terms are not clearly defined. But, these are words that should ideally be clarified with each survivor respondent. Meanings should not be assumed—particularly not when the respondents are not speaking their mother language. For example, when conducting a second interview with a survivor who had given multiple causal attributions of "miracle," continued clarification revealed that "miracle" was merely a figure of speech for this respondent and did not imply the work of a deity. In fact, just the opposite was the case; the survivor admitted losing his faith after the war. It was not possible to reinterview all of the survivors for clarification, but the six who were reinterviewed for this study provided a great deal of nuanced insights into complex concepts many of us assume we know the meanings to, and take for granted, such as "fate," "luck," and "miracle."

Of note is the fact that "God" or "miracle" were not cited at all by Eitinger (1964) as either a category or subcategory. Schiff (1997) noted this as well and suspected Eitinger subsumed God under the category for chance and fate. Eitinger (1964) included the category "help of others," or what he called "was with friends and relatives." The other categories he included are "own efforts," "did not participate," and "the question was not asked or the answer was not satisfactory" (p. 78). Of all of these categories of causal attributions, the largest by far was mere chance—perhaps due to the broad boundaries of the category (Eitinger, 1964).

Matussek's (1975) study, which included both Jewish and Gentile survivors, including political prisoners, gave categories that included "discipline and self-control," "chance or luck," "camaraderie with fellow inmates," "family memories," "religious faith," and "faith in political convictions"

(p. 32). Categories like "help from others" were conspicuously absent. Matussek did not explain how he phrased the questions meant to elicit "reasons for survival," how he arrived at his categories, or what was included in them. For example, under the category of "religious faith," it is unclear whether he included statements of clear and direct divine intervention, such as "God helped me," as well as statements of religious practice, which do not always make a clear connection between faith in God and practice of ritual, such as "I prayed a lot, and that helped." The two biggest categories in Matussek's sample, very close to each other in frequency, were discipline and self-control (22.8%) and chance or luck (21.1%), categories that are internal and external, respectively. He noted that "interviewees often gave no reasons for their survival, but equally often other interviewees cited more than one reason" (p. 32).

Schiff's (1997) study included the following categories, in order of frequency, and did not differentiate them as internal and external attributions: "destiny," which "involves the workings of a force that is greater than oneself; known by other names such as the divine, the miraculous as well as fate" (p. 78); "no explanation," which means that the survivor could not give an explanation; "help," which included aid from friends as well as Gentiles; "luck," which "includes all variations on the theme of chance"; and "personal characteristics," under which heading he subsumed both agency and nonagentic characteristics, such as age, appearance, and gender. These categories could be further refined and meanings more carefully delineated. Schiff essentially did what he criticized Eitinger for; he made his categories too broad and ill defined, but perhaps that can be explained by the small size of the sample.

Suedfeld (2003) clearly separated causal attributions into internal and external categories. Internal categories included "determination, hope, and persistence," "secretiveness," "being careful," "intelligence," "good health," and "strong sense of identity," among others (p. 27). Under external attributions, he included "social support," "fate, luck, chance, God," "help from family," "help from Gentiles," "hiding," "age," and "Aryan appearance," among others. Similar to the earlier studies, he included fate, luck, chance, and God in a single category, even though his sample size was arguably large enough to further refine this category ($N = 143$). In contrast, he separated "help from others" into several different categories: social support, help from family, help from friends, and help from Gentiles (Suedfeld, 2003).

Methodology

A content analysis was conducted on 95 survivor interviews to try to establish patterns of causal attributions within the sample. The interviews were systematically combed for every causal attribution related to the war and every statement related to the search for meaning after the war. After conducting the content analysis, six survivors were reinterviewed to ask more nuanced questions about their responses. They were asked the specific questions: "How did you survive the war?" and "Why did you survive the war?" and these interviews, not surprisingly, led to more nuanced understandings of those survivors' causal attributions.

In retrospect, it might have been more useful to phrase the how question as Suedfeld (2003) did: "What factors do you think were important in your surviving the Holocaust?" because even when separating out the how and why questions in this way, the differences were not always apparent to the survivors. As we have seen, even native English speakers often conflate these terms.

While most survivor respondents in the TTP sample for this study were not directly asked the questions: "How did you survive the war?" and "Why did you survive the war?"—and if they were, they were not asked the questions in any systematic or consistent manner—the survivors' interviews were nevertheless full of causal attributions regarding survival. For a smaller percentage of respondents, statements of meaning and purpose after survival were expressed, as well.

Finally, it is important to note that this study was not concerned with historical "facts" or with what outside observers may consider as the "objective" reasons why and how someone survived the Nazi horrors. The objective reasons for survival are perhaps ultimately unknowable. Rather, as Schiff (2005) also emphasized, this study was concerned with the belief systems of the survivors themselves, the meaning they put to their experiences, the narratives they told, the words they chose, and the understandings they came to after many years of struggle.

Findings

For the current study, the external (Figure 5.1) and internal (Figure 5.2) attribution categories were obtained and are listed next in order of frequency, from most commonly cited to least.

External Attributions

1. Help of others, a category that includes relatives, friends, and Gentiles, although this could be further refined into two categories: relatives/friends and Gentiles.
2. Luck, which includes the Yiddish word *mazel*, connoting "in the stars," which often implies an outside force.
3. God, which includes God's direct intervention, God's desire for the survivor to live, or the survivor's faith in God.

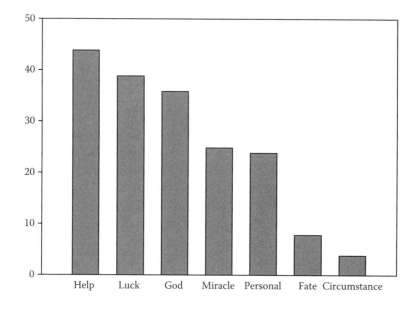

Figure 5.1 External attributions for survival.

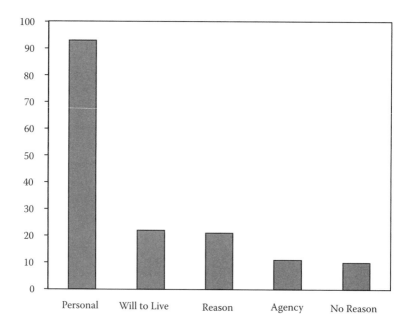

Figure 5.2 Internal attributions for survival.

4. Miracle, which does not always imply a deity, but can be, in some cases, merely a figure of speech. Also included in this category are dead relatives the survivor feels are watching over him or her; dead relatives coming in a premonition or dream; and a *malach*, or angel—described as a being in human form, who steps into the survivor's life to direct him or her to safety and then disappears from sight.

5. Personal characteristics, a category that includes appearance, or "passing as Aryan," and age (youth), characteristics that are not a function of the individual's agency.

6. Fate, which includes the concept of *Bashert*, or something that is "meant to be" or predetermined.

7. Random circumstance, or pure chance, conceptualized as different from "luck," resulting from entirely random situations that have no predetermined plan behind them.

Internal Attributions

1. Personal characteristics, a parallel category to that included in external attributions, but implying a more active role than the external attributes of "appearance" or "age." Subsumed in this category are intelligence; skill; the ability to run quickly; hypervigilance; knowledge and facility with languages other than Yiddish; charm, which was used to the survivor's advantage to elicit help from others; optimism; and lack of fear.

2. Will to live, or "survival instinct," what survivors described as an almost-primal need to hang onto life, no matter what.

3. Reason to live, which includes following the directives of family members to survive; staying alive to tell the world what happened; desire to reunite with family members; desire for revenge (this last being a surprisingly small number).

4. Agency, which includes making decisions, taking risks, claiming at least partial credit for one's own survival or for the survival of others.

5. No reason, either because it is not found in the narrative or the respondent actually said, "I don't know how I survived."

The main finding concurs with Suedfeld's (2003) study: There were far more external than internal attributions. The largest external attribution category, help of others, was also the largest in the Suedfeld study, which, if he had conflated social support, help from friends, help from family, and help from Gentiles, would have been even larger. Also similar to Suedfeld's study, luck and God are the next largest external attribution categories, although Suedfeld made these into one category. Still, the pattern is similar in our study; survivors seemed more willing to credit external factors for their survival than they were to credit themselves.

As in Matussek's (1975), Schiff's (1997), and Suedfeld's (2003) studies, the majority of our respondents gave multiple attributions for survival, often mixing internal and external attributions, and often within the same sentence. For example, Efraim, who survived in hiding in Poland, escaping many *Aktions* [German for round up and deportation of Jews to extermination camps] of the Nazis, said:

> Who was lucky, or alert enough, or had luck enough, or had a place to hide, could survive again and again and again. That's what happened to me. I was maybe very alert, very quick reactions, and had a lot of luck. I survived many Aktions.

Almost in one sentence, we find the internal, personal characteristics of hypervigilance and quick reactions and the external attributions of luck and having a hiding place.

Norman, who survived several camps, said:

> Was I that lucky? I wasn't the smartest guy. I had no big education. But I see that a person doesn't have to go to college to have sense, to make decisions. But I know one thing: That in dire times like this, the human being became an animal. The instinct for survival takes over and there's nothing stronger than your survival instinct.

Norman articulated a sense of agency in talking about his survival. He did not seem to credit luck, but rather the decisions he made as well as an instinctual drive or will to survive.

Only 15 in our sample gave single, consistent attributions, mentioned either once in the interview or several times. Of these, most credited help from others, and almost all of these were child survivors who credited their parents or another adult. For example, Pearl, who survived Auschwitz, said:

> I don't think I would have survived if my mom wouldn't have been with me. And I don't think I would have survived if my sister wouldn't have been with me. And I think each of us wouldn't have made it alone. First of all, you'd have no reason to try. I was quite ill. And without my mom, without my sister, I know I would have never made it.

Other single attributions included the following:

God: "God was with me. God was holding a hand above my head, that I should live."

Miracle: "My survival was absolutely a miracle. An intervention by
the Almighty."
The will to live: "The will to live. The will to go on and live. That's all.
I didn't have some expectations, big ones. Just to go on and live."

Rather than puzzling over multiple attributions and their implied or
actual inconsistencies, it would seem more useful to puzzle over those survivors who were able to give single, consistent attributions. What might
contribute to their surety in offering a single cause to explain such a chaotic, inexplicable, catastrophic event as the Holocaust? Surely, the multiple
explanations for survival the majority of survivors offered, the "maneuver-
ing back and forth between possibilities," was exactly what Schiff (1997)
said it was; it served as a mechanism for "integrating the story of survival"
(p. 81). Our sample indicated that, in most cases, survivors were still puzzling over how they survived. In the midst of the inconsistencies of causal
attributions, they were wrestling with worldviews and philosophies of life.
Judith spoke of the ramifications of randomness:

So often it was really completely random whether somebody survived or didn't survive. And I suppose maybe in some way this
feeling of randomness probably gives you a little bit of a feeling of
insecurity. You can't really believe in an ordered universe that if you
do everything by the rules nothing bad will happen to you. Maybe I
have more of a sense of an element of chance in existence than some
people would as a result of this.

Why do the survivors in our sample seem to have such difficulty claiming agency? Agency in our sample does not seem related to either gender or
Holocaust experience. Those who credited themselves even partially with
their own survival are fairly evenly divided between men and women,
although one could speculate that women might be less likely to "own" a
sense of agency. Esther said:

I always make sure we have bread. I was the one. Nobody else, just
me. I felt smart. My grandfather gave me that idea. He said, "If you
were a man, you'd be a rabbi."

Esther's quotation may give us a clue regarding why some survivors were
able to credit themselves for their survival. As a child, she was given a
strong sense of self-efficacy by her grandfather. She felt she could be effective in the world and had a strong belief in herself before the Holocaust
descended on her and her family. Perhaps this is one reason why she may
be better able than some others to credit herself. She also survived with
family members, and this may be a factor, as well.

Douglas said:

> Naturally I give myself credit. If I wouldn't be there, my wife wouldn't be with me, and she wouldn't have survived, either.

Not only was Douglas able to claim some credit for his own survival, he was able to state clearly that he helped his wife survive. Douglas, like Esther, had a strong sense of self-efficacy even before the war.

Those who claimed agency also run the gamut of Holocaust experiences. Someone who spent the war years in hiding might be better able to credit him- or herself with survival because of the myriad decisions, risk taking, and day-to-day efforts to survive than an individual who spent time in a concentration camp, where one was confronted almost daily with a series of tragically "choiceless choices," as Langer (1989) so poignantly described. But, our sample is fairly evenly divided between concentration camp experiences and spending the war in hiding.

Survivor respondents gave us possible explanations for the general reluctance to claim that their own actions resulted in surviving the Holocaust. First, as Barbara told us:

> You knew that if you will escape, if you will run away, even if you'll find a place where to hide, that because of saving yourself, 10 other innocent people would later on die.

In such lethal circumstances, how can an individual claim agency?

More than this, perhaps, there may have been an inability or unwillingness for many to claim agency because that would imply they were smarter, more decisive, or ultimately more worthy than those relatives and friends who did not survive, what has been described as "narrative humbling." "Drawing distinctions between oneself and the dead is problematic" (Schiff, 1997, p. 86).

More important, perhaps, giving external attributions, such as luck, random circumstance or chance, and other people, takes away some of the onus or burden of guilt. Not survivor guilt in the sense of feeling personally responsible for the deaths of others—a charge survivors have understandably resented that has peppered the pathologizing literature regarding them—but guilt in the sense of feeling a need to justify one's own existence when so many were killed.

In addition, perhaps, by taking credit for one's own survival, that individual is vulnerable to the question: Could I have saved others? Abdication from agency may be a more adaptable response in this situation. It may be safer to put the credit "out there," rather than "in here." Placing responsibility outside oneself is an adaptive narrative, perhaps, in the case of

Holocaust survivors, and one that may allow the survivor to alleviate whatever burden he or she may feel in personal survival.

Yet, it is also important to note that both internal and external attributions given by our respondents play an adaptive role. In the cases of Esther and Douglas, for example, they seem to have been able to hold onto their strong sense of self-efficacy after the war and take some pride in their own survival.

What can we learn from this that is applicable to other traumatic events in the lives of our clients? In the following case study of Sharon, we see how it took many years before she could make attributions for her own survival, after first taking more than two decades to begin to process the events.

Clinical Application: Sharon

Sharon was 21 years old when she was in a near-fatal car accident, hit by a drunk driver on Christmas Eve. The accident caused her to have a "near-death experience," 200 stitches in her face, and a shattered arm and leg. Her arm was so crushed—"in 100 pieces"—that the doctors were at first convinced that it needed to be amputated to save her life. However, they were able to save both her life and her arm. Her face was remarkably unscarred considering the extreme nature of the lacerations.

Now a psychiatric nurse practitioner in her early 50s, married with three grown children, Sharon looks back on that experience and describes her survival in almost mystical terms, but also in the mixed causal explanations that include both internal and external attributions. "I feel like it's a miracle. I had the conscious thought to wear a seatbelt and unlock the door. And I'm strong, capable, and refused to give up. And … I was not alone in the car. God was with me." Her doctors, mystified about how she could have possibly survived such a crash, credited her "extremely large bones and hard head."

After the accident, Sharon spent "40 days and 40 nights" in traction and in excruciating pain. She calls this period "my wilderness," giving it a Biblical reference. She had to relearn how to walk, how "to hold my head up. It was so humbling. But it was a spiritual journey. I knew I was not going to let this destroy me because I'm blessed."

When asked if she gives herself credit for surviving, she says that it was her "heart and her faith" that got her through it. "Heart," she defines as "the inner gut knowledge that I can get through stuff." She says she grew up knowing that about herself. She also grew up with a strong faith in God. "Faith is just there for me. When the accident happened, I immediately started praying. … All through my life different things have happened that bring Scriptures alive to me. In my practice—I can't imagine having a practice without a faith. I don't feel alone when I'm with my patients. I feel supported."

Sharon could not talk about the accident for years. She suffered from many of the symptoms of posttraumatic stress disorder (PTSD), including hypervigilance, avoidance, and nightmares from which she would awake screaming. Ten years ago—and 20 years after the accident—she underwent EMDR (eye movement desensitization and reprocessing) therapy. As her symptoms lessened, it became easier for her to talk about the accident and to make sense of it. However, she has been left with lifelong pain from her shattered ankle and has been significantly curtailed physically because of that. She has also suffered memory loss. "I've lost pieces of my life. This is what makes me cry." She mentions one other negative impact: "I expect more of others than I think they are capable of giving."

For many survivors of traumatic events, it seems, there are multiple attributions for survival that include both internal and external components. Sharon names many attributions for why she survived the crash: miracle, God, her own conscious choice to wear a seatbelt and unlock the door, her strength, her determination not to give up, her large bones. But, it is clear that she mostly credits God for her survival, an external attribution that has enabled her to find peace despite her ongoing suffering. God was with her in the car, God is with her when she treats her patients, and God informs her life. She has clearly found a great deal of comfort in that certainty, even as she draws on her own considerable strength.

Sharon took many years to come to the understandings she now holds of how she survived. Her narrative appears to be an adaptive one, even though she still finds it difficult to talk about the accident 30 years later. In her mix of internal and external attributions can be found a nuanced understanding of survival that speaks to years of struggle to find an answer. The multiple mix of personal strength and determination plus faith in a deity coalesced for Sharon into several answers that she can hold together without contradiction. However, we need to keep in mind that it took her many years to come to this understanding.

The next case example, Jody, demonstrates how a young woman continues to struggle for understanding after coming out of the numbing fog of substance abuse.

Clinical Application: Jody

Jody is a 30-year-old woman who has been diagnosed with major depressive disorder, recurrent, as well as PTSD and obsessive-compulsive disorder (OCD). In addition, she has struggled with alcohol and narcotic dependencies. She is the single mother of two small children, only one of whom is currently in her custody.

Jody's childhood was a nightmare of severe physical abuse by her father, physical abuse and neglect by her mother, and sexual abuse by her brother over many years. In addition, she was raped violently at knifepoint when she was 16 and sustained several serious knife injuries.

> I cannot recall a time when I was told by either of my parents that they loved me. I was certainly never hugged or shown any type of affection. My main job in the family was to clean the house and take care of my younger siblings. If my chores weren't completed to my mother's satisfaction, I was punished severely by both her and my father. I was beaten so badly once that I was unable to go to school for weeks. The rest of the time I tried to hide my injuries from my teachers and friends. I was told every day that I was ugly, fat, useless, stupid, a waste of everyone's time.

> Jody's brother sexually abused her from the ages of 7 through 12. He threatened to kill her if she told their parents, and she lived in fear of her life throughout those years. She developed severe urinary tract infections, wet the bed nightly, and was punished for it. Yet, she never told her parents about the sexual abuse until she was 12. Neither parent believed her, and her brother remained in the household, discontinuing his sexual assaults but continuing to threaten her.

Jody was raped violently at knifepoint when she was 16. The perpetrator was never found. She became pregnant with her first child the same year (not by the rapist) and dropped out of high school. She is still not sure who the father is. Her pregnancy was met with derision and seen as further proof to her parents of her worthlessness. She became dependent on opiates and used alcohol, drugs, and sex throughout her teens to numb herself. Pregnant with her second child before the age of 20, she became addicted to opiates and was an alcoholic. She began cutting and attempted suicide once while pregnant with her second child. Her firstborn was taken into custody by the Department of Health and Human Services (DHHS) when she was reported to them by her parents. Her second baby went through opiate withdrawal symptoms and had to be hospitalized for several weeks after birth. That child was also taken by DHHS and put into foster care.

Jody spent 5 years in and out of various drug and alcohol treatment programs, both inpatient and intensive outpatient programs. She relapsed, on average, once every 6 months for several years. She is currently being treated for the trauma underlying her substance abuse after having managed to maintain her sobriety for 3 years. She was able to regain custody of her firstborn child and is hoping to gain custody of her other child. Her mother died of cancer 3 years ago, and Jody has severed her relationships with the other members of her family of origin, whose continued verbal and emotional abuse led to several of her relapses. She has begun a journey through her traumatic childhood with her therapist and struggles to understand how she survived her childhood abuse.

> I don't know how I got through those years. I mean, I blamed myself—I still blame myself—for what my parents and my brother did to me. I'm beginning to see that maybe it wasn't all my fault; but if it wasn't my fault, why did they treat me like that? And why did I put up with it for so long? I'm so stupid for putting up with it!

When her therapist suggested that she was just a child and that the adults and her older brother should bear the burden of blame for her abuse, Jody nodded.

> I know that inside my head. I mean, I think I understand that that's really who is to blame. But I don't *believe* it yet in my soul. I don't

know when I'm ever going to believe that. I *want* to believe it, but I don't know how to get there. I bet it would be a huge relief to have that burden of responsibility off of me!

When asked by her therapist how she thinks she endured all the suffering of her childhood, Jody says

I numbed out. I mean, I just tried to find a way to get real numb—sex, drugs, alcohol, cutting, anything that would put me in that "zone" where I didn't feel anything anymore. I found my way out in men, and the drugs and alcohol they gave me. I don't know if I was trying to find love so much as I was trying to escape from my life.

Is this an internal or external attribution? On the one hand, Jody's words speak to a clear choice to "numb out," and she sought out men and substances (external) that would help her get there. The state of being numb (internal) eased the pain and made it bearable.

But, she also credits her newly found faith. As she attends NA (Narcotics Anonymous) and AA (Alcoholics Anonymous) meetings on a regular basis, Jody has gotten in touch with her Higher Power, when she had stopped believing in the Christian God of her childhood.

I used to think God abandoned me. I mean, where was He when I was going through all of that? Why didn't He stop some of that hell for me? Now, I think He was there all the time and was just helping me find my way out—of the abuse and out of drugs and alcohol. I guess I got myself into the mess, but He helped me find my way back out. If I didn't have God in my life, I don't think I would have made it.

When asked about what role her own determination to quit drugs and alcohol and to regain custody of her children played in her own survival and what role her own personal characteristics played in her survival of the abuse of childhood, Jody was less than willing to credit her own agency, demonstrating almost nonexistent self-efficacy.

I don't know. I mean, I'm such a screw-up. I don't think it had anything to do with me. I think I just got scared when my kids were taken away by the state, and I decided I had to do something to get them back. That wasn't my decision. I think maybe God was punishing me, or something, by having my kids taken away and then showed me that I needed to get straight to get them back. It wasn't me. I had nothing to do with it. And as for getting through my childhood? I'm telling you: I zoned out. That's the only thing I can think of that got me through.

Is Jody giving internal or external attributions? Is her narrative adaptive or maladaptive? How might a therapist work with the client to deepen the narrative? Will it help, long term, for Jody to settle on the external attribution of "God" for her own survival from childhood abuse? Or, will she eventually find her way to her own agency, her own internal strength that allowed her to endure, saw her through to safety and eventually find the determination to maintain her sobriety and regain custody of her children?

Survivors of the Holocaust teach us that, in working with our clients who suffer from other forms of trauma, we should be there to listen as the posttrauma narrative emerges. We may never know what final attributions our clients will settle on for themselves, but we can be there as witnesses as they struggle to understand what their internal role was in survival and what external forces they believe came into play. Sometimes, we are simply there to help them write the story. It is ultimately their decision what form their narrative will take, and whether it will be adaptive or maladaptive cannot immediately be determined. The ultimate attribution or attributions they make—internal or external or mixed—often takes years, and even decades, to be decided.

The Search for Meaning

This study's second, related research question is how survivors understood *why* they survived the Holocaust, for what reason or purpose. This is a topic that has not been adequately addressed in the literature. In other words, how do survivors answer the painful existential questions: What meaning have I found in my own survival? Why did I survive when so many of my family members and friends did not?

The search for a reason, or the search for meaning, is according to Frankl (1959), considered to be "the primary motivational force in man" (p. 54). Quoting Nietszche, Frankl believed that "he who knows the 'why' for his existence, will be able to bear almost any 'how'" (p. 127). Thus, Frankl felt that the need for an individual to have a meaning or purpose in life actually helped some Jews survive the concentration camps; those who did not have such a purpose or reason to go on living were less likely to make it to the end of the war. The "will to meaning" therefore had survival value for Frankl. It is "the reaching out beyond ourselves for something other than ourselves. Under the same conditions, those who were oriented toward the future, toward a meaning that waited to be fulfilled—these persons were more likely to survive" (p. 97).

Whether Frankl was correct in this assertion, the psychological literature indicates that those who are able to find meaning after trauma cope better and are more resilient than those who do not. Those who continue to struggle for meaning, or who cannot find it, are considered somehow less adaptable and resilient (Herman, 1997; Janoff-Bulman, 1992; McCann & Pearlman, 1990; Meichenbaum & Fitzpatrick, 1993; Miles & Crandall, 1986; Morelli, 1996; Schwartzberg, 1993; Tedeschi, Park, & Calhoun, 1998). However, for some crimes against humanity, finding meaning is not always possible (Silver, Boon, & Stones, 1983).

In fact, the ability to find meaning in the wake of extremely traumatic events may be far more difficult than making a causal attribution for one's survival. The answers understandably involve an often-intense, existential struggle. Indeed, as the Nobel Prize-winning author Toni Morrison (1970/1994) articulated, "Since why is difficult to handle, [perhaps] one must take refuge in how" (p. 7). The struggle to find meaning in one's survival after enduring the senseless cruelty of the Nazis and their collaborators and after so many of the survivor's loved ones were killed is not always ultimately "resolved." Does that mean that those survivors who have not found meaning and purpose after extremely traumatic events are somehow less resilient?

The survivor may be left with an uncomfortable feeling of needing always to justify one's own life, by doing enough "good deeds," for example, or having a positive influence on the world. To reinvoke Frankl (1959), "Each man is questioned by life; and he can only answer to life by *answering for his own life* [italics added]; to life he can only respond by being responsible" (p. 172). Surely survivors were starkly and brutally "questioned by life" in the Holocaust, and some answered for their lives by searching for meaning and purpose in the aftermath.

Only 18 in our sample were able to articulate finding a meaning and purpose for their lives after their survival of the Holocaust. This is in significant contrast to those who were able to find causal attributions for the how of their survival. Of those 18, 6 gave more than one meaning. The categories are shown in Figure 5.3.

The biggest category, to continue the Jewish people and the chain of Jewish tradition, was articulated by Cynthia, who survived Auschwitz as an adolescent:

> You know something, what went through my head, back as a child of 15, 16, then? I want to get married. I want to bring a new generation. I want to show that there's still some Jews. ... I feel that God put me on this earth to accomplish something. And if I would [give up my religion], then Hitler won. And I don't want Hitler should win. I want to bring a new generation and a religion, and they should multiply what we lost.

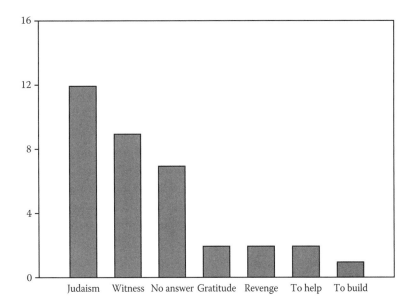

Figure 5.3 Meaning of survival.

Bluma has found meaning in remembrance. She considered herself a witness. She spoke of Emanuel, a young doctor who survived the Warsaw ghetto, only to find himself on a train to Auschwitz. Bluma told of how she was suffocating on the train from the crush of bodies, the heat, and the stench. Emanuel, a friend of hers, noticed a small opening at the top of the cattle car and made a wider hole, big enough to jump out. He convinced Bluma and two other young people to escape with him. They jumped from the train. Bluma only sprained her ankle, but the other three young men were shot by Nazi guards. Emanuel was eviscerated by bullets.

As he lay dying, he said, "There is no way I can make it. I'll be dead in a few minutes. Run, run—we are close to a town. They must have alerted the SS. Please, please, run and live. Live! How else will anybody ever remember me? Everybody else is dead." I never did forget Emanuel. I keep up his yahrzeit anniversary (anniversary of his death) and Yizkor (memorial service for the dead) every year, just like for my parents and brother, on the ninth of Av. Because I never knew the name of his father, I say, "Emanuel ben Israel." If there ever was a true son of Israel, he sure was him.

Edith, who survived the war as a 13-year-old alone in the forest and dodging Ukrainian bullets, has also found meaning in remembrance and believed her mother's letter to her was a reminder to tell the world about what happened to the Jews.

If I survived, I should tell the world what those beasts did to the Jews. And that sort of helped me go public, when I started speaking at schools, and wherever I go, because I feel that was a message from my mother. I had a mission, because of the letter my mother gave me. My mother had thrown me a message that I must survive. ... One of us has to survive, and one of us has to tell the world.

While some survivors could be very articulate and clear about the meaning or purpose they have found in their survival, others could be just as articulate in describing their very painful individual struggles to find meaning. As Frank articulated:

I go through these guilt feelings sometimes ... when I think about ... and wonder about my life. What have I accomplished? There are probably children that were killed there who probably could have contributed a lot more to the world than I have or ever could. And yet on the other hand, I look and I see I've got a wonderful wife, I've got three lovely children. I suppose we did our share to an extent. But I often wonder: Why me? Why did we survive? It's a bit of a guilt trip. More than a bit, sometimes.

Frank "responds by being responsible" (Frankl, 1959, p. 172), spending a great deal of his time in altruistic pursuits, searching for reasons to justify his existence. His response is a good example of TTP sample respondents who were still searching for meaning in their survival, almost 60 years after the war.

The message from these survivors to clinicians working with other survivors of trauma is that the search for meaning can sometimes take many years, and that often there is no answer to the question: "Why me?" Does that make those who can find no meaning in their trauma less resilient? In the following case study of Joe, we see that it took many years for him to come to a sense of meaning and purpose after the Vietnam War, and that sense of meaning was found after another traumatic event of his life: the loss of his job.

Clinical Application: Joe

Joe is an African American man in his late 50s, from a large northern city, who came into therapy because of what he called "intrusions" about the Vietnam War. His flashbacks and nightmares were interrupting his concentration during the day and his sleep at night. He was also reporting depression, having just learned that he would be laid off from his blue-collar job that had been a large part of his life for almost 30 years.

Joe was raised by his mother; his father left when he was 2, and he never knew him. His mother, a hard-working woman of strong religious convictions, taught him that he could be whatever he wanted to be, and that he had to believe in himself and his abilities. "Everything I am, I owe to my Mom." Joe gained a strong sense of himself and his own self-efficacy, which would benefit him in the war to come.

The day after graduation from high school, Joe was drafted into the army and shipped off to Vietnam at the age of 18. He served his tour of duty and received several medals for courage under fire. He witnessed many of his buddies killed and maimed and was wounded severely himself, surviving many traumatic situations. "We did the right thing in 'Nam. I don't have any regrets about my tour of duty. We did the right thing. And the war taught me to be prepared for life. You had to have a plan, or you died." When he returned home, he was spit on by antiwar protestors and called a war criminal. In pain and disgust, he threw away his uniform and his medals.

While he was serving his first year in the service, he was notified by a commanding officer that his father had died, the father he had never known. This is a big regret in his life, that he never got to know his father "man to man." After the service, Joe worked for several years at odd jobs, then met a young woman and fell in love. They married and had four children, all of whom, he was proud to say, graduated from college, something he never was able to do himself. He struggled with alcohol and substance abuse through the years. But he said the war's horrors receded, and he didn't have any of "these intrusions" until he was notified of the impending loss of his job because the plant was closing.

Joe had been looking forward to retirement in a few years, along with paying off his house and his children's student loans. He felt stunned and lost—without a job for the first time in his life. But the refrain that he kept repeating to his therapist was: "What will those guys do? Some of them still have small children or kids in college. What will they do? They're so unprepared. They don't have a plan. You got to have a plan! You *die* without a plan. I can't stop thinking about them. They're my buddies. What will they do?" The lessons of Vietnam—to have a plan or you died—seem to have been reenacted in his experience of the layoffs in his factory.

In his life narrative, it was evident to his therapist that Joe may have been suffering from survivor guilt—despite his protestations to the contrary. The substance abuse for years after the war, a common comorbid condition in people suffering from PTSD, may have been a way to cope with both the traumatic memories and the guilt of having survived when many of his friends had not. His belief that he and his fellow soldiers "did the right thing" in Vietnam was a way for him to make sense of how 18-year-old boys could kill and maim. Further, the war taught him you had to have a plan for life. It was having a plan and following through with that plan that is the causal attribution he makes for his own survival. It was very clear to Joe: Without a plan, you die.

Despite his internal causal attribution for his survival of the war years, and despite his apparent belief that he did the right thing, the layoffs in his company of himself and his younger coworkers brought the war years back and triggered his PTSD. He agonized over the plight of his coworkers, and seemed more concerned with them than he did with himself and his own precarious financial situation.

His therapist helped him reframe his job loss as a time for healing from the war, for rethinking his life and his goals, and perhaps for trying something totally different, something he had wanted to do his whole life and had not had a chance to do. At midlife,

Joe found himself in Erikson's psychosocial crisis of "generativity versus stagnation" (Erikson, 1966). The pull for him was toward generativity—toward giving back to his community. "I'm tired of working with my hands. I want a job where I can use my brain a little more. And you know what? You're going to think this is crazy. But I want to go back to the inner city where I was raised and be a mentor to some of those Black kids there. Maybe I can be a coach, maybe I can teach them something, anything. They need to be prepared for life. It isn't easy being a Black man in America. They need all the help they can get."

The search for meaning in survival continues for Joe, well into midlife. His therapist encouraged his search for meaning, by making a contribution to the youth who had not yet known war. He could teach them to "be prepared for life." As therapists, we need to recognize that the search for meaning after trauma is often lifelong, and that new traumatic events can force the search toward a new urgency. Meanings grow and change over a lifetime and are developed, discarded, and augmented. When working with clients who face new crises in their lives, we can help support them in the search and help them reframe their new crises as opportunities for change.

Conclusion

Regarding causal attributions for survival, this study seems to indicate that external attributions may be psychologically "safer" for this particular population of Holocaust survivors, more adaptive, and therefore will be far more common than internal ones in their narratives. By attributing one's survival to something "out there," often vague and nebulous and beyond one's control or ultimate understanding, survivors were able to alleviate some of the onus of survival itself, including survivor guilt.

It could be argued that many survivors would feel it tremendous hubris to credit themselves in any way with their own survival. To give themselves credit would make them somehow better, smarter, and by implication, more "worthy" than murdered family members and friends. Yet, some people could give themselves credit, and perhaps those are the people who went into the war with a strong sense of self-efficacy, a belief in their own abilities to get out of it alive. Further, perhaps people who did not have a strong belief in God going into the war would be less likely to attribute their survival to God, or to concepts like fate or luck, which imply some sort of belief system in something vaguely out there. As Schiff (1997) pointed out, an external attribution such as fate or destiny can also imply a "chosen-ness" that some survivors may have found uncomfortable.

Still, as one of our respondents articulated, external attributions for one's survival are also not so easy to accept, especially in relation to the question of God's role in the Holocaust, a topic that is beyond the scope of this chapter. In some cases, it would appear from this survivor's quotation, it is best to live without an explanation.

If I was to accept that God was part of my surviving, then … how do I explain the part that so many did not survive? If God had to do with one, then God had to do with the other. And I just couldn't accept either explanation. (Barbara)

Regarding the search for meaning in survival, this study raises questions that call for further exploration: Why were some survivors able to find meaning and purpose in their survival while others were not? Is the inability to find meaning related to the severity of the trauma or the extent of the losses? Did those who were able to find meaning survive with several family members intact? What is the relationship between having feelings of survivor guilt and the inability to find meaning in survival? What is the relationship between age at the onset of trauma and the ability to find meaning afterward? Were those people who had strong religious belief better able to find meaning in their suffering than those without belief or vice versa? When do survivors come to a sense of meaning—soon after the Holocaust years, later, or at the end of life? Does that meaning change over time? Does the inability to find meaning indicate, as the psychological literature tells us, that such a survivor is coping and adapting less well, is less resilient, than those who have been able to find meaning for their lives? Perhaps there is strength to be found in the struggle itself.

The causal attributions and the search for meaning made by Holocaust survivors can help inform our clinical work with survivors of other traumatic events. Therapists should be aware of the various internal and external attributions survivors of trauma make to describe how they endured and see those attributions as adaptive, evolving ways in which their clients learn, over time, to make sense of their own survival. It may well be the case, as it is for Holocaust survivors, that multiple attributions are more common than single attributions in our clients' narratives. Whether internal, external, or a combination of both, therapists should help their clients explore whether their attributions are adaptive or maladaptive. We may find that external attributions function as more adaptive than internal ones, in some cases, and should be open to exploring these avenues with our clients.

In addition, we should be aware of our clients' ongoing search for meaning in their traumatic experiences and do our best to encourage that exploration as an important step toward healing. To paraphrase Frankl, knowing the why or the meaning for one's existence after trauma can often help an individual bear with the trauma itself. Healing can surely be found in the meaning that is found; however, there is strength to be found simply in the search. For some traumatic life events, there may be no meaning to be found afterward; the search may be enough. Indeed, if the why is hard to get to, some survivors will "take refuge in the how" (Morrison, 1970/1994, p. 7).

References

Ayalon, L., Perry, C., Arean, P. A., & Horowitz, M. J. (2007). Making sense of the past: Perspectives on resilience among Holocaust survivors. *Journal of Loss and Trauma, 12,* 281–293.

Bandura, A. (1999). Social cognitive theory of personality. In L. A. Pervin & O. P. John (Eds.), *Handbook of personality: Theory and research* (pp. 154–196). New York: Guilford Press.

Bandura, A. (2004). Self-efficacy. In N. B. Anderson (Ed.), *Encyclopedia of health and behavior* (Vol. 2, pp. 708–714). Thousand Oaks, CA: Sage.

Bloom, S. (1997). *Creating sanctuary.* New York: Routledge Press.

Butler, R. N. (1963). The life review: An interpretation of reminiscence in the aged. *Psychiatry, 26,* 65–76.

Courtois, C. A., & Ford, J. D. (2009). *Treating complex traumatic stress disorders: An evidence-based guide.* New York: Guilford Press.

Eitinger, L. (1964). *Concentration camp survivors in Norway and Israel.* Oslo: Ferlag-Vorstat.

Erikson, E. (1966). Eight ages of man. *International Journal of Psychiatry, 2,* 281–300.

Finkelstein, L. E., & Levy, B. R. (2006). Disclosure of Holocaust experiences: Reasons, attributions, and health implications. *Journal of Social and Clinical Psychology, 25,* 117–140.

Frankl, V. (1959). *Man's search for meaning.* New York: Washington Square Press.

Herman, J. (1997). *Trauma and recovery.* New York: Basic Books.

Janoff-Bulman, R. (1992). *Shattered assumptions.* New York: Free Press.

Langer, L. (1989). The dilemma of choice in the death camps. In J. K. Roth & M. Berenbaum (Eds.), *Holocaust: Religious and philosophical implications* (pp. 222–233). New York: Paragon House.

Matussek, P. (1975). *Internment in concentration camps and its consequences.* New York: Springer-Verlag.

McCann, L., & Pearlman, L. A. (1990). *Psychological trauma and the adult survivor: Theory, therapy, and transformation.* Philadelphia: Brunner/Mazel.

Meichenbaum, D., & Fitzpatrick, D. (1993). A constructivist narrative perspective on stress and coping: Stress inoculation applications. In L. Goldberger & S. Breznitz (Eds.), *Handbook of stress: Theoretical and clinical aspects* (pp. 706–723). New York: Free Press.

Miles, M. S., & Crandall, E. K. (1986). The search for meaning and its potential for affecting growth in bereaved parents. In R. H. Moos (Ed.), *Coping with crises: An integrated approach* (pp. 235–243). New York: Springer.

Miner, M. H., & McKnight, M. (1999). Religious attributions: Situational factors and effects on coping. *Journal for the Scientific Study of Religion, 38,* 274–286.

Morelli, P. T. T. (1996). Trauma and healing: The construction of meaning among survivors of the Cambodian holocaust. *Dissertation Abstracts International, 57*(9-A), 4133.

Morrison, T. (1970/1994). *The bluest eye*. New York: Plume.

Orenstein, S. W. (1999). Predictors of explanatory style among Holocaust survivors. *Dissertation Abstracts International: Section B: The Sciences and Engineering, 59*(10B), 5583.

Peterson, C., Seligman, M. E. P., & Vaillant, G. (1988). Pessimistic explanatory style is a risk factor for physical illness: A 35-year longitudinal study. *Journal of Personality and Social Psychology, 55*, 23–27.

Schiff, B. (1997). *Telling survival and the holocaust*. Unpublished doctoral dissertation, University of Chicago.

Schiff, B. (2005). Telling it in time: Interpreting consistency and change in the stories of Holocaust survivors. *International Journal of Aging and Human Development, 60*, 189–212.

Schiff, B., & Cohler, B. J. (2001). Telling survival backward: Holocaust survivors narrate the past. In G. Kenyon, P. Clark, & B. deVries (Eds.), *Narrative gerontology: Theory, research, and practice* (pp. 113–136). New York: Springer.

Schwartzberg, S. S. (1993). Struggling for meaning: How HIV-positive gay men make sense of AIDS. *Professional Psychology: Research and Practice, 24*, 483–490.

Seligman, M. E. P., Abramson, L. Y., Semmel, A., & von Baeyer, C. (1979). Depressive attributional style. *Journal of Abnormal Psychology, 88*, 242–247.

Silver, R. L., Boon, C., & Stones, M. H. (1983). Searching for meaning in misfortune: Making sense of incest. *Journal of Social Issues, 39*, 81–102.

Specht, J., Egloff, B., & Schmukle, S.C. (2011). The benefits of believing in chance or fate: External locus of control as a protective factor for coping with the death of a spouse. *Social Psychological and Personality Science, 2*, 132–137.

Suedfeld, P. (2003). Specific and general attributional patterns of Holocaust survivors. *Canadian Journal of Behavioural Science, 35*, 133–142.

Suedfeld, P., Soriano, E., McMurtry, D. L., Paterson, H., Weiszbeck, T. L., & Krell, R. (2005). Erikson's "components of a healthy personality" among Holocaust survivors immediately and 40 years after the war. *International Journal of Aging and Human Development, 60*, 229–248.

Taylor, S. E., Lichtman, R. R., & Wood, J. V. (1984). Attributions, beliefs about control, and adjustment to breast cancer. *Journal of Personality and Social Psychology, 46*, 490–501.

Tedeschi, R. D., Park, C. L., & Calhoun, L. G. (1998). *Posttraumatic growth: Positive changes in the aftermath of crisis*. Mahwah, NJ: Erlbaum.

Weiner, B. (1986). *An attributional theory of motivation and emotion*. New York: Springer Verlag.

Wilson, J. P., Friedman, M. J., & Lindy, J. D. (Eds.). (2001). *Treating psychological trauma and PTSD*. New York: Guilford Press.

CHAPTER 6

"If Somebody Throws a Rock on You, You Throw Back Bread"

*The Impact of Family Dynamics on Tolerance
and Intolerance in Survivors of Genocide*

NANCY ISSERMAN

Introduction

When asked the question, "Does the Holocaust affect your political views?" a surprising number of survivors interviewed for the Transcending Trauma Project (TTP) clearly stated that they do not harbor any hatred toward the national groups that perpetrated crimes against them and their families. Irrespective of their experiences during the Holocaust, about one third of the survivors in the sample were able to separate out their emotional responses toward the perpetrators of the specific crimes against them from their views of all Germans, Poles, or other groups that collaborated with the German Nazi government. On the other hand, about the same number of survivors expressed hatred toward their perpetrators and the entire national group that participated in the destruction of their families and their lives. This is not an unexpected response even now, over 50 years after the Holocaust, given what the survivors experienced.[1]

While the political science and sociological literatures attribute political tolerance to age, education, and religious affiliation, among others (Alozie, 1995; Bobo & Licari, 1989; Karpov, 1999; Maykovich, 1975;

Stouffer, 1967; Wilcox & Jelen, 1990), an analysis of individual survivors using qualitative data points to the importance of family-of-origin relationships as one factor influencing tolerance in the victims of genocide toward the perpetrators.

In my study of the political beliefs of the survivor respondents of the TTP (Isserman, 2005a), the identification of the influences on tolerant beliefs about the genocide perpetrators arose from an examination of the narratives about prewar family-of-origin life. These prewar stories revealed the importance of family-of-origin relationships in the formation of political beliefs of tolerance and intolerance. An analysis of the TTP interviews compared the survivors who expressed tolerant views to a group of survivors with intolerant views. Tolerant and intolerant survivors were identified after tracking their statements about other ethnic, political, and religious groups. In particular, quotes in the interviews about Germans, Poles, Ukrainians, and other European groups who sought to exterminate the Jews in World War II were important in determining the beliefs in tolerance.

This study found that the quality of relationship between the survivors and their family-of-origin caregivers played a major role in influencing survivor attitudes toward other groups.[2] The results showed that survivors who evidenced positive relationships with their family-of-origin caregivers also held tolerant attitudes toward the perpetrators of the genocide; conversely, the survivors who had troubled relationships with their family-of-origin caregivers expressed intolerance toward the perpetrators. This finding arose from an analysis that applied a five-factor continuum of behavior between the caregivers and the child to describe the nature of the caregiver–child relationship. This five-factor rating, the quality of family dynamics paradigm, grew out of the grounded theory work of the TTP. The paradigm (Hollander-Goldfein & Isserman, 1999) described five sets of patterns of interaction/attachment between the parent/caregiver and the child that directly influenced political beliefs in adulthood. This connection between family-of-origin relationships and political beliefs has not been fully explored in the social science literature on intolerance.

In the political science literature, psychological insecurity is a key component of political intolerance (Davis, 1995; Eisenstein, 2006; Marcus, Sullivan, Theiss-Morse, & Wood, 1995; Peffley, Knigge, & Hurwitz, 2001; Sullivan, Piereson, & Marcus, 1982). However, the definition of psychological insecurity and an understanding of its contribution to political intolerance have not been clearly defined. This chapter proposes that psychological concepts and recent theories about intergroup behavior help to define psychological insecurity and thus explain influences on tolerance in ways that the traditional political science literature has not.

To help explain psychological insecurity and its impact on intolerance, two theories are important, one from psychology and one from the intersection of political psychology and intergroup relations. These two, attachment theory and terror management theory (TMT), will help clarify the concept of psychological insecurity and its relationship to intolerance. One theory, attachment theory, examines how the relationships between children and their primary caregivers influence adult behavior and explains the behavior of the secure and insecure child. (Bretherton, 1992; Collins, 1996; Main, Kaplan, & Cassidy, 1985). TMT describes how the interaction of attachment, self-worth, and cultural belief systems comprise a world-view that may be defensive or open to those who hold different worldviews. TMT explains on a group level the relationship between attachment styles in the family of origin and the views of secure and insecure adults toward other groups (Burke, Martens, & Faucher, 2010; Greenberg et al., 1990; Hart, Shaver, & Goldenberg, 2005; Mikulincer & Shaver, 2001; Weise et al., 2008). Linking attachment theory to TMT helps describe how family-of-origin relationships affect the adult survivor's political beliefs. Thus, attachment styles reveal positive or negative family-of-origin relationships, and these relationships are linked to specific views of tolerance or intolerance in the adult survivor.

The data for this chapter on political tolerance came from a subsample of 18 survivors of the population of 95 in the TTP.[3] The subsample was divided into three equal groups of six survivors each. The three groups were intolerant, limited intolerant, and tolerant survivors.[4] In this research study, *tolerance* in Holocaust survivors was defined as the capacity to endure associations with individuals or groups, specifically the perpetrators and the ethnic groups to which they belonged. Given the war experiences suffered by the survivors at the hands of the perpetrators, it would not be surprising for survivors to normally dislike or hate members of the perpetrators' ethnic groups. However, tolerant survivors do not hold hostile attitudes toward persons on the basis of their ethnic, religious, or political group affiliation. The TTP interviews provided clear examples of tolerant beliefs, for example:

> I realize that people have behaved very cruelly towards the Jews, but I realize that it's not because each and every one of them is a cruel individual; it's because they were taught from childhood to hate Jews, and these are the effects from teaching hatred. If these same human beings would have taught tolerance and kindness and love, I'm sure we would live peacefully with our Christian neighbors. (Barbara)

> We were taught early on in our lives to know that we were good children—that the hatred of the Jews was not a personal hatred. (Fruma)

Limited intolerant survivors confined their intolerance to the perpetrators or the specific groups representing the perpetrators. They otherwise held tolerant attitudes toward most other groups. For example, one survivor declared,

> [In addition to hating the Poles] only the German groups. The Jew-hating groups. But no other group. Maybe not Jew-hating group; any hating group. I have the same feelings. All those groups and cults and everything, religious groups which are built on hate to other religions, I have hate to them. [But otherwise she noted that she judged each individual as an individual.] (Tova)

Intolerant survivors expressed a more generalized hatred. Their hatred is first toward the perpetrators and the groups representing the persons who destroyed their families, livelihoods, and homes, during and right after World War II continuing to the present time. Yet, they also expressed hatred toward ethnic, racial, and religious groups outside their own group. Examples of intolerant beliefs are:

> The Poles are anti-Semites. … Because Poland is anti-Semiten to hell. … They will write on your door, you know, "the Jews," the Zhid was such a terrible thing, Zhid. You know, Zhid is a Jew in Polish. Zhid is like a … like a elephant. The Pollaks, they kill you for a dollar. (Ivan)

> I can never be a friend with a German person, never. I can never trust a German person. As far as Gentile people … I am friendly to them but I cannot really be a good friend to a Gentile person. … Because even the Gentile person stood by. Everyone stood by and let us be killed. (Charlotte)

Thus, in the TTP data the survivors who expressed beliefs about tolerance or intolerance could be placed in three groups: tolerant, limited intolerant, or intolerant. What are the factors influencing the political belief patterns of tolerance or intolerance in survivors? This question is the focus for this chapter.

Review of the Political Science Literature on Intolerance

Psychological Insecurity and Intolerance

For the past 50 years, political science scholars have suggested that psychological factors contribute to political intolerance. In studies using quantitative methods to look at groups of people, scholars have shown that psychological insecurity is the main factor in predicting political intolerance (Davis, 1995; Eisenstein, 2006; Marcus et al., 1995; Peffley et al., 2001; Sullivan et al., 1982). As early as 1960, Rokeach and others who followed him (Duch, & Gibson, 1992; Eisenstein, 2006; Rubenstein, 1995) defined psychological insecurity as comprising dogmatism, low self-esteem, and mistrust (Rokeach, 1960). Yet, in this published body of research the reasons why or how dogmatism, low self-esteem, and mistrust lead to political intolerance are not elucidated. How do these traits constitute psychological insecurity? How does psychological insecurity lead to political intolerance?

Psychological Factors

The political science and political psychology literatures discuss two groups of psychological factors that influence intolerance: personality traits and psychological insecurity. Self-centeredness, low self-esteem, the authoritarian personality, mistrust, pessimism, and dogmatism are some of the personality traits linked to intolerance (Knutson, 1973; Rokeach, 1960; Sullivan et al., 1981, 1982; Sullivan & Transue, 1999). Many studies focused on these personality traits—especially the authoritarian personality (Adorno, Frenkel-Brunswik, Levinson, & Sanford, 1950)—as contributors to intolerance. Others, like the work of Sullivan et al. (1982) and Sullivan and Transue (1999), identified three of these traits—low self-esteem, mistrust, and dogmatism—as comprising the concept of psychological insecurity. Sullivan et al. then noted that psychological insecurity is one of three explanations of intolerance; the other two are perceived threat and political ideology or commitment to democratic institutions. Research has shown that survivors who are intolerant perceive the world to be a threatening place, which they verbalize by stating that they expect another Holocaust to happen (Isserman, 2005a). Tolerant survivors do not incorporate perceived threats into their worldview.[5] Neither Sullivan's work (1982) nor that of others writing about psychological insecurity (Davis, 1995; Eisenstein, 2006; Marcus et al., 1995; Peffley et al., 2001; Sullivan et al., 1982) fully define it or explain how it relates to intolerance.

Several research studies, using quantitative methods, reported that the best predictor of intolerance is dogmatism; that is, the more close-minded people are, the more intolerant they are (Gibson, 1992; Rokeach, 1960). Rokeach formulated the dogmatism scale and found high correlations between it and that of Adorno's scale measuring anti-Semitism (Rokeach, 1960; Rubenstein, 1995). The most relevant attribute of dogmatism is the tendency to dichotomize beliefs into "strict categories of acceptance and rejection" (Duch & Gibson, 1992). Duch and Gibson concluded that people who are more dogmatic are quite hostile to beliefs that differ from their own, in part because these beliefs threaten them. Individuals who exhibit the attribute of dogmatism or psychological insecurity also exhibit anger stemming from the perception of threats from groups other than their own, while at the same time evidencing a tendency to stereotype (Duch & Gibson, 1992).

Delving deeper into the concept of psychological insecurity, additional quantitative studies concluded that people whose physiological and psychological security needs have not been met tend to exhibit significantly less tolerance than those whose needs have been met (Golebiowska, 1995). Conversely, individuals whose psychological needs have been met and are in satisfying and committed adult relationships have been shown to view potentially negative situations as less threatening (Collins, 1996). Thus, the literature points toward a connection between intolerance and the child's unmet needs. These unmet needs in the adult lead to anger or insecurity in response to perceived or real threats from others who hold different beliefs. Yet, what leads individuals to have unmet psychological needs or what these unmet psychological needs mean are two topics not addressed in the political literature on tolerance (Isserman, 2005a).

Some scholars move away from the concept of psychological insecurity entirely and discuss a predisposition to authoritarianism that, coupled with conditions of threat, lead to political intolerance (Stenner, 2005). Adorno et al. (1950) and others (Stanford, 1973; Stouffer, 1967) briefly addressed the issue of family relationships as a factor in creating an authoritarian personality. In their studies, they predicted that poor psychological functioning contributes to intolerance. Their research mentioned that individuals with authoritarian personalities often came from dysfunctional families in which they had conflicted relationships with their fathers. These studies observed this connection but did not pursue an in-depth exploration of the relationships in the family of origin to intolerant attitudes. The exception is Stenner, who suggested that "physical punitiveness in childhood may be associated with increased authoritarianism in adulthood" (p. 172). She speculated that it may be "as simple as a child's learning that physical force and coercion by authority are appropriate means to 'influence' another's behavior" (p. 172). Thus, according to Stenner, a child who experiences physical force and coercion in his or her early relationships may develop an authoritarian personality in adulthood. She concluded that people who exhibit an authoritarian personality also exhibit intolerance toward others.

The Importance of Attachment Theory and Family-of-Origin Relationships as a Factor in Political Intolerance

The data in this chapter point to the importance of the qualitative experiences of a child's development within the family of origin. The qualitative experiences are shaped by the attachment style of the child to his or her primary caregiver—usually the parent, although sometimes another significant adult in the child's life. This relationship guides the understanding that the child develops of his or her experience and behavior within the family of origin (Bretherton, 1985). Styles of attachment observed in children appear useful for describing individual differences in adult styles of relating. Thus, individuals who have experienced secure attachments in their family of origin usually find themselves in satisfying and committed adult relationships that allow them to view potentially negative events in a less-threatening way (Collins, 1996). Exploring this idea further will help elucidate an understanding of the impact of the quality of family-of-origin relationships on the development of psychological insecurity and intolerance.

Attachment Theory and Family-of-Origin Relationships

In the 1950s, John Bowlby developed the concept of the "internal working model" as part of attachment theory. The internal working model is an integral component of the attachment behavioral system that guides the child's behavior based on past experiences (Bowlby, 1973, 1969/1982). In the internal working model, the mental health of the child depends on the child experiencing a consistent relationship with a nurturing caregiver (Bowlby, 1969/1982). Bowlby defined the model noting that the child, with available and supportive parents who encourage autonomy, views himself or herself as able to cope and be worthy of help. A child whose parents are unresponsive, who abandon or threaten to abandon the child, will view himself or herself as unworthy and unlovable (Ainsworth, 1979). Attachment develops from the biological necessity of the developing infant to stay in close proximity to his or her primary caregiver, which Bowlby had observed in nature as well as in human beings. The relationship between the primary caregiver and the child is a reciprocal one in which the attachment provides a feeling of safe haven and security for the child. This safe haven, which has been called the secure base of attachment, facilitates exploration of the child's inner and outer worlds (Ainsworth, 1979).

A child learns what he or she feels through a process of social feedback; attachment relationships are a primary source of this feedback (Gergely & Watson in Allen, 2005). Ricks (1985), building on Bowlby's theory, noted that when parents are available and supportive a child is secure. When the parents are not available or supportive, the child is insecure. Patterns once established are self-perpetuating (Main et al., 1985). The nature of the attachment not only governs a child's experience of relationships in the family of origin but also has an impact on the child's behavior toward other people into adulthood (Allen, 2005).

Siegel (1999) elaborated on attachment in the family of origin. He hypothesized that repeated patterns of interactions between children and their parents create patterns in the developing brain that form impressions in the memory, shaping behavior, emotions, and perceptions. During early development, a parent and child relate to each other's feelings and intentions in ways that establish these patterns. The early Ainsworth studies (Ainsworth & Bowlby, 1991) suggested that healthy, secure attachment requires that the caregiver have the capacity to perceive and respond to the child's psychological state. This capacity would serve to fulfill the child's security needs. Thus, the relationship between the parent or primary caregiver and the child is a crucial component in creating an insecure or a secure personality in the child. Researchers have also noted that styles of attachment observed in children appear useful for describing individual differences in adult styles of relating. Main, Kaplan, and Cassidy (1985) and others adapted Ainsworth's infant attachment patterns to adults and created the Adult Attachment Interview (AAI). The AAI describes the interviewees' early childhood attachment relationships in their own words and uses these descriptions to arrive at an understanding of the adult's attachment capabilities (Main, 1996). Thus, examining the attachment patterns in the family of origin creates a picture of an adult's sense of security. How does this shed light on intolerance?

Terror Management Theory and Attachment Theory

TMT appears to provide a framework that explains—on an intergroup level—the relationship between attachment theory, psychological insecurity, and intolerance. According to TMT, individuals strive to achieve both high self-esteem and, at the same time, a view of the world as predictable, orderly, and meaningful.[6]

TMT proposes that individuals acquire self-esteem from their family-of-origin interactions with their primary caregivers (Hart et al., 2005). The theory then speculates that, in the aggregate, the attachment patterns of individuals in a group united by ethnicity, religion, or other similar characteristics affect the views of that group toward other groups (Greenberg & Kosloff, 2008). One way of understanding this is through the concept of worldview. As mentioned, worldview consists of traits that shape an individual's view toward others.[7]

Several quantitative research studies have been conducted confirming that attachment style influences how people respond to threats to their worldview (Burke et al., 2010). These studies posed several scenarios to different groups to try to understand how attachment affects worldview. The studies concluded that threats to the attachment system elicit defensive actions (Hart et al., 2005; Mikulincer & Shaver, 2001) and may increase death-related thoughts (Florian, Mikulincer, & Hirschberger,

2002). There was also evidence that threatening self-esteem causes greater attachment and worldview-related defenses (Fein & Spencer, 1997; Mikulincer, Birnbaum, Woddis, & Nachmias, 2000).

Thus, according to TMT research, worldview is impacted by attachment and by self-esteem and shapes how secure people view the world (Greenberg et al., 1990; Mikulincer, 1997). Two other studies have looked at families and their political attitudes and concluded that the nurturing family would hold liberal views and the strict-father family would hold conservative views (Wiese et al., 2008). Thus, people who experience secure relationships hold values of tolerance and compassion, and those who experience insecure relationships and authoritarian values do not (Wiese et al., 2008).

However, TMT research has examined group responses through quantitative methods. Using qualitative research methods to discern the nature of the relationship between the individual child and the parent through interviews will elucidate how attachment theory and TMT explain individual responses. The qualitative research methodology used to analyze the TTP data provides a framework for seeing how these theories relate and lead to understanding the concept of psychological insecurity, the key component in intolerance in the adult. This focus is absent from the current literature, and in recent TMT articles, the researchers have called for studies looking at individual behavior (Hart et al., 2005). By studying individual behavior, the missing links between family-of-origin relationships, psychological insecurity, and tolerance will be uncovered.

To summarize, the attachment relationship between the child and his or her primary caregivers creates for the child a worldview that governs his or her interactions with others who hold different beliefs, values, and worldviews. People who have experienced positive relationships with their primary caregivers are more secure and have higher self esteem, which partly protects them against threats to their worldview and feelings of vulnerability. These positive feelings of self-worth create individuals who have developed effective emotion regulation devices and positive models of themselves and others. As a result, they evidence more openness, less defensiveness, and a reduction in dogmatism and authoritarianism (Hart et al., 2005; Mikulincer & Shaver, 2001).

People who have experienced less-secure or negative relationships with their primary caregivers more strongly defend their worldview against any threats and are less tolerant of others who hold different views (Hart et al., 2005; Mikulincer & Florian, 2000). Exploring the nature of family-of-origin relationships would consequently shed light on the origin of tolerant or intolerant beliefs in individuals. To do this, the TTP created an instrument, the quality of family dynamics paradigm, that analyzes and categorizes family-of-origin relationships.

The Quality of Family Dynamics Paradigm

The nature of attachment in the child can be discerned through the application of the quality of family dynamics paradigm (Hollander-Goldfein & Isserman, 1999). This paradigm uses five factors to determine patterns of interaction that influence attachment styles between the parent/caregiver and the child. Tracking the family-of-origin relationships identifies which children experienced security through met psychological needs and which children experienced insecurity through unmet psychological needs. Through this tracking, the TTP data support the idea that secure attachments in childhood are key in influencing tolerant beliefs, and insecure attachments in childhood are key influences on attitudes of intolerance. In this qualitative assessment, descriptions of relationships and stories about the relationships in the family of origin are used to reveal the nature of the relationships.

The five dimensions of parent–child dynamics that describe the family-of-origin attachment relationships along a continuum are as follows:

Closeness ↔ Distance

Empathy ↔ Self-centeredness

Validation ↔ Criticism

Expressive of Positive Emotions ↔ Expressive of Negative Emotions.

Open Communication ↔ Closed Communication

This particular study only used four of the five dimensions for its analysis. The fifth dimension, open/closed communication, is not examined in this chapter. The open or closed nature of the communications in the family is not important as the analysis looks at all the available stories. The contents of every story about family-of-origin relationships contributed to the analysis. For the remaining four dimensions, the following positive and negative definitions apply:

- **Closeness**: There are close, frequent, helpful, and positive contacts and ties with family-of-origin members.
- **Empathy**: The child experiences the adults in the family as caring and understanding, responding to the child's needs and feelings, including making sacrifices on behalf of the child.
- **Validation**: The adult caregivers support the child's feelings, thoughts, needs, and behaviors; are encouraging, complimentary, and may express pride in the child.
- **Expressive of positive emotions**: Love, happiness, satisfaction, and affection are expressed verbally or physically between the adult caregivers and child.

- **Distance**: There are cold, infrequent, and negative contacts between family-of-origin members; family-of-origin relationships are not close, and the child has little involvement in family members' lives.
- **Self-centeredness**: The adult caregivers are focused on their own needs and desires to the partial or complete exclusion of the needs and desires of the child; the adults are experienced as self-absorbed, neutral, or inattentive to the child and may be selfish or even damaging to the child's well-being.
- **Critical**: The adult caregiver's interactions with the child are negative, dismissive, and unsupportive of the child's feelings, thoughts, needs, and behaviors and may include the expression of disappointment in the child.
- **Expressive of negative emotions**: Predominantly negative emotions are expressed within the family-of-origin relationships, including anger, resentment, criticism, disappointment, rage, and dissatisfaction; the child may feel unloved, "bad," unwanted, guilty, or unworthy.

Results

Based on the political science literature that links psychological insecurity to intolerance and the attachment and TMT literature that link parent–child relationships to insecurity in adults, this study posited that negative attachment ties between survivors and their families of origin would be more prevalent in the interviews of the intolerant survivors. Indicators of negative attachment ties revealed insecure relationships between the survivor and the family of origin and affected the survivor's relationships with other groups as an adult. Conversely, indicators of positive attachment ties between the survivors and their families of origin would be more prevalent in the interviews of tolerant survivors. Positive attachment ties created secure relationships in the family of origin, which lead to adults holding positive views towards other groups.

Methodology

The relationship between the survivor as a child and the primary caregivers was revealed through an analysis of content and frequency of stories that the survivor told about his or her family of origin. Two researchers examined all the stories and classified each according to the factors in the quality of family dynamics paradigm. A particular relationship vignette may have been rated as "close," while another vignette may have been rated as "distant." When the stories told of the interactions between the primary caregiver and the child were primarily described according to the positive factors in the quality of dynamics, then this relationship was labeled as healthy and reflecting a secure attachment. When negative parent–child dynamics defined the relationship, they were classified as insecure attachment and poor-functioning relationships. Each story was placed on a chart representing the eight factors in the paradigm.

The interviews of the six survivors who were in the intolerant group contained fewer stories of positive qualitative dynamics than the other two groups. Unless a family was severely dysfunctional, there were almost always some positive narratives in the TTP interviews about the family of origin from the child's perspective. Yet, in the intolerant survivor group the number of the negative narratives about family relationships equaled the number of the positive narratives, and the overall number of narratives, positive or negative, was low. Compared to the other two groups, the number of narratives reflecting closeness or expressions of positive emotions between the survivors and their adult caregivers was low. In addition, intolerant survivors appeared to remember few empathic or validating narratives about their family-of-origin relationships. In summary, the intolerant survivors reported few positive stories about their relationships with their parents. Some examples follow.

Karl described a distant relationship with his mother through the following quotation:

> With my mother, it was somewhat more distant, because I didn't see much of her. … And I think we had breakfast together. But I don't remember having dinner together.

A statement reflecting a critical relationship noted:

> They [his parents] wouldn't hit me. But I remember they were screaming the hell out of me. (Ivan)

Examples of narratives reflecting expressions of negative emotions stated that

> I felt I was afraid of my father; if I would do something wrong I would get it. (Theodore)

> My mom hit me more than my father. … She didn't like anything that I did. (Charlotte)

> My father remarried; and I went away, and my brother went away, and the only two sisters left were left at home. And they didn't have a nice way of living because they were not treated like my mother used

to treat them. And they were always depressed and not too happy. But nobody was happy that time in those conditions all together. So those are the memories of my [family]. (Tom)

Moreover, as noted, the intolerant survivors told far fewer total narratives about family-of-origin relationships in their entire interview than in the interviews of the other two groups. It is as if the survivors in the intolerant group did not have many positive stories to share, so they were less inclined to share any stories, negative or positive, with the interviewer.

In both the limited-intolerant and the tolerant survivor groups, narratives of positive family dynamics were numerous, and the narratives of negative dynamics were much fewer. All four positive family dynamic components—closeness, empathy, validation, and positive expressions of emotion—were prevalent in the limited intolerant survivor interviews. Each category usually contained several examples. These examples were for the most part strong, clear, unambiguous statements about the family's positive dynamics. One example describing positive relationships in the limited intolerant category was as follows:

I got everything from my father, beside love. Love, attention, advice. ... He always took me in his arms, he cuddled me if I cried. ... If I came home, he wouldn't work. ... He would run ahead, meet me. "Give me your report," and run with that report to his neighbor. "Well, what did I tell you? It's the same as last year! It's excellent from top to bottom." He would show it to everybody. (Eva)

In the tolerant survivor group, the statements of positive family dynamics were even stronger and more numerous. Some examples of statements reflecting positive close family relationships are as follows:

To the children, my father was such an affectionate person. I mean, when he came home, he found room on his lap for all the kids to sit on. And he was a very exceptional individual. (Barbara)

We were all leaning on him. My father was our idol. (Nate)

Validating statements and expressions of positive dynamics were also strongly worded:

I remember he was warm; he was always taking care of me. And when I was near him, I always knew that I'm protected. (Ella)

My father was our guiding light. He was everything for us. ... We looked up to him for some kind of miracle. (Nate)

Table 6.1 Narrative Differences in Political Beliefs According to the Family of Dynamics Paradigm Factors

Family Dynamic Aspects	Intolerant	Limited Intolerant	Tolerant
Closeness	11	49	38
Empathy	4	14	25
Validation	4	19	11
Positive emotional expression	10	32	48
Total Positive Narratives	**29**	**114**	**122**
Distant	11	8	2 (7)[a]
Critical	5	2	0 (2)[a]
Self-centered	2	1	1 (4)[a]
Negative emotional expression	14	6	6 (15)[a]
Total Negative Narratives	**32**	**17**	**9 (28)[a]**

[a] The numbers in parentheses are higher because of one individual who had a poor relationship with her mother and sister prewar but who received significant positive emotional support from her father and grandmothers who lived with her. The other set of numbers represents the other five individuals in the group and more clearly shows the contrast between the intolerant and tolerant survivors.

While the positive stories were quite plentiful, few examples of narratives of negative family dynamics existed in the interviews of the tolerant survivors. One interview in fact contained no negative narratives. One interview contained only one negative story. Three other tolerant survivors' interviews contained only a few negative narratives. These patterns are shown in Table 6.1.

Thus, the data showed that numerous positive narratives and few negative narratives were found in the tolerant and the limited intolerant survivors' interviews. Survivors who reported positive narratives had formed secure attachments to their caregivers, which were reflected in their relationships not only with family members but also toward others. In addition, the empathy, validation, and expressions of positive emotions that these survivors received, especially from their parents, gave them the capacity to have greater empathy for others. One manifestation of this empathy was the development of an attitude of tolerance for others outside their own group. One survivor stated that her father told her:

"I know it's terrible to suffer," he said, "but will you be happier if you will turn into the type of individual that have hated us?" He says, "It's not right. That's why we suffered, because others hated us. If you will become a hateful person, you'll only hurt yourself, and not the people that you hate." And he was absolutely right. (Barbara)

Another noted:

We learned to put up with negative behaviors toward us and not to overreact, but to grin and bear it. We censored ourselves—i.e., think twice before you act out. … We learned early on to tolerate differences—even if we hated them. We lived in hope that things would be better. She continued later in the interview to add, "I was horrified about the racial issues here in America, and I had joined the League of Women Voters, although I was a bloody foreigner. And for equal housing, and I had worked for all kinds of interracial intergenerational ways." (Fruma)

Still a third tolerant survivor stated that she believed the United States should interfere in Bosnia:

I don't accept anymore that we should just be bystanders and watch people suffer because of their differences. (Mimi)

In summary, as revealed in the quotations about family dynamics, when the relationships between the survivor and the family-of-origin members clustered more on the negative end of the continuum and psychological security needs were not met, intolerant attitudes predominated in the survivors. In contrast, when the relationships between the survivors and their families of origin clustered on the positive end of the continuum and psychological security needs were met, tolerant attitudes predominated in the survivors.

Messages of Tolerance

While analyzing narratives about the family-of-origin dynamics, another unexpected finding emerged. Some tolerant and limited intolerant survivors reported receiving messages from close family members—often parents, but sometimes a sibling or grandparent—that functioned as a guide for their future tolerant attitudes. The messages may have been given to them just prior to the war, in the normal course of growing up, during the war, or after the war. These messages of tolerance were reported in two tolerant survivor interviews and three limited intolerant survivor interviews. In a previous paper using a slightly different sample of the TTP survivors, the number of messages of tolerance in these groups was even higher

(Isserman, 2005b). In the six intolerant survivor interviews examined in this chapter, no messages of tolerance existed. The five examples of these messages of tolerance follow:

> And my parents were able, after the war, to give me that comfort and strength to be able to turn that hate that I felt against the whole world, and especially all those Christians who have collaborated with the Nazis, to turn it around in a positive force. I had many discussions with him [her father] after the war about hating those people, and he always stopped me. He never let it go any further. (Barbara)

> We were taught early on in our lives to know that we were good children—that the hatred of the Jews was not a personal hatred. (Fruma)

And in similar words from a third survivor:

> I never heard from my mother or father any messages of hate towards any other religion or nationality. (Eva)

Two additional survivors credited their parents with influencing them to hold tolerant beliefs:

> [I] didn't grow up to hate people. ... It's the way I was brought up, to trust people. People are good. (Tova)

> My mother used to teach us. I will never forget. ... If somebody throws a rock on you, you throw back bread. ... You never throw back a stone. Never throw back a rock. And that's the way she taught us. And I will never forget when she used to tell us this that we should never be mean. Even somebody's mean to us we should try to be nice and you could work it out. (Hinda)

This evidence suggests that where there are positive relationships between the caregivers and the survivors, messages of tolerance from family-of-origin members to the survivor were passed on and guided the survivors' adult worldviews.

Conclusion

The impact of family-of-origin relationships on political beliefs was revealed through the TTP survivor interviews. The nature of the attachment between the primary caregiver in the family of origin and the survivor has been shown to have an impact into the adult years. Parental and other family-of-origin relationships and experiences in childhood provide the basis for interpersonal functioning beyond childhood (Kabeera & Sewpaul, 2008).

This study focused on understanding the factors that influence tolerance in individuals. Political science research has defined psychological insecurity as a key component in intolerance without clearly analyzing how the two concepts are connected. The relationship of psychological insecurity to intolerance becomes clear when examined through the lens of attachment theory and TMT and using the quality of family dynamics paradigm to reveal the nature of attachment relationships in the survivor's family of origin. The factors of the quality of family dynamics paradigm facilitate an understanding of the family-of-origin relationships that the survivor experienced. These factors on a continuum from positive to negative help us to analyze the quality of the attachment relationships between the survivor and his or her primary caregivers.

From this analysis and by using the findings of TMT studies, we are then able to understand which individuals will exhibit psychological insecurity and intolerance and which individuals would exhibit psychological security and tolerance in the TTP population. In this study, survivors with intolerant beliefs evidenced negative or troubled family-of-origin relationships when their stories about their relationships in their families of origin were analyzed through the quality of family dynamics paradigm. The troubled relationships reflected insecure attachments with unmet psychological needs. Attachment theory and TMT then suggest that these individuals will be more likely to view potentially negative events or people who hold different worldviews in a threatening way. The threats to their worldview result in an increase in psychological insecurity and lead to an increase in intolerance. Their statements about groups and persons confirmed this as they reflected hatred and intolerance toward others of different ethnic, religious, or racial groups. In comparison, survivors with limited intolerant or tolerant political beliefs evidenced positive family-of-origin relationships and thus felt secure enough as adults to reach out to others who were from different groups or who held different views than their own.

Thus, this study explained some of the missing gaps in previous literature on tolerant beliefs through examining the beliefs of individuals who survived genocide. Analyzing family-of-origin relationships using the quality of family dynamics paradigm and applying attachment theory and TMT to the results provides a theoretical framework for understanding how psychological insecurity influences intolerance in victims of persecution.

Notes

1. In his publications on South Africa (Gibson, 2004; Gibson & Gouws, 2000), James L. Gibson concluded that intolerance is generated at very low levels of perceived threat, and thus one would expect intolerance to be pervasive in a group of individuals who had suffered political persecution as did the Holocaust survivors.

2. In an unpublished dissertation (Isserman, 2005a), I found the following: Tolerant survivors did not view the world as a threatening place; while all survivors' worldviews consisted of mistrust towards others, optimism, and other-directed statements, only tolerant survivors directed their altruism toward non-Jews. All survivors exhibited strong in-group identity; tolerant survivors were slightly less conservative on public policy issues than the others, and more tolerant survivors survived through hiding and with family members, facilitating the transmission of the message of tolerance from family-of-origin caregivers to the survivors.

3. Eighteen cases of 95 survivor interviews in the original TTP study were selected to be in the subsample of this study. The 18 were chosen based on the following criteria: Their views on tolerance were thorough, detailed, and clearly stated in the interview; their interviews were complete documents discussing pre-, during, and postwar years according to the semi-structured interview guide; and they had completed the Jewish Identity Survey (JIS). In addition, although representativeness is not important in a qualitative study, the demographics of the 18 cases were not different from the rest of the 95 TTP survivors or different from the demographics of the 2000 special report on survivors of the National Jewish Population Survey (NJPS: Kotler-Berkowitz, Blass, & Neuman, 2004).

4. The definitions of tolerance resulted from the coding of the survivor interviews through the N4 qualitative computer coding program, an older version of NVIVO. Any statement about tolerance or intolerance in the interviews was highlighted and coded into two overlapping categories: "people, groups" and "tolerance." Interviews lacking any statements on tolerance or if the statements were so vague that a position on tolerance could not be clearly discerned were eliminated from consideration in the study.

5. For a fuller discussion of the relationship between perceived threat and political ideology to political intolerance, see my unpublished dissertation (2005a).

6. Janoff-Bulman (1983) and others focused on the aftermath of trauma when this worldview is shattered and victims experience vulnerability.

7. The components are trust/mistrust; optimism/pessimism; other-directed/self-directed; and altruism.

References

Adorno, T. W., Frenkel-Brunswik, E., Levinson, D. L., & Sanford, R. N. (1950). *The authoritarian personality*. New York: Norton.

Ainsworth, M. D. S. (1979). Infant-mother attachment. *American Psychologist, 34,* 932–937.

Ainsworth, M. D. S., & Bowlby, J. (1991). An ethological approach to personality development. *American Psychologist, 46,* 331–341.

Allen, J. G. (2005). *Coping with trauma: Hope through understanding.* Washington, DC: American Psychiatric.

Alozie, N. O. (1995). Political tolerance hypotheses and white opposition to a Martin Luther King holiday in Arizona. *The Social Science Journal, 32,* 1–16.

Bobo, L., & Licari, F. C. (1989). Education and political tolerance: Testing the effects of cognitive sophistication and target group effect. *Public Opinion Quarterly, 53,* 285–308.

Bretherton, I. (1985). Attachment theory: retrospect and prospect. *Monographs of the Society for Research in Child Development, 50,* 3–35.

Bretherton, I. (1992). The origins of attachment theory: John Bowlby and Mary Ainsworth. *Developmental Psychology, 28,* 759–775.

Bowlby, J. (1973). *Attachment and loss: Vol. 2. Separation.* New York: Basic.

Bowlby, J. (1982). *Attachment and loss: Vol. 1. Attachment* (2nd ed.). New York: Basic. (Original work published 1969)

Burke, B. L., Martens, A., & Faucher, E. H. (2010). Two decades of terror management theory: A meta-analysis of mortality salience research. *Personality and Social Psychology Review, 14,* 155–195.

Collins, N. L. (1996). Working models of attachment: Implications for explanation, emotion, and behavior. *Journal of Personality and Social Psychology, 71,* 810–832.

Davis, D. W. (1995). Exploring black political intolerance. *Political Behavior, 17,* 1–22.

Duch, R. M., & Gibson, J. L. (1992). Anti-Semitic attitude of the mass public: Estimates and explanations based on a survey of the Moscow oblast. *Public Opinion Quarterly, 1996,* 1–28.

Eisenstein. (2006). Religious motivation versus traditional religiousness: Bridging the gap between religion and politics and the psychology of religion. *Interdisciplinary Journal of Research on Religion, 2,* Article 2, 1–30. Retrieved January 20, 2011, from http:www.religjournal.com/pdf/ijrr02002.pdf

Fein, S., & Spencer, S. J. (1997). Prejudice as self-image maintenance: Affirming the self through derogating others. *Journal of Personality and Social Psychology, 73,* 31–44.

Florian, V., Mikulincer, M., & Hirschberger, G. (2002). The anxiety-buffering function of close relationships: Evidence that relationship commitment acts as a terror management mechanism. *Journal of Personality and Social Psychology, 82,* 527–542.

Gibson, J. L. (1992). The political consequences of intolerance: Cultural conformity and political freedom. *The American Political Science Review, 86,* 338–356.

Gibson, J. L. (2004). *Overcoming apartheid: Can truth reconcile a divided nation?* Cape Town, Africa: Russell Sage Foundation, Institute for Justice and Reconciliation.

Gibson, J. L., & Gouws, A. (2000). Social identities and political intolerance: Linkages within the South African mass public. *American Journal of Political Science, 44,* 278–292.

Golebiowska, E. A. (1995). Individual value priorities education and political tolerance. *Political Behavior, 17,* 23–48.

Greenberg, J., Solomon, S., Veeder, M., Pyszczynski, T., Rosenblatt, A., Kirkland, S., & Lyon, D. (1990). Evidence for terror management theory II: The effects of mortality salience on reactions to those who threaten or bolster the cultural worldview. *Journal of Personality and Social Psychology, 58*, 303–318.

Greenberg, J., & Kosloff, S. (2008). Terror management theory: Implications for understanding prejudice, stereotyping, intergroup conflict, and political attitudes. *Social and Personality Psychology Compass, 2*(5), 1881-1894.

Hart, J., Shaver, P. R், & Goldenberg, J. L. (2005). Attachment, self-esteem, worldviews, and terror management: Evidence for a tripartite security system. *Journal of Personality and Social Psychology, 88*, 999–1013.

Hollander-Goldfein, B., & Isserman, N. (1999). Overview of the Transcending Trauma Project: Rationale, goals, methodology, and preliminary findings. In P. David & J. Goldhar (Eds.), *Selected papers from a time to heal: Caring for the aging Holocaust survivor* (pp. 77–89). Toronto: Baycrest Centre for Geriatric Care.

Isserman, N. (2005a). *"I harbor no hate": The study of political tolerance and intolerance.* Unpublished doctoral dissertation, City University of New York.

Isserman, N. (2005b). Identifying individual determinants of intolerance in Holocaust survivors. In J. Steinert & I. Weber-Newth (Eds.), *Beyond camps and forced labour* (pp. 557–565). Osnabrueck, Germany: Secolo Verlag.

Janoff-Bulman, R. (1983). A theoretical perspective for understanding reactions to victimization. *Journal of Social Issues, 39*, 2, pp: 1–17.

Kabeera, B., & Sewpaul, V. (2008). Genocide and its aftermath: The case of Rwanda. *International Social Work, 51*, 324–226.

Karpov, V. (1999). Religiosity and political tolerance in Poland. *Sociology of Religion, 60*, 387–402.

Knutson, J. N. (1973). Personality in the study of politics. In J. N. Knutson (Ed.), *Handbook of political psychology* (pp. 28–56). San Francisco: Jossey-Bass.

Kotler-Berkowitz, L., Blass, L., & Neuman, D. (2004). Nazi victims residing in the United States. United Jewish Communities Report Series on the National Jewish Population Survey 2000–01, report 2.

Main, M. (1996). Introduction to the special section on attachment and psychopathology: Overview of the field of attachment. *Journal of Consulting and Clinical Psychology, 64*, 237–243.

Main, M., Kaplan, N, & Cassidy, J. (1985). Security in infancy, childhood, and adulthood: A move to the level of representation. *Monographs of the Society for Research in Child Development, 50*, 66–104.

Marcus, G. E., Sullivan, J. L., Theiss-Morse, E., & Wood, S. L. (1995). *With malice toward some: How people make civil liberties judgments.* Cambridge, UK: Cambridge University Press.

Maykovich, M. K. (1975). Correlates of racial prejudice. *Journal of Personality and Social Psychology, 32*, 1014–1020.

Mikulincer, M. (1997). Adult attachment style and information processing: Individual differences in curiosity and cognitive closure. *Journal of Personality and Social Psychology, 72*, 1217–1230.

Mikulincer, M., Birnbaum, G., Woddis, D., & Nachmias, O. (2000). Stress and accessibility of proximity-related thoughts: Exploring the normative and intraindividual components of attachment theory. *Journal of Personality and Social Psychology, 78*, 509–523.

Mikulincer, M., & Florian, V. (2000). Exploring individual differences in reactions to mortality salience: Does attachment style regulate terror management mechanisms? *Journal of Personality and Social Psychology, 79*, 260–273.

Mikulincer, M., & Shaver, P. R. (2001). Attachment theory and intergroup bias: Evidence that priming the secure base schema attenuates negative reactions to out-groups. *Journal of Personality and Social Psychology, 81*, 97–115.

Peffley, M., Knigge P., & Hurwitz, J. (2001). A multiple values model of political tolerance. *Political Research Quarterly, 54*, 379–406.

Ricks, M. H. (1985). The social transmission of parental behavior: Attachment across generations. *Monographs of the Society for Research in Child Development, 50*, 211–227.

Rokeach, M. (1960). *The open and closed mind.* New York: Basic Books.

Rubenstein, G. (1995). Authoritarianism in Israeli society. *Journal of Social Psychology, 135*, 237–240.

Siegel, D. J. (1999). *The developing mind.* New York: Gilford.

Stanford, N. (1973). Authoritarian personality in contemporary perspective. In J. N. Knutson (Ed.), *Handbook of political psychology* (pp. 139–170). San Francisco: Jossey-Bass.

Stenner, K. (2005). *The authoritarian personality.* Cambridge, UK: Cambridge University Press.

Stouffer, S. (1967). *Communism, conformity, and civil liberties.* New York: Wiley.

Sullivan, J. L., Marcus, G. E., Feldman, S., & Piereson, J. E. (1981). The sources of political tolerance: A multivariate analysis. *The American Political Science Review, 75*, 92–106.

Sullivan, J. L., Piereson, J., & Marcus, G. E. (1982). *Political tolerance and American democracy.* Chicago: University of Chicago Press.

Sullivan, J. L., & Transue, J. E. (1999). The psychological underpinnings of democracy: A selective review of research on political tolerance, interpersonal trust, and social capital. *Annual Review of Psychology, 50*, 625–650.

Weise, D. R., Pyszczynski, T., Cox, C. R., Arndt, A., Greenberg, J., Solomon, S., & Kosloff, S. (2008). Interpersonal politics: The role of terror management and attachment processes in shaping political preferences. *Psychological Science, 19*, 448–456.

Wilcox, C., & Jelen, T. (1990). Evangelicals and political tolerance. *American Politics Quarterly, 18*, 25–46.

CHAPTER 7

A Minyan of Trees

*The Role of Faith and Ritual in Postwar Coping and
Its Relevance to Working With Trauma Survivors*

JENNIFER GOLDENBERG

Introduction

The Holocaust narratives of the Transcending Trauma Project (TTP) articulated survivors' ongoing struggles with some of the most compelling questions confronting them after the war: Where was God during the Holocaust? Why didn't he save my family members? Why did I survive when so many I loved were killed? These existential questions weave throughout the interviews as a disturbing subtext.

In their attempts to find answers to these questions, survivors' prewar faith systems were lost, retained, or significantly altered. Despite questions regarding God's role in the Holocaust, faith or ritual practice became important long-term strategies used by the majority of our survivor respondents to cope with the massive losses suffered in the war. This is a response that appears, on the surface, to be counterintuitive; one would think that more survivors would have lost their faith or discontinued Jewish practice after the massive trauma they had undergone, particularly since they were specifically targeted for group extermination precisely because they were Jewish. Why, then, did most of the survivors in this study conserve aspects of their faith and practice? What roles did faith and ritual practice play in the posttraumatic coping of Holocaust survivors?

The question of faith after the Holocaust has been written about by survivors themselves, as well as by nonsurvivors and Gentiles (Bauer, 2001; Hass, 1995; Haynes & Roth, 1999; Helmreich, 1992; Roth & Berenbaum, 1989; Wells, 1995; Wiesel, 1990). More recently, the role that faith plays in coping after various forms of trauma has been explored by researchers studying the aftermaths of political persecution (Lehtsaar & Noor, 2006), terrorism (Kelly, 2006; Plante & Canchola, 2004), and natural disasters (Marks, 2009), as well as of veterans treated for posttraumatic stress disorder (PTSD; Fontana & Rosencheck, 2004). However, more research clearly needs to be done.

In a special issue on religion and spirituality in forced migration, Gozdziak and Shandy (2002) noted the dearth of systematic research on the role of religious belief and practice in the journeys of refugees.

> Despite the diversity of religious and spiritual beliefs and practices that sustain many refugees and forced migrants in their processes of displacement, migration, and integration into the host society, contemporary considerations among both researchers and policy makers tend to neglect the role of religion and spirituality as a source of emotional and cognitive support, a form of social and political expression and mobilization, and a vehicle for community building and group identity. (p. 129)

There have been several large surveys of religious belief and practice after the Holocaust. An early study by Brenner (1980), using a random sample of 708 survivors in Israel, attempted "a systematic inquiry … [into] how surviving European Jews construed and interpreted their Holocaust experiences and how they were affected religiously, in their faith and practices, by what they had undergone" (pp. 3–4). It is notable that Brenner found that, rather than becoming atheists or agnostics, many survivors changed their view of God to a more impersonal Being who is not directly involved in human affairs.

Helmreich (1992), in a later sociological survey of Holocaust survivors living in America, seemed to support Brenner's conclusions. He found that

> the majority of believers did not become atheists, but there was a definite decrease in the number of believers. Moreover, for most the Holocaust created grave doubts about the nature of God and His relationship to human beings even as the survivors continued to believe in Him. (p. 238)

Helmreich found that most survivors in his sample remained connected to the Jewish community for various reasons, including their continued faith in God, their desire to preserve connection to tradition and their previous lifestyle, and their desire to identify with the contemporary

Jewish community (Helmreich, 1992). The research of both Brenner (1980) and Helmreich found that many survivors retained their faith. However, neither of them explored some possible factors contributing to this retention of faith and practice. The interviews from the TTP provide a more complete and nuanced understanding of this phenomenon.

The TTP explored, as one of its many areas of inquiry, the postwar faith and ritual practice of the survivors interviewed and the impact of the Holocaust on their belief systems. Isserman's (2005) study based on TTP interviews found that for survivor families with strong positive family relationships, there was a pattern of continuity in lifestyle and values between the generations. In contrast, for survivor families with problematic relationships, there seemed to be a pattern of discontinuity in lifestyle and values. Isserman found that survivors who came from families in which positive family dynamics predominated kept to the same levels of religious observance as their families of origin.

In analyzing the responses of our respondent survivors, this researcher (Isserman, 2005) noted how important a role both faith and ritual practice played for almost everyone in the long-term process of their posttraumatic adaptation. The survivors in our study came from a wide spectrum of religious beliefs prewar—from secular and assimilated to ultra-Orthodox. However, the vast majority came from what we may term "traditional homes," that is, their parents were observant Jews who believed in God, kept the Sabbath and kosher laws, and were fairly regular in synagogue attendance. Postwar, approximately half of the survivors the TTP interviewed retained some semblance of a belief in God. The other half, while not clearly stating their belief, or while expressing it in more ambiguous terms, still identified themselves strongly as Jews and were involved in and committed to Jewish ritual practice, synagogue, and community to varying degrees.

Examination of the narrative data suggests a pattern related to the quality of family relationships in childhood and adolescence before the war with religious belief and practice after the war. This is a theme to explore in the study of trauma survivors in general and points to the interrelationship between family-of-origin attachments and faith and ritual practice after trauma. Tracking the following vignettes will reveal the emotional foundation of faith and ritual practice based in attachment experiences.

Most of our survivor respondents were in the developmental stage of adolescence or young adulthood going through the war. They were, therefore, old enough before the Holocaust to have formed a fairly well-developed belief system based on their parents' beliefs. A smaller percentage were young children. However, even those in the youngest cohort still retained a strong Jewish identity and some semblance of belief or ritual practice after the war. Confronted with horror and massive losses, many survivors changed their understanding of God, if not abandoning their belief altogether. But, traditional practice, which is expressed as behaviors shared with other family members, remained more intact for many survivors. Why?

For some of these child, adolescent, and young adult survivors, the quality of their attachments with their parents seems to have either helped or hindered them in their retention of faith and in their desire to practice Jewish rituals. In fact, the evidence in these interviews points to a relationship between strong familial prewar attachments and the conservation of faith or ritual practice after the war. Conversely, those who had negative relationships with parents and insecure attachments were more likely to transform their belief systems and, in at least two cases, even any form of Jewish ritual practice altogether (Goldenberg, 2008).

Trauma theory posits that after a traumatic event many of our assumptions about self, other, and worldview are shattered (Janoff-Bulman, 1992). During the recovery period, trauma survivors first try to assimilate the trauma into their already-existing belief systems. People are, first and foremost, cognitive conservationists (Pargament, 1997) in the sense that we cope with stressors in a way that will retain the familiar cognitive schemata we have about self and world. Our cognitive schemata include our faith systems. Individuals try to rebuild shattered assumptions and belief systems about the world posttrauma by assimilating the traumatic experience into a safe, familiar, pretrauma worldview. But, when the trauma cannot be successfully assimilated, the pretrauma paradigm undergoes a process of accommodation, or a total reworking of established beliefs, to accommodate to the new posttrauma reality (Janoff-Bulman, 1992).

Janoff-Bulman (1992), basing her discussion on Piaget, referred to this posttraumatic process as "assimilation/accommodation." Pargament, in his work on the psychology of religion and coping (1997), used the comparable terms "conservation/transformation."

What role might the quality of pre-Holocaust family relationships play in either the conservation of prewar belief or its transformation? Can any associations be made between positive family relationships and the retention of Jewish faith and practice after the war, or the reverse—that negative family relationships played a role in the transformation of belief and practice?

Conservation of Faith and Ritual Practice

A small percentage of the survivors we interviewed had belief systems that were ostensibly unaltered by their Holocaust experiences. These survivors, for the most part, were able to continue their religious practices and hold on to their faith after the war, in an apparently effortless assimilation of their traumatic experience into their preexisting belief systems. For example, Ita, who survived Auschwitz as a teenager, reported a steadfast faith in God before, during, and after the war. Her faith was and continued to be an unshakeable coping strategy.

> If I wouldn't have the belief like that, I wouldn't have gotten through. I always talk to Hashem [God]. I got a lot of this from my parents. Because I grew up in this kind of a home, that's where I got my steadfastness. … I was always, always praying to Hashem, talking to Hashem, he should help me.

Ita was an only child, and after her parents were taken away, she survived the war both in hiding and in Auschwitz. Her parents communicated with her through letters up until their deaths, and some of those letters survived the war with her. She keeps her parents' letters in a sealed box and to this day has been unable to take them out and reread them. But, she remembers vividly the strong messages of faith her parents gave her in those letters. Commitment to her faith after the war may actually have come from her positive attachment to her parents, which was expressed as loyalty to them. Retaining her faith, and retaining her loyalty to her parents by taking their messages of faith to heart throughout her postwar life, seems to have played a large role in helping her cope with their loss.

> I didn't have the feeling, like some people, maybe they were very religious before the war, and after the war they threw it all out. … I never had that. I was always praying to God, talking to God, he should help us. [I got it] from the upbringing, from the school … and from my parents. My father always wrote to me, I should have faith, I should always trust in God. So I had that.

Cedric also came from a close family before the war. He believed that his faith and practice were not only retained, but actually strengthened by his experiences in the Holocaust.

> [The Holocaust] didn't change [my faith]. I became more stubborn about remaining a Jew. I said I'm going to remain a Jew—I'll believe in God. I'll bring my children up as Jews. … Our generation, the European generation, went through the worst catastrophe that can happen to mankind. And yet there were very few who gave up Jewishness. And I think that is a lot to our credit that we remain Jews and we believe in God and raise our children to believe in God. … It meant that Hitler did not succeed. *Am Yisroel chai.* The people of Israel live. That was our strength.

Because many of the survivor respondents in the TTP were in the developmental stage of adolescence when they entered the war, they were old enough to have already formed more-than-rudimentary faith systems before going into that prolonged period of trauma. The majority of them were old enough to have formed secure attachments with significant people in their lives. It is notable how descriptions of faith and ritual practice are often embedded in the descriptions of important attachment relationships.

For example, Cynthia talked about climbing into bed with her grandmother on cold winter evenings and hearing her say her prayers, at bedtime and in the morning.

> That grandmother came in every morning to say Modeh Ani, that morning prayer, with us, with the children. I still say that prayer every morning that she taught me.

Into her 80s, Cynthia remained an Orthodox Jew.

Gerda talked about praying to her mother, who had died when she was very small, before the war. Her only memory of her mother was sitting with her and praying a particular prayer as the sun went down on the Jewish Sabbath.

> I remember one moment, when she hold me in her lap, sitting next to the window. On Saturday, between day and night, you know at twilight, there is a prayer, "God from Abraham and Yaakov." I don't remember her face; I remember feeling her hand in my hand. And I remember saying after her. This is the only thing I remember [about my mother], not that somebody told me. This I really remember, and I feel it. This was always with me.

The meanings survivors gave to these memories are powerful ones. Prayer and rituals connected them with the beloved people they lost. By continuing those ritual moments—by themselves or with their own children and grandchildren—they honored the dead and, in a sense, kept the dead alive (Goldenberg, 2008).

It would appear that through the predictability of ritual, and the practice of it within a group setting with other Jews who had gone through similar circumstances, survivors found strength in the familiar practices of their Jewish tradition. These were important, comforting echoes of their prewar lives, homes, lost family members, and friends.

The central importance of ritual practice was poignantly highlighted by Jeffrey. While suffering the exigencies of life as an underground partisan fighter, often alone and hiding in the forest, he still found a way to remember his murdered father's memory, counting trees to form a *minyan*, or quorum of 10 needed to say particularly important Jewish prayers.

> I used to take 10 trees and make a minyan, and say Kaddish for my father. Even though I had no [Jewish] calendar, I never missed a day.

Tova confirmed the importance of Jewish practice as a means of coping with postwar reality. She made a clear juxtaposition of family and faith.

I think you cannot leave your family, and you can't leave your religion. You have to adjust to the best of your ability [after the war] to respect your religion. Because certain things in life are dictated by religion—like when a child is born, or they're married, or their death. If you believe in it or not, you say Kaddish, you still observe it.

Once in the United States, the reestablishment of Jewish community in particular, and specifically within a synagogue framework, was particularly critical as a coping strategy, as Tom explained:

I started to have less faith in God after I saw … how they killed those people in ghettos and all over. … Still, when I came over here I wanted to be with Jewish people for some reason, regardless what I [believed]. … That's why I joined [a synagogue]. … I felt more comfortable with the synagogue people than the people I was surrounded with [i.e., non-Jews].

For survivors of more recent genocides and ethnic conflicts, loyalty to dead family members' beliefs and ritual practices may play a crucial role in coping with massive trauma and loss. This loyalty is reflective of the positive attachments that the survivors had with the dead members of their families of origin. We need to be cognizant of and sensitive to that when working with such clients.

Case Study: Timothy

Timothy is an example of a survivor of political persecution and torture whose faith was rooted in his positive attachment to his family of origin—in this case, his grandfather. He is a South African torture survivor, seeking asylum in the United States, and is suffering from chronic PTSD. For the past 20 years he has experienced recurrent distressing flashbacks, nightmares, psychological distress on seeing disabled people, and on reading about social unrest and injustice, both in South Africa and in the rest of the world. He is terrified of government authorities. He is easily overwhelmed by noise, sirens, crowds, and loud voices. He avoids almost everything except the people and places that are mandatory: work and family.

Timothy was born in South Africa in 1957, near the Botswana border. He was one of 10 children. His father died when he was 5 years old, and he was sent to live with his aunt and uncle. His upbringing centered on Christian values and hard work, and he found immense comfort in the Bible, which he read often throughout his childhood. His grandfather spoke to him about life before apartheid and instilled in him a sense of history. Timothy developed a deep and abiding attachment to his grandfather, who implanted in him a love not only of God but also of the history and people of South Africa. His grandfather served as a father figure after his own father died and was a mentor and role model throughout Timothy's life (his grandfather lived to be 109).

Between 1975 and 1977, the family's property was confiscated by the apartheid government. Blacks lived in constant fear; there were many killings in the villages. Timothy became a member of the ANC (African National Congress) and was given a special mission to join the South African Defense Force, work his way through the ranks, and eventually overthrow the government. A hard worker, he was promoted to the highest rank, with more than 1,000 troops under his command. In the meantime, he married and had two children.

During the 1988 coup, Timothy was captured and severely tortured for several years while in prison. During that period, Timothy read the Bible many times, a practice he had developed in adolescence. This continued to be a strong source of coping for him. He felt close to God while he was in prison and speaks of his time in solitary confinement as one of "serene peace."

After he was released from prison in 1994, his outspoken views about corruption within the new government led to threats of assassination. He and his family fled to the United States in 1997.

Once in the states, the family became very active in their new church community. Timothy worked as a janitor for the church while waiting for his working papers. He has a strong belief in God and an intense commitment to helping humankind. He did not lose his faith after his experiences. However, the past is ever present in Timothy's life; his years of torture and imprisonment are part of his psyche. Many of his coping strategies and attempts to heal himself are spiritual and based in his deep attachment to his beloved grandfather. This relationship sustained him throughout his many ordeals.

Case Study: Susan

The case of Susan, a young woman in her 20s who came into therapy due to PTSD from a recent rape, illustrates the importance of ritual practice within a faith community as a compelling adjunct to trauma therapy. She is an example of a trauma survivor with positive family-of-origin relationships that led her to rely on faith to cope with the aftermath.

Susan is also a survivor of chronic sexual abuse from the ages of 7 to 14 by a family member. She presents as a young adolescent boy—both in her manner and affect and in the clothes she wears—as if she were frozen in the developmental stage when the abuse occurred. In addition, she suffers from social anxiety and has a significant history of substance abuse. Susan spent her adolescent years and early adulthood abusing drugs and alcohol, surviving several serious car accidents in which drugs and alcohol were involved. Eventually, while heavily intoxicated, she was raped by a new acquaintance. She had been clean and sober for 30 days before coming into treatment.

As a child, Susan attended church with her family. "I believed in God when I was a child. But I think that during the years of the sexual abuse, I lost my faith. I mean, maybe I didn't quite lose it, but it got covered up with stuff. I left. Maybe *HE* didn't ever leave. I went back to God the day after the rape. I was so ashamed. I needed the church again."

She prayed that she was not pregnant and promised God to be sober and to live a more spiritual life. "Now it's different. I feel His full presence. I will get bursts of happiness just looking at the sun or at the flowers. When something happens you have to make the right decision. I think I made the right decision by going back to God."

Susan joined a local church. She says that her mother was her inspiration. "I always was the closest one to my mother of all my siblings. She used to single me out for special treats when I was a kid. She wanted me to go to a new type of church, and I went in order to please her, as well as to help myself after the rape and to help keep me sober." Susan, in this description, connects her close attachment with her mother to her openness about reconnecting with her faith. She was soon referred for therapy, and as the therapy progressed it triggered flashbacks of the earlier sexual abuse that she had not forgotten but had suppressed.

During this time, the church became a refuge for Susan and a useful adjunct to therapy, serving as a strong base of social support as well as a source for spiritual meaning. She used it to overcome her social anxiety as well. The therapist watched Susan's role in the church unfold and saw that it gave her more mastery over her life. Her involvement with her faith community has helped give her the strength to continue her path out of substance abuse and move beyond her frozen state shaped by her childhood victimization.

All of these examples—of Holocaust survivors as well as of more current trauma survivors, illustrate the connection between strong family-of-origin attachments and the retention or conservation of pretrauma faith and practice. Clinicians, many of whom are uncomfortable talking about matters of faith with their clients, should be more open to exploring these avenues of coping and more cognizant of how they are often rooted in positive, pretrauma attachments.

Transformation of Faith and Ritual Practice

Other survivors changed their conception of God after the Holocaust. In the face of massive trauma and loss, they could no longer believe in the interventionist God who characterized their prewar faith. If God were an interventionist God, why didn't he intervene? Yet, these survivors were unable to reject their belief systems, so they transformed their God from a deity who directly affects one's daily existence, to a more distant God, relatively uninvolved in human affairs. In this way, survivors were able to assimilate their traumatic experiences into their prewar belief systems and still retain their belief in God.

Tova, who survived several concentration camps while hiding her infant son, expressed both her struggle with her faith and her newly forged belief in a "different" God.

[Before the war] I believed that everything comes from God. After the Holocaust, this changed. … If you're going to take it that it's God's will, then most religious people were killed. Very few stayed alive. And most of the people who were rough and tough from my town, the worst element, survived. So if it is the good God which

rewards people for being good, and for observance, then how would
I explain that? So I have to find an explanation for myself. ... I believe
in a certain power [now]. A different God. A spirit.

Another survivor described her reconceptualization of God in this
way:

> I realized that we cannot blame God, nor can I accept the fact that
> what happened to us is a punishment for our nonobservance. ...
> It's the moral teachings of the Torah, and the ethical behavior that
> we must display at all times, that is the essence of our teachings of
> Judaism. And in this respect, I feel that I have found God again, but
> not in the sense of what the Orthodox might call God. To say that
> God has the power over each individual to punish us for every little
> transgression? We would never accept such a God. Nor would we
> forgive him for the things he has done. (Barbara)

Approximately 10% of the survivors in our sample totally rejected their
prewar faith. In these cases, we found that the survivors reported troubled
relationships in their families of origin. These survivors did not exhibit
loyalty to retaining the beliefs or practices of their family members. No
longer believing in God, their assumptions about the world and their
faith underwent profound transformations. Reworking their schemata to
accommodate the trauma they experienced, they expressed a belief system more in consonance with ethical humanism, while still retaining their
Jewish identity and connection to Jewish community and tradition.

> Any rational person would not believe in a God who would per-
> mit these things to happen. ... We still have the seders. We did the
> cultural things, but that's all. ... Other than that, pay no attention,
> because [the practice of Judaism] is meaningless, because there is no
> God. The idea is to live a moral life if you can. I do belong to a temple
> just to keep it alive, and I think we have to sustain these centers of
> Jewish learning. (Harry)

Tamar, who aborted her child and survived the Lodz ghetto and various
labor camps, stated poignantly:

> Where was God when they took the little babies, little children, and
> put them to crematorium? Where was God? How can an Orthodox
> Jew answer me this? That's why we don't believe—because we saw
> too much.

Wilma articulated her struggle with the role God played in the Holocaust
and came to the conclusion that she should simply avoid the question, and
that other survivors have done the same.

There are only two ways you can go. Either you say, "Where was God?" and then you shed your faith. Or you are willing to admit that human intelligence is limited, and there are certain things we don't understand. I guess we all stayed away from [the question of] where was God [during the Holocaust].

Sophie said:

There's no answer. You can ask and ask over and over again, and you get no answer. I envy those people who are religious because they have something to lean on. They have an answer. God wants it. It's God's will. It's a way to explain to yourself. But you know the difference, and you can believe in it or not. (Sophie)

Ella, whose beloved father was killed during the war, still prays to him in her old age. Although she says she always believed in God, and still believed in God after the war, it seems from her interview that she prayed to her father more readily and more frequently than she prayed to God. Her relationship with him was a secure one, whereas her attachment to her mother (who survived with her) was insecure. Her mother was, in fact, quite physically and emotionally abusive to Ella throughout her childhood.

I remember he was warm. He was always taking care of me. And when I was near him, I always knew that I'm protected. In fact, even to this day I pray to his spirit whatever is there. I say, "Help me, please." … [I was] very close to him. It helps me very much.

It is interesting to note that Ella prays to her father, who died in the early years of the war. She severed herself from the Jewish community after the war and therefore did not engage in Jewish ritual practice. She associated the latter with her mother, who was abusive to her before the war as well as after and with whom she has cut off ties. She is an example of a survivor whose troubled family-of-origin relationship had an impact on her ritual practice.

The most dramatic evidence of a transformation of a faith system came from the only survivor from the TTP who converted to Christianity from Judaism. Eva's father, whom she loved very much, died of tuberculosis when she was 9, and her mother, who was severely mentally ill, was incapable of parenting her. Thus, Eva's faith was challenged even before the war. During the war, Eva felt that the Jewish God had abandoned her, so she turned to a new belief in Christianity.

In fact, this survivor's transformation of faith, or conversion, took place *during* the war, and almost suddenly, the way she tells it, rather than in the gradual conversion or transformation over time that seems to have taken place for the other survivors. When Eva was in hiding, and enduring multiple rapes while hiding alone in a barn, she prayed for her safety, and she specifically prayed that she would not get pregnant from the rapes. Were she to become pregnant, it would have been much more difficult for her to survive.

> I prayed. I prayed. I suppose there are some people who become saints and some people dedicate their life to Christianity completely. But those Catholic girls that I knew, I don't think any one of them believed more than I did, and I prayed. My favorite saint was Saint Theresa, and I prayed to her constantly, and to the Holy Mother, and I begged them to take care of me. That's all. I didn't say, "Do this or do that." Just, "Take care of me." [Crying.] I suppose it helped. And another thing happened. I got my menstruation. And I just went down on my knees in the morning, and I thanked God, and I prayed again.

Case Study: Judy

Judy is another example of someone whose negative family-of-origin relationships hindered her use of faith and practice as coping strategies. A woman in her late 60s, she lost her daughter to breast cancer when her daughter was 37. Judy was raised in a totally nonobservant Jewish family, although she grew up in a predominantly Jewish community. She did not have close relationships with either of her parents and had a particularly problematic and difficult relationship with her mother. Thus, her family-of-origin relationships were more on the negative end of the continuum, and she was also raised virtually without Jewish faith or ritual practice. After marriage, Judy moved from city to city as her husband's job sites changed, and she views the search for Jewish community as an ongoing theme during those years. "I think I always sort of believed there was a God up there. Somebody up there. I'm not sure exactly when it began to gel." After her marriage, Judy went to Israel with her husband for a full year. "I really felt like I was home. It was like one big community—a family."

Once home in the states, Judy became more involved in Jewish life, becoming active in her synagogue and sending her children to Hebrew school, while attending adult education classes herself. "I think I believed in God then. I took the prayers very seriously. And I was always searching for Jewish community."

When her daughter got sick, she felt her Jewish community was not supportive of her or her family. "That soured me. I felt like a leper." She stopped going to services. After her daughter's death, she lost her belief in God.

> My faith is gone now. I just don't believe in anything. I just don't know anymore. I don't see God as punishing people. If He's there, He's not involved in this kind of stuff. I just don't know if faith is even a possibility for me anymore. If I were to believe in God, how could you believe He was responsible for that? What would be the point?
>
> I used to believe in heaven; now I don't know where Rachel is. I think of her in the ground. It would have been comforting to think of her in heaven. I'm not sure that I believe when I die that I'll see her again. I used to get a great deal of comfort from that. There is no meaning in her death for me. I don't know. Maybe if I

had come from a family that believed in God, maybe I could have fallen back on it. Would I have used it to cope? I don't know. I can't yet make a family Passover seder again. The empty chair is just too empty.

Remarkably, both Rachel and Judy never asked the "why" question. "I never asked, 'Why my daughter? Why did this happen to our family?' Because I know bad things happen in the world. And it just happened to happen to us."

Judy credits her therapist with helping her bear the grief. "You go through so many different phases of grief, and she just encouraged me every step of the way. 'This is what it is right now. What is going to help you get through the next day, week, etc.?' She helped me stay with my coping skills. She was always very supportive and empathic. She told me to go with those who help you and forget about the rest."

What also helped was Judy's involvement in the TTP. She has worked on the TTP research team for several years, including the years leading up to Rachel's death. "I often think of survivors, and if they could live through it, I could, too. I didn't lose a whole family. They are truly my role models, and that's the most helpful of all—working on the project. They went on and built families and lives. It's people I truly believe in."

It is interesting to note that for the survivors Eva, Ella, Tamar, and Harry, qualitative prewar family relationships can be described as mostly negative. Did these negative family relationships contribute—at least partially—to their inability to retain their prewar faith and ritual practice afterward? Surely, there were also other contributing factors, such as the level of prewar observance and belief systems of family members, the severity of war experiences, age at the time of the Holocaust, and postwar life. But, it seems clear from our sample that most of those survivors who had close, warm family attachments—relationships with parents that were described by them as open in communication, empathic, affectionate, and other-directed—were more likely to retain their prewar beliefs or Jewish ritual practices they had learned from their parents. Moreover, as we have seen, many of their statements directly connected close, positive prewar relationships with their own postwar beliefs and the continuation of the rituals they learned from their parents.

The examples given here demonstrate the varying degrees of struggle survivors have had over the years with existential belief systems about God and with the decisions made about Jewish ritual practice and belonging to Jewish communities during the years of postwar rebuilding. Each has struggled to find a way either to assimilate the traumatic experiences by conserving preexisting beliefs or to accommodate or transform those belief systems to make room for the new, cruel reality and life in the aftermath.

It is important to note that, whether professing unwavering faith, forging new conceptions of God, or totally rejecting their beliefs, for almost all of the survivors we interviewed, the practice of some form of Judaism—with or without a belief in God—and a connection to Jewish community, remained critically important components of coping and adaptation. The preservation of community and traditional rituals enabled survivors to feel that neither their pre-Holocaust sense of self nor was the legacy their parents had left them was not completely destroyed. They found comfort in the familial familiarity of the rituals. As Shoshana told us:

> All I say is the Shema (prayer affirming God's oneness). My father used to say we don't have to pray. Just say Shema before you go to bed. I did this always, and I still do. It has the meaning for me that I am with my family, that it's part of the tradition.

However, some of the survivors questioned their faith and their parents' faith even before the war, particularly the older ones in the sample, who had begun to frequent Zionist and secular youth groups and were therefore exposed to different and more secular ideas. This questioning, of course, is a normative task of adolescence, as parents' beliefs and values are held up to skepticism and scrutiny. But, even the few who had begun to question their faith before the war seemed to have retained a strong belief into old age. The majority seemed, in fact, to have gone to great lengths to retain their faith despite the horrors they had endured and, for some, *because* of the horrors they had endured.

The messages and values—including religious and moral values—parents imparted to their children before the war became a source of strength for survivors to draw from after the war. Lessons were taught and absorbed on a regular basis in many of these families, including lessons of faith and religious practice. They seem to have played a large role in these survivors' long-term postwar coping and adaptation.

One could hypothesize that the severity of the trauma during the Holocaust had an impact on the retention or the discarding of faith after the war. In other words—and although it is difficult to categorize Holocaust experiences in a hierarchy of suffering—those survivors who had more extreme experiences or more prolonged trauma in the concentration camps might have had a greater tendency to lose their faith than those who were less traumatized. However, this seems not to be the case in the TTP sample. A more important role seems to have been played by loyalty of the survivors to the dead—loved ones, parents, grandparents, siblings—and a strong desire to continue in the traditional ways handed down by their families. This loyalty to parents and grandparents' belief systems is embedded in strong, secure attachments that were formed before the war.

Conclusion: The Familial Familiarity of Faith and Ritual Practice

It may be that holding on to the familiar in an unfamiliar post-Holocaust world was a fundamental, foundational, and pervasive coping strategy for these survivors. Family, community, and way of life were destroyed, but the beliefs, practices, and values of those families and communities were the powerful vestiges that remained. Forced to learn new languages, live in new countries, build new communities, and create new families, survivors tried to retain their faith and hold on to the familiar rituals, as life rafts in uncharted waters.

Surely, as we have seen for survivors of other types of trauma, holding on to the familiar in an unfamiliar posttrauma world can also be a fundamental coping strategy (Gozdziak & Shandy, 2002). We, as clinicians, need to be more cognizant of this strategy and do more to help support and foster it in our clients. We can learn from these Holocaust survivors' experiences to be acutely aware of the critical role that belief and ritual practice may play in many of our clients' lives. Too often, perhaps, we do not explore these avenues with our clients; in fact, some of us may actually avoid discussion of faith and spirituality in therapy (Canda, Nakashima, & Furman, 2004; Gilligan & Furness, 2005; Nelson-Becker, 2005; Nelson-Becker, Nakashima, & Canda, 2007). The example of Katherine and her clinician is a case in point.

Case Study: Katherine

Katherine came for psychotherapy following her release from a state hospital; she had been in and out of inpatient care for several years. She was referred to a senior staff person at a community mental health agency. Katherine was diagnosed with major depressive disorder, schizoid affective disorder, and borderline personality disorder. Establishing trust was difficult and prolonged.

Katherine was the younger of two siblings. Her parents were practicing Catholics; although she did not attend Catholic schools, she participated in the sacraments and was held to the tenets of Catholicism in her home. She was a strong student who eventually went on to college, where she majored in literature.

When Katherine was 12, she became involved in a youth activities group and quickly engaged with the male leader. She remained involved with this group through high school and became the "special friend" of the group leader, who was grooming her for child pornography. She was used in many pornographic films while in high school. The relationship ended while she was in college, and she had her first psychotic break. She reengaged briefly with Catholicism at that time but felt she had sinned so deeply that she would never be forgiven, and she moved away from any form of organized religion or spirituality.

Katherine was progressing well in therapy, so when her therapist had to move out of state, they both agreed to terminate. Three years later, the therapist was contacted again by Katherine, who wanted to tell her about her "massive life decision to enter the convent. I have thought about becoming a nun for several years, and with God's hand have been accepted into the Dominican Sisters." Her therapist was astounded, and her own words provide a poignant recrimination of why so many of us as clinicians simply do not ask.

We had never talked about this spiritual struggle. Why, my goodness why, had we never talked about this? Did she bring it up, and I missed the cue? Did she not bring it up because she thought I wouldn't understand or approve? Did she know that at that time religion was not discussed in therapy? Was she protecting me from this spiritual struggle she was enduring? What did I learn about myself from this—that I was more comfortable talking about trauma than religion? Was my own conflicted Catholic background so confounding that I simply couldn't go there? I still don't know. But the questions remain: Why didn't she say anything, and why didn't I ever ask?"

By neglecting to ask, either consciously or unconsciously, we are missing out on a large aspect of some of our clients' coping strategies. No matter what our own struggles with faith have been—whether we are believers, nonbelievers, or agnostics—being able to ask the questions regarding faith, spirituality, and ritual practices, as well as asking about the crises of faith after trauma are critical components in our clinical work. We should recognize that, in fact, when struggling with questions of belief after severe trauma, there is comfort to be found in the familial familiarity of ritual and in the participation with others from similar faith communities in those ritual practices.

In sum, Holocaust survivors as well as other trauma survivors often use faith and ritual practice as coping strategies to help anchor them. They do this quite creatively at times, as in the case of Jeffrey, who summoned a "minyan of trees" to honor the dead. These strategies were often forged within the matrix of positive, loving family-of-origin relationships. It is important to explore the evolution of faith issues for *all* survivors of traumatic events. These case examples show how pretrauma belief systems and comforting rituals may be called on after the terrible events survivors of many different types of trauma have lived through. Surely, it is part of our role as clinicians to help our clients explore their posttrauma belief systems, give them a voice and a safe place to express their existential struggles, or, perhaps, simply ask the questions.

References

Bauer, Y. (2001). *Rethinking the Holocaust.* New Haven, CT: Yale University Press.

Brenner, R. R. (1980). *The faith and doubt of Holocaust survivors.* New York: Free Press.

Canda, E. R., Nakashima, M., & Furman, L. D. (2004). Ethical considerations about spirituality in social work: Insights from a national qualitative survey. *Families in Society, 85,* 27–35.

Fontana, A., & Rosencheck, R. (2004). Trauma, change in strength of religious faith, ad mental health service use among veterans treated for PTSD. *The Journal of Nervous and Mental Disease, 192,* 579–584.

Gilligan, P., & Furness, S. (2005). The role of religion and spirituality in social work practice: Views and experiences of social workers and students. *British Journal of Social Work, 36,* 617–637.

Goldenberg, J. (2008). *The feelings of my family are with me: The posttraumatic coping of adolescent survivors of the Holocaust.* Unpublished doctoral dissertation, Bryn Mawr College, Bryn Mawr, PA.

Gozdziak, E. M., & Shandy, D. J. (2002). Editorial introduction: Religion and spirituality in forced migration. *Journal of Refugee Studies, 15,* 129–135.

Hass, A. (1995). *The aftermath: Living with the Holocaust.* Cambridge, UK: Cambridge University Press.

Haynes, S. R., & Roth, J. K. (Eds.). (1999). *The death of God movement and the Holocaust.* Westport, CT: Greenwood Press.

Helmreich, W. B. (1992). *Against all odds.* New York: Simon & Schuster.

Isserman, N. (2005). *"I harbor no hate": A study of political tolerance and intolerance.* Unpublished doctoral dissertation, City University of New York, New York City.

Janoff-Bulman, R. (1992). *Shattered assumptions.* New York: Free Press.

Kelly, T. A. (2006). The role of religion, spirituality, and faith-based community in coping with acts of terrorism. In B. Bongar, L. M. Brown, L. E. Beutler, J. N. Breckenridge, & P. G. Zimbardo (Eds.), *Psychology of terrorism* (pp. 137–152). Oxford, UK: Oxford University Press.

Lehtsaar, T., & Noor, H. (2006). The role of religion in coping with the trauma of political persecution: The case of Estonia. *Religion in Eastern Europe, 26*(3), 44–57.

Marks, L. D. (2009). Faith, crisis, coping and meaning making after Katrina: A qualitative, cross-cohort examination. In K. E. Cherry & J. L. Silva (Eds.), *Lifespan perspectives on natural disasters: Coping with Katrina, Rita, and other storms* (pp. 195–215). New York: Springer.

Nelson-Becker, H. (2005). Religion and coping in older adults: A social work perspective. *Journal of Gerontological Social Work, 45,* 51–67.

Nelson-Becker, H., Nakashima, M., & Canda, E. R. (2007). Spiritual assessment in aging: A framework for clinicians. *Journal of Gerontological Social Work , 48,* 331–347.

Pargament, K. I. (1997). *The psychology of religion and coping.* New York: Guilford Press.

Plante, T. G., & Canchola, E. L. (2004). The association between strength of religious faith and coping with American terrorism regarding the events of September 11, 2001. *Pastoral Psychology, 52,* 269–278.

Roth, J. K., & Berenbaum, M. (1989). *Holocaust: Religious and philosophical implications.* New York: Paragon House.

Wells, L. W. (1995). *Shattered faith: A Holocaust legacy.* Lexington, KY: University Press of Kentucky.

Wiesel, E. (1990). *From the kingdom of memory: Reminiscences.* New York: Schocken Books.

PART III
Parenting Patterns

CHAPTER 8

Parenting in Survivor Families

Critical Factors in Determining Family Patterns

NANCY ISSERMAN, BEA HOLLANDER-
GOLDFEIN, and LUCY S. RAIZMAN

Introduction

One of the most significant psychosocial variables in psychological develop-ment is the family. Current research is exploring multiple factors influenc-ing stress reactions in children (Brom & Kleber, 2009). One line of research has explored the connection between the quality of the marital relationship between the parents, the quality of each parent's relationship with the child, and the impact on the child (Cowan et al., 1985; Cowan, Cowan, Ablow, Johnson, & Measelle, 2005; Cowan, Cowan, Pruett, & Pruett, 2007). Cowan and Cowan (2010) proposed that the quality of relationships between family members reflects the three-generational family patterns, both parents' rela-tionship with the child, the balance between life stresses and social supports, and the inner perceptions and transactions that partners bring to their rela-tionship as a couple. In their research, they found that a key factor in the adaptation of the child to school was the quality of the couple's relationship.

Moreover, the spillover hypothesis predicts that a breakdown in parent-ing occurs when spouses are preoccupied with their own problems and do not have the time, energy, or capacity to be attuned to their children's needs (Cox, Paley, & Harter, 2001). The quality of family dynamics paradigm discussed in Chapter 6 includes self-centeredness as one of the five factors defining the parent–child relationship.

Cummings and others have studied emotional security theory (EST) and its connection to the impact of the marital relationship on the child. They noted that stability in the interparental relationship creates a secure base for the child to explore other relationships (Cummings & Merrilees, 2010). EST is a transactional process, emphasizing the impact of repeated marital conflict on the child's functioning. Frequent exposure to conflict over time may lead to maladaptive functioning in the child (Cummings & Merrilees, 2010, p. 31).

Others have also studied the impact of marital conflict on the family. Low and Stocker (2005) studied the impact of marital conflict, parents' depressed states, and hostile parenting style on children. Using statistical techniques that analyze cause-and-effect relationships, they found that when the parent–child bond was healthier (i.e., less hostile) the child was better adjusted in spite of the intensity of marital conflict and the severity of parents' depressed states. This research is part of a growing literature pointing to the significant role of caregiving relationships in the mediation of adversity in the lives of children and adults (Cowan & Cowan, 2010; Gewirtz, Forgatch, & Wieling, 2008; Power, 2004).

Understanding the impact of trauma on survivors and the subsequent impact on parenting style is essential to the study of the intergenerational transmission of trauma. In acknowledging that the quality of parent–child relationships mediates the impact of stress on children, it follows that the impact of parental trauma on children is mediated by the quality of the survivors' parenting and the quality of the attachment between parents and children. The study of parent–child relationships from both parent and child perspectives is an invaluable resource for understanding family dynamics. Descriptions of the dyad and how the parent and child view each other runs through the life histories conducted by the Transcending Trauma Project (TTP) team. The accumulation of evidence yields rich descriptions of each intergenerational dyad.

A key to understanding the nature of the intergenerational dyad is to examine the nature of the attachment between the parent or caregiver and the child. This chapter examines the attachment patterns of the survivors and their children to gain knowledge about which factors pre-, during, and postwar contributed to parenting style and attachment. By tracking the patterns within each family, we gain a better understanding of which factors influence a positive family environment and which factors influence a negative family environment in survivor families. This approach enables the analysis team to utilize the language of the interviewees in describing their significant relationships.

The importance of attachment theory in analyzing parent–child relationships and to the creation of the quality of family dynamics paradigm was reviewed in Chapter 6. The view of the TTP of survivor families comes out of a family dynamics perspective, the principal framework used to analyze the survivor family interviews (Bar-On et al., 1998; Boss, 2001; Walsh, 2003; Weingarten, 2004).

The accumulation of evidence from the analysis process of the survivor narratives yields rich descriptions of each intergenerational dyad. We found families in which both parents were reported by the child to have a positive impact on the child's life and families in which both parents were reported by the child as negative in their impact, as well as families in which the impact of the parents' behavior on the child was mixed. However, the categorization of the families into three distinct groups, positive, mixed, and negative, using the quality of family dynamics paradigm, is a new contribution to the fields of trauma and Holocaust studies research.

The quality of family dynamics on the positive end of the continuum—closeness, empathy, validation, expressive of positive emotions, and open communication—clearly parallels descriptions of positive parenting in the mental health literature that fosters positive psychological development in the child (Gewirtz et al., 2008). According to attachment theory, this style of parenting fosters a secure attachment style (Bowlby, 1969, 1988; Ainsworth, Blehar, Waters, & Wall, 1978; Main, 1999). The quality of family dynamics on the negative end of the continuum—distance, self-centeredness, criticism, expressive of negative emotions, and closed communication—describes parenting that has a negative impact on the development of the child. In this case, the style of parenting fosters an insecure attachment style. As depicted in Table 8.1, the dynamics that foster secure attachment also influence the capacity to regulate emotions and the development of positive self-esteem. The qualitative relational dynamics that foster insecure attachment serve to impede the capacity to regulate emotions and the development of negative self-esteem (Bretherton, 1992; Hazan & Zeifman, 1999; Rovers, 2006; Siegel & Hartzell, 2003; Zeifman & Hazan, 1997).

The theory of interpersonal neurobiology suggests that biological development as determined by early nurture forms the foundation for adult development (Siegel, 1999; Siegel & Hartzell, 2003). Early attachment and

Table 8.1 Qualitative Relational Dynamics

Positive Parenting Mediating Parent	Negative Parenting Emotionally Distressed Parent
Closeness	Distance
Empathy	Self-centered
Validation	Criticism
Expressive of positive emotions	Expressive of negative emotions
Open communication	Closed communication
Secure affect, positive attachment, regulation of self-esteem	Insecure affect, negative attachment, dysregulation of self-esteem

the impact of parenting throughout childhood significantly contribute to the psychological profile of the adult. The challenge is to discern the developmental impact on a child and to understand the pattern of attachment styles in the child's family of origin.

Description of the Sample

Of the 65 families interviewed, there were 50 families, constituting 215 interviews, that included the parent and child generations. In almost all cases, there were no grandparents and in some cases only limited extended family due to the destruction of Jewish families in the Holocaust. Many survivors were the sole surviving members of their families who married other sole surviving members of their families. The parents were often the only real or potential caregivers available to the child. Therefore, for Holocaust survivor families, there was a paucity of extended family members to provide positive influences when problems surfaced in the home environment. This meant that the parenting relationships were often the only nurturing relationships that existed in the family. This included the absence of siblings since several survivor families—20% of our sample— only had one child after the war. This intensified parental effects in those families with little extended family.

Methodology

A charting process (see Chapter 3) reorganized the narrative data into a format that clearly revealed the quality of parent–child relationships. By tracking the description of all the family members who were interviewed, we (the authors of this chapter) placed families into groupings. Specific information in the interviews tracked included the narrative descriptions of each parent and child in the family; descriptions of the interactions between the individual parents and the child; the description of the parental marital relationships; the description of the dynamics of the family; and the picture of daily life in the family, all from both child and parent viewpoint.

The Family Pattern Parameters in the TTP Sample

The 50 intergenerational TTP families were analyzed and placed into three types of survivor nuclear families: positive, negative, and mixed families. Families were categorized based on the following criteria: the descriptions of each of the parents in the parent–child relationship according to the quality of family dynamics paradigm; the parents' marital relationship; the existence of targeting one or more children in the family; the description of the child's adult mental health status; and the nature of relationships in the child's nuclear family. From these broad markers, the TTP research team identified several factors that revealed the pattern of the family relationships. The description of the parent's or spouse's behavior in the family toward the child and the emotional state of the parent(s), the existence or absence of conflict in the parental marriage, the identification of targeting a child by either parent for which the child experienced a negative impact as a result of the targeting; the description of the child's adult mental health and relationships; and the existence of empathy in the child toward the experience of his or her survivor parent(s) are the key factors that, when tracked through the interviews, illustrate the family interaction patterns.

The first factor that arose from the narrative descriptions was the picture of each parent by the child or by the parent. How was the parent described? How did the survivor parent describe him- or herself? How did the survivor describe his or her spouse? Were the descriptions positive, negative, or a mix of both? Of particular importance to note was the characterization of either parent as depressed or angry.

The second factor consisted of the descriptions of relationships in the survivor's nuclear family, otherwise known as the child's family of origin. These descriptions were revealed in the stories that the child reported in the interviews. The stories were analyzed according to the quality of family dynamics paradigm to determine the nature of attachment that existed between the parents and the child. The paradigm, discussed in detail in Chapter 6, consists of a five-factor continuum of relationship descriptions: closeness to distance, empathy to self-centeredness, validation to criticalness, expressive of positive emotion to expressive of negative emotion, open communication patterns to closed communication patterns. The application of the paradigm to the family relationships between the child and the parent revealed whether the parents served as good role models or ineffective role models according to the child's perspective.

The third factor contributing to the characterization of the family was the nature of the marital relationship between the survivor parents. The absence or presence of marital problems and the degree to which they played a role in the family dynamics contributed to the classification of the family according to the three categories.

The fourth factor defining the three types of families considered whether the child was targeted by either distressed parent. This factor focused on families in which one or both parents were angry or depressed and expressed that anger or depression through actions that directed to the child. In most circumstances, the child perceived the parent's actions as damaging to the child's self-image or worldview. However, in a few cases one parent was able to mediate the negative impact of the other distressed parent's targeting (see Chapter 9 for a more full discussion of the mediating parent pattern).

The fifth factor was the description by the adult child of his or her current mental health status and relationships. Did the child experience significant problems in his or her adulthood in forming positive relationships in the nuclear family? Did the child report mental health problems that had an impact on his or her adult life?

The last factor analyzed whether the child expressed empathy toward his or her survivor parent regardless of the parent's behavior toward that child. Empathy toward the survivor parent consisted of an awareness of the trauma that the parent experienced and an understanding of the role that it played in his or her life.

Overall, a critical element of determining which pattern the family followed relates to the distinction between self and other on the part of the parent. The parents who were able to put their children's needs first and somehow hold back on their own needs could provide the nurture and sustenance that the children needed to develop in healthy ways while acknowledging their parents' difficulties. In mixed families, this ability on the part of the parents was inconsistent, while the negative families suffered most from the parents' anger and depression. The children, troubled by the conflict in their relationships, were burdened by the knowledge that their parents suffered greatly. Yet, they resented them for the ways in which they were mistreated. These patterns are not unusual, and we propose, based on our clinical experiences, that they parallel the distinctions in nonsurvivor American families.

In categorizing the family patterns, one third of the TTP sample was comprised of families with strong positive family relationships. This speaks to the capacity to rebuild life in ways that we would not have predicted based on the enormity of the trauma the parents experienced. At the same time, however, the negative families could not overcome the negative impact of the parental trauma. In these families, the parents' suffering was not sufficiently ameliorated, and the children felt burdened by their parents' struggles, often to the point of their own emotional distress. In contrast, in the mixed families, parental anxiety and anger spilled into aspects of family life that adversely affected the children even though the positive aspects of the parenting relationships did somewhat ameliorate the repercussions of the parents' behavior.

Examples of the Three Categories of Families From the Interviews

Positive Families

Several factors contribute to a picture of families with positive aspects of coping that provide a template for the patterns that produce more resilient and healthy children. The positive families were characterized by healthy parent–child relationships. The parents were described by the children in positive words like *loving* and *caring*. Neither parent was labeled angry or depressed. When analyzing the description of the parent–child relationship according to the paradigm, the stories told by the child in the interview cluster on the positive end of the continuum. The relationships were characterized as close, empathic, validating, and expressed in positive emotional terms. Open communication patterns existed in the parent–child relationship. The child described the parental marriage as good or relatively trouble free. No signs of either parent targeting any child in the family were present. The adult child described his or her current situation in positive terms, often noting the influence of the parents as positive role models, as sources of support, and as having successfully transmitted their values or belief systems to the child. In our study, 11 of the 50 families fell within the positive category.

The following two representative examples from the interviews demonstrate the strong positive patterns of parenting and attachment from the total of 11 families in this group.

The A Family

The A family, a male survivor in his 70s, a female Holocaust survivor, also in her 70s, and their only child, an adult son in his 40s, were interviewed. The parents, retired at the time of their interview, lived in a suburb of a large city and had both worked in their own businesses that at times strained their family life. The son described his father as very hardworking, strong willed, caring, affectionate, and warm. He characterized the mother as a positive influence, expressive, warm, and nonjudgmental. They had a long marriage that the son called a "friendship and a good one," close, loving, very affectionate, and fairly successful at compromising and communicating despite normal arguments and conflicts.

The son, educated and professionally employed, was married with two children. He considered his parents loving and involved and as "outstanding people with outstanding values." The son described his mother as closely connected and devoted to him. According to his interview, the parents experienced some fearfulness and difficulties in separating from their son's life. Yet, he reported that he was raised to respect his parents and was sensitive to their well-being, calling them daily. He reflected on his parents' marriage:

> After 45 years of marriage, to be able to talk to one another is an achievement unto itself … they're probably the closest they've ever been. … A combination of their life experiences and now achieving an age where … they both need each other more. … They got along fairly well, and I never felt the insecurity of a turbulent family relationship.

The son stated that to him family is the most important value as a result of his parents' war experiences. Other key values, like education, financial security, and success, derived from his parents' work ethic and were a huge influence in his life. When there were difficult times in his father's business, the son reported that the father would say to him:

> I'm a survivor. I've survived worse so I will get through this. … So from that comes optimism, the message of maybe even in situations where you think you can't control your destiny, maybe you can.

The son reflected on the impact of being a child of survivors and had a generally positive, optimistic, and trusting attitude about others:

> I'm a stronger person as a result. … I'm able to cope … better with a lot of situations than most people that I know. … So, I would say that it really was a significant factor in my life, and continues to be, and I expect that it will always be. But interestingly enough, as horrible as it may sound, I think I'm a better person for it.

It is important to note how much respect, admiration, and empathy were conveyed by the son for his parents and to note also the expression of gratitude for the life he lives with his own nuclear family. He is an example of the strength of positive parenting and the resiliency of the parents, who survived horrific experiences that as a result affected his development in constructive ways.

The C Family

The C family included one survivor parent, the mother, and an American-born father, both in their 70s, with two adult daughters in their mid-30s who were interviewed. The father was viewed by his daughters as a sweet and kind man, understanding, mild mannered and pleasant, quiet, persistent, and hardworking.

The daughters described their mother as a very positive role model, bright, loyal, responsible, kind and "really strong … a guiding light." The mother reflected on the importance of not arguing in front of their children, as well as other values. She possessed a "strict voice to discipline her good children who listened, and [she] appeared more serious than their father when it came to rules" and expectations for her two daughters regarding education, friendships, and family values. The mother was viewed as "active; the spokesperson" and a little overprotective, one who worried about her daughters. She described her daughters as "good children [who] listened."

The parents were affectionate with one another and fairly demonstrative toward their children. The mother expressed a desire for her children to be normal:

> I … felt … we wanted our life to move on, and not just stay in that situation and constantly live the Holocaust. So I really did not become active [in Holocaust-related support groups]. When we had the children, we wanted them to have a very normal … [upbringing]. … I was hoping that we could just raise them to be normal, healthy American children, and not have to pay the price, emotionally what we had gone through. I don't know if I succeeded. I many times hope I did, but I'm not sure.

She added:

> [I did not want my children] to be not assimilated in the sense that they shouldn't
> know who they are, but in the sense that I wanted them to be no different than all
> the children of that age; To be able to enjoy and laugh, and just have fun with all
> the small things. Look at the stars and just be happy instead of always worrying
> about what happened to their mommy or daddy. That was my main goal: to make
> sure that they truly don't pay the consequences of the Holocaust.

The younger daughter recalled that "my parents were always there for me and real supportive." She added that, "I had more of a normal childhood [than that of other children of survivors] and continued to be a child through my childhood."

The older daughter expressed admiration and empathy toward her mother, whom she described as "a hero." She felt more of a sense of obligation and responsibility to be grateful and appreciative of her life than her American school friends. She honored the importance of her mother's survival by creating a work of art with the words: "From darkness to light, from captivity to freedom, to be free again."

The reflections by the mother in the C family provided an example of the distinction between "self" and "other." She was able to focus on her children's needs and to provide nurturing and caretaking for the children to develop in healthy ways. The daughters from the C family strongly demonstrated the impact of their mother's resilience and their parents' marriage that enabled them to successfully parent and provide a positive and healthy family environment for their own children.

The Negative Families

In the negative families, the negative parenting was the predominant influence on the children, resulting in significant problems coping in adulthood. The child's description of the parents included a characterization of one or both parents as angry or depressed. The parent was described in such terms as "critical," "angry," "depressed," "worried," or "anxious," words that revealed a negative affect. The relationship between the child and parent as analyzed through the quality of family dynamics paradigm was described as one in which the parent was distant, critical, self-centered, and exhibiting negative emotions. Communication patterns were closed between the parent and child. The parents' marriage was characterized as distressed or conflicted, with moderate-to-severe problems. Targeting of a child in the family may have been present. If so, efforts by either or both parents to mediate the targeting were insufficient and ineffective. The targets were typically either the oldest child or all of the children. This points to one possible interpretation that oldest children are most vulnerable to their parents' emotional difficulties after extreme trauma.

We found several of the families in our sample in which the eldest child suffered emotional or physical abuse from a parent. In these families, there often existed a similar pattern of an angry parent, frequently a mother who was a sole survivor of her family and who gave birth to her eldest child shortly after the war. The child described his or her adult life in negative terms, often noting resentment toward the distressed or angry parent, trouble in establishing secure relationships with others or a spouse, lack of support by the parents, and significant problems in coping. The child usually did not exhibit empathy toward the survivor as a result of the Holocaust. In our study, 13 families of 50 demonstrated the patterns described in the negative family category.

The families in the negative dynamics category differed greatly from those with positive family dynamics. The analysis revealed that these families were not able to overcome the damaging impact of the parental trauma, and that the children felt burdened by their parents' experiences, leading to their own emotional distress. Here are three representative examples and vignettes from the interviews that demonstrate the highly negative patterns of parenting and attachment from the group of 13 families.

The F Family

The F family, a female child Holocaust survivor in her early 70s, her American-born spouse, and two of their three adult children were interviewed. The father and husband, a man many years older than she, American born, educated, and successfully employed in a profession, was distant, noncommunicative, and someone who maintained a "laissez-faire" attitude toward his parenting role in the family. The father was described as supportive and as generally caring, but a man who "did not know his children" and who did not intervene much in his children's lives. The mother was described by her children as highly critical, depressed, anxious, angry, and a caregiver who had a strong sense of family. She admitted the destructive impact of her behavior on the family as an angry, critical, and perfectionist wife and parent.

The survivor confirmed that she had problematic relationships with all three of her children and that these relationships were somehow related to feelings of guilt.

> A lot of my guilt is learned, inherited or second generation because definitely guilt is a real problem for me. All of them suffered from my tragedy, and all of my kids were quite rebellious.

The daughter, a married woman in her late 30s, and her brother, the middle son, unmarried and also in his late 30s, were both educated and professionally employed. Both acknowledged that their mother regretted being a harsh disciplinarian, overly strict with her first son, their older brother, who was at the time of the interview unmarried in his 40s, educated and employed in another city. The daughter witnessed her mother's abusive behavior toward her older brother and considered him traumatized as a result of his childhood experiences. She saw herself as independent, "the good child" growing up, rebellious as a teenager, and strong willed and defined herself as a "typical, good, Jewish woman, taking care of everyone else." The daughter realized she also was an angry person who yelled frequently at her own daughter and had many difficulties coping with both her marriage and parenting of her two children. She felt overwhelmed, guilty, and overprotective and coped poorly with the challenges of motherhood. She struggled with bouts of depression, low self-esteem, and poor self-care and experienced little sense of success in her life. She reflected: "I have a lot of feeling lost. I have a sense of aimlessness. I'm still aimless."

The brother described himself in his interview as open, witty, lacking self-esteem, struggling with mistrust and insecurity in friendships, and failing in relationships with women. Despite his family's poor communication skills and much stress at home dealing with his older brother, childhood health problems and other losses of relatives helped him become empathic to the pain of others. He observed that: "My mother complains a lot; this family doesn't talk, it internalizes a lot, and maybe she does, too."

He suffered with depression and did not view his life as successful. He described his father as loving, bright, distant, shy, and quiet, yet said they rarely communicated or expressed emotions with one another. The son tried to please his father and live up to his parents' expectations by choosing the same career as his father. He tried to protect his mother from her painful traumas by avoiding communication about the Holocaust. Yet, he did not link difficulties in his present life to the past influence of his mother being a Holocaust survivor who suffered with symptoms of depression and anxiety. He complained about his father's lack of involvement but denied the extent of the emotional impact.

> I always resented—not resented, that's too strong a word—my father's laissez-faire attitude. It would have been better if he'd helped some with guidance. But that was his style. I have no complaints about that.

In these children, emotional expression was reactive or constricted. Analyzing the family with the paradigm revealed relationship patterns that cluster on the negative side of the continuum. Parented by an emotionally distressed mother who crossed the line into abuse and a distant father who reinforced closed communication, these siblings had little in their family experience to mediate the impact of their parents' negative behavior.

The Z Family

The Z family, the survivor widow and mother, in her 70s, and her only child, an adult daughter in her 40s, were interviewed. The daughter described the deceased father and husband as an adoring, sweet, loving, forgiving, and supportive man who communicated positive messages of caring to her. The father, a non-Holocaust survivor, had a role in the marriage and family as a peacemaker who attempted to balance the mother and wife's harshness yet failed at "playing the mediator."

The mother was described by the daughter as angry, critical, controlling, demanding, rigid, aloof, emotionally distant, and unaffectionate. The daughter recounted stories of her fear of her mother's anger and remembered "scary memories of her mother's scenes," which included being slapped by her. She referred to her mother as "the queen," who never apologized and held grudges. The daughter described the ways her mother rigidly structured and controlled her life, leaving her feeling depressed, angry, and struggling with a lack of self-esteem during her childhood. She commented that she would give in to please her mother to avoid further conflict. Her father tried to soften the damaging impact on her life of her mother's selfish behaviors.

However, her father's lack of assertiveness in both challenging and mediating her mother's controlling behaviors and decisions had a negative impact on the daughter's sense of competence and worthiness. Her father's refusal to advocate on his daughter's behalf when he disagreed with his wife contributed to his ineffective mediation of the mother's anger. Despite the daughter's descriptions of her family life as an oppressive and restrictive environment, one that made her feel sad and unhappy, she indicated that she admired her mother's resourcefulness during her war experiences, respected her strength to survive the trauma, and expressed understanding of her mother's weaknesses of character as a partner and parent.

The painful and negative impact on the mother and daughter's relationship characterized the family as negative even with the remarkably compassionate feelings of the daughter. In this family, the suffering of the mother was not sufficiently buffered by the father, and the daughter felt damaged by the trauma in the postwar adaptation.

The G Family

In the G family, a survivor in her 70s was interviewed as well as her first child, an adult son, in his 30s. The survivor mother, a widow, was severely depressed and suffered health problems. The mother was described by the son as critical, distant, cynical, fearful, a worrier, self-sacrificing, and suffering from low self-image and guilt regarding her highly conflicted relationship with one of her children. She admitted to a prior abortion she caused herself during the war and subsequent physical and emotional problems after the war that contributed to her not being able to attach easily with the birth of her first child. The mother indicated that she was happy when she married her husband and with the births of her two children and loved both of them despite significant personality differences between them. The mother had lost her own mother when she was born. This early loss and subsequent deprivation of a primary caretaker bonded her to her older sister, whose death she witnessed during the war. She felt tremendous guilt about surviving when others in her family died and reflected on how these significant losses before and during the war embittered and damaged her, affecting her ability to cope and parent:

> Every time when I pray to myself, oh, I wish something good should happen to me ... always bad things happen to me. A lot of things are bothering me, but I have to forget, that's all. I have to take day by day and whatever will be, will be. What can you do?

Her daughter, who reportedly suffered from mental illness, also contributed to the survivor's difficulties in coping with her life and to her difficulties in her relationships with her husband and son. Her son witnessed his mother's anger in her frequent episodes of fighting and yelling with his sister.

He described himself as a caregiver who felt neither he nor his wife and grandchild received any love or affection from his mother. The daughter was overwhelmed by stories of the mother's horrific war experiences and was not protected from excessive communication about her mother's traumatic memories and nightmares.

The nuclear family dynamics included a troubled marital relationship marked by frequent shouting and much sibling rivalry, mostly revolving around the extra attention the daughter was shown because of her mental health problems. The mother, also, felt guilt and sorrow that her daughter and son were not close. Furthermore, her husband's war experiences resulted in depression and anger. As a result, the G family could not overcome the negative impact of the parental trauma. Thus, in this family the damaging behaviors of the parents were not sufficiently mediated, and the child felt burdened by the war trauma.

The Mixed Family Category

The mixed families fell in between these two extremes and were character-ized by mixed positive and negative influences. Consequently, children in the mixed group reflected healthier functioning in coping with adulthood and fewer significant problems in life than those in the negative families, but also evidenced a greater number of adverse influences than those in the positive families. In the mixed family category, each of the five fac-tors consisted of both positive and negative characteristics. The parents were described in terms reflecting both ends of the paradigm continuum and often included an angry or depressed parent. The parents' marriages ranged from good to mild or moderately distressed but were not described as severely distressed by the child. While targeting of a child in the fam-ily may have been present, there may also have been some attempts at mediation by the less-symptomatic parent. These attempts to mitigate the effects of targeting were not totally successful, however, and the child exhibited some signs of the damaging impact of the targeting. The child's adult life showed in general some negative influences from the problems of the parents either in nuclear family relationships that were troubled or in the child's mental health status. Although many of the children did not exhibit empathy toward their parents as a result of their war experiences, even when empathy was present it did not make a difference in the family relationships. In our study, 22, or almost half, of the 50 families, the largest group, were placed in the mixed family category.

In 100% of the mixed families in the TTP sample, there was an emotion-ally distressed parent, manifesting angry or depressed emotional reactions and behaviors as described by both the adult children and the other parent. The study of the narrative material revealed three characteristics that differ-entiated the children in the mixed group from the children in the negative group. The first characteristic was that the descriptions of the emotionally dis-tressed parents, although mostly negative, did include some positive aspects. The second characteristic was that in one third of the parental partnerships at least one parent was described in mostly positive terms. The third charac-teristic was that the adult children in the mixed group reported fewer prob-lems in their adult lives than were reported by the children in the negative group. As a result, these characteristics created overall patterns that contrib-uted toward more healthy parenting relationships and family environments when compared to the negative families. While impossible to quantify, the qualitative analyses revealed that, in a majority of the families, the angry or critical parents demonstrated some measure of positive interaction with the children. In these families, the other parent was not described as emotionally distressed. Thus, they exhibited more positive parenting behavior, although not quite enough to compensate for the impact of the emotionally distressed parent. The adult children in this group discriminated among their parenting experiences, attributing positives and negatives to both parents. In addition, their problems were less pervasive, allowing them to achieve some measure of success and happiness in their adult lives.

It is important to note that in over half of the families in this category the data revealed a pattern of emotionally distressed parents targeting children with their symptoms, as in the negative group. The pattern of targeting was similar as well, with the targets typically being the oldest child or all of the children. This again points to the possible interpretation that oldest children are most vulnerable to their parents' emotional difficulties after extreme trauma. Finally, there was a much higher level of empathy present in the children in three quarters of the families in this group, with more children empathic to their parents' Holocaust experiences in contrast to the children in the negative group.

The T Family

In the T family, a total of five members, were interviewed. This included the survivor mother, the survivor father, and their three children, two sons and daughter. The father survived the war with one younger brother and his parents, having lost his beloved older brother, a partisan. The father, a hardworking businessman, was devoted to providing for his family. Yet, he was consistently described by his adult children as angry, unemotional, distant, strict, unaffectionate, and possessing a controlling and domineering personality. They further characterized him as having a relentless work ethic, physically abusive, tough, bullheaded, and stoic and as not showing loving feelings or pride toward his three children during their childhood.

The mother in the T family was described by her adult children in positive and negative terms, as loving, caring, emotional, and a peacekeeper and yet passive in terms of dealing with her husband. She was also described as a worrier, nervous, and insecure. The mother exhibited a closeness with her four older sisters, with whom she survived the death camps, believing strongly in the importance of the family in her life.

The oldest son described his mother as

always nurturing and always there for me. She was there to bring up the kids, and … she did a great job with doing that. … She was proud of me no matter what I did.

Although he remarked that his father had mellowed in recent years, he noted, "My father didn't really show love or anything like that. My father worked a lot and didn't spend much time with me."

He decided against joining his father in the family business and instead found professional success and a secure marriage with three children. His teenage son's chronic illness affected his ability to relax and be happy or optimistic about the future. The middle child, a daughter in her late 30s, single and successfully employed as a professional, described her father as enraged about what he experienced during the war. She stated that she felt she relived her father's suffering and losses by listening to his stories about the war. She remembered walking out of the room because she became so overwhelmed by his negative emotions and her sadness. Although her father had a hard time showing emotions like love and pride, she reported that she adored him now as he had made efforts to soften toward his children. The daughter also commented that during her childhood she witnessed the tensions between her parents. She described her mother as a mediator between her father and the children, but it was not a consistent role on which the daughter could count. Her mother's conflict about effectively negotiating with her father was combined with the mother's own anxiety and worry about their lives. "The more anger I saw, the more my father would withdraw, and my mother she'd scream and yell and plead and beg."

The youngest son, single and in his middle 20s, was completing college and worked closely with his father. He described his father as a man who tended to hold in most emotions and was still unable to tell his son that he was proud of his accomplishments. The son struggled with his own indecision about education and career choice, yet attributed his desire for financial independence and his work ethic to his father. He was determined to please his father despite his parent's often opinionated and disapproving comments. He could identify with his mother's coping style. "I'm a worrier. I have a lot of insecurities. If I don't have anything to worry about, I find something to worry about. I'm more like my mother that way."

The youngest son observed the self-sacrificing role his mother played in accommodating to his father and doing what she could to avoid conflict. He saw his father in the European tradition of the male role model who held all the power and made the major decisions in the family. As a result, the son concluded that his parents did not communicate openly or effectively with each other or with him.

The daughter had the most to say about her mother, describing her as a bright, strong, and capable woman, loving and open with her feelings toward her children. As an adult, she saw her mother as less submissive compared to during her childhood. She felt the need to be protective of her mother for as long as she could remember.

> I guess I always saw my mother as very dependent ... but if there was anything that was ever a struggle my mother had to be the one to give in. So that wasn't a very good lesson to have learned and ... the more I saw that the more independent I became. That was just not going to be me. ... My mother would talk about her worry to me. She would always tell me what she was worried about. My father would withdraw, but we knew to stay away from him because he was worried. And my mother always had to be there for my father.

The daughter expressed empathy in discussing the close and supportive relationship she had with both of her parents despite their past interference in her life when she considered marrying a non-Jewish man. She described herself as highly responsible, decisive, self-reliant, with difficulty in accepting that she also has anxiety-related fears about her life as a single career woman and in relinquishing what she cannot control.

The holding back [of emotions] … just comes from always needing to be in control, take care of things … maybe when I was a kid it came from not allowing myself to be happy because how could I be happy when I should be feeling pain?

In summary, the mother in the T family was described as a mediator who tried to protect her children from her husband's anger, criticism, and withdrawal and seemed to have been moderately effective in buffering the negative effects when the father's verbal attacks targeted the children. All three children expressed compassion toward their parents despite suffering from the negative effects of their father's anger, criticism, and rejection.

The L Family

In the L family, two members were interviewed, the survivor and one child. The female Holocaust survivor, 75 years old, married her first husband, 11 years older, after the war, and they had three children—two sons and a daughter. The husband lost his first wife during the war and was described by his wife as a very strict disciplinarian, cold, cruel, distant, and depressed. He died when his sons were in their 20s, and the mother remarried another Holocaust survivor whom she described as an angry and very depressed man. The second husband also died several years prior to the interview, after a long illness. The child described the mother, who acted as the peacemaker in family relationships, as an extremely devoted wife to both her two husbands. The child viewed her as affectionate, optimistic, responsible, giving, overprotective, and overpowering. She would intervene on behalf of the children because discipline from the father was often severe, and she would plead with him not to hit the children.

The oldest son married late in life. He was a successful businessman and actively involved in charitable activities. He described his father as studious, religious, quite charming to others as well as humorous, critical, angry, sad, and unhappy. He observed: "To me he was cold and distant. I rarely had a conversation with him, any sort of meaningful conversation. Really quite rare." His father's frequent criticism of him and lack of praise was hurtful and damaging to his self-esteem. He remembered that his father belittled his accomplishments and did not approve of or involve himself in his son's interests while the son was growing up. "Even with other children, he would be quite charming and joking and playing around, but it's something he never did with me."

The son recalled that his father had no career or educational expectations for him since his father's only goal was that he be religious. He observed that his mother never criticized him; instead, she praised him and tried to soften the criticism from his father. His mother was a worrier, anxious, and overprotective his entire life. The father targeted and directed his negative emotions toward his children, apparently, the son thought, as a result of his struggles with depression and sadness over early losses in his life during the war. In contrast, he saw his mother as strong and admired her ability to accept life and cope with parenting by

always putting on a happy face. I've never seen my mother fall apart. The only time I saw my mother really get upset is when I personally would be very upset about something, and a rare occasion, my mother would be very upset because I would be so upset.

In the L family, the transmission of emotional damage from the angry and possibly depressed father was minimized and buffered by the mother's caretaking and mediating presence. The theme of the importance of children, family ties, and commitment to one another was also evidenced in the mother's nurturing and caring role. Yet, she was not able to fully mediate the impact of the father's criticisms and negative behavior on the son's self-image.

Conclusion

The seven case examples provide compelling and rich descriptions of the impact of parental trauma that critically influenced children's development and lives in later adulthood and their overall coping and sense of physical and emotional well-being. Analyzing the families in terms of the five parameters (description of parents, description of parent–child relationship according to the quality of family dynamics paradigm, description of the parents' marital relationship, identification of the presence in the family of a target child, and description of the child's adult nuclear family relationships and mental health status) resulted in three categories of families: positive, negative, and mixed.

While the patterns are not so unusual and, we believe, are similar in nonsurvivor or nontrauma populations of American families, what is noteworthy is that one third of the sample was reported as having strong, positive, and healthy family relationships. This reflects the resilience and capacity to rebuild life in ways that we would not have predicted based on the nature of extreme trauma and the difficulties in coping with postwar life transitions and events.

The observation about the positive families that distinguished values between self and other is also important to explore. The parents who were able to protect and support their children's needs first and focus less on their own needs could provide the nurture and responsiveness that the children needed to develop in healthy ways while acknowledging their parents' difficulties and challenges. In mixed families, this capacity on the part of the parents was more inconsistent, while the negative families suffered most from the impact of the parents' symptoms of anger, depression, and lack of emotional availability. The children, distressed by the conflict in their parents' marriage and family relationships, were burdened by the knowledge that their parents suffered significantly from trauma and loss.

The analysis of the TTP interviews shows that the parent–child relationships in the formative years had an impact beyond childhood into the adult life of the child. Examining parent–child relationships not only through the viewpoint of the parent but also through the perspective of the child illustrates the impact of the parent's behavior and mental health on the adult child's psychological well-being. And as discussed in the next chapter, one parent's impact on the child may be great enough to mitigate problems resulting from living with an angry or depressed parent.

References

Ainsworth, M. D. S., Blehar, M. C., Waters, E., & Wall, S. (1978). *Patterns of attachment: A psychological study of the strange situation.* Hillsdale, NJ: Erlbaum.

Bar-On, D., Eland, J., Kleber, R, Krell, R., Moore, Y., Sagi, A., et al. (1998). Multigenerational perspectives on coping with the Holocaust experience: An attachment perspective for understanding the developmental sequelae of trauma across generations. *International Journal of Behavioral Development, 22,* 315–338.

Boss, P. (2001). *Family stress management: A contextual approach.* Newbury Park, CA: Sage.

Bowlby, J. (1969). *Attachment.* New York: Basic Books.

Bowlby, J. (1988). *A secure base: Clinical applications of attachment theory.* London: Routledge.

Bretherton, I. (1992). The origins of attachment theory: John Bowlby and Mary Ainsworth. *Developmental Psychology, 28,* 759–775.

Brom, D., & Kleber, R. (2009). Resilience as the capacity for processing traumatic experiences. In D. Brom, R. Pat-Horenczyk, & J. D. Ford (Eds.), *Treating traumatized children: Risk, resilience, and recovery* (pp. 133–149). New York: Routledge.

Cowan, C. P., Cowan P. A., Heming G., Garrett, E., Coysh, W. S., Curtis-Boles, H., & Boles, A. J. (1985). Transitions to parenthood. His, hers, and theirs. *Journal of Family Issues, 6,* 451–481.

Cowan, C. P., Cowan, P., Pruett, M., & Pruett, K. (2007). An approach to preventing coparenting conflict and divorce in low-income families: Strengthening couple relationships and fostering fathers' involvement. *Family Process, 46,* 109–121.

Cowan, P. A., & Cowan, C. P. (2010). How working with couples fosters children's development: From prevention science to public policy. In M. S. Schultz, M. K. Pruett, P. K., Kerig, & R. D. Parke (Eds.), *Strengthening couple relationships for optimal child development: Lessons from research and intervention* (pp. 211–228). Washington, DC: American Psychological Association.

Cowan, P. A., Cowan, C. P., Ablow, J., Johnson, V. K, & Measelle, J. (2005). *The family context of parenting in children's adaptation to elementary school.* Mahwah, NJ: Erlbaum.

Cox, M. J., Paley, B., & Harter, K. (2001). Interparental conflict and parent–child relationships. In J. H. Grych & F. D. Fincham (Eds.), *Interparental conflict and child development: Theory, research, and applications* (pp. 249–272). New York: Cambridge University Press.

Cummings, E. M., & Merrilees, C. E. (2010). Identifying the dynamic processes underlying links between marital conflict and child adjustment. In M. S. Schultz, M. K. Pruett, P. K., Kerig, & R. D. Parke (Eds.), *Strengthening couple relationships for optimal child development: Lessons from research and intervention* (pp. 27–40). Washington, DC: American Psychological Association.

Gewirtz, A., Forgatch, M., & Wieling, E. (2008). Parenting practices as potential mechanisms for child adjustment following mass trauma. *Journal of Marital and Family Therapy, 34*, 177–192.

Hazan, C., & Zeifman, D. (1999). Pair bonds as attachments: Evaluating the evidence. In J. Cassidy and P. R. Shaver (Eds.), *Handbook of attachment: Theory, research and clinical applications* (pp. 336–354). New York: Guilford Press.

Low, S. M., & Stocker, C. (2005). Family functioning and children's' adjustment: Associations among parents' depressed mood, marital hostility, parent-child hostility and children's' adjustment. *Journal of Family Psychology, 19*, 394–403.

Main, M. (1999). Attachment theory: Eighteen points with suggestions for future studies. In J. Cassidy & P. R. Shaver (Eds.), *Handbook of attachment: Theory, research and clinical applications* (pp. 845–887). New York: Guilford Press.

Power, T. G. (2004). Stress and coping in childhood: The parents' role. *Parenting: Science and Practice, 4*, 271–317.

Rovers, M. W. (2006, September/October). Overview of attachment: A continuous tread. *AAMFT Family Therapy Magazine,* 8–11.

Siegel, D. J. (1999). *The developing mind.* New York: Guilford Press.

Siegel, D. J., & Hartzell, M. (2003). *Parenting from the inside out.* New York: Tarcher Putnum.

Walsh, F. (2003). Family resilience: A framework for clinical practice. *Family Process, 42*, 1–18.

Weingarten, K. (2004). Witnessing the effects of political violence in families: Mechanisms of intergenerational transmission of trauma and clinical interventions. *Journal of Marital and Family Therapy, 30*, 45–59.

Zeifman, D., & Hazan, C. (1997). A process model of adult attachment formation. In S. Duck & W. Ickes (Eds.), *Handbook of personal relationships* (2nd ed., pp. 179–195). Chichester, UK: Wiley.

CHAPTER 9

"Like a Bridge Over Troubled Waters"

Divergent Parenting and the Mediating
Influence of Positive Parental Attachment

BEA HOLLANDER-GOLDFEIN, NANCY
ISSERMAN, and LUCY S. RAIZMAN

Introduction

As noted in Chapter 8, the Transcending Trauma Project (TTP) found that in the interviews, the impact of parental trauma critically influenced children's development and lives in later adulthood by affecting their overall coping and sense of physical and emotional well-being. The extensive analysis of relationships between parents and children and how these relationships had an impact on the transmission of trauma yielded three groupings of qualitative family relationships. Survivor families with predominantly negative relationships tended to display emotional difficulties in the second generation. Survivor families with predominantly positive relationships led to greater psychological health in the second generation. Families with mixed patterns of positive and negative relationship qualities between both parents and children resulted in a complex interplay of positive qualities and emotional difficulties for the children. A smaller, fourth group of families revealed a different pattern. In these families, the healthier parent was successful in mediating the negative impact of the emotionally distressed parent on the children. The children who experienced this successful mediation reported that the angry or depressed parent had a relatively limited adverse effect on their lives. They described in great detail the positive impact of the mediating parent on their success as adults.

But, how does this mediating influence work? Both parents undoubtedly influenced the offspring, but which parenting influence prevailed and why? If neither parenting style prevailed, then what was the balance between positive and negative effects?

Review of the Literature

This is an important inquiry for the field of marriage and family therapy in light of Walsh's (1998) observation that "most studies of resilience have focused on children of a seriously disturbed or abusive parent, dismissing such a child's entire family as dysfunctional" (p. 6). By integrating systemic, ecological, developmental, and trauma perspectives, Walsh (1998) made the case for the necessity of "a complex interactional model" (p. 12), referred to as "the family resilience approach," when attempting to understand the resilience of an individual within a family. This approach takes into account all the intersecting relationships and critical developmental factors that influence family members. While not directly addressing the issue of differential impacts from divergent parenting styles, the family resilience approach would include, by definition, our examination of each parent-child dyad.

Divergent parenting is present throughout the TTP sample, as it is present in most families. The observation that adults parent differently is not a surprising finding, although the recognition and the description of the range of impacts of divergent parenting on children have not been thoroughly explored (Amato & Rivera, 1999; Cassano, Adrian, Veits, & Zeman, 2006; Jacob & Johnson, 1997; Phares & Compas, 1992; Phares, Fields, Kamboukos, & Lopez, 2005). This chapter contributes to the study of this phenomenon utilizing an in-depth qualitative analysis.

The TTP sample containing 50 parent-child families allowed the research team to study each individual within the parent-child dyad separately. This is in contrast to much of the prior research and clinical writings, which have typically referred to parental impact without differentiating the impact of paternal involvement and have analyzed impact through a single source of data (Amato & Rivera, 1999). Some studies have explored parent–child interaction and examined the impact of maternal or paternal depression or parent alcohol-related illnesses on the child. These studies, while looking at the impact of the impaired parent, have not also investigated the healthy parent's ability to mitigate the distressed parental impact on the child (Barber, Stolz, Olsen, & Maughan, 2005; Fauber, Forehand, Thomas, & Wierson, 1990; Jacob & Johnson, 1997; Keller et al., 1986). The use of the terms *parents* and *parent–child relationship* do not discriminate between the parents in terms of their potentially different impact on children. For example, the Low and Stocker (2005) study, mentioned in Chapter 8, examined families in which both parents were depressed. Therefore, the influence of a nondepressed parent could not be studied. Pederson and Revenson (2005) looked at the role of family attachment style in mediating the impact of parental illness on adolescent well-being. Again, parents were assessed as a unit, and the possibility that each parent had different attachment styles was not addressed.

Rarely has there been a study of the impact of the "other" parent on the child, the parent who does not have the "problem" (Cassano et al., 2006). In fact, some studies stated that family functioning can mediate the effects of interparental conflict but not mediate any conflicts in the child–parent relationship (Unger, Brown, Tressell, & McLeod, 2000).

While studies of resilience have contributed to our understanding that any nurturing relationship within a child's life can foster positive adaptation (Werner & Smith, 1992), and while the field of child development has contributed to our understanding of the constructive role played by the parent–child relationship in mediating the impact of stress and trauma, neither literature has focused on the mediating quality of divergent parenting (Walsh, 1998). In a well-functioning family, the existence of divergent parenting may not be problematic, either because the parents are similar in their parenting style or because the divergent styles may be complementary and enriching for the child. In problem cases, in which one parent is emotionally distressed and interacts with the child in ways that are harmful, the emotionally distressed parent is the "stressor" who negatively impacts the psychological development of the child. In these cases, it is possible that the nondistressed parent may have a positive, neutral, or negative impact on the child, which may mediate or exacerbate the influence of the distressed parent (Raizman, 2001).

Studies have begun to explore the impact of each parent on the child (Marsiglio, Amato, Day, & Lamb, 2000). Cowan, Cowan, and Knox (2010) found that fathers who exhibited secure attachments from their family-of-origin relationships were able to protect their children from the negative impact of the mothers' insecure attachment. Other studies concurred in this finding (Lee, Bellamy, & Guterman, 2009). Cowan, Cowan, Ablow, Johnson, and Measelle (2005) also found that mothers with secure attachment ties were not able to provide a buffer against their husband's insecure model of relationships to maintain a marital/parent–child relationship that was positive. Specifically, in this study the researchers explained their contrasting findings by speculating that fathers can act as protectors when mothers exhibit a depressive style. But when fathers exhibit insecure modes of relationships, they are often angry or hostile, and these behaviors are more difficult for women, even those with secure attachments, to handle (Cowan et al., 2005).

To truly understand the child's experience and subsequent development, it is important to study the influence of the nondistressed parent. This rounds out the picture of family life and reveals the parenting patterns that explain individual differences among the children and why families with similar problems function differently. The TTP data containing interviews with in-depth descriptions of family members and family dynamics gave us the opportunity to explore the impact of the nondistressed parent on the family dynamics and child–parent relationship.

As mentioned in Chapter 8, in almost all cases in the TTP sample, there were no grandparents and in some cases only limited extended family due to the destruction of entire Jewish families and communities in the Holocaust. The parents were often the only real or potential caregivers available to the child. Therefore, for Holocaust survivor families there was a paucity of extended family members to provide positive influences when problems surfaced in the home environment. This meant that the parenting relationships were often the only nurturing relationships that existed in the family. This reality served to intensify parental effects.

Results

The fourth pattern of families uncovered in the TTP data, the mediating parent pattern, was defined by the existence of a healthier parent who succeeded in mitigating the negative impact of the emotionally distressed parent on the children. There were 4 intergenerational families of 50 that followed this pattern. Similar to the group of negative families and the group of mixed families, in each of these families there was a clear emotionally distressed parent described by the adult children and the other parent. But, unlike the groups of negative and mixed families, the nondistressed parent was described in *exclusively* positive terms. In this group of families, the positive qualities of the nondistressed parent were reported by the adult children to be effective in compensating for the negative parenting of the emotionally distressed parent. The success of the nondistressed parent's compensation was described in great detail by the adult children. They succinctly articulated the negative experiences with the emotionally distressed parent, the positive experiences with the other parent, and how the positive experiences helped them overcome the impact of the negative influences. The descriptions within the life histories were so explicit and consistent across the four families that this pattern clearly deserves special attention, not only as a finding, but also as a potential model for nondistressed parents attempting to raise children with a distressed coparent. Although some research has stated that women, even those with secure models of attachment, may find it difficult to contend with angry husbands who lash out at their children (Cowan et al., 2005), the analysis of the TTP data on mediating families shows that it is a difficult, but attainable goal for one individual to mediate the negative parenting of the other parent even if that other parent is an angry father.

The mediating family group is divided into three families in which the mother was the mediating parent and one family in which the father was the mediating parent. In two families, the fathers were angry, and in one family, the father was depressed. In the fourth family, the mother was depressed. Thus, in three families the mother was the positive influence. This is in contrast to many other families in the TTP sample in which the mother was the healthier parent but was unable to compensate for the negative interactions of the father. Therefore, gender alone does not determine whether an individual will be a successful mediator within the family. Other factors play a role in deciding the success of the mediating parent to compensate for negative family dynamics. This chapter explores these factors that facilitate the success of the mediating parent within the troubled family environment.

The children in the four families described their mediating parents as primarily responsible for the psychological health that the children experienced in adulthood. In this group, parental marriage was described as generally happy in two of the cases and moderately distressed in the other two. When compared to the negative and mixed family groups, these marriages were less severely distressed marriages among the mediating parent families. Thus, the more positive parent lived with less marital discord. The children experienced a greater likelihood of viewing more positive than negative parental interactions—or at least there was some balance and therefore the presence of positive affection between the parents. As a result, less overall negativity existed in the family environments. This is an important factor when understanding the potential for mediation in families with a distressed parent. Subject to further investigation, it may be that the relative moderate level of marital distress made it possible for the mediating parent to utilize enough emotional energy and emotional space in the family system to convey positive messages to the children about their worth and to enact positive parenting behaviors. On the opposite end of the continuum, therefore, our findings support the work of others that high levels of marital distress make it impossible for the healthier parent to have a significant impact on the parenting environment for the children in spite of their best intentions. (Cowan et al., 2005, 2010; Fauber et al., 1990)

In terms of other family dynamics, only one family in the positive mediating group reported the negative targeting of children by the emotionally distressed parent. In two of the families, the daughters took on the role as caregiver for the parents. We observed that all the children we interviewed in these families expressed empathy for their parents' difficulties, recognizing that, to some extent, their difficulties were the result of their victimization in the Holocaust. The lower rate of targeting the child could have created a psychological environment that was more conducive to empathy for the distressed parent. It could also allow the child to absorb positive messages. In addition, it may be that in less-negative environments it is easier for children to exhibit empathy toward difficult parents since the positive parent is modeling empathy as well as successfully mediating potential emotional injuries (see Table 9.1)

Examples from these four case studies demonstrate the important influence of the role of a mediating parent in families with an emotionally distressed parent. The key finding is the consistently negative description of the emotionally distressed parent and the consistently positive description of the mediating parent. These firsthand descriptions provide evidence that the children are able to distinguish between their parents' influence on them. Moreover, the symptoms of the more emotionally distressed parent do not notably affect the second generation when compared to the positive impact of the mediating parent. In fact, according to their own words, the children viewed themselves as well adjusted and successful in their present lives. The positive descriptions of the healthier parents clearly point to the powerful role they played as mediators of the negative family dynamics. This is not to say that these children did not have issues to resolve related to the angry or depressed parent's impact on them. Nevertheless, they could enter their adult lives with greater strength, resilience, and positive self-esteem due to the efforts of the nurturing parent. These characteristics form the foundation from which the adult children drew their emotional resources to cope with the challenges of adulthood and to deal with the negative aspects of their lives.

The W Family

In the W family, quotations from the three sisters illustrate the similarity of perceptions about the parents shared by the siblings. The oldest daughter was the closest confidante of the mother and described her father as angry, critical, rigid, domineering, distant, and unaffectionate.

> He never showed affection, never, never. … I have a picture of him holding me on his lap when I was about 4. If I didn't have that picture I could tell you that I never sat on my father's lap, and my father never kissed me. … I know it isn't true, but that's what I am left with.

> She felt that she could not please her father. His critical posture upset her, especially coupled with his dedication to religious practice that seemed to her to be more important to him than his relationship with her and her sisters. Despite much success

Table 9.1 Profile of Successful Mediation Families

Father Angry [1,2]	Father Depressed [2,3]	Mother Angry	Mother Depressed [2,3]	Both Angry and Depressed	Both Parents Positive and Negative Influence	Other Parent Positive Influence	Good Marriage	Moderate Distressed Marriage	Bad Marriage	Target Child	Caretaker Child	Empathy
2	1	0	1	0	0	4	2	2	0	3 No 1 All	2 Daughters	4 Yes
25%	13%	0%	13%	0%	0%	100%	50%	50%	0%	25%	50%	100%

Positive mediation families N = 4, 8% of the total data sample.

[1] *50% of distressed parents described as angry (2 males and no females).*

[2] *50% of parents described as emotionally distressed: one parent in each family.*

[3] *50% of distressed parents described as depressed (1 female and 1 male).*

in her professional life as a university professor, a satisfying second marriage, and two children, the oldest daughter reflected:

> I felt … throughout most of my life I was a disappointment to my father in a lot of ways, and the way I could make it up to him was to be really good in school. It was forever that wish to do the right thing, to make him really proud of me.

This statement demonstrates the daughter's wish to please her father, which seemed only to be possible through school performance. The middle daughter, known in the family as the father's favorite, described him as angry, strict, and uncommunicative. She noted that her father would not talk to his wife or children for days as punishment.

> Silence is a killer, and that's probably one of the worst forms of punishment I know. When my parents argued my father just wouldn't talk to my mother, and he thought that punishing her by not eating the meal she prepared was the punishment that she deserved. He really, looking back, was very dysfunctional. … My father showed anger. I'll never forget he smacked me in the face and bent my braces. He had a temper. One of us had locked ourselves in a bedroom, and he broke the door down to get us. And I remember occasionally he would hit us with a strap.

The youngest daughter, the most tearful of the three sisters during the interview, described her father as angry, quick tempered, distant, critical, and unaffectionate.

> My memories of my father were not so warm. His role was more to provide, and I have memories of him being angry at not being able to provide the way he would have liked to. And having worked so hard, and also working on the Sabbath, that was very painful for him. When I think back on it now, I understand his anger.

The mother was perceived as a worrier who advocated on her children's behalf and served a crucial nurturing and mediating role in the family between the children and their difficult father. The ways their mother conducted her life became a role model for her daughters. The oldest daughter revealed:

> I have to call her [Mother] every single day. I have to call my sisters every single day. … We are very close, and my mother is my best friend. Sometimes I think about the possibility of losing her, and I just don't know how I could possibly deal with it. We are too symbiotic. We are connected beyond what I think is normal. She completely made up, as much as she could, for what my father couldn't provide.

This is a clear statement about the mother's capacity to compensate for what the father did not provide. But, there is also a statement about family relationships that are so close that they are described as "symbiotic." This raises the question of whether a parent–child relationship that is "too close" may provide many positives to the child but ultimately end in hampering the processes of growth and individuation. It is certainly true that relationships, when too close, can exert a negative influence, but it is unclear what too close means when the child's well-being has been dependent on the mother giving beyond the call of duty to compensate for the angry, critical, rejecting father. The closeness of their relationship may have been intensified due to the role it played in counterbalancing the negatives. In this case, the daughter was doing quite well in her adult life and described few personal difficulties. The balance between the positive influences of the mediating parent and the potential for the relationship to be too close and possibly constricting requires further study. However, other than feeling the need to call the mother and sisters daily, little in this interview uncovered any long-term adverse effects of the close relationship.

A study of parent–child relationships in Holocaust survivor families found that behaviors that could be described as enmeshment (Podietz et al., 1984), and would therefore be expected to negatively affect family members, actually functioned in positive ways in these families. The researchers therefore redefined these behaviors as "engagement." Calling daily was one of the behaviors that they observed in survivor families, which functioned positively for the parents and children and not in a harmful manner as might have been expected. Behaviors of connection, when enacted in healthy attachment relationships, have a different emotional valence in survivor families for whom the children are the anchor in their new lives posttrauma (Podietz et al., 1984).

The middle daughter reflected,

> My mother was the one who gave me the warmth as a child. I could cry to her. She would hug me … kiss me. She was there for me. My mother had to carry out my father's wishes, and if they weren't carried out, then he would blame her. It was unheard of for him to sit down with us and talk about feelings. We didn't have feelings. We were the children who had to listen. Again, my mother was the mediator. She knew we had feelings, but she was expected to carry out my father's wishes, yet she felt for us.

The youngest daughter observed, "My memories of my mother were warm, very warm."

The W daughters described their family dynamics, particularly their father's anger and mother's ability as a caregiver who mediated their father's negative behaviors and helped them cope with and accept disappointments in their lives. As the oldest daughter asserted:

> I feel … because of the miracles that happened to my mother, because of her faith and giving me the feeling I could accomplish whatever I needed to, I am pretty positive. … I take things in small pieces, I do what I can. … My parents gave me the tools, the skills, to persevere to make it on my own, and not by their intention, but by situation.

Her experience helped her shape an optimistic worldview.

> I have this idea that there is some sort of destiny out there that is preestablished for me, and that if I follow my path and seize the opportunities that are put in my way, then I'll arrive at this wonderful place where I'm supposed to be.

The middle daughter raised two daughters as a single parent, supported herself as a mental health professional, and remarried. She also observed that

> My mother would always just pick up my chin and say, "It's going to be all right, Mamala, and don't worry and you'll do it. You'll make it." She provided that outlook. … Yeah; I think that's where it comes from, although now things are different. But as a child, she certainly gave us the encouragement, … She's just

a wonderful catalyst for everything good. She has her faults, but I've learned so much from her. … She is the most incredible human being I've ever known.

Subsequently, she revealed:

I gained a sense that I could do anything. I just think if I make up my mind, I will overcome this, or anything that gets in my way, that's half the battle. It's a sense of survival that I have that nothing's going to knock me down.

The youngest daughter had struggled through problems in her marriage with two children and found gratification in her employment as a nurse. She also expressed an optimistic outlook on life's possibilities.

Life isn't always fair, but I truly believe you get your just reward. I have high expectations of myself, and I in turn have a very high expectation of those around me.

This family is an example of how the impact of the father's critical, negative emotions and constricted affect was effectively mediated by the nurturing and caring presence of the mother. Considering that his anger targeted every member of the family, it is particularly noteworthy that the mother managed to impart love, validation, and positive self-esteem to each daughter. They clearly saw the pressure she was under to accommodate to her husband while advocating on their behalf. They realized how she must have sacrificed her individuality for the sake of balancing the needs of husband and children. All three daughters noted the strong bond their mother had with her four sisters and with all of them. Through her example, she showed them the value of family ties, commitment to loved ones, and loyalty during difficult times. The daughters also revealed admiration for their mother's hope and resilience and for her planning during the war. Her dominant coping style of acceptance is summed up by the quotation, "That's life." While the extreme trauma experienced by both parents in the Holocaust certainly affected the children's lives, the nurture and devotion of their mother enabled them to develop in healthy ways in spite of the parental trauma.

The I Family

In the I family, a survivor and two children were interviewed. The adult daughter described her deceased father as religious, chronically depressed, very sad, anxious, "always working and never home" because of the demands of the family business. The daughter discussed her father's discomfort and avoidance in dealing with conflicts in the business.

He was afraid of confrontation, afraid it would make him sicker, so there would be more [pain] to bear. … It was unrelenting, his pain. He had emotional difficulties and was depressed and anxious over my lifetime, and he would go in and out of that, being more and less severe.

She added that her father's feelings were obvious to her due to her own heightened sensitivity to her parents' struggles in supporting the family. While she did not recall her father telling her directly that he loved her, she noted that he was very proud of her. She remembered him with fondness, stating, "He was a soft man, slight of build, thin, simple, straight, honest, and hardworking."

The daughter reflected that she was sensitive to her father's emotional vulnerability at a very young age, learned to be a caregiver like her mother, watching helplessly as her father suffered from anxiety and depression. She felt a great deal of compassion and deep connection to the three survivors in her family, which included her parents and half-brother. Her mother worked in the family's business, and when her father wanted even more help from the children in the business, she objected by saying, "The kids are not going to be in the business; they are going to have another kind of life."

The daughter described the mother as strong, courageous, affectionate, loving, and responsible; an even-tempered person who did not like anger or confrontation; totally self-sacrificing to her husband; and particularly sensitive to not causing pain to those she loved. Her mother was also a worrier, yet the daughter did not feel burdened by talking to her mother about problems.

> We're both other oriented, which is the shrink way of putting it, so we can be in the kitchen together without any conflict.

The daughter observed that she learned to be an emotional caregiver for both parents due to her father's depressions and due to the emotional burdens of the war and the enormous stress of the business.

> I could endure and be there. . . . I was trained to be there because I had to be, and I was not injured on the way, and that's very important. Being with a parent's pain is different than the pain of being injured by the parent.

With regard to the family dynamics, the daughter reported that her parents did not directly criticize her. She felt accepted and supported. Because the father's problems were never turned against the children in the family, the mother's mediating influence succeeded in protecting them from the pervasive sadness and prevented them from feeling responsible for the father's emotional distress. The message from her was "be normal."

> Their pain did not get expressed as hurting me with their burden. They didn't turn it into attacks on me, directly or indirectly, verbal or nonverbal. I got the message that I can be normal. . . . I didn't go crazy. . . . Because certainly a lot of things were painful enough to create other kinds of difficulties. And so I think I had my ways of working them through because it didn't become stuff that hurt me, that put me down, or that attacked me, or left me bleeding.

The daughter's description of what she admired in her mother was her integrity and her strong sense of identity.

> She lived in the world, worked very hard, and balanced work and family, and all this emotional heaviness.

In the daughter's lengthy interview, she gave credit to her mother's strong influence in shaping her own sensitivity to others' pain.

> At her core is someone who affirms life . . . and who was balanced between her own needs and others, those in her care. Always took care of the other.

The fact that the father in the I family did not attack his daughter as a result of his depressed emotions was very important for her. Not serving as his target allowed her to feel compassion for him and experience a positive connection with him. She felt his love even if it was not shown in a demonstrative way. His caring for the family was acknowledged, and his inability to show it because of his emotional suffering was understood with compassion.

The mother was a strong, nurturing, empathic, and validating presence. She sacrificed her personal needs in favor of the well-being of the family. The daughter admired her mother for her ability to be a role model of caring, strength, and resilience. Consequently, her father's depression did not negatively impact her self-esteem or make the daughter feel burdened by the responsibilities of being an emotional caregiver. Her sensitivity to the pain of others prepared her well for her career in psychology and for coping with life's disappointments and challenges.

As a result of her mother's caregiver efforts to mediate the impact of her father's depression, the role of caregiver was a comfortable role for the daughter. She expressed this deeply embedded quality of caring for others in her work as a psychotherapist and in her role as a mother. Her positive sense of relationships, her capacity for closeness and empathy, and the validation she received in childhood gave her the tools to achieve greater balance and mutuality in her adult relationships.

The confluence of factors described and the satisfactions that the daughter described in her adult life as a therapist and mother—both caregiving roles—raise the question of how her mother's self-sacrifice operated as a role model for the daughter. In fact, this is a question that may be asked about each of the families since the mediating parent exerted enormous effort to make sure that the children were all right, which can only be accomplished through self-sacrifice. Perhaps self-sacrifice is a common denominator when an adult helps a child overcome the difficulties of his or her environment.

The D Family

In the D family, the daughter, an only child, and the father were interviewed. The mother refused to be interviewed. Despite the many difficulties experienced during her childhood, the adult daughter described her family relationships as very positive and close. She accepted that what happened in her life came from living with a distressed mother.

> My mother has a way of giving double messages no matter what she said or did. So even when she said optimistic things, I remember this. … You could hear the terror in her voice. I remember a lot of tension. I remember how we felt worried [she and her father].

She was acutely aware of the family's struggles of coping with her mother's chronic depression and its impact on her parents' marriage after their liberation from the Holocaust. While she understood that her parents suffered significant losses of family members and experienced extreme trauma, she knew few details about their war experiences and felt protective of them. She described her role in the family.

> I always felt an obligation to be happy because of all the misery that my family endured. … But I never had any sense of guilt. [But] I wasn't [really] happy because I was carrying a lot of baggage.

She characterized her mother as emotionally reactive, and as a result her mother would withdraw into her own sadness into periods of "cutoffs" that accompanied her depression. "A very, very insecure, unsure person … just devastated by a sense of inferiority, unhappy, hysterical." She observed that her parents' marriage was often conflictual: "They struggled. … there was no negotiation. … I don't remember rational negotiation. Everything was so fraught with emotion."

At the same time, she spoke of the relationship she had with her father, whom she described as "warm, generous, calm, with a sense of humor, and was a hero to her [mother]." She viewed him as a stoic, resourceful individual who could handle adversity and provide a stabilizing presence for her, which created a sense of optimism in her life. She commented:

> My father was not afraid of death; he's not afraid of pain. He doesn't cringe. … He looks at a situation in the face. He has other weaknesses, and we all do. I'm not idealizing him, and I don't want to discuss my sense of my father's weaknesses … but he has guts and stamina.

She saw her father's influence as providing calmness and balance. He also provided "that kindness, honesty, and generosity [that were] were hallmarks of my home." The mother's dependency, emotionality, and reactivity were stabilized by the calmer, balanced caregiving of her father, who tended to shoulder the family's stressors, moderating the impact of her mother's suffering and emotional neediness. In addition, the daughter's boundary setting and values helped her maintain an empathetic connection to her family while maintaining her independence.

Her father's personal qualities as a healthy, validating, and accepting parent, combined with his ability to provide support, helped to buffer her from the adverse impact of her depressed mother. Although her mother had difficulty containing her own negative emotions, the behavior did not get expressed as harsh criticism or personal attacks on the daughter. Her mother did not directly target her as a result of her depressed mood, and the damaging aspects were diminished by her father's strongly mediating presence. Her father's behavior made it possible for her to feel greater empathy and compassion toward her parents' struggles. Consequently, she was able to separate and develop her own sense of self.

The D family raises the issue of gender and the differential impact of an impaired father versus an impaired mother. Is there a differential impact of an impaired father or mother on a son versus a daughter? Does gender matter regarding the parent who is able to successfully mitigate the impact of the impaired other parent on the child? Some research seems to point in this direction (Amato & Rivera, 1999; Cowen et al, 2005; Marsiglio et al., 2000). The reality that the daughter in the E family grew up with a depressed and often-unavailable mother raises challenges that are different from the parallel situation of the I family, in which the daughter was raised with a depressed and often-unavailable father. Gender identification seemed to play out differently in these two cases. It is often difficult for a child when the mother is not the emotional caregiver, but studies of resilient children revealed that any "positive" caregiver can fill this critical role in a child's life (Werner & Smith, 1992). The role modeling of the parents' marriage in the D family may, however, have had an impact on her adult, significant relationship. In this case, we see that the daughter's marriage failed. Nevertheless, we read of her strength and perseverance in getting through this difficult challenge, perhaps because of her father's influence as someone who was strong and afraid of nothing. To her, he was a hero, and he modeled for her the qualities of being heroic.

The daughter's independent spirit, intelligence, self-awareness, and determined pursuit of educational and professional goals helped her deal with painful personal disappointments. She confronted failure in her own marriage and the challenges of single parenthood. The adult daughter in the D family was a strong example of a person with her own strength, resilience, and ability to cope with the challenges in her life.

The V Family

In the V family, the interviews of the Holocaust survivor mother and her daughter were less rich in detail, but the pattern of a mediating parent can be discerned from the clear descriptions given by the child. The deceased husband/father was described as unhappy, distant, emotionally unexpressive, strong willed, old fashioned, and overprotective. The daughter described her father as exhibiting unpredictable outbursts of anger, a volatile temper, and moody behavior that dominated the family environment. The mother, who married her husband later in life, remarked that he was depressed much of his life, with emotional and physical health problems. He survived the Holocaust as the lone survivor of his family of origin. The mother described him as a quiet, introverted, and "not a happy person."

The mother noted that she had a long and "difficult marriage." She reported he "was a hard man to live with." The stressors of everyday life caused him a great amount of tension; he would withdraw into silence and "wouldn't talk to me for days."

The adult daughter, an only child, characterized her mother as loving, caring, open, and strong. The daughter viewed her as "a pretty tough lady" who balanced the impact of her father's verbal abuse and criticism with love and devotion. The daughter gave credit to the mother, acknowledging her as a close and solid presence that helped the daughter cope as she moved into adulthood. The mother's values performed an important role in encouraging the daughter to persevere. She grew up to be an independent, optimistic, honest, and grateful person. The daughter married and worked with her husband in a family business. She described herself as a positive presence for her own children.

> I always thought I was pretty fortunate really to be born, considering what my parents went through, met each other, and [that] I was the product of that was pretty special. I always felt pretty strongly about their situation. ... They really had to struggle with making a living, and they struggled to have a happy life, and it's hard to relate to that, because life has been pretty easy for me. But knowing what they went through makes me appreciate life more. ... I'm sure it made me stronger, too. I just can't let myself get upset about anything in life because I saw my parents having to be strong about life, too.

The V family illustrates the mediating influence of the mother, whom the daughter described as her "best friend" and "role model." The daughter attributed her father's emotional despair to the horrors he witnessed during the war. She was compassionate about her father's suffering while keeping her distance from his anger. Her mother protected her consciously and deliberately, leaving her relatively unscathed by her father.

The daughter's story raises the issue of how and if relationship patterns in one's family of origin are repeated in the nuclear family. Due to the mother's successful mediation, in this case the pattern of the parents' troubled marriage did not repeat itself. The daughter worked with her husband in a family business, and instead of repeating the pattern of her parents' difficult employment relationship, she and her husband functioned together very well. The mediating parent not only had a positive impact on the psychological development of her daughter but also profoundly affected the quality of relationships in the next generation.

Discussion

In the four case studies of the W, I, D, and V families, the narrative descriptions reveal a parental pattern in which the emotional difficulties of one parent, which could have fostered serious problems in the child, are juxtaposed against the mediating effect of the other parent's love and nurture. As a result, the mediating parent facilitated healthy development in the child.

In summary, our first finding is the observation of the mediating parent dynamic. It seems that the nurturing parent not only must exhibit many of the positive five factors of the quality of family dynamics paradigm necessary for positive psychological development—closeness, empathy, validation, expressive of positive emotion, and open communication—but also be willing to overfunction and thereby sacrifice some measure of "self" for the sake of the children (see Chapter 6 for a full discussion of the paradigm). The parent, we conclude from these examples, must be able to establish a close and positive attachment and must be able to express love and affection while modulating the negative reactivity that may be generated by the difficulty of the situation. Limitations in any of these areas would make it even more difficult to compensate for the negative input from the other parent.

Children who are "fortunate" enough to have a mediating parent report gratitude and appreciation to the parent who helped them cope with the emotionally distressed parent. That a child can grow up in a household with a depressed or angry parent and yet feel positive about self and attached to others is an important observation. The emotional and psychological dynamics that contribute to this outcome incorporate the elements of positive parenting with the challenges of coping and adaptation.

Our second finding is that the extent of the severity of targeting the child by the emotionally distressed parent is critical to the health of the child regardless of the quality of that parent–child relationship. If the child is only in proximity to the parent's difficulties but not targeted by the parent, the child is freer to develop an empathic bond with the emotionally distressed parent. This occurs even though the parent's ability to securely attach is compromised by his or her poor mental health. It would appear that the greater the capacity for mediation on the part of the other parent, the stronger the bond that can develop between the child and the emotionally distressed parent.

In comparison, as discussed in Chapter 8, the analysis of the negative and mixed families point to a pattern in which the child targeted by the emotions of a troubled parent is at much greater risk for long-lasting negative effects into adulthood. The child not only grows up in a damaging emotional environment but also feels personally rejected and blamed. In these cases, there is little room for an empathic understanding of the parent in any way other than an intellectual understanding that the parent has been severely traumatized. The child is torn between loyalty to a victimized parent and the psychological need for distance and emotional safety. These are the tragic cases in which the survivor parent is twice victimized, first by the perpetrator and then by the abandonment of children who cannot tolerate the emotional negativity related to the parent's mental state. In families in which there is consistent targeting of a child, the other, healthier parent is going to be less effective in compensating for the adverse effects even when there is great effort to protect the child (see Chapter 8 for a full discussion of this pattern).

Our third finding is that the capacity for empathy is influenced by the extent of positive parenting that the child experiences even in an environment influenced by the problems of an emotionally distressed parent. The children of survivors who received more positive parenting revealed a greater capacity to handle their parents' difficulties with compassion than did children of survivors who experienced more negative parenting. In the first case, the children often praised their parents for being role models of love, courage, and resilience. In the second case, the children often talked about feeling emotionally burdened.

Acknowledging that attachment style is codetermined by the relationship between a child and each parent raises questions not yet answered by existing theory. Johnson (2003) acknowledged that attachment styles are often mixed because they are the result of "qualitatively different relationships with different caregivers" (p. 10). Siegel (1999) clearly acknowledged the contribution of each parent (caregiver) to the attachment capacity of the developing child. He stated, "In particular, these patterns of brain function—these states of mind—become activated within the context of a specific relationship. One child can have distinct attachment strategies for each parent" (p. 77). This observation predicts the development of distinct attachment strategies within the same individual, but there is no existing language within the literature to describe these "combinations" that meld into "mixed" attachment patterns, causing inconsistencies in significant relationships. These questions have even greater significance in the context of a child raised by an emotionally distressed parent and a more stable parent, both of whom are survivors of extreme trauma, as our four case studies have demonstrated. In these cases, divergent parenting assumes different levels of meaning since both parents are experiencing the aftereffects of their traumatic exposure on a personal level and in the marriage. In addition, the emotional tone of the family environment is often influenced by residual feelings of anxiety, sadness, and grief.

The question of nature versus nurture is significant when addressing the intergenerational impact of divergent parenting styles. What is learned behavior and what is an expression of a child's genetic predisposition is an important question when attempting to disentangle the effects of divergent parenting and intergenerational transmission of trauma. According to Siegel and Hartzell (2003), the capacity for secure attachment is primarily shaped by relationship experiences and not genetics. Their perspective points to the dominant impact of "nurture" on a child's development, specifically in terms of attachment styles, self-esteem, and identity (Fosha, 2000; Greenberg, 2002; Hesse, 1999; Luborsky & Crits-Cristoph, 1990). This emphasizes even further the critical nature of parenting relationships in the development of the child.

Another dimension of attachment important for the understanding of the qualitative findings is "earned secure attachment." This speaks to the phenomenon that even when an individual grows up in an unsupportive household, it is possible for that person to become a securely attached adult through various routes of self-growth and therapy (Byng-Hall, 1999, p. 626). Siegel and Hartzell (2003) described earned secure attachment as the result of therapy, mindfulness, and good attachments later in life.

The qualitative investigation of divergent parenting revealed the reality that for some Holocaust survivor families, the healthier parent has the potential to mediate the negative impact of the less-healthy parent. The TTP data demonstrated that from the vantage point of children raised by an emotionally distressed parent and a mediating parent, the latter was crucial to their well-being. In addition to formulating the mediating parent dynamic, this research points to the importance of focusing on the interaction between each parent and each child when studying family adaptation to stressful experiences and traumatic events. The assessment of the overall impact of the parental subsystem (or caregiver subsystem) obscures the individual contribution of each parent to the child's development and therefore obscures the positive influence of the healthier parent.

The potent impact of a mediating parent should not be underestimated and needs to be understood if the field of marriage and family therapy is to truly comprehend how families and individuals cope with extreme stress. Somewhere in the mix of family dynamics and life events, as negative as they may appear to the observer, is the possibility of a counterbalancing influence that provides positive nurture, closeness, empathy, validation, and positive affective expression. To whatever extent these qualities are present, in either parent, the child experiences elements of secure attachment that offer hope for healthy adult attachments. If these qualities are absent, the child is vulnerable to the negative effects of relationships characterized by distance, narcissism or self-centeredness, criticism (rejection), negative affective expression, and closed communication. Growing up in this kind of interpersonal environment foreshadows emotionally distressed adult attachments.

When the healthier parent succeeds in exerting the primary influence on the child and overcomes the influence of the more troubled parent, the former is clearly functioning as a "mediating" parent. The strength of the impact is determined by the intensity of the relationship with the healthier parent and the extent to which that parent is willing and able to intercede on behalf of the child. The mediating parent needs to assert emotional dominance over the negatively charged interactions with the other parent if he or she is to achieve greater influence on the child and buffer any long-term negative effects.

The adult children in this chapter clearly described the mediating parent as the healthier parent of the two. They attributed to this parent the successful compensation for any adverse family dynamics through his or her loving attitude and positive support. The mediating parents described in these families not only had the capacity for caring and attachment but also perceived the importance of compensating for the negative impact of the emotionally distressed parent. Often, the healthier parent assumed a supportive role with the emotionally distressed spouse in addition to the mediating role with the children. This may be one explanation for why the marriages in the successful mediation group were described in more positive terms than in the negative and mixed groups. The mediating parent sacrificed his or her own needs in service of the healthy development of the children. This unrelenting focus had its rewards in the subsequent mental health of the children. Mediation, it seems from these examples, often requires significant devotion to have an impact great enough to compensate for the distant, critical, emotionally negative, and closed parent. The self-reflective function of the more nurturing parent helps the child come to some understanding of the emotionally distressed parent. By offering the child a context within which to comprehend the more troubled relationship with the other parent, the child can cope more effectively with this reality. Fonagy et al. (1995) conducted extensive research on the relationship between attachment, psychological functioning, and resilience. They found consistent evidence to support the conclusion that "the ability to reflect promotes resilience, robs traumatic stressors of their pathogenic force, and has the power to interrupt the intergenerational transmission of predisposition to pathology" (p. 255).

The success of the mediating parent was also identified by the five positive factors of the quality of family dynamics paradigm (see Chapter 6) that the mediating parent demonstrated in the interactions with the children. In addition to expressing appreciation for the caring and love given to them from the mediating parent, the children attributed the positive quality of their adult experiences to the guidance and nurture they received during childhood. The interviews clearly revealed that the children were aware of how different their lives would have been had they not received the care and loving attention of the parent who exhibited the capacity to prioritize and advocate for their needs. In summary, the mediating parent dynamic emerged from the analysis of the divergent parent–child relationships. The adult children described their parents as acting "like a bridge over troubled waters." This phrase captures the experience of being lifted out of the negative environment and protected from the pain below by the support of the "bridge." It reflects the sentiments of those children who found themselves fortunate enough to have the support of a mediating parent. The adult children reported that it was the relationships with the mediating parent that gave them the psychological tools to feel good about themselves, to engage in healthy adult relationships, to successfully nurture their children, and to succeed in life.

Case Examples From Clinical Practice

The following two clinical cases describe the mediating parent dynamic. These cases possess similar emotional and relational dynamics to the families portrayed through vignettes from the life histories conducted by the TTP. In therapy, knowing how these dynamics worked in the childhood of the client was important for the therapist's understanding of the relational dynamics that were enacted in the therapy session.

Since these are current therapy cases, the clients are still working on relationship problems and personal challenges in their lives. Therefore, the long-term impact of divergent parenting, particularly the influence of the problematic parent–child relationship, is more apparent because it is often a major focus in treatment. The successful mediating families in the community sample interviewed by TTP did not emphasize the residual negative impact of divergent parenting either due to the mediating parent's success in helping the child cope with the negative impact or because the long-term negative impact had been experienced as manageable by the adult child. This marks the difference between a clinical sample and a community sample. In a clinical sample, the problem areas are understood to be at the forefront.

In each of these cases, the therapist clearly observed the developmental contribution of the more positive parent to the client, providing a source of psychological strength that would not have been observed had there not been successful mediation. The core of strength imparted by the mediating parent enabled the therapist to more effectively help the client work with the residual negative impact of the distressed parent. It also allowed the therapist to work more effectively with other problems in the client's life.

The first case example is representative of a number of cases presented by the therapists with whom we consulted. Change the nature of the distressed parent's psychological disturbance, change the gender of the parent who is distressed, hold constant the efforts of the other parent to help the child cope, and you have a template for the childhoods of many clients who come to therapy. A number of cases that came up in collegial conversation fit the overall description of mediating parent with similar dynamics but different facts. It is important to note when discussing situations in which a parent is psychologically distressed, that cases involving physical and sexual abuse would probably not fall into the category of mediating parent. The experiences of physical and sexual abuse seem much less amenable to mediation due to the nature of the injury inflicted on the child, although positive caretaking from any source offers emotional refuge for the child. Often, we have found that the other parent in cases of child abuse is intentionally unaware, afraid himself or herself, or relatively impotent in his or her impact. We assume that the possibility of sufficient mediation to compensate for the abuse would be unlikely in such circumstances.

Case Example: Competence and Independence

This case was recommended by the therapist as an example of a mediating parent. It is a long-term case that has addressed many issues related to the client's marriage, work situation, and family of origin. It started out as marital therapy and progressed to individual therapy for both partners. The client's husband was described as devoted to her, but he refused to have a child with her when they married because he already had children from a prior marriage and could not accept having another child. This was a source of pain and disappointment for the client and brought them into therapy. She was committed to her marriage but at times found it emotionally empty. The marital therapy focused on communication and connection. The therapeutic work on the client's family of origin is the focus of this case summary. The client reported that the father did an exemplary job in helping her cope with her mother, who suffered from a mental illness as well as with her own physical health issues. His consistent, positive support enabled her to become competent and successful in the world.

The client suffered from a condition that required extensive medical care. This in and of itself was a significant challenge in her life, which she described as something she was in control of as an adult due to her father's constant support. Because of her mother's mental illness, it was her father who encouraged her and helped her throughout her life. His message to her was that, in spite of her medical condition, she could do anything she wanted to do, and he succeeded in helping her feel like a normal person. Her mother was emotionally volatile and often verbally abusive. The mother yelled at the client when she was a child that the client was ugly and that no one would ever marry her. Her father's support served to limit the impact of these messages. A constant source of anxiety for the client was the reality that she never knew what kind of mood her mother would be in when she returned from school. Her father encouraged her to handle her mother's tirades by not reacting and to try to figure out what disturbed her mother so that she could avoid these situations. She followed these directives and succeeded in keeping her mother's emotional tirades at bay, responding more strongly to her father's loving support.

The client's father was described as kind and enthusiastic to a fault. All the siblings agreed that he was a superior man who helped them feel good. The children agreed that he did a good job of parenting. The client took on his role in the family and even though she was the youngest, she was the matriarch of the family. She assumed this role early in her adult life since her father died when she was in her 20s. The therapist described the client as viewing her father as a saint, and that she adopted the expectation of acting even more saintly.

The exploration of her inner emotional life thus was difficult for the client. A breakthrough for her was the realization that her emotional life had been contained to "handle" her mother, and that her wish to be more saintly and her position as the matriarch felt natural to her on one level, but that inside she was beginning to feel the burden of these roles and the absence of other emotions.

The awareness of the price paid for having a father who helped her cope with her medical issues and her mother's illness set off a complex set of feelings. She came to recognize the irony that her father, who helped her have a successful life, also modeled the avoidance of feelings. To address her marriage and her residual family feelings, she had to acknowledge the angry feelings toward her mother for the verbal abuse and emotional neglect she experienced. She also needed to acknowledge feelings about her father that were not exclusively centered on gratitude. The client came to understand that she absorbed the messages from her father about normalcy to an extreme, and that she translated them into the need to be better than normal. During therapy, she recognized this as a burden in her life, and that she needed to relinquish some control to experience a range of feelings and reactions to gain the ability to experience normal feelings in response to day-to-day events.

By exploring the dynamics of her family relationships on a deeper level, she was able to realize that along with the positive support, she was also influenced by her father's coping style of avoidance of feelings. This became her coping style as well. In fact, she reported never crying throughout her life. Therapy probed the emotional level of her childhood experiences, which then opened the door to her emotional life. This became an important growth experience for her.

The mediating parent role in this case was important to give this client a positive foundation in her psychological development. It helped her succeed in various capacities in her life. She felt "normal," which would never have happened without her father's strong resolve to help her fulfill her potential and live a life of her choosing. However, the relative success she achieved in her life depended on her ability to contain her emotions. Now, in therapy, with support, she could explore her emotions, trusting that she had a firm foundation that will sustain her.

A common theme for therapists to address with clients with a distressed parent is the exploration of suppressed feelings related to the pain caused by this parent. The combination of mediating parenting and empathy for the troubled parent often masks these feelings until such time in adulthood when therapy related to other problems provides the opportunity for self-examination. In the case outlined, the father dealing with an emotionally impaired wife and a child burdened with significant medical issues was challenged to find a coping strategy that was effective for him. Often, the coping style of the parent becomes a role model for the child, and on an unconscious level. This is similar to the H family from TTP, for whom self-sacrifice was modeled for the daughter by the mediating parent. In this case, as with the H daughter, the internalization of the healthy, mediating parent's coping style has had mostly beneficial effects, but as an extreme position, it is bound to cause problems as well.

Case Example: It Is Never Too Late

The next case is an example of the mediating parent who had a partial impact in childhood and became more important in adulthood. The client credited her father for helping her create a different family from that of her childhood.

The client, in her early 40s, returned to individual treatment as recommended by her teenage daughter's therapist due to a number of stressors related to her daughter's struggles with developmental and neurological deficits. The client blamed herself for needing help on how best to be an advocate for her daughter with medical professionals during many years of in-home counseling and day and residential treatment programs. The therapy enabled her to reflect on how she coped with the crises over the previous 10 years involving her daughter's care.

Her exploration of family-of-origin problems raised the issue of conflict avoidance and what it was like to be the youngest daughter of eight children. Her father's violent temper was directed toward her older brothers, and she was often "in the middle," protecting her brothers from her father's rages. She could get away with this because she was "her father's favorite ... since he didn't hit girls." Her mother was described as angry, distant, reactive, and overwhelmed by the family's financial problems, which made it impossible for her to focus on the welfare and safety of her children. In addition, she was "scary, quick to criticize, screamed a lot, always upset, and not nurturing." The compensating relationships in the family were with two older siblings, who were protective and comforting toward her despite the insecure and chaotic family environment.

When her father became disabled and could no longer work, the daughter became his primary caregiver. Her mother was then forced to return to work. The father brought nurturing qualities to his relationship with her that she was not receiving from her mother. The client described her father as "making me feel special, always taking my side, nurturing and proud of me." When her mother worked weekends, her father "took good care of me," and the qualities of the relationship with her father seemed to buffer her from the sense of complete abandonment.

As the client grew older, her father behaved in a more loving, caring, and dependable fashion when she asked him to babysit for her two children until she returned from work. She depended on him to care for them, and he was helpful and reliable. The consistent caring relationship with her father, even though it occurred when she was already an adult, buffered her from the feelings of abandonment by her mother. While she understood her role in her family of origin as that of "trying to be good," she also felt like "an outsider that didn't fit in." As part of her development, she learned to validate her own experience and "stand up for herself." As an adult and parent, she advocated on behalf of her children, and with her attachment to her father and her own resilience, she affirmed her strength as a positive and loving parent in her nuclear family. Although this does not exactly follow the pattern of mediation in childhood described in previous vignettes and case examples, it does describe how affirmation and support can have an impact even for an adult, who benefits from a parent's nurturing support related to current life struggles. In this case, the father took care of the client's children and kept them safe while she was at work. This offered her a great deal of security, which compensated for the many years when her father was not a nurturing or a reliable care-taker. The foundation of being the favorite daughter who used her status to protect her brothers may have set the stage for the improved relationship later in her life. She could have turned away from her father, but there was enough of a foundation of positive con-nection that enabled the client not only to let him into her adult life but also to place him in charge of her children.

In this case, Rubin's work, *The Transcendent Child* (1996), offers insight into children who seem to overcome adversity by choice. The client described herself "as an outsider that didn't fit in." Rubin described multiple examples in which individuals in troubled families felt as if they did not fit in and made the decision to search for a healthier way to live. Rubin suggested that the possibility of another way to shape their lives enables children to choose a better life. This describes the last case, although the client also experienced a relationship with her father that improved significantly over the years and that in her adulthood became a significant source of help and support. The therapist considered this an example of mediation. The negativity of her mother was rejected in favor of a loving connection with her children, which the father helped the client achieve. In this case, parental mediation came later in life. Byng-Hall (1999) pointed out, specifi-cally in terms of earned secure attachment, that "the influence of early attachment or later relationships can be modified" (p. 626), in this case for the better.

Implications for Clinical Practice

The importance of exploring each parent–child relationship is not only relevant for the understanding of child development but also has signifi-cant implications for marital and family therapy. In couple therapy, doing a comprehensive genogram and attachment history of the family of origin during the early phase of treatment would reveal the presence or absence of a mediating parent in one partner's or both partners' childhood. Knowing this reality would provide the therapist with the knowledge, irrespective of the problems presented in the therapy, that this client has a secure founda-tion and a reservoir of potential for positive coping and growth, in spite of adverse life circumstances.

In family therapy, it would be especially important when treating chil-dren to assess their relationship with each parent separately. Asking chil-dren to describe the quality of the relationship with each parent along with asking about parental styles of discipline, decision-making approaches, conflict management, parental roles, and communication styles between the parents will yield a picture of how each parent interacts with the child. Eliciting the nature of the interaction with each parent separately will reveal possibilities for healthy interactions that can be encouraged by the therapist for the sake of the child. It is often difficult to influence both parents in their interactions with their children, but even if one parent responds by learning to be more empathic, supportive, and validating, there is hope that the child can benefit from the effective positive influence of this parent. In such a case, it may be possible, assuming that the more negative parent does not "target" the child, that the positive parent can mediate the adverse impact on the child of the distressed parent, and that the child can actually learn to be empathic toward the parent who is suffering emotionally.

Both to assess the parent–child relationship and to encourage parents to improve their parenting practices for the child's well-being, the quality of family dynamics paradigm is useful. As discussed in previous chapters, the paradigm consists of the five dynamics of closeness-distance, validation-criticism, empathy-self-centeredness, open communication-closed communication, and expressive of positive emotions-expressive of negative emotions. A therapist may assess each parent-child dyad according to the five-factor paradigm to identify useful resources and how the relationships need to improve.

If the parent capable of more positive interactions with the child is willing to take on more responsibility, it seems possible to foster the child's resilience and growth through effective parental mediation. Expecting that both parents grow into positive roles with their child is of course the goal, but when this is not realistic, it is still valuable to help the child through the efforts of one parent. Conducting this assessment early in therapy informs the therapist about the attachment potential of each client in the couple or the family and contributes to the development of an appropriate treatment strategy. Supporting a mediating parent is an effective therapeutic strategy. When a mediating parent is effective, a child can truly be nurtured toward healthy growth and development.

References

Amato, P., & Rivera, F. (1999). Paternal involvement and children's behavior problems. *Journal of Marriage and the Family, 61*, 375–384.

Barber, B.K., Stolz, H.E., Olsen, J.A., & Maughan, S.L. (2005). Parental support, psychological control, and behavioral control: Assessing relevance across time, method, and culture. *Monographs of the Society for Research in Child Development, 70*, 1–151.

Byng-Hall, J. (1999). Family and couple therapy: Toward greater security. In J. Cassidy & P. R. Shaver (Eds.), *Handbook of attachment: Theory, research and clinical applications* (pp. 625–648). New York: Guilford Press.

Cassano, M., Adrian, M., Veits, G., & Zeman, J. (2006). The inclusion of fathers in the empirical investigation of child psychopathology: An update. *Journal of Clinical Child and Adolescent Psychology, 35*, 583–589.

Cowan, P. A., Cowan, C. P., Ablow, J., Johnson, V. K., & Measelle, J. (2005). *The family context of parenting in children's adaptation to elementary school.* Mahwah, NJ: Erlbaum.

Cowan, P.A., Cowan, C., & Knox, V. (Fall 2010). Marriage and fatherhood programs. In S. McLanahan, R. Haskins, C. Paxton, & I. Sawhill (Eds.), *Fragile families: The Future of Children,* (pp. 205–230) 20/2. Princeton University-Brookings Institute.

Fauber, R., Forehand, R., Thomas, A. M., & Wierson, M. (1990). A mediational model of the impact of marital conflict on adolescent adjustment in intact and divorced families: The role of disrupted parenting. *Child Development, 61*, 1112–1123.

Fonagy, P., Steele, M., Steele, H., Leigh, T., Kennedy, R., Matoon, G., et al. (1995). Attachment, the reflective self and borderline states. In S. Goldberg, R. Muir, & J. Kerr (Eds.), *Attachment theory: Social, developmental and clinical perspectives* (pp. 233–278). Hillsdale, NJ: Analytic Press.

Fosha, D. (2000). *The transforming power of affect.* New York: Basic Books.

Greenberg, L. S. (2002). *Emotionally focused therapy: Coaching clients to work through their feelings.* Washington, DC: American Psychological Association.

Hesse, E. (1999). The Adult Attachment Interview: Historical and current perspectives. In J. Cassidy and P. R. Shaver (Eds.), *Handbook of attachment: Theory, research and clinical applications* (pp. 395–433). New York: Guilford Press.

Jacob, T., & Johnson, S. L. (1997). Parent-child interaction among depressed fathers and mothers: Impact on child functioning. *Journal of Family Psychology, 11*, 391–409.

Johnson, S. M. (2003). Introduction to attachment: A therapist's guide to primary relationships and their renewal. In S. M. Johnson & V. E. Whiffen (Eds.), *Attachment processes in couple and family therapy* (3–17). New York: Guilford Press.

Keller, M. B., Beardslee, W. R., Dorer, D. J., Lavori, P. W., Samuelson, H., & Klerman, G. R. (1986). Impact of severity and chronicity of parental affective illness on adaptive functioning and psychopathology in children. *Archives of General Psychiatry, 43*, 930–937.

Lee, S., Bellamy, J., & Guterman, N. (2009). Fathers, physical child abuse, and neglect: Advancing the knowledge base. *Child Maltreatment, 14*, 227–231.

Low, S. M., & Stocker, C. (2005). Family functioning and children's' adjustment: Associations among parents' depressed mood, marital hostility, parent-child hostility and children's' adjustment. *Journal of Family Psychology, 19*, 394–403.

Luborsky, L., & Crits-Cristoph, P. (1990). *Understanding transference: The core conflictual relationships theme method.* New York: Basic Books.

Marsiglio, W., Amato, P., Day, R. D., & Lamb, M. E. (2000). Scholarship on fatherhood in the 1990s and beyond. *Journal of Marriage and the Family, 62*, 1173–1191.

Pedersen, S., & Revenson, T. A. (2005). Parental illness, family functioning and adolescent well-being: A family ecology framework to guide research. *Journal of Family Psychology, 19*, 404–409.

Phares, V., & Compas, B. E. (1992). The role of father in child and adolescent psychopathology: Make room for daddy. *Psychological Bulletin, 111,* 387–412.

Phares, V., Fields, S., Kamboukos, D., & Lopez, E. (2005). Still looking for poppa. *American Psychologist, 60,* 735–736.

Podietz, L., Belmont, H., Shapiro, M., Zwerling, I., Ficher, I., Eisenstein, T., et al. (1984). Engagement in families of Holocaust survivors. *Journal of Marriage and Family Therapy, 10,* 43–51.

Raizman, L. (2001). *The role of the mediating parent in intergenerational transmission.* Paper presented at Council for Relationships conference on Transcending Trauma, Philadelphia. December 2001.

Rubin, L. B. (1996). *The transcendent child: Tales of triumph over the past.* New York: HarperCollins Books.

Siegel, D. J. (1999). *The developing mind.* New York: Guilford Press.

Siegel, D. J., & Hartzell, M. (2003). *Parenting from the inside out.* New York: Tarcher Putnam.

Unger, D., Brown, M, Tressell, P., & McLeod, L. E. (2000). Interparental conflict and adolescent depressed mood: The role of family functioning. *Child Psychiatry and Human Development, 31,* 23–41.

Walsh, F. (1998). *Strengthening family resilience.* New York: Guilford Press.

Werner, E. E., & Smith, R. S. (1992). *Overcoming the odds: High risk children from birth to adulthood.* Ithaca, NY: Cornell University Press.

PART IV

Intergenerational Transmission to the Children of Survivors

CHAPTER 10

"The Elephant in the Room"

Survivors' Holocaust Communication With Their Children

SHERYL PERLMUTTER BOWEN, JULIET I.
SPITZER, and EMILIE S. PASSOW

A central paradox is survivors' abiding wish to tell their story (primarily as a debt of survival to those who were lost) and their despairing belief that it is, at heart, untellable.

—Wajnryb, 1999, p. 85

To speak of horror endured by Jewish survivors of Nazi persecution is difficult. It is an important yet challenging task to move beyond the details of Holocaust facts and experiences to explore the relationships that were constructed out of the ashes. Yet another challenge is to examine how we mine the memories and excavate the processes of making meaning of life after the Holocaust. If these experiences are ultimately "untellable," survivors "cannot share what they have experienced with others, [and they] experience themselves at a distance as well as a relationship of being excluded in relation to those who themselves did not experience something similar" (Rosenthal, 2003, p. 924). Yet, some do talk about what happened to them in the Holocaust.

As we know, patterns of family communication have an impact on family dynamics and the tenor of a household (Cowan & Cowan, 2009; van Ijzendoorn, 1992). In the case of Holocaust survivors, some shared pieces of their stories, while others treated the Holocaust like the proverbial "elephant in the room" that no one talked about. In this chapter, we first offer a brief review of the literature regarding Holocaust communication in families and then describe the data analyzed for this project. We identify three groups of motives for sharing Holocaust memories and several motives survivors have had for choosing to be silent. Finally, we point to some implications of this work.

Many scholars, among them Adelman (1995); Epstein (1979); Halik, Rosenthal, and Pattison (1990); Eitinger and Major (1993); Mor (1990); Robinson and Winnik (1981); and Sagi-Schwartz et al. (2003), have studied parents and children of the Holocaust and have revealed that similar social and emotional patterns seem to occur across many Holocaust families: parental overprotection; parental overinvolvement, leading to problems of individuating for their children; children feeling different because of their immigrant parents; difficulty expressing anger at parents because of the extent of their suffering; and overidentification as a way for the children to accept their parents. In reviewing literature on this subject, Waxman (2000) revealed both transmission of trauma and subsequent symptomology, as well as resilience and strength in survivors and their offspring.

Okner and Flaherty (1988) also cited literature reflecting differential effects of communication, both positive and negative, depending on the amount of detail, the frequency, the style of reporting on the part of the Holocaust survivor, and the age of the children when they heard their parents' stories. It is clear that no one pattern of communication occurs, and there is no single pattern of effects; however, Eitinger and Major (1993) noted that "children benefit most when there is not too much communication and yet the Holocaust is not a taboo subject" (p. 634). Wiseman and Barber (2008) found negative effects from a lack of communication about the Holocaust:

The reasons survivors give for talking or keeping silent about the Holocaust defies simple interpretation. Similarly, the impact on their children of being or not being told can vary widely. Moreover, decisions about talking about their experience often were not either/or situations, but also included choices about whom to tell and in how much detail. Frequently, the survivors' concern about the impact of their spoken memories on the family contributed to these decisions. In turn, children of survivors (COSs), whether directly told of their parents' traumatic experiences or not, construct some image of what happened to their parents. Hirsch (1996) called these constructs "postmemory":

Postmemory characterizes the experience of those who grow up dominated by narratives that preceded their birth, whose own belated stories are displaced by the stories of the previous generation, shaped by traumatic events that can be neither fully understood nor re-created. (p. 662)

As in all families, COSs are imbued with cultural transmission through what their parents say or what they obviously omit. The socialized messages (Wajnryb, 2001) can include dicta that carry more weight even than a regional or family heritage. These children, for example, often recall being told precepts such as, "Eat, you never know where your next meal is coming from," or "They can never take knowledge away from you." Such statements are both cautionary and existential in nature and reflect the traumatic experiences of the parent as well as the message they want to emphasize to the next generation about priorities the children should adopt.

Sometimes, the details of the parent's liberation, emigration, and beginning life anew are glossed over in deference to the importance and sheer magnitude of what the survivor remembers about the Holocaust. In many survivor families, children cling to any fragments of their parents' memories, especially those children who have grown up without grandparents. Some of these immigrants endured unspeakable traumas in labor and death camps, on death marches, or in hiding; in watching strangers, neighbors, or family members killed before their eyes or chosen for the "other" line, the line that led them to their deaths. Nevertheless, many survivors of the Holocaust went on to rebuild their lives, marry, have children, make a living, and grow old. Some of these immigrants talked incessantly to their children about their lives in Europe; some never talked at all (Bowen & Spitzer, 2005).

Wajnryb and others have noted the silences and allusions to traumas of the Holocaust that were not fully discussed in a linear fashion when children were in their parents' households. The stories that the second generation received were "deeply embedded in a relational and emotional context which gave them a meaning far greater than the words alone contained. Silence and semi-silence, indeed the suppression of language, served to transmit messages as well" (Wajnryb, 2001, p. 35). Some children received the message that they were not allowed to ask direct questions, or that some topics were taboo in the household. Interviews from the Transcending Trauma Project (TTP) are replete with examples of the nonverbal cues that might trigger depression, tears, or withdrawal in a survivor parent, of which the children were overtly or subliminally aware. Moreover, these occasions, which included not only sad events such as the anniversary of a family member's death but also happy ones such as the birthday of a third-generation grandchild, paradoxically awakened feelings of loss and even despair.

In some cases, survivors who were silent with their families talked to other people, either fellow survivors or even general audiences, when the survivors agreed or volunteered to be public speakers. In other cases, survivors shared their Holocaust experiences with their family members but did not talk to outsiders. In still other cases, survivors were open about their experiences with both families and the public. Finally, there were survivors who chose complete silence.

Methodology

For this study, we looked at a subset of the data from the TTP, specifically statements from our interviews with survivors and their families indicating whether and why they talked about the Holocaust. We analyzed 31 of the 50 sets of interviews that included at least one survivor parent and at least one COS, for a total of 87 interviews. We arrived at the 31 sets through the following process: In approaching the TTP database, we first considered whether the families interviewed had open or closed communication climates, as judged by the triads who had analyzed each family group and as had been reported in the synopses (see Chapter 3 for a fuller explanation of the triads). We then searched the transcripts of the interviews to discover whether the interviews included any mention of sharing or avoiding talking about the survivors' Holocaust experiences. Only 31 of the 50 intergenerational sets fit these criteria. Then, the statements about communication were coded using a list of reasons for sharing and a separate list for silence.

The research team initially had generated lists of motives from a broader knowledge of our interviews and from more general Holocaust literature. We modified these lists inductively as we coded the data. Although survivors did not always identify their own motives, their interview narratives directed our inferences. We also examined the narratives of COSs based on transcripts and synopses for their reports of communication within their families and coded any statements that reflected motives. We should point out that some survivors and children noted multiple motives.

As discussed in Chapter 3, interviewers asked questions that often invited nuanced responses from the interviewees. Circular or triangulated questioning of family members across interviews attempted to discern what each family member knew about the survivors' prewar and war experiences. Some direct questions were asked to clarify how the respondent perceived the communication about the Holocaust in the home. In fact, asking different family members about one another has been one way of discovering how the stories have been told (or not told). Questions were posed in various ways to elicit not only recall but also deeper insight concerning the interviewee, if possible.

As we continued to work with the motives that emerged from the data, we noted whether the motives were directed primarily toward another or at self. For example, as we discuss further in this chapter, sometimes survivors shared their stories so that their children would work for social justice and "never again" allow a Holocaust to take place. Sometimes, the survivors spoke so that they themselves would feel known or would be recognized as human. We also observed a tension between emotional expression and the desire for emotional protection that created another layer in the motives for sharing as well as motives for remaining silent about the trauma of the Holocaust.

Finally, we examined what parents and children said about their general communication patterns and those regarding the Holocaust to see which communication patterns correlated with positive, negative, or mixed family dynamics. These evaluations were rooted in the quality of family dynamics paradigm and the patterns of family dynamics that the research team had developed, discussed more fully in Chapters 8 and 9, respectively. These constructs, we should note here, include an empathy-self-centeredness scale. What is significant about these observations is that they allow us to see potential dilemmas some survivors experienced in deciding whether or how to relate their experiences and to whom.

Initially, as reported by Bowen and Spitzer (2005), we identified 10 motives. With further work, we saw that these motives could be condensed into three major categories. First, there are those sharings that were more fact based, whether self- or other oriented. The other-oriented motives were to memorialize or honor the past or simply to respond to questions. The self-oriented motives simply revealed more about the survivor self.

The second grouping of motives for communicating involved those that had a lesson or a clear emotional loading. These included teaching to remember the facts, fulfilling an obligation to a dead family member or important person in the survivor's life, instilling courage or character development, encouraging preparedness, or nurturing gratitude and appreciation for the advantages of the present. The motives for sharing in this second category, we noticed, are all other related and span the entire chronological spectrum: present, past, and future,

Finally, the third category of sharings was those that seemed excessive to the listener and did not take the other into consideration. In these cases, the survivor was "stuck" or trapped in time (and therefore focused on the past) and wanted to share to "unload." In the following sections, we explain the motives for sharing in each of the three categories more specifically, with support from many quotations taken directly from the interviews.

Motives for Sharing

Telling the Story

Memorializing Perhaps the most prominent motive that children and parents gave for talking about the Holocaust was to honor the past by remembering. Sometimes, conversation memorialized a specific person or a lost way of life. Olivia, a female COS, put it this way:

> My mother described to me in a lot of detail about Auschwitz and what it was like and what it looked like. She would volunteer information without my asking. If something would remind her of something, she would tell me. Sometimes I would ask a question, but more often it just came up. She thought it was important for me to know.

This family was generally open, and in addition to taking the initiative in starting a discussion about the Holocaust, the survivor mother responded to direct questions.

At times, such talk can appear to be sheer nostalgia, and the agenda can vary from wanting to relate history to sharing personal experience with others. According to COS Isabel,

> They used to tell when I was a little kid, like war stories. All their friends would be Holocaust survivors, and like other parents play golf or tennis, or went to the movies, my parents told stories.

Similarly, a male COS reported:

> He used to always tell us stories, when we were little before we went to sleep. He used to tell us stories, either about the war or after the war, about his childhood. … It's an incredible experience, it's incredible to hear it, and it's incredible in the sense to be part of it. … It's great to listen to it. And he always said he was going to tape all these stories and so forth, and he never really got to it yet. Because, slowly, slowly, there are not many more people from that era to talk about it. Like yes, I am a part of it, but it's impossible to have all that information that he has, and to pass it on. (Karl)

Implicit here is the emphasis on the growth that one can experience by witnessing, transmitting, and receiving the information. When the information is conveyed naturally, the listener may be able to bond with the teller and create continuity of memory.

Response to Direct Questions   As discussed, the pace at which parents and children talked about the Holocaust varied tremendously. Some survivors only responded to their children as they asked about the war experiences and were cognizant of telling their children only as much as the children could handle at the time. In one parent-child pair, the child concurred that the material had been presented "at my own pace." Included in the interview with female survivor Wilma is the following:

Interviewer: How did you deal with the war with your children?
Wilma: … I didn't speak about it, but C, the older one is always very inquisitive, and she got a hold of one bit of one snippet of conversation either between my husband and myself or with my mother. And she pressured and pressured and pressured and then finally one night I sat down on her bed and I started answering questions and got deeper and deeper and deeper into it and at 2:00 in the morning I was still sitting on her bed. And then she cried impossibly, and I think I've always blamed myself for part of what has made her life kind of difficult and that she is hypersensitive. She is extremely leery of the non-Jewish world. … But in the meantime, I think that I, I put a lot more emotional baggage on her than she was ready to take and yet it was question by question. So, the only way I could have avoided this is to refuse to answer questions.

Responding to direct questions, in fact, often occurs in families considered to be open generally in their communication. Sometimes, however, the responses to direct questions meander into more emotionally and psychologically loaded territory.

Self-Revelation Sometimes, the survivor reports his or her experiences incidentally as they come up; other times, the survivor wants the listener to know directly about parts of his or her life. COS Nancy noted:

My mother never spoke about what hurt her, what she did not have, or what she lost. She never spoke about the missing pieces. She always spoke in ways she became a hero, and she, for the sixth-grade graduation, the topic was heroes. My son wrote about his hero, who was his grandmother, and my daughter in junior high school, wrote pieces about interviewing my mother. So the way we were taught about the Holocaust was never a burden, it was very important, it has been very directive in our attitudes, but it wasn't a burden, and a lot of things that we've done because of it, I think were positive things.

Here, imparting facts or lessons about the Holocaust was at best secondary. Rather, the primary motive for sharing was the desire to be known, or appreciated, to be acknowledged or understood as an individual, as someone who has had specific experiences and who responded to them in particular ways. As we shall demonstrate, this part of telling the story, whether memorializing, in response to direct questions, or as a form of self-revelation, seems to be the most direct and effective way of sharing memories about the Holocaust.

Telling the Story: Lessons to Be Learned

Teaching History   Sometimes, survivors talked about their experiences in a pedagogic way, so that the listener would learn the facts about what happened and various implications that the survivor saw in these facts and events. Female survivor Edith said:

> But I speak extemporaneously, from what I remember sometimes. I used to come home, and I would say, "Oh, I meant to say this, and I forgot!" … And my husband said, "Whatever you remember. They don't know what you forgot. The students heard. They've learned. They know the tortures the Jews went through."

Noah, a male COS, reported the following:

> And then of course, there was another tremendous message about how important it was to be a Jew. My mother would say to me, "Never forget you're a Jew, because even if you do forget, other people won't." And I'd hear stories about people in the concentration camps and how there were people in the concentration camps who were the children of intermarriages who didn't know they were Jewish; had no idea they were Jewish. And the Nazis rounded them up, did to them what they did to us. So, never ever forget that you're Jewish because you can never hide from it, and you shouldn't hide from it, you shouldn't be ashamed of it, you should be proud of it. So, I had an extraordinary sense of Jewish identity. … It's hard to remember a time I didn't know … and they didn't keep their experiences in the war secret.

Such disclosures usually are other directed and can express the desire to either or both memorialize the past or try to find meaning in the experience reported. Moreover, this type of telling often has an ethical component that connects past, present, and future, for the goal of describing the past is to evoke an attitude or action in the listener that will affect the future.

Fulfill an Obligation   In some cases, survivors promised that if they survived, they would tell their story or the story of the family members who perished. At times, this motive contributed to fulfilling a parent's directive to keep the faith and survive, to never forget what happened to them, and to help prevent any other Holocausts from occurring. Clearly, the sharing that took place with this background sometimes had heavy psychological loading. Consider the words of female survivor Edith:

> I was in the labor camp. But before my mother was shot, she was detained someplace for a day or two. Somehow or other she managed to scribble on a little piece of paper, a note, and I don't know how I got it, but I wish I had it. And she said to me, "My dear child. You are young. Hopefully you will survive. But when you survive, remember to tell the world how the Germans treated the Jews and how we suffered." And I think, if it weren't for that note, I couldn't speak today about it. It's almost as if I had a message from her. As much as it hurts, as painful as it is, you must tell them, hopefully to prevent another genocide.

Harry, a male survivor, said in his interview that he had been writing an autobiography.

> It's important for my children and mostly my grandchildren, so that they know what the background is. And they have to know. They don't think they need it now. They will need it 30 years from now, and I won't be around to tell them, so they might as well have it.

In cases such as Harry's, the survivor feels an obligation toward the future, rather than toward the past alone.

Instill Courage and Character Development   The lessons of the Holocaust are many, and sometimes sharing Holocaust experiences is a way to perpetuate the lessons across the generations, to instill courage and character development. Male survivor Frank put it this way:

> Those memories are very, very hard. That's something that never leaves me. And I don't know if I'd want it to leave me. Fifty-five years to my children, it's like 2,000 years. But I tell them it's been in my lifetime, some terrible things have happened. I tell them to be strong, to be secure in themselves, and never to take anything from people, anything anti-Semitic. Just not to take it.

Inculcating Preparedness   The phrase *never again* often is heard as a primary lesson of the Holocaust, but it has many dimensions. In some cases, the survivor puts the listener on alert to be aware of anti-Semitism in particular. In other cases, the survivor generalizes the dangers of prejudice and encourages the listener to actively protest injustice as it arises globally. While she was talking about her public speaking, survivor Barbara expressed this sentiment:

> I realize that people have behaved very cruelly towards the Jews, but I realize that it's not because each and every one of them is a cruel individual; it's because they were taught from childhood to hate Jews, and these are the effects from teaching hatred. If these same human beings would have taught tolerance and kindness and love, I'm sure we would live peacefully with our Christian neighbors; they would not have behaved so cruelly toward us. This is a result, and that's why I try to always emphasize, when I talk to them, they have to stop, even in their own families. When they hear a derogatory joke made about, whether it's about Jews, or Blacks, or any other ethnic group, they should not just sit and laugh along and have fun, but it has to be stopped and explained that there is no such thing as, "I'm better than somebody else."

Nurturing Gratitude and Appreciation   On a more positive note, survivors often want listeners to appreciate what they have now. Pearl, a female survivor, asserted the following:

> I always felt I didn't want to tell my children more than what they could comprehend at their age; they knew very early about the Holocaust because they would ask questions. "Did you have any brothers?" and I would tell them yes; they wanted to know what happened to them. "Where are they?" and I would say that they died, that they where killed in Germany during the war. I also wanted them to make sure that they love and appreciate this country, because this is the country, I think is the best on earth.

As we demonstrate in the following, the impact of these stories also can be negative when they are transmitted in a heavy-handed, didactic way.

Telling the Story: Compulsive

Stuck in Time   Occasionally, the children reported that their parents demonstrated a lack of perspective and shared their stories obsessively. This situation can occur early in the life of the COS. One son recounted that his survivor parents and uncle talked about the Holocaust all the time in the home. Sometimes, such "flooding" can happen when both the survivor and the COS are much older. In the case of Isabel, the COS reported that as her mother's Alzheimer's disease progressed, it was as if a "screen lifted," and stories that the daughter had never heard poured out. Another COS, Oren, said:

> What I remember in my home is, what I remember is a weight. There was always something hovering over the house. They were never more than a conversation away from recalling something in the Holocaust. Ever. And it was that way my whole life. Now I make the place sound like it was a funeral home. It wasn't at all. Not in the least. But there wasn't a holiday, there wasn't an occasion, where a memory wasn't stirred about something that took place there. There wasn't a holiday where there wasn't a yahrzeit candle lit because for some reason or other, there were always roundups of Jews or pogroms or something that coincided with a particular holiday. And until I got married ... I never realized that holidays were supposed to be happier times than they were in my house. And I'm making it sound like it was very morbid. It wasn't at all. Hardly. But it was just very, it was unusual. It was always there. It was *always* there. (emphasis in original)

Unload Often, at the end of life especially, the survivor has a personal need to review, describe, and sometimes evaluate past events—to unload. In his interview, the COS Noah told the interviewer that his parents started telling him stories about the Holocaust when he was 7 or 8:

> It's hard to remember a time I didn't know. I think it got stronger over the years ... They didn't keep their experiences in the war a secret. They were always very open—which is different from most survivors, and my uncle talked an awful lot about it, too.

Similarly, COS Rita described the following:

> They both opened up and started telling stories. And they insisted that I should be the one to chronicle all of this, and I took notes. But the things they said were always incomplete. There was always times when I took notes that they would digress, and then it would become personal like, "You're like this one or that one." I would lose patience. I don't think it was the right time for them. It may have been, and it wasn't the right time for me. I can't tell you. I was in my early 30s. And then they started opening up, telling me lots and lots of stories. But what bothered me was they didn't match. And then I was too young to understand why at that point. ... My father would tell me the same story three different times, three different ways. And the same thing with my mother when I would sit down with her.

Thus, as described, the reasons for the survivors' talking about their traumatic experiences were both numerous and complex. In addition, telling alone is itself not predictive of healthy family dynamics. Our research would indicate that the manner of telling is an important differentiating factor. What we identified as the first motives for telling—memorializing, responding to direct questions, and the desire for self-revelation—seem to be the most healthy for family relationships. By contrast, what we have termed the second and third group of motives for telling—lessons to be learned and compulsive telling—can often be detrimental to family systems.

Motives for Silence/Not Sharing

In coding comments about communication in the interviews, we discovered a spectrum of reasons that survivors gave for not sharing. Many of the reasons for not talking about their Holocaust experiences involved presumed emotional protection in silence that could protect both the survivor and the potential listener. Sometimes the survivor was silent because he or she was anticipating a negative perception by the listener. And sometimes, survivors did not want to or could not remember.

Emotional Protection By far, the most frequent reason given for not talking about Holocaust experiences was emotional protection. Sometimes, the emotional protection was of oneself, as in the cases of survivors Bonnie and Chava:

> No, no. To single people, yeah. In fact, one time the president in our synagogue was asking me, they have a Sunday morning breakfast, to tell them something what I went through. I told them, I cannot do it because I'm getting emotional on this stuff from here. (Bonnie)

Survivor Chava gave a similar explanation for her decision to remain silent:

> Yeah, but I never liked to talk about it. I really don't, because … I want to forget it. But you know, you don't forget that. So I don't want to talk about it.

Other times, survivors chose to be silent to protect others:

> We never talked in the presence of the children that my sister was killed, my mother was killed. We didn't want to implant in them something that they would dream. Like I dream. When they were

teenagers or older, I don't recall if they ask special. My children, I would say he is very sensitive. He didn't want to hurt us. Sometimes, my children didn't know even that my husband was married, and he had two children they were killed. My husband said it is better not to talk about it. … Because when a child listen that a brother is killed, as a little baby, it is emotional; he could get disturbed. And we didn't want that his mind should go around. A child has a mind, too. Oh, he was killed, my brother. Was killed. Maybe I will be killed. … So we were thinking about it is not good to feed the child while they are young with something unpleasant. But now my daughter-in-law has a whole library about the Holocaust, and her grandson asks. (Hinda)

At another point in her interview, she said:

We talk very little, very little. We want to be human beings again. And if we would start to talk about our problems during the war, and about the loss of our dear ones, we wouldn't be able to cope with the situation we were in.

Eva, another survivor, in turn, was sensitive to her daughter's need not to hear her mother's memories:

Quite a few times, I started to talk with my daughter, but every time I would say: "Honey, can we sit down somewhere; I would like to talk to you about something," she would say, "Mom, you are not going to tell me something about yourself again, eh, because I really don't want to know."

In turn, children held back from asking their parents about their past for fear that they would upset them or themselves. COS Rita's comments, for example, reflect the intent to protect both self and parent:

As a child, I never wanted to know anything, and my parents fell apart. They were too vulnerable; whenever anything was raised. … It was not presented as matter of fact information—it was loaded—and that was too much for all of us.

Since overidentification of a child with a parent also can involve a desire to protect the parent from further trauma, COSs often feel they are caught in a bind between wanting to know, yet not wanting to hurt the parent. The parent simultaneously may want to shield the child from knowing about the extent of the damage he or she suffered. Bar-On (1995) called this situation a "double wall": "The survivors tried to 'spare' their children from the horrors they had experienced, and the children, who felt their parents recoiling, built their own 'wall' alongside that of their parents, abstaining from asking questions or initiating a conversation about what they had gone through" (Litvak-Hirsch & Bar-On, 2006, p. 466). The following quotation by COS Oren is a straightforward example of this double bind:

Oren: They were very free talking about their experiences. But I never asked … and the reason that I never asked about it was I knew how difficult it was, how painful it was for them to talk about it. So why force it?

Interviewer: So it was hard to ask.

Oren: Well, it wasn't hard. I just didn't. They would have answered. That wasn't the problem at all. They were very open and free about it. They certainly weren't ashamed of anything, of their experiences. But I just never asked, because I knew it was too painful for them to talk about, so I didn't.

Survivor Edith showed the awareness that others were trying to protect her:

My in-laws never asked me. And I used to be hurt that they didn't. And they were afraid. They were protecting me.

Not Asked   Many interviewees responded that they simply were not asked about their Holocaust experiences, that no one was interested. The "conspiracy of silence" right after the Holocaust has been well documented (Danieli, 1980, 1981). Survivors said they would have talked but were never directly asked and did not think others would want to hear what they had to say. Abram, a male survivor, claimed:

I have not one friend from American people, Jews from America; all that I associate with is only people from Europe. Americans didn't want to know. Nobody asked us. And they said to us in the beginning, "And you went through what?" So we could not communicate with them at all; it was just impossible. Nobody would say "I would like to listen to the story of what you went through," nobody.

Female survivor Mimi said of telling others:

My friends were immature. They were silly teenagers, and the most important thing was the latest song or dance or color bow in their hair. And they knew nothing about the Holocaust. It would have been of no interest whatsoever for them to hear about it. And if I would have mentioned it, they wouldn't have believed it.

Anticipated Negative Reaction   We see the survivors not wanting to have to defend the reality of their experiences. Anticipating disbelief, lack of interest, or repulsion, many survivors chose to keep quiet. More often than not, this motive also underlies not wanting to talk about the Holocaust even with people outside the nuclear family.

Survivor Wilma said that she tried to talk to others, but soon stopped because of the reactions she received:

I did very shortly after we came here, within the first year and a half or so, [when] I could handle the language a little better, a little more competently. But … the reactions I got were like an icy shower, and I clammed up; after that I spoke to no one.

Survivor Chava pointed out:

Like I said, the American Jews didn't even believe it to begin with. My own aunt didn't believe it.

As Wajnryb (2001) noted,

The topic (talking about massive personal tragedy) becomes, as it were, a participant in the drama. As there is no proper venue for the talk, no social domain in which participants can slip comfortably into pre-constituted roles, the topic itself appears larger than life. It fills up the available space left void by an absence of roles, participants and scripts. It takes over, turning into an *over*-presence. It's as if the space becomes monopolized and swallowed up by the topic. And the listener is overwhelmed—not knowing what to say, where to look, what to think, how to feel, how to respond; wanting to make it go away. (p. 100, italics in original)

Failure of Memory   Survivors sometimes cannot or do not want to remember. Harry, a male survivor put it this way:

There is nothing to say [about thoughts and feelings during the Holocaust] because I don't really recall. Everybody reacts differently to moments of stress, and my reaction is very simple. I close up and ignore it. And therefore I really have no recollection.

Not Wanting to Dwell in the Past   Some survivors used silence as a way to move beyond their Holocaust experiences. Consider this excerpt from an interview with male survivor Karl:

Interviewer: I'm wondering about the fact that [you've] … lived, essentially as a non-Jew for so many years. During those years, [was the] Holocaust … out of your awareness?

Male survivor Karl: It was neatly suppressed. … I ran across an old girlfriend [from college]. … She mentioned that [I didn't talk] about the Holocaust and what happened to [me]. She said, "I wondered why you never talked about it." She said she could remember asking questions, and I would give her answers, but … not volunteer any further information. So I guess what I did was I suppressed all that. But again, that was by example, partly. My father didn't talk about it a whole lot. … Maybe because the business of getting on with life was all that pressing that you know, as they say in Hebrew, "ein breichah [sic Ein breirah]." You have no choice. You go on. You do what you needed to do to survive, and to keep on going. And it's tough surviving in this country. It's tough enough for me.

Female survivor Pearl said:

I sort of felt that we wanted our life to move on, and we wanted our children to have a very normal life, and not have to pay the price, emotionally, for what we had gone through, so my main goal was to provide them with a normal upbringing.

Female survivor Eva saw the future in her child: "I didn't feel the need to talk to anyone about what I lived through, because from the moment my daughter was born I had someone to live for. The rest did not matter." Sometimes, this motive for silence could be paired with a desire to assimilate into American culture. Some survivors felt that "moving on" demanded acting like an American and not dwelling in the past.

We do not claim that this list of motives for sharing or silence is exhaustive. While the initial list of motives was developed based on the research team's extensive familiarity with the entire pool of interview data as well as with scholarly literature and memoirs of the Holocaust, the research team suspects that there may be additional motives for remaining silent. We suspect that some survivors may feel that they would not have been understood because of a language barrier, either wanting to express themselves in Yiddish or another language, and listeners would not understand. Further, survivors may have felt shame because of actions they had to perform or things that happened to them. They may have felt guilt because on some level they might not have seen either their survival or some of their actions as justifiable. We also suspect that some survivors may have felt paranoia or deep fear that it would be dangerous or threatening to share their experiences. We draw on Wajnryb (1999) again to summarize some of these issues:

> The pain of Holocaust survivors is a complex amalgam of emotions: grief for personal losses and for the obliteration of a world that was, frustration at ongoing health problems, a debilitation originating in years of extreme deprivation and abuse; shame at what was experienced and witnessed, perhaps at what had to be done, in some cases, to survive; guilt at surviving when so many did not; rage at the experience of wanton cruelty; a learned inability to mourn, born of a survival-driven need to suppress normal emotional responses to abnormal events; and bitterness that justice was never served. (p. 87)

Finally, similar to one of the motives for sharing, some survivors seemed to see an ethical reason *not* to share; that is, they did not wish to burden the listener to prevent the listener from learning to hate the Nazi perpetrators as well as others.

As part of our study, we examined whether families were identified by the researchers as having open or closed communication *in general*, and then whether communication about the *war* was open or closed. One might infer that underlying the interest in communication is an assumption that talking is "good." However, what we found is that how and why one talks about his or her experiences is more important than talking in and of itself. Moreover, in the eyes of the survivors we interviewed, the motives for sharing and the motives for silence are both legitimate. Important as it may be, communication is but one aspect of relationships that affect perceptions and well-being of trauma survivors and their families.

Relationship of Communication to Overall Family Dynamics

The present study incorporated not only a descriptive analysis of the motives expressed by survivors and their children, but also an attempt to connect the communication motives with the overall quality of family dynamics. The TTP analyzes relationship dynamics across family units, based on the 15 categories demarcated in the synopses, using what we term the quality of family dynamics paradigm (Hollander-Goldfein & Isserman, 1999) The paradigm contains five dimensions or continua along which the individual and family dynamics can fall. The five dimensions are (a) closeness-distance, (b) empathy-self-centeredness, (c) validation-criticism, (d) expressive of positive emotions-expressive of negative emotions, and

(e) open communication-closed communication. In the present analysis, we focused on the last of these dimensions, that of communication, and looked at not only the content of the communication within survivor families, but also the relational dynamics that are associated with that communication.

The families were also categorized by the TTP team on the basis of five factors: (a) the type of descriptions of their parents that the child gave or that the survivor(s) gave about each parent in the family; (b) the nature of the descriptions of the family relationships; (c) the description of the parental marital relationships; (d) the presence of a child targeted by either parent and experiencing a negative impact as a result of the targeting; (e) the description of the child's adult mental health and relationships; (f) the existence of empathy in the child toward his or her survivor parent(s). Of the 31 families considered for the specific analysis reported in this chapter, 7 were considered in the positive category of overall family dynamics and impact on the next generation. Thirteen were considered in the mixed category, and 11 in the negative category.

In correlating aspects of general communication and family dynamics, we can say definitively that the motives we have identified as the first group of motives for telling the story (memorializing, responding to direct questions, and self-revelation) seemed to contribute to healthier relationships between survivors of trauma and those with whom they shared their stories. This type of sharing allowed the survivor of trauma to feel known and enabled the listener to hear the story appropriately, that is, *without feeling pressure*. The listener may indeed feel moved, but not pressure at being told emotionally charged and difficult information. Survivors thus could experience themselves as full human beings, not defined exclusively in terms of their Holocaust experiences. Consequently, the barrier between them and their loved ones was able to dissolve.

Every family in the "positive overall" category had open general communication, and if there was any sharing of experiences around war, it was not compulsive. Any communication reported about the Holocaust was told appropriately (as in the first two groups of motives for telling). While we see a relationship between open communication and appropriate telling of trauma experiences in four of the seven open families, we can pose some additional questions: Do these findings suggest that appropriate telling per se will lead to a less-negative impact on the (child) listener? What does this type of sharing engender in the child? Does the sharing reflect the parents' acknowledgment of the child as an individual? Is it a sense that the parent trusts the child with difficult information? Is it a sense that the child is loved enough to be treated with honesty? Does the listener end up feeling loved and valued as a result of being entrusted with these stories?

However, open communication in general does not guarantee healthy, positive family dynamics. Several families who were identified as having open general communication nevertheless were categorized in the mixed impact group, but there was inappropriate telling or no telling of Holocaust experiences. This was the case for 6 of the 13 mixed families examined in this chapter.

Other families in the mixed group did not fit into a clear pattern, suggesting that communication is neither the only nor necessarily the most important dimension in promoting healthy family relationships. Additional potentially important variables yet to be examined in these mixed families include (a) inconsistent communication patterns, including very different styles used by the mother and father during childrearing; (b) variables that account for differing reports from different children in the family, such as birth order and the proximity of a child's birth to time of immigration or other pivotal events in the family's history, the parents' sense of adjustment to their new lives, and the economic status of family; (c) personal changes that the survivor and child undergo as they reach adulthood or move toward the end stages of life. These factors need further investigation. On the basis of our current research, we can say that our project includes a number of families who changed their patterns of communication, particularly when grandchildren asked and were told about the Holocaust experiences. We also see the positive influence of therapy in both COSs and their parents. In some of the families we interviewed in which the children's upbringing might have been mixed or negative, after therapy, the adult children were doing well. This outcome demonstrates the human quality of resilience and the capacity of some to survive and thrive even in the most difficult circumstances.

Finally, we should point out that when families reported both closed communication in general and closed war communication, they also tended to be families with a negative family dynamic. This was true for 5 of the 11 families in the negative group. Yet, other negative families had mixed or unboundaried communication and inappropriate telling of Holocaust experiences, with no discernible pattern. This finding reinforces our observations regarding the importance of both the nature and the perceptions of communication within family systems.

As a result of these findings, we want to emphasize that the motives for communicating about the experiences related to the Holocaust are far more varied and complex than the notion of "never again," the most frequently, if not exclusively, cited motive for why Holocaust survivors share their stories. Embedded in the desire to ensure that the Holocaust never happens again is also what we call the "ethics of empathy": Because they suffered, many of the survivors wanted to prevent others from suffering.

This orientation is both other directed and future directed—a very resilient, hopeful, and empowering combination. While there is nothing in a survivor's power to change what has happened in the past, he or she might be more inclined to recount the trauma if he or she knew that retelling does not have to be or lead to a repetition of feelings of helplessness. Instead, the telling can promote a sense of meaning and personal value. Used in the therapeutic setting, the framework we have described can thus help shift the therapist's and the client's understanding of what can happen as a result of sharing: The narrative is no longer strictly a way of releasing negative feelings or sharing or unloading a burden. Instead, it can become a means of release from being "stuck in time," a means of transcending a sense of permanent victimhood. In other words, the telling itself can be reconceived as part of a process of empowerment. Assuming that the client would benefit from revisiting or speaking about the trauma, the therapist can direct the client toward this orientation and help the client open communication about the trauma. If done appropriately (i.e., using the first group of telling motives), such open communication may allow more profound connection with others as the client may feel more understood or "known."

Similarly, by explaining that some survivors have chosen to share their stories as a way of honoring the past and those who are no longer here, the therapist may be able to motivate a client to find value in retrieving the memory of those who have been lost, if the loss of a loved one (perhaps even the loss of a previous sense of self) is what constitutes the trauma. We are not advocating that retelling is the best therapeutic approach for everyone. Therapists need to be cautious in their approach and evaluate each case according to its circumstances.

Suggestions for Further Research

While we have categorized the motives for communication described into two groups (one for sharing and one for silence), they can also be grouped according to a number of other parameters. One primary pattern that emerged from the interviews we examined is that the motives for both sharing and not sharing were either self-oriented or other oriented. While no consistent pattern has emerged thus far, further research could investigate the question of whether those whose motives for sharing or silence were other oriented were more successful in rebuilding their lives than those who chose communication based on self-oriented motives.

We also noticed a temporal pattern among the motives for sharing and for silence. While some were focused on the past (i.e., what happened in the Holocaust), others were focused on the future and what the survivors hoped for the future, not only for themselves but also for the world (i.e., social justice and the elimination of genocide). Further research could reveal whether temporal orientation has any role in mental health.

Similarly, we did not systematically investigate the role of gender in the communication patterns within these or any of the families interviewed for the TTP. No doubt there are other variables that we have yet to consider in these complex and layered communication phenomena. We present only some of the multiple threads in the tapestries of families living in the aftermath of Holocaust trauma with the hope that our findings both illuminate our subject and are applicable to other variations of trauma based on radical displacement.

References

Adelman, A. (1995). Traumatic memory and the intergenerational transmission of Holocaust narratives. *Psychoanalytic Study of the Child, 50*, 343–367.

Bar-On, D. (1995). *Fear and hope: Three generations of the Holocaust.* Cambridge, MA: Harvard University Press.

Bowen, S. P., & Spitzer, J. (2005). Survivors sometimes tell their stories: Motives for sharing and motives for silence. In J.-D. Steinert & I. Weber-Newth (Eds.), *Conference proceedings: Beyond camps and forced labour: Current international research on survivors of Nazi persecution* (pp. 545–556). Osnabrueck, Germany: Secolo Verlag.

Cowan, P. A., & Cowan, C. P. (2009). Introduction to the special issue. Couple relationships: A missing link between adult attachment and children's outcomes. *Attachment & Human Development, 11*(1), 1–4.

Danieli, Y. (1980). Countertransference in the treatment and study of Nazi Holocaust survivors and their children. *Victimology: An International Journal, 5*, 355–367.

Danieli, Y. (1981). Families of survivors of the Nazi Holocaust: Some short- and long-term effects. In C. D. Spielberger, I. G. Sarason, & N. Milgram (Eds.), *Stress and anxiety* (Vol. 8, pp. 405–421). New York: McGraw-Hill.

Eitinger, L., & Major, E. F. (1993). Stress of the Holocaust. In L. Goldberger & S. Breznitz (Eds.), *Handbook of stress: Theoretical and clinical aspects* (2nd ed., pp. 617–620). New York: Free Press.

Epstein, H. (1979). *Children of the Holocaust: Conversations with sons and daughters of survivors.* New York: Putnam.

Halik, V., Rosenthal, D. A., & Pattison, P. A. E. (1990). Intergenerational effects of the Holocaust: Patterns of engagement in the mother-daughter relationship. *Family Process, 29*, 325–339.

Hirsch, M. (1996). Past lives: Postmemories in exile. *Poetics Today, 17*, 659–686.

Hollander-Goldfein, B., & Isserman, N. (1999). Overview of the Transcending Trauma Project: Rationale, goals, methodology, and preliminary findings. In P. David, & J. Goldhar (Eds.). *Selected papers from a time to heal: Caring for the aging Holocaust survivor.* (pp. 77–89). Toronto: Baycrest Centre for Geriatric Care.

Litvak-Hirsch, T., & Bar-On, D. (2006). To rebuild lives: A longitudinal study of the influences of the Holocaust on relationships among three generations of women in one family. *Family Process, 45*, 465–483.

Mor, N. (1990). Holocaust messages from the past. *Contemporary Family Therapy,* *12*, 371–379.

Okner, D. F., & Flaherty, J. (1988). Parental communication and psychological distress in children of Holocaust survivors: A comparison between the US and Israel. *International Journal of Social Psychiatry, 35*, 265–273.

Robinson, S., & Winnik, H. Z. (1981). Second generation of the Holocaust: Holocaust survivors' communication of experience to their children, and its effect. *Israel Journal of Psychiatry and Related Sciences, 18*, 99–107.

Rosenthal, G. (2003). The healing effects of storytelling: On the conditions of curative storytelling in the context of research and counseling. *Qualitative Inquiry, 9*, 915–933.

Sagi-Schwartz, A., van IJzendoorn, M. H., Grossmann, K. E., Joels, T., Grossmann, K., Scharf, M., et al. (2003). Attachment and traumatic stress in female Holocaust child survivors and their daughters. *American Journal of Psychiatry, 160*, 1086–1092.

van Ijzendoorn, M. H. (1992). Intergenerational transmission of parenting: A review of studies in nonclinical populations. *Developmental Review, 12*, 76–99.

Wajnryb, R. (1999). The Holocaust as unspeakable: Public ritual versus private hell. *Journal of Intercultural Studies, 20*, 81–94.

Wajnryb, R. (2001). *The silence: How tragedy shapes talk.* Crows Nest, Australia: Allen & Unwin.

Waxman, M. (2000). Traumatic hand-me-downs: The Holocaust, where does it end? *Families in Society: The Journal of Contemporary Human Services, 81*, 59–64.

Wiseman, H., & Barber, J. P. (2008) *Echoes of the trauma: Relational themes and emotions in children of Holocaust survivors,* Cambridge: Cambridge Press.

CHAPTER 11

Holocaust Narratives and Their Impact on Adult Children of Survivors

HANNAH KLIGER and BEA HOLLANDER-GOLDFEIN

Introduction

This chapter[1] discusses the process the Transcending Trauma Project used to ask Holocaust survivors for their life histories. The impact of key narratives told by survivors and heard by their children and grandchildren is explored with a focus on development, socialization, and identity formation. We are particularly interested in how people adapt in the aftermath of trauma and how they construct and communicate memory and meaning as individuals and within their communities. We elicit testimonies that are fluid rather than fixed, open to the expression of deeper personal meaning and self-exploration. As survivors' narratives are heard, particularly within the family, their stories about traumatic events teach the listeners more than just how to cope with trauma, but more broadly how to be in the world. The listener, in turn, selects, remembers, and internalizes (albeit not consciously) the stories that later may translate into life lessons.

The historical accuracy of autobiography is less the point than the ways in which the traumatic events and meaning of survival are remembered, reported, and assimilated. Meanings heretofore unarticulated are generated in a context and environment cocreated by the interviewee and the interviewer. Participants in this process have expressed appreciation for the questions that no one has ever asked them before.

The in-depth interviews conducted by the Transcending Trauma Project shifted the angle of vision from documenting external conditions to recording and analyzing the internal realities of survivors' lives, especially the personal and emotional significance of events before, during, and after the Holocaust. We asked about the memory practices of survivors to probe not only what happened to them but also mainly what happened within them. We asked interviewees to incorporate issues and descriptions significant to them. Our interviews were open ended and included discussions of family of origin, key life events, cultural affiliations, and religious and moral belief systems.

In asking survivors for their life histories, our query focused on how they rebuilt their lives, the methods they used to cope, and the ways in which their beliefs, attitudes, and values affected their will to live and, later, to start over and rebuild. Speaking from one's inner self for the first time is a powerful, often-affirming experience. Thereby, the interviewer and interviewee are both transformed by the interpersonal process. From this perspective, speakers listen to themselves and watch others listen acceptingly to their narratives that incorporate, often for the first time, their inner private experiences. Moreover, we witness the power of these narratives to reveal the value systems of those who share the memories of trauma, as well as the impact on the value systems of those who hear the stories of survival.

For children of survivors, listening to the experience of survivor parents has multiple consequences. For the second generation listening to traumatic memories, they are hearing not only what the parent went through but also who the parent or grandparent is. When a particular attribute of a survivor parent is clear and emotionally compelling, this attribute can become an organizing value system in the developing identity of the child that is expressed throughout the unchartered territory of his or her life. The workings of this process emerged in the analysis of intergenerational interviews. We have framed this process as the transmission of pivotal narratives.

We raised the following questions: What makes a narrative pivotal? How does the developmental stage of the listener/receiver of the story determine the impact of the stories? Similarly, how does the developmental stage of the survivor/storyteller at the time of the telling determine the impact of the stories? Does the relationship between the survivor and the child of the survivor/listener determine how the stories are integrated? What accounts for differences among siblings' responses to the same stories heard? Is it in the repetition of the same stories over and over again, or perhaps in the silence broken with one particular story, that makes a narrative pivotal?

In the cases described here, we trace the metamorphosis of pivotal family narratives recalled and now recounted by children of survivors. The first example is the story by Iris, a child and grandchild of survivors. The story is one of several narratives that have had a profound impact on her. The memory begins with the long death march of Iris's grandmother toward the end of World War II:

And she takes her shawl and puts it over her head and walks away from the hundreds, perhaps, women, that are being marched at gunpoint. And she took an out, she took the choice, she took control of her destiny, and as I interpret it, very calmly decided how she's going to determine the rest of her life, whatever it is.

As the interviewer asked Iris to consider the meaning of this choice, she reflected:

And she has said and has written that you know, she consciously made this very logical decision. If she turns around and walks away she'll get shot in the back, and it will be over. And if she makes it, she'll get to be with her kids. And there is some courage in that ... that incident evokes for me courage, control, solitude; the self-reliance that I think informs a lot of what I do in my life.

Asked to probe further about her own life, Iris underlined her own intuitive sense about being separate, the imperative to not be part of a crowd.

I see that scene, and I imagine her as being, if there are four or three women across in a line, she was obviously on the edge. So I know that whenever I'm in a crowd, I am reluctant to get into the center. I always stay on the edge. I'm conscious of where the exits are all the time. All the time.

Throughout her life, Iris has been cast as an oppositional rebel for her refusal to adhere to the rules. She shared her awareness of this judgment of her behavior with resentment and pain as revealed by tears welling up in her eyes. But, in the context of the pivotal memory of the grandmother who had enough and left, Iris's behavior needs to be understood as a strong and suitable reaction. Her apartness is less defiance than it is her inherited mode of survival. Making this connection, spontaneously, in the course of the interview provided an inner sense of self-recognition. For Iris, the recognition provided a much-needed salve for private doubts about her inner motivations. She knew she was not an oppositional rebel but could not explain the compelling drive within her. She continued later in the interview:

> There's a defiance in general about rules and especially in crowds. But it sort of filters in all parts of my life. That following what everyone is supposed to be doing somewhere in my consciousness means sure and certain death. That it's up to, if I want to survive, I have to be on my own as a solo player, away from the crowd. I think that plays out a lot in my life. It's not, I have not consciously done this, but if I were to outline the path my life has taken, in terms of career, for instance, I manage to do things in a roundabout way, not from start to finish. I'm not assigning this experience of my grandmother's as the reasons I live the way I do. But it is interesting to note. And I think there's a connection that, that nothing in my life has been start to finish. ... And there's something that I still hold, that if you keep running, you're safe.

Establishing her own path and finding the routes of her choosing are pieces of Iris's legacy. In fact, when asked by the interviewer to connect this most profound and resonant memory to "a trait of yours, an aspect of yours, a defining quality of you. Not just you reacting to war stories, but a war story that became, as you say, a self-defining aspect of your identity," she stated:

> That would be it. And as I mature and understand myself more with each passing month and year, and as I fine-tune my truths, it becomes more and more clear. [Crying.] And I feel like I'm on that. ...I'm behind her in those footsteps. In a way, the path has been paved. I'm not rebelling; I'm following a path.

In the telling of that story, in the context of the research interview, a critical clarification of self in relation to story occurred. The memories became messages about how one's core values, while rooted in a past that is painful, move forward to a more valid interpretation and a purpose routed in moral and personal choices.

In a second example, Charna reviewed a story she had always known about her mother's war experience:

> It is at that first selection ... that the drama of what happened between mother and her mother and her baby took place. There were three groups. One was the people sent to the trains into the death camp. Another group was the young people who could work, and then another group were those family members of the people in the work

camp. … So anyone connected to the people in the work camp was still being allowed to reenter the work camp. And they had children, that group. So my grandmother, in I think the chaos of that moment, I can't imagine it feeling anything other than terribly frightening, my mother was holding my brother in her arms. He was 8 months or 9 months at the time. Her mother was trying to take the baby away from my mother, saying to her, "I'll take care of the baby, and you can go work." Well, the unstated reality was, my grandmother knew she was going to her death, and that the baby would go with her, but at least my mother would have a chance to live.

Hearing her mother recapture the moment yet again on a recent occasion, Charna was reminded of her mother's choice to refuse to relinquish her infant child. She described this latest retelling:

But what she said poignantly, clearly, in words this summer which I knew was always part of the story whether she said it or not [pause, crying], was the unwillingness on my mother's part to have any role in her mother's death.

For Charna, the daughter of the woman who could not tolerate any role in another's suffering, the message was clear. It was clear even without the explication of a larger meaning system by the parent about how the decision was made. The interview process helped define what she saw as a "very deeply embedded part of me." She continued:

It was like looking in the mirror when she told me that. And again, it's like I always knew it, and I always knew the message, but there's something when you take the time to really focus on it and pay attention and put all the words on it.

The pivotal memory assumes its place as a guiding principle for her own standard of behavior. In the unfolding of her own narrative, Charna was drawn to the abiding power of the unspoken but ever-enacted value statement acquired from her mother's testimony:

But I think I was very … [pause, crying] I'm not sure why this is so emotional. [Pause.] But I think I was even more exquisitely attuned to and avoidant of and unwilling to cause anybody pain. [Pause.] At all. In any way.

Her essential identification with the central principle of empathy for people, what her interviewer termed "a universal, governing, dominant law in your very core being," was enunciated in numerous examples throughout her interview. With the interviewer as guide, Charna contemplated her own choices as lifelong continuities emergent from the pivotal telling of trauma.

In another example, Noam, Ted's father, recounted how his watch-making skill saved his life in the barracks. In a pivotal moment, a Nazi observed as Noam fixed the watch in front of his eyes, threatening to kill him if he failed. Subsequently, Noam worked as a watchmaker in the camps and prided himself in having accomplished this feat. Ted praised his father's dexterity in the life-or-death situation and felt that his own ability paled in comparison:

> The thing is, the first time I ever opened and took apart a watch, I just completely destroyed it. I was given an old watch to destroy. There was no doubt in his mind [his father's] that I was going to destroy this watch.

Yet, what the children concluded they learned from their parents' stories was, as Ted remarks, "in the final analysis, ways to define meaning in their experiences, and to make them have meaning for us in a way that could be useful in our lives." As the pivotal story resonates intergenerationally, affecting each of the children, somehow survival and the skill of watchmaking became intertwined. On the one hand, we see the message being transmitted literally, that is, fix the watch quickly or die. Yet, while the message that is transmitted is that the very skill of watchmaking is essential and valuable, it is also possible that the essential message that leaves the deepest impression is not the pain of the event or the pain of other experiences, but the imperative of survival.

The impact of telling the trauma is contrasted, in the next case, with the powerful legacy of not telling, where silence about deeply held painful secrets pervades the family. Mona, a daughter of Holocaust survivors, claimed not to have "a memory of a story told to me by either of them that I would say was a pivotal one." Only in adulthood did Mona learn that her mother had a husband and a child who died of starvation in Siberia during the war and with that knowledge came a clearer understanding of her mother's withdrawal and her distance. Mona confirmed the sentiment of other children of survivors, that the most important event in her life happened before she was born, yet in this instance "the way [these] memories and stories were transmitted … was through silence." The interviewer offered the possibility that "the impact was not what she told you, it's who she was because she didn't tell you." Mona responded:

> Right. I could not make sense of her inability to connect emotionally, physically, and so I internalized bad feelings about myself. … Had

the stories been made available earlier ... it would have generated quite a bit of sadness ... perhaps even overwhelming sadness, but I think it would have helped me be more compassionate of her and of myself.

When asked to think about the ways in which her mother's silence had informed her behavior in her own life, Mona took a moment to reply:

It's difficult for me to be angry and to confront people. I grew up without expressing anger because it would have hurt her to have done that with her. I had a sense of being damaged because she couldn't connect to me. If I have feelings, if I get angry, I feel guilty. It's a challenge to validate my feelings and have feelings of anger, to confront people. ... I deal with it all the time. I'm more sensitive to my own feelings and the feelings of others. This whole scenario goes through my head—"Why are you angry? Don't be angry!" My inclination is to be silent; my challenge is to work on that because that's what I learned growing up.

Pivotal narratives, verbally communicated or nonverbally conveyed, play a role in identity formation. From these examples, we see how the experience of trauma, and its memory and telling, must ultimately take us to the intersection of survival and identity. An integration of both the positive adaptation and the negative sequelae of surviving extreme trauma is needed and is possible by looking at the survivor and the survivor's family. In other words, we are studying what it means to decode the text to understand the individual and then recontextualize the text to understand the family. The preliminary findings indicate that the approach has been successful in eliciting a more fully integrated life history. Individual differences emerged while illuminating significant familial and group themes. Without undermining or underestimating the tragedies and trials that individuals and communities experienced, a legacy of resilience and resourcefulness becomes apparent when family units can be investigated. As poignant narratives are shared on a deeper level, with oneself and with significant others, life themes emerge as representations of belief systems that are guided by human connection.

The capacity for transforming trauma may depend on the capacity, ultimately, to negotiate memory, to recognize the personal teachings that are embedded in the process of sharing stories whether or not the speaker or listener is consciously aware of the messages imparted and to integrate these narratives through life-affirming belief systems. By gathering the narratives of all generations, this study speaks to the complex process of surviving. The lessons of the Holocaust are many, among them the capacity of individuals to use their memories to weave a narrative of survival that forms the foundation of meaning.

Summary and Clinical Application of Pivotal Narratives

The utility of using directive questions to find pivotal narratives in sessions with clients has been explored by clinicians who are affiliated with the Transcending Trauma Project, as well as by professionals who have attended workshops at which our data are discussed. A deliberate focus on family stories that resound through the generations, if only one asks, has helped clients who seem to be "stuck" or somehow unable to move beyond their current relational stance either with the therapist or with a family member. In such cases, when clients are invited to access unique stories of their lives that had never been told in therapy, these stories and their exploration shed light on the issues at hand in new ways. The therapist's approach can shift based on these stories, claimed one clinician who felt as if she had been pushing against the identities at the core of her clients, despite a treatment of almost 2 years, until the pivotal narrative was revealed. Moreover, the pivotal narrative process had a deep impact on the clients, who were able to recognize new strengths in themselves on their therapeutic journeys.

Individual Case: Anna

As with the case of adult children of survivors described in this chapter, clinicians can approach the search for lessons learned from pivotal narratives as a gateway to uncovering key identity markers that shape their clients' decisions, even when these influences remain below the surface or are as yet unrecognized. In one example, Anna came to therapy to improve her relationship with Tom, who she had been dating seriously for a few years. Raised in a traditional Catholic family, Anna worked as a physical therapist and lived on her own in the city. She and Tom never lived together; however, they talked time and again about marriage and raising a family. They each visited and spent time with their respective families, living close by and feeling connected to their parents and siblings. They were considered and treated like long-term partners in each household, and their future as a couple seemed pretty much sealed. Although Anna spoke with great concern for Tom and with mainly joyous anticipation about the time they spent together throughout the week, she described an incident about 1 year before coming to therapy in which she kissed another man at a party. That betrayal, as she described it and about which she still felt guilty, led Anna and Tom to cancel a planned joint vacation and, in general, precipitated a kind of questioning about the viability of the relationship.

During therapy sessions with her counselor, Anna often asked for direct advice about what to do about Tom: Were they a good match? Should she stay with him? Sex was less frequent than she wished, her observations of Tom's inability to really be curious about her was becoming more troublesome, and she was more aware of her impatience with his lack of initiative, even as she admired him for the strides he had made in his own life and career. As the therapy continued, the doubts were voiced steadily, but still the overall stated intention was to make it work with Tom. And, then, in the week following her sister's wedding reception, Anna came in and announced that she was going to end the relationship with Tom. What had been clarified for her? What sense of herself and who she was had come to light as an unavoidable core of being?

In the deepening work between therapist and client, who were seeing each other on a weekly basis, at a midpoint in the work, the counselor asked Anna if there were any pivotal stories that had been expressed in the family and passed along intergenerationally. Anna answered without hesitation and relayed a story she knew about her paternal grandparents, born in Poland and active in the Polish underground resistance during World War II. She knew they had been unhesitatingly convinced of the need to help fight the Nazi invasion of Poland and then never doubted the merit of their actions. Theirs was a genuine altruism, unimpeded by any second thoughts, fostered by a calling for authenticity and mutual respect that marks a hero. This is the clarity Anna brought to her work, to her friendships, even as she was also pulled by the more passive instincts that characterized her maternal lineage.

Pointing to these dual legacies helped Anna understand her emotional dilemma and the doubts she sometimes felt about her wish to be heard and honored for her indefatigable hero's heart. Recognizing the imperative of her drive for pursuing her vision helped her explain to herself the impatience she felt with anything less in her relationship with Tom. Since making the decision to end the relationship, which she did with clarity and conviction, she more willingly embraced as a strength her capacity to see and feel what others around her may choose to neglect or shun as she embraces her commitment to connecting deeply with others in ways that feel she is being more true to her sense of self.

Couples Case: Bob and Barbara

Having couples hear each other's pivotal narratives can also be a therapeutic strategy for clinicians to adopt on behalf of their clients' progress as partners. When Barbara and Bob first came for counseling, their level of distress was quite high, focused on a conflictual dynamic that they could both recite and repeat in the room. The experience of the couple was characterized by a predominant pattern in which Barbara would criticize and demand more attentiveness from Bob, at which point he would shut down and disengage. Barbara, taking this personally as a signal from Bob that she was not important enough to warrant his focus, would inevitably break down into tears with emotional outbursts of hurt and humiliation. For his part, Bob would be baffled and, even worse, angered, by this dramatic response, which felt to him like punishment for his attempts to soothe and bring calm to a situation that threatened the growing closeness of the pair.

To help move the therapy along, it was useful to frame the problem and their instinctual reactions as something they inherited, based on their histories and family of origin. Eventually, the couple began to accept that their cycle of conflict was reflective of their past, and not only that each of them was, in effect, undermining the security of the relationship. Rather, together we tried to understand more fully what we observed in the room together: Barbara, in distress, exhibited high anxiety, which led her in pursuit of Bob, who then chose the path of avoidance and disconnection. As the couple successfully experienced de-escalation and its benefits, there was far more readiness to explore the feelings underneath the behaviors and to make more explicit the pain, humiliation, and shame that froze the interaction between the two of them.

Over time, Barbara and Bob began to identify defenses and vulnerabilities grounded in significant family-of-origin influences based on pivotal narratives each of them could readily recite. For Barbara, we learned about developments that resulted in the intergenerational legacy of trauma and resilience that she carried. Her mother's great-grandparents came from Ireland, and her grandmother's father died when he was young. Her great-grandmother raised five children, the only Catholics in their urban neighborhood, who were admonished to succeed and be exemplars of good behavior. All received an Ivy League education and were deemed to be very smart according to family lore. Only Barbara's grandmother married, at age 30, however, whereas another sister was remembered to have died alone. Barbara's grandmother came to live with the family, then passed away a few years before Barbara's own mother died from cancer. In relaying her history, another key theme was the family's decision to take in foster children through Catholic Charities and then to adopt several of these boys as Barbara's younger siblings. Probing further about this, I learned that there had been 12 pregnancies, 7 miscarriages, and 3 or 4 stillborn infant deaths. All this, and more, led us to conclude that Barbara carried the mixed legacy of privilege and struggle, the power and predicament of knowledge, the stark reality of life in the face of death.

For Bob, who was well aware of the transmission of pivotal themes throughout four generations in his family, he could speak with clarity about the repetition intergenerationally of expectations that had an impact on his daily interactional pattern. He could effortlessly retell the adventures of his clan several generations back, highlighting the gain and loss of inherited wealth by men in the family, beginning with his great-grandfather. Ultimately, his own father, despite being told he was not college material, made his way through college and law school to land a comfortable position now as a partner in a Chicago law firm. On his mother's side, Bob was aware of a propensity of men to eschew college in favor of military service or blue-collar labor. Bob was typically more curtailed in his narratives; however, in therapy he was finding his voice and was becoming less afraid of the choices he was contemplating, which now included law school and marriage to Barbara following his own career in the military.

While we are still synthesizing this mix of past and present, both Barbara and Bob have come to see their reliance on and alliance with, albeit unknowingly and unwittingly, inherited ways of being in the world. Their individual development and the family system from which they come will, they now acknowledge, have importance for therapy. Thus, with a poignant sense of wonder and some humor, this sea-loving, boat-owning couple can talk metaphorically about the fleet of beliefs and attitudes on whose wings they sail that affect the presenting problem as they try to navigate and self-regulate their own route. It has been important to establish a therapeutic atmosphere of empathy, responsiveness, and trust that facilitates the partners' capacity to change in light of their adaptive earlier responses to trauma in their families' history. What each garnered from their past and from our exploration of the legacy of these narratives was a more nuanced sense of the socializing intergenerational impact of these lessons on their identity formation and who they are because of these stories.

Concluding Thoughts

Through questions and interventions, including some that focus on the ways in which clients experience and have feelings about the therapist's presence and role vis-à-vis our coevolving relationship, the exploration of pivotal narratives can challenge the premise and tackle the promise of providing a direction for understanding and growth that is nonblaming and that draws on clients' own resources and creativity. Individuals and couples can learn to listen carefully in new ways to descriptions of the problem and the effect it is having on their life and relationships. At the same time, they gain a better sense of the beliefs and behaviors that stand in the way of bringing about their desired solution, particularly because client and therapist have been able to trace these constraining attitudes and beliefs to their source as central themes in the family of origin and culture. Giving clients feedback at the end of sessions that summarizes their progress and encourages them to continue the changes that they have themselves suggested has also proven helpful. Thus, by depathologizing their dilemma and guiding the pivotal narrative process by picking up and pointing out qualities, values, intentions, or actions that can be defined as positive, thereby highlighting an appreciation of these capacities and expanding on their resourcefulness, it is possible to imagine a different, more positive future.

Note

1. Selected sections in this chapter are reprinted from "Texts of trauma, texts of identity: The narrative legacy of Holocaust survivor stories," *Doubletake/ Points of Entry,* Spring/Summer, 40–44, 2007.

Bibliography

Basham, K., & Miehls, D. (2004). *Transforming the legacy: Couple therapy with survivors of childhood trauma.* New York: Columbia University Press.

Brenner, I. (2004). *Psychic trauma: Dynamics, symptoms, and treatment.* Lanham, MD: Aronson.

Collins, N., Guichard, A., Ford, M., & Feeney, B. (2004). Working models of attachment: new developments and emerging themes. In W. S. Rholes & J. A. Simpsons (Eds.), *Adult attachment: Theory, research, and clinical implications* (pp. 196–239). New York: Guilford Press.

DeMaria, R., Weeks, G., & Hof, L. (1999). *Focused genograms: Intergenerational assessment of individuals, couples, and families.* New York: Routledge.

Feld, B. (2004). Holding and facilitating interactive regulation in couples with trauma histories. *Psychoanalytic Inquiry, 24,* 420–437.

Garland, C. (Ed.). (1998). *Understanding trauma: A psychoanalytical approach.* New York: Routledge.

Gerson, M. (1996). *The embedded self*. Hillsdale, NJ: Analytic Press.

Herman, J. (1992). *Trauma and recovery*. New York: Basic Books.

Janoff-Bulman, R. (1992). *Shattered assumptions: Towards a new psychology of trauma*. New York: Free Press.

Johnson, S. M. (2002). *Emotionally focused couple therapy with trauma survivors*. New York: Guilford Press.

LaCapra, D. (2001). *Writing history, writing trauma*. Baltimore: Johns Hopkins University Press.

Pietromonaco, P., Greenwood, D., & Barrett, L. (2004). Conflict in adult close relationships: an attachment perspective. In W. S. Rholes & J. A. Simpsons (Eds.), *Adult attachment: Theory, research, and clinical implications* (pp. 267–299). New York: Guilford Press.

Solomon, M., & Siegel, J., Eds. (1997). *Countertransference in couples therapy*. New York: Norton.

Van der Kolk, B. A., McFarlane, A. C., & Weisaeth, L. (Eds.). (1996). *Traumatic stress: The effects of overwhelming experience on mind, body, and society*. New York: Guilford Press.

CHAPTER 12

A Systemic Perspective of Coping and Adaptation

The Inextricable Connection Between Individual and Family

BEA HOLLANDER-GOLDFEIN

Introduction

The fields of traumatic stress, Holocaust studies, developmental psychopathology, and systems theory have contributed to an expanded knowledge base of which factors are related to coping and resilience. Researchers across these fields of study have advocated for the need to investigate the interrelationships among these factors and how they explain survivorship. The particular focus of the Transcending Trauma Project (TTP) has been to propose a conceptual framework that enables us to study a life from a life history. Since the TTP was developed in the early 1990s, it has been our goal to utilize the life histories gathered from Holocaust survivors and their family members to gain a better understanding of coping and adaptation after extreme trauma. From our work, we suggest that utilizing the information available in a life history provides the broadest possible perspective for understanding the interplay between the processes of development and the capacity for handling life crises and trauma.

The TTP model, which is the conceptual framework presented in this chapter, integrates the research findings of the TTP with contributions from the academic fields listed (Aldwin, 2009; Brom, Pat-Horenczyk, &

Ford, 2009; Allen, 2005; Courtois & Ford, 2009; Figley, 1989; McCann & Pearlman, 1990; Valent, 1998; van der Kolk, McFarlane, & Weisaeth, 1996; and Wilson, Harel, & Kahana (1988). This integration has aided us in developing a model of coping and adaptation after extreme trauma that incorporates continua of behavior that account for individual differences in traumatic stress responses, in the recovery process and in the transmission to the next generation. Studying differences among families and how they nurture and socialize children helps to explain variations in adult coping and adaptation. The development of the TTP model has progressed over years of gathering and analyzing information provided by the TTP life histories. We hope that the model presented in this book will make a contribution toward a better understanding of how human beings cope with adversity differently and why these differences exist. The model offers mental health practitioners a developmental framework for understanding the sources of influence contributing to posttraumatic symptoms that go beyond the trauma itself. It enables the practitioner to conceptualize the multidimensional nature of traumatic effects by focusing on varied aspects of human functioning. In so doing, therapeutic intervention can focus on the traumatic symptoms while addressing contributing factors from earlier in the survivor's life.

This chapter is organized in two sections. Section 1 presents the TTP model and explains the domains of human experience that comprise the model. The discussion includes the work of key authors in attachment theory, family resilience, systems theory, interpersonal neurobiology, and developmental psychopathology as an extension of the review of literature in Chapter 1. The TTP model is actually two models in one. The first part of the model is focused on the Holocaust survivor and tracks family-of-origin experiences. The second part is focused on the child of the Holocaust survivor and tracks how the survivor experience affected the next generation. The model describes domains of life experience and the progression of developmental impact from one domain to the next. This is not to imply determinism since it is impossible to predict with certainty a particular psychological outcome from specific experiences. It is possible, however, to track patterns of influence among factors in one developmental stage and the impact of those influences on the expression of factors in the next developmental stage. The TTP model incorporates factors that research and clinical practice have pointed to as key influences in human development without any presumption that the model, at this stage in its development, is all inclusive.

Section 2 presents how the TTP model offers a framework for exploring trends in the interrelationships between developmental factors, family dynamics, identity traits, and risk/protective factors that influence coping, adaptation, and resilience. Four life histories, charted on the TTP model, are presented for discussion. These include two parent-child dyads, one from the positive family group and one from the negative family group (see Chapter 8). By studying these contrasting pairs, we hope to convey how the first part of the model reveals patterns of developmental experiences that contribute to differences in the coping and adaptation of the survivor. The second part of the model focuses on transmission and sheds light on ways in which the survivor parent influences the child's capacity to cope and adapt in adulthood. Further examination of this process and its potential for revealing the interrelationships of factors that influence coping and adaptation in survivors and their children will be an important extension of this work.

Section 1

Part 1: The Transcending Trauma Model

Systems theory is the basis for our investigation of individual functioning, parent–child dynamics and family interactional processes to better understand how a human being copes with adversity and trauma. The TTP research team purposely constructed the semistructured interview for conducting deepened life histories to reveal the familial context for the interviewees' experiences. The systemic framework advocates that to more fully understand human development it must be contextualized within relationships that influence not only psychosocial domains of behavior but also the expression of genetic inheritance (Kaffman & Meaney, 2007; Kagan, 2010; Suomi, 2000).

The domains of the TTP model reflect the multifactorial nature of development. Many aspects of human functioning change, grow, and develop within the context of multiple relationships and multiple environments, as the individual encounters developmental milestones involving the mind–body connection. Each developmental stage is the prelude for the emergence of the next stage. This process is equally true for the family as it goes through its own developmental stages. Multiple factors are constantly interacting to influence the development of each child within the family. Siblings experience their families differently due to the additional factors that differentiate them from each other, such as gender, temperament, and "fit" with each parent.

Conceptualizing the complexity of the interplay among factors that influence human behavior is where the field of psychology and its related disciplines are positioned today. Traumatic stress research has historically documented the negative sequelae of extreme trauma only to discover significant variability among survivors due to the complex interplay of factors that influence survivorship. The study of individual differences among trauma survivors reveals a continuum of experience spanning from positive to negative adaptation, with most individuals falling somewhere in between. Based on the accumulated knowledge from traumatic stress research, it has come to be accepted that pretrauma experience directly influences the individual's posttrauma adaptation. The investigation of pretrauma experience illuminated the functioning of risk and protective factors that contribute to the individual's position on that continuum (Garmezy, 1983; Rutter, 1990). Concurrent with these advances, the field of resilience emerged in an attempt to explain why some people survive well and others do not and how the phenomenon of posttraumatic growth operates differently for each survivor. This research has identified risk factors, protective factors, resilience traits, and posttraumatic growth related to posttrauma adaptation. The current challenge for the field is to observe and describe the processes by which these factors, traits, and characteristics interrelate with each other to generate the responses of individuals and families to normative and adverse life circumstances (Calhoun & Tedeshi, 2006; Greene, 2002b, 2006; Wilson, 2006).

Scientific inquiry, through the development of structural equation modeling and, more specifically, path modeling, can now study the direction of influence that variables have on each other when studying the psychological impact of an event on human behavior (Hoyle, 1995). The extent of influence that psychosocial factors have on each other is qualified by the distinction between mediating factors that have a direct impact and moderating factors that have an indirect impact on responses to particular events. The qualitative investigations conducted by TTP have revealed patterns of interrelated factors associated with coping. The TTP model proposes patterns of influence that could potentially explain the processes that contribute to how people cope and why they cope differently. The empirical study of these patterns, utilizing path analysis techniques, provides the means by which to study the complexity of how developmental factors, family dynamics, and identity traits influence coping and resilience in trauma survivors.

Masten (2007) stated the importance of identifying the processes and pathways of influence that mediate and moderate resilient adaptation. Layne and his colleagues (2009) presented clear and concise visual graphics that depict pathways of influence among psychosocial factors affecting human behavior. These researchers have made significant contributions to understanding the association among factors in human experience that acknowledge the variability of experience and facilitate the study of human differences.

Presented in Table 12.1 is the first part of the transcending trauma model, which is focused on the survivor. Each domain of the model is explained in terms of defining concepts and the role of that domain in human development.

The TTP model is built on a developmental framework that tracks development from infancy to adulthood. It was created by TTP to fulfill the goal of learning about the life experiences of survivors before the trauma of the Holocaust to understand their postwar adaptation and the impact on their children. The model provides a conceptual framework for the study of a life from an extended life history. The findings from the TTP qualitative

Table 12.1 Survivor's Foundation of Psychosocial Development Before the Trauma

FROM BIRTH TO ADULTHOOD: PRETRAUMA PREWAR

Domain 1

Biology: Genetic Predisposition, Temperament, Potential, Intelligences

Domain 2

Survivor—Foundation of the Individual Self, Interpersonal Neurobiology
Early nurture: Attachment to caregiver
Compensatory attention: Affection from other adults

Domain 3

Survivor—Foundation of the Relational Self
Indicative of Attachment Relationship With Parents (Caregivers)
Quality of Family Dynamics Paradigm, Family of Origin
Closeness—*Distance*
Empathy—*Self-centeredness*
Validation—*Criticism*
Open communication—*Closed communication*
Expressive of positive emotions—*Expressive of negative emotions*

Domain 4

Survivor—Family-of-Origin Interactional Processes Related to Positive Adaptation and *Maladaptation*[a]

Belief Systems
Make meaning of adversity vs. *Senseless loss, failure, blame, shame, despair*
Positive outlook vs. *Powerless, helpless, overwhelmed*
Transcendence and spirituality vs. *Spiritual distress, injustice, disconnected, punishment*

Organizational Patterns
Economic and institutional resources vs. *Resources depleted or unavailable*
Family and community connectedness vs. *Vital bonds lost, exploitation, and social isolation*
Flexibility vs. *Rigid, autocratic, unstable, enmeshed, conflicted*

Communication and Problem Solving
Clarity of communication vs. *Ambiguous information, secrecy, distortion, denial*
Collaborative problem solving vs. *Blocked problem solving, no planning, overwhelmed*
Open emotional expression vs. *Blocked emotional sharing, gender constraints, no respite*

Domain 5

Quality of Survivor's Parents' Marriage
Good, moderately distressed, highly distressed, divorced

(Continued)

Table 12.1 (Continued) Survivor's Foundation of Psychosocial Development Before the Trauma

Domain 6		
Positive and *Adverse* Life Events		
Risk and Protective Factors		

Domain 7		
Survivor—Identity Formation		
Personality and Skills	**Cognitive Schema**	**Affective Functioning**
Character traits	Meaning systems	Range of emotional
Coping styles	Beliefs and faith	experiencing
Skills & education	Roles in family and in	Affect regulation
	society	Self-reflection and
		self-awareness

Domain 8
Survivor—Country of Origin; Racial, Ethnic, & Cultural Background;
Gender and SES

IMPACT OF THE TRAUMA ON THE SURVIVOR

Domain 9
Severity of the Trauma

Domain 10	Domain 11
Posttrauma Impact	**Posttrauma Adaptation**
Physiological vulnerability: Physical injuries	**Balance Between Self and Other Determines Quality of Relational Functioning in the Nuclear Family**
Hypervigilance: Mistrust, suspicion, lack of safety	
Vulnerability: Anxiety, fearfulness, impending danger	Establishing connection in significant relationships
Emotional reactivity: Emotions that come on suddenly and are not modulated by thought or circumstance	Being aware of feelings and able to modulate their expression
Identity and role disruption: Who am I now?	Cognitive functioning Reaffirmation of identity
Shattered beliefs about self and the world	Memories are available and neither obsessive nor blocked
Explanatory style: Pessimistic and negative attributions	Integrating the story of one's experience
Crisis of faith in G-d	Explanatory style: Optimistic and realistic attributions
Unresolved mourning	Reconstruction of belief systems
PTSD: Intrusion, avoidance, arousal, dissociation	Acceptance of life's realities and finding meaning
Vulnerability to psychiatric disorder	Opportunity to utilize potential, talent, and skills
Relationship alienation, isolation, and loneliness	"Self-reflective function"

Table 12.1 (Continued) Survivor's Foundation of Psychosocial Development Before the Trauma

Domain 12
Characteristics of Coping – Described in Life Histories
<u>Temperament: Personality characteristics</u>
<u>External attributes</u>
<u>Positive beliefs about self</u>
<u>Pretrauma challenges</u>
<u>Faith and general beliefs</u>
<u>Focused endurance</u>
<u>Active and instrumental coping</u>
<u>Social connection: Relationship orientation</u>
<u>Family connection</u>
<u>Defense mechanisms</u>

Note: In Table 12.1, positive factors are <u>underlined</u>; negative factors are *italicized.*
[a] Used with permission. Walsh, F. (2007). Traumatic loss and major disasters: Strengthening family and community resilience. *Family Process, 46,* 212. John Wiley & Sons Ltd. © 2010.

analyses of 275 life histories contribute to the conceptual foundation of the model and provide evidence for the importance given to particular developmental milestones. This model is not designed to emphasize strengths or weaknesses. It is designed to expand our understanding of both resilience and traumatic injury on the continuum of human behavior.

It is our belief that all Holocaust survivors carry within them qualities of resilience as well as the lingering injury from their overwhelming losses and physical torture during World War II. For many Holocaust survivors, the capacity to move beyond their suffering and rebuild successful lives is extraordinary and seems to overshadow what Krell, himself a child survivor, has called the "depression of the soul" (1998). For other survivors, who were unable to rebuild their lives, their lifelong depression and psychiatric disorders resulted in long-term hospitalization (Laub, 2005). In contrast, the sample of survivors interviewed for TTP were married with families and were functioning in the varied roles that constituted their lives with mixed levels of success and distress. They participated willingly and could engage in a verbal exchange and an extended conversation about their lives before, during, and after the war. They could respond to questions about their thoughts, feelings, and inner experiences. Therefore, on the continuum from extraordinary to nonfunctional, the TTP sample was comprised of survivors and family members who were on the more functional end of the continuum.

Early in our work, the landmark research conducted by Valliant (1977) on adult development cautioned us to be wary of external judgments. Vaillant studied a cohort of male undergraduates at Harvard University who were identified as most likely to succeed in their future lives. A striking case in his sample was a man who became extremely successful and prominent in his career, but whose family life was very distressed. This led the researchers to reexamine the definition of a "successful life" to include the private as well as the public persona. They found that the appearance of a successful life or a distressed life cannot be accepted at face value. This has implications for our study of Holocaust survivors. To achieve a balanced understanding of success and distress in a survivor's postwar life, our model considers information about personal, marital, and family functioning in addition to information about work and community involvement. It addresses both the public and private dimensions of the survivor's life.

Glicksman and his colleagues (2003) raised a different caution. They pointed to the importance of studying the life of survivors as a trajectory that may have many twists and turns, at times demonstrating great resilience and at other times demonstrating difficulties in adjustment. TTP has taken this into account by tracking the life course of survivors from childhood through old age. We include not only experiences of the family of origin and the nuclear family, relationship functioning and individual functioning, cognitive and emotional functioning, but also belief systems and personality characteristics together with the presence or absence of key attributes of resilience.

To find a meaningful language to assess the balance between positive and negative qualities in survivors' lives, many of the factors used to assess coping and adaptation on the TTP model are described on a continuum or as a comparison. The challenge of the complexity of human functioning is represented by the reality that no two people standing next to each other at the Auschwitz death camp came from the same background, and they did not rebuild their lives in the same way. While they shared a common horrifying experience in a death camp and most likely shared the reality of extensive losses of loved ones, they did not experience the same developmental influences in childhood or the same biology. They also did not share the same potential for coping and adaptation in their postwar lives.

DOMAIN 1

SURVIVOR BIOLOGY

GENETIC PREDISPOSITION, TEMPERAMENT, POTENTIAL, INTELLIGENCES

Biology Domain 1 of the TTP model is biology. While acknowledging the general absence of data about the biological predisposition of the individuals in this study, we have noted those qualities that have a biological base and are described in the life histories. Fundamental to the fulfillment of the biological bases of behavior is the quality of family relationships, especially the caregiver relationship. Psychology and related fields have come to acknowledge that the argument of nature versus nurture is spurious, and that the reality is closer to nature interacting with nurture (Kaffman & Meaney, 2007; Siegel, 1999; Suomi, 2000). Therefore, it is a premise in the study of human development that the fulfillment of a child's potential for positive psychological growth and healthy physical development is dependent on the interaction between the quality of relationships with caregivers and genetic endowment (Schore, 1994). The expression of talent is also fostered by the quality of relationships with caregivers, which is limited by temperament and genetic endowment (Kagan & Snidman, 2004). Sociocultural factors exert their influence in terms of overt manifestations of behavior, motivation, and value orientation. (Kagan, 2010).

DOMAIN 2

SURVIVOR—FOUNDATION OF THE INDIVIDUAL SELF, INTERPERSONAL NEUROBIOLOGY

Early nurture – Attachment to caregiver
Compensatory attention – Affection from other adults

Foundation of the Individual Self   Domain 2 of the TTP model focuses on the development of the individual "self." This early stage of human development provides the foundation for the emergence of characteristics in the individual that will influence coping and adaptation later in life. The sense of self begins to form as a result of the mutual interactions between an infant and the infant's caregivers. The fulfillment of basic physical needs fosters physical stability and emotional security, while the fulfillment of emotional needs fosters psychological, emotional, social, intellectual, and physical development. It is within this relational environment that the full expression of genetic potential is nurtured (Schore, 1994; Siegel, 1999; Siegel & Hartzell, 2003).

Nurturing family relationships throughout childhood is important to sustain ongoing psychological health. If positive nurture is disrupted due to the loss of the primary caregiver or if a child is subjected to neglect or abuse, then the child's development will be negatively affected. Early positive nurture is critical to the well-being of the individual over a lifetime and even in the face of devastating experiences later in life. The foundation laid down by positive early nurture serves as a baseline of psychological health. If early nurture is not provided by the mother or father, then a surrogate caregiver can successfully step in to take on the caregiving role. Compensatory attention that comes from other sources of adult caregiving is extremely important to a child at every stage of development. Positive caregiving at any point in time can build on the foundation of even the smallest elements of positive nurture that occurred early in life (Walsh, 2006; Werner & Smith, 1992). This care may come from grandparents, extended family, friends, teachers, religious leaders, or community members. Whatever the source, supportive empathic attunement from a caring person, at any point in one's life, promotes and reinforces healthy emotional functioning. If a child grew up in a dysfunctional family and experienced troubled relationships and difficult social circumstances, empathic attunement from caring people can foster reparative experiences. This enables the person to utilize underdeveloped psychological and genetic potential for healthier functioning.

Advances in the scientific understanding of the development of the brain and the formation of the mind have been referred to as *interpersonal neurobiology* (Siegel, 1999). This term captures the reality that relationships form the basis for the development of the self. The interaction between the experience of self within significant relationships and inborn temperament ultimately leads to the development of the adult personality (Kagan, 2010). Attachment theory pre-dates the new brain science and has been validated by discoveries related to brain function and development. Attachment theory explains how early childhood experiences with primary caregivers result in secure or insecure attachment styles, which form templates for adult relationships and the development of personality characteristics. These templates influence how the individual engages in relationships throughout the life span (Bowlby, 1969; Cassidy & Shaver, 1999). The quality of early caregiving relationships is also predictive of how the individual will parent his or her own child. The Adult Attachment Inventory (AAI) was designed to assess early attachment styles from the adult report of early attachment relationships. Research has validated that this instrument accurately predicts the attachment style that will characterize the future relationship between the adult and his or her unborn child. The assessment of an adult's early attachment experience is accomplished by eliciting stories about the dynamics of significant relationships throughout the life of the person (Ainsworth, Blehar, Waters, & Wall, 1978; Bowlby, 1988; Bretherton, 1992; Hazan & Zeifman, 1999; Main, 1999; Zeifman & Hazan, 1997b). The life histories conducted by TTP function similarly to the AAI in terms of describing significant family members and by eliciting stories about experiences with these significant family members throughout childhood. The repetition of themes across stories provides the basis for observing positive and negative bonds with parents and others.

Secure attachment in childhood fosters the capacity for closeness in human relationships. It allows for the cognitive appraisal of life in positive terms and the affirmation of goals and values. Secure attachment facilitates the capacity to be flexible and adaptive as well as the ability to regulate emotions so that they are manageable and appropriate. Finally, it fosters the capacity to be self-aware and aware of others and helps support the belief that life is imbued with meaningful experience. Secure attachment can be the basis for one's willingness to care for others beyond one's own needs (Hazan & Zeifman, 1999). These qualities directly impact how well an individual manages life challenges and responds to adversity. Anxious and avoidant attachment relationships disrupt the healthy development of the qualities listed. A child growing up with insecure attachment will be less prepared to manage life constructively and less able to respond to adversity effectively.

How then do we explain the phenomenon of children growing up under adverse circumstances within troubled families who succeed in building successful adult lives? There have been numerous studies of these resilient children. The longitudinal investigation conducted by Werner and Smith (1977, 1982, 1992, 2001) found that these children have appealing qualities that attract adults to come to their aid. These adults provide nurture, encouragement, and guidance that enable the child to access healthier functioning and make constructive choices for their futures. Rubin (1996), interviewing what she called transcendent children as adults, observed that each one had a caring adult at some point in their lives, and each one consciously chose a different life path than one would have predicted based on the children's families. They deliberately sought out role models and opportunities to live a better life. Attachment theorists have called the outcome of this process *earned attachment* (Hesse, 1999).

In the TTP sample, survivors were asked to describe their families and in particular their relationships with their parents and other caregivers. It was our goal to ascertain the quality of attachment that the survivor experienced in childhood and track the interrelationship between attachment and other developmental factors related to coping and adaptation. In addition to descriptions of family life and parenting relationships, survivors described encounters with caring adults who were influential in their lives. During the war, many survivors described times when parents or siblings took extraordinary care of them and risked their lives on their behalf. They also reported that strangers cared for them in ways that ultimately saved their lives. These acts of caring had a profound impact on the survivors and reaffirmed that they were human and that life still had meaning. While constituting only a small percentage of war experiences, these social connections helped sustain survivors in their struggle to endure their suffering.

The life histories of survivors contain the normal complexities of human development. Multiple factors are always at play in a child's life and within the family. As we track the lives of survivors and their children on the TTP model, you will notice trends in the balance of relationship qualities. The balance between constructive and destructive qualities in early nurture raises the concept of "good enough parenting" (Winnicott, 1960). Since perfect parenting does not exist, the concept of good enough acknowledges the reality that as long as there are positive influences in a child's life, the child will derive whatever benefit is possible from these positive sources of psychological health, provided that the negative influences are not overwhelming.

Neuroscience and attachment theory offer another important consideration for the focused study of life histories. Both point out that life stories are different in quality based on an individual's early attachment. The stories shared by those Holocaust survivors who experienced positive attachment with caregivers are longer and richer in detail and contain more emotional language than the stories of those who did not. They also reveal a greater capacity for self-awareness and the awareness of what others are experiencing (Fonagy, Steele, Morgan, Steele, & Higgit, 1991). Those individuals raised with caregivers who were not good enough and caused the child to feel emotionally insecure, anxious, and fearful tended to tell fewer stories, which were shorter in length, minimal in detail, relatively devoid of emotion, and lacking indications of self- and other awareness (Siegel, 1999).

Tracking life histories of survivors on the TTP model reveals patterns of influence across developmental stages. As the child matures, actual parenting behaviors become important in terms of their influence on the development of personality traits, belief systems and affect regulation. All of this occurs while the child is learning life skills and gaining knowledge about the world. Parenting behaviors are the means by which the attachment relationship is expressed during later stages of development.

DOMAIN 3

SURVIVOR—FOUNDATION OF THE RELATIONAL SELF

INDICATIVE OF ATTACHMENT RELATIONSHIPS

QUALITY OF FAMILY DYNAMICS PARADIGM, FAMILY OF ORIGIN

Closeness – *Distance*
Empathy – *Self-centeredness*
Validation – *Criticism*
Open communication – *Closed Communication*
Expressive of positive emotions – *Expressive of negative emotions*

Note: In this box, positive factors are underlined; negative factors are *italicized*.

Foundation of the Relational Self: The Quality of Family Dynamics Paradigm   Domain 3 of the TTP model focuses on parent–child relationships and how they function. These relationships foster secure and insecure attachment, which is registered in the body as the sensations of safety and threat. As the child matures, parent–child and other caring adult relationships continue to enhance the growth of the self by influencing self-esteem and by encouraging the emerging identity of the child. The capacities to be in relationship with another human being need to be nurtured so that neural pathways are developed that sustain healthy relating over a lifetime. Relationships contribute to the experience of nurture and support in childhood and of love and intimacy in adulthood. Children need to develop the capacity to be close to someone and the skill to relate well if they are to experience happiness and fulfillment as adults.

Operating from a grounded theory methodology, TTP developed the semistructured interview to include an intensive exploration of significant relationships in childhood (see Chapter 3). We probed with open-ended questions and sought the descriptions of these relationships in the survivor's own words with their own judgment of what was positive and what was negative. We recorded the descriptions of parent–child relationships and then sought to label the patterns of parenting that were revealed during the analysis process.

Our analyses revealed five qualitative family dynamics on a continuum from positive to negative that describe the majority of interactions between parents and children recorded in the survivor life histories. These five family dynamics are listed on the domain of the TTP model labeled "Foundation of the Relational Self" because they foster positive development in the child and promote the capacity for close relationships later in life. As discussed in detail in Chapter 6, these qualitative family dynamics are: closeness versus distance, empathy versus self-centeredness, validation versus criticism, open communication versus closed communication, expressive of positive emotions versus expressive of negative emotions. We conceptualize these parent-child behaviors as the specific mechanisms that promote psychological growth and personality development. They are among the caregiving behaviors that promote secure and insecure attachment in childhood that is the foundation for adult bonding later in life.

On the positive end of the continuum, these parenting interactions promote positive self-esteem, feelings of trust and freedom of emotional expression. The emotional quality and cognitive messages inherent in these interactions contribute to the child's capacity to be in relationship with significant others and are the foundation for adult bonding later in life. On the negative end of the continuum, these parenting interactions promote negative self-esteem, mistrust, and emotional withdrawal. Here, the interactions contribute to the child's avoidance of close relationships as a means of self-protection. The qualitative examination of the life histories revealed clearly that the relationships between parents and a child are influenced by the psychological level of functioning and the parenting style of each individual parent. Simultaneous to the research efforts of the TTP, the work of Cowan and Cowan (2000, 2002, 2005) and others effectively switched the focus of family studies and developmental psychopathology from the almost-exclusive focus on the mother as caregiver to the assessment of both parents in terms of their parenting impact (Schulz, Pruett, Kerig, & Parke, 2010). When both parents are psychologically healthy and utilize positive parenting, the effects on the child are positive. For parents who are distressed and utilize negative parenting behaviors, the effects on the child result in a broad range of difficulties. Tracking childhood relationships with both parents is challenging when one parent engages more positively and the other more negatively on these five dynamics. Many factors, including gender, parenting behaviors, vulnerability and temperament of the child, and the specific problems of the negative parent determine how mixed parenting affects the developing child. These patterns have been tracked by the TTP through the analysis process (see Chapter 8).

Researchers in the field of developmental psychopathology have focused on parenting practices not only in terms of healthy development but also specifically in terms of helping children cope with adversity. Gewirtz, Forgatch, and Wieling (2008) "propose that parenting practices are potentially the most salient target of intervention in promoting children's resilience post trauma" (p. 178). The recognition that intervention with traumatized children should focus on the family system reinforces the emphasis of Gewirtz and her colleagues on parenting practices that can prevent symptomatic behavior and reinforce resilience in children confronting traumatic events. The parenting practices that Gewirtz et al. advocated are based on the research findings of Patterson and his team that demonstrated the effectiveness of five parenting practices (PTMO: Parent Management Training–Oregon Model) with children who manifest behavior problems (Patterson, DeBaryshe, & Ramsey, 1989; Patterson, DeGarmo, & Forgatch, 2004; Patterson, 2005). PTMO is based on promoting structure, security, and emotional warmth. The quality of family dynamics paradigm of the TTP model correlates with two of Patterson's criteria: security and emotional warmth. Structure, which fosters skill development and responsible behavior, is the third component of Patterson's paradigm of effective parenting. The focus on structure and its role in development is a good transition to the next level of the TTP model.

DOMAIN 4

SURVIVOR FAMILY-OF-ORIGIN INTERACTIONAL PROCESSES RELATED TO <u>POSITIVE ADAPTATION</u> AND *MALADAPTATION*[a]

Belief Systems

<u>Make meaning of adversity</u> vs *Senseless loss, failure, blame, shame, despair*
<u>Positive outlook</u> vs *Powerless, helpless, overwhelmed*
<u>Transcendence and spirituality</u> vs *Spiritual distress, injustice, disconnected, punishment*

Organizational Patterns

<u>Economic and institutional resources</u> vs *Resources depleted or unavailable*
<u>Family and community connectedness</u> vs *Vital bonds lost, exploitation, and social isolation*
<u>Flexibility</u> vs *Rigid, autocratic, unstable, enmeshed, conflicted*

Communication and Problem Solving

<u>Clarity of communication</u> vs *Ambiguous information, secrecy distortion, denial*
<u>Collaborative problem solving</u> vs *Blocked problem solving, no planning, overwhelmed*
<u>Open emotional expression</u> vs *Blocked emotional sharing, gender constraints, no respite*

Note: In this box, positive factors are <u>underlined</u>; negative factors are *italicized*.
[a] Used with permission. Walsh, F. (2007). Traumatic loss and major disasters: Strengthening family and community resilience. *Family Process, 46*, 212. John Wiley & Sons Ltd. © 2010.

Family Interactional Processes and Adaptation   Walsh's (2007) model of "Family-of-Origin Interactional Processes Related to Positive Adaptation and Maladaption" is placed here in the TTP model because it describes important family processes related to belief systems, organizational structure, communication, and problem solving. Her model is based on the premise that how families negotiate these processes will directly reflect the capacity of the family to adapt to changing demands and to cope with adversity. This in turn will directly affect how the children will learn to adapt and cope. It will also influence the choices that the children make as adults when they are responsible for handling the demands of their own nuclear families. The family processes listed on the model are part of day-to-day life and foster the developmental growth of children by engaging them in these ongoing tasks and experiences. Children learn these tasks from role modeling and from direct interactions with parents (Walsh, 2003b, 2006).

From the time that the developing child can function cognitively and emotionally, beliefs, values, and spiritual ideas are conveyed to the child simply by being part of the family. The organizational structure of the family communicates messages about generational responsibilities, roles played by the different members, and guidelines for adapting to change and challenge. The structure of the family dictates closeness and distance and how members relate to each other. It also dictates how much a family connects with the community and the outside world.

Communication and problem solving are essential functions of a family, and how well a family engages in these functions has a significant impact on the well-being of its members. Communication is a constant and takes place on verbal and nonverbal levels. Clarity of communication is necessary for family members to feel understood. Problem solving is an essential function of family life. The absence of problem solving leaves the family unprepared for demands and subject to extreme stress. Rigid planning can be harmful and divisive. In a traditional household in which parents make decisions for children or the father makes decisions for everyone, taking the other family members into account is a constructive process. Even a defined hierarchy of decision making can be a collaborative process that conveys respect, understanding, and love to each family member.

Open emotional expression is the last task in Walsh's model and serves the broadest needs of the family. It is crucial to healthy psychological development and is an expression of the bonds within the family. It is closely linked to the developmental domains that preceded this domain. Positive early nurture and qualitatively positive parent–child interactions will serve to keep the emotional life of a family open and expressive. Poor early nurture and negative parent–child interactions will serve to shut down the emotional life of a family. Either outcome has a ripple effect on the family and will affect beliefs, organizational patterns, communication, and problem solving.

Walsh's model of family functioning was chosen for the TTP model, not only because of its scope, but also because it frames family processes in terms of a continuum of behavior from the positive to the negative. Paralleling the presentation of the quality of family dynamics paradigm (Domain 3), which is also conceptualized on a continuum, this framework makes it possible to compare positive and negative patterns of behavior. It also enables the TTP to take a retrospective look at how coping and adaptation expressed later in the lives of Holocaust survivors is related to their descriptions of how their families of origin handled interpersonal processes.

The integration of Walsh's conceptualization and the conceptualization by TTP expands on our understanding of family functioning. The interactional processes of families are based on the negotiation between two parents (caregivers). If the parents (caregivers) are psychologically healthy and interact with their children utilizing behaviors from the adaptive side of the continuum, then the model would predict that the family members would cope relatively effectively when challenged by trauma. If the parents (caregivers) are psychologically distressed and the family utilizes behaviors from the maladaptive side of the continuum, then the family members would tend to respond in maladaptive ways when challenged by trauma.

Greene (2002b, 2010a, 2010b, 2010c) integrated the study of Holocaust survivors and family systems theory in her extensive study of survivorship. Her family resilience template, which overlaps many of Walsh's constructs, assesses how families utilize assets, confront threat, implement survival skills, rise above the challenge, cope with accumulated risk, access resources and strengths, and construct a common worldview. Walsh's model, the result of her investigation of positive and distressed families, and Greene's model, the result of her investigation of Holocaust survivors, are both significant contributions to the study of coping, adaptation, and resilience. The development of the Holocaust survivorship model specifically contributed to the field of resilience by substantiating the observation that a large number of Holocaust survivors have succeeded in rebuilding their lives and that they have demonstrated extraordinary resilience.

Over the 20-year span of the TTP, the view of survivors, within the broader mental health field, has radically shifted from a pathology orientation to a resilience framework. This shift has been supported by ongoing research into the survivor experience. The questions that motivated the development of the TTP are the same now as they were at its inception. Our goal has been to better understand the differences among survivors and to understand how these differences came to be. To the body of work published by Greene, Armour, Hantman, Graham, and Sharabi (2010d), we contribute an understanding of how survivors differ from each other—how relative strengths and weaknesses coexist, how prewar upbringing differentially affected postwar adaptation, and how resilience takes various forms.

DOMAIN 5

QUALITY OF SURVIVOR'S PARENTS' MARRIAGE

Good, moderately distressed, highly distressed, divorced

Quality of Survivor's Parents' Marriage   The quality of the parents' marriage is a factor that mediates the overall influence of parenting on the development of children. This factor is presented in Domain 5 of the TTP model. The role of this mediating factor in the TTP sample became apparent when we assigned survivor families to groups designated as positive, mixed, and negative families (see Chapter 8). This was done to facilitate a comparative understanding of how key factors such as coping strategies, resilience, and emotional experiencing are related to the overall functioning level of the families. Profiles of the families revealed that the negative group had a higher percentage of survivor marriages described as highly distressed, while the positive group had a higher percentage of marriages described as good or moderately distressed.

The broader question related to the TTP sample is the nature of the distress in the marriage. Under normal circumstances, distress in marriage is typically the result of unhappiness, incompatibility, or external stressors causing tension in the marriage. For Holocaust survivors, however, distressed marriages could be the result of traumatized functioning, which causes negative interactions between the spouses. The survivors in the TTP sample bore the emotional burdens of their traumatic experiences in the war, which manifested in various ways depending on their psychological makeup. We do not yet understand how a distressed marriage resulting from parental traumatization affects children differently from a more conventionally distressed marriage. For example, children of survivors who reported compassion for their parents' suffering during the war appeared to be more compassionate and less reactive to their parents' marital problems. This may temper the negative impact because the conflict is understandable even though it is still difficult to bear. We are unaware of research that has disentangled the effects of emotional incompatibility versus the effects of traumatic stress on marriage and parenting.

The research of Cowan and Cowan (2005), discussed in Chapters 8 and 9, revealed that distressed marriages have a negative impact on parenting. Parke, Schulz, Pruett, and Kerig (2010) also presented a model of family functioning that linked marital satisfaction with quality of parenting. They explained that even parents who are good enough based on their capacity to relate to their children constructively may parent more negatively as a result of being in a distressed marriage. Cummings and Merrilees (2010) have shown through their research that distressed marriages have a negative impact on children separate from the effect on parenting. Their theory of "emotional security" proposes that parents who engage in overt interpersonal conflict create an insecure environment for their children. They observed that in response to overt marital distress, children either blamed themselves for their parents' arguments or saw themselves as responsible to fix the marriage. Either assumption caused the child to feel anxious about the parental conflict and insecure about the future. In addition, children who are mature enough to understand feel sad about the hurt that the parents are inflicting on each other. As a result, developmental milestones in childhood are compromised by feelings of insecurity. For this and other reasons, children witnessing ongoing marital distress without sufficient compensatory experiences are vulnerable to problems in adulthood.

Many Holocaust survivors experienced factors conducive to marital distress, including the fact that they tended to marry quickly after the end of the war. Their losses, insecurity, and desperation prompted a quick connection that they hoped would alleviate the loneliness and provide a partner to share an unknown future. These quick connections are referred to as "marriages of despair" (Danieli, 1985). Interestingly, survivors may not have described their marriages as unhappy, but their children reported witnessing significant conflict. Children also reported being affected by their parents' conflicted marriages. The degree to which the impact was negative was mediated by the quality of their relationships with each parent and their empathy for their parents' trauma (see Chapter 9).

Secondary traumatic stress disorder is the concept in the trauma literature that explains what happens to a spouse who is the caregiver for a symptomatic partner (Figley, 1998). This concept points to the process by which individuals who are in close proximity to someone experiencing posttrauma symptoms have the potential of being traumatized by exposure to those symptoms (Gilbert, 1998). This pattern has been observed in many proximal relationships to traumatized individuals. Lev-Wiesel and Amir (2001) found that one third of the Holocaust survivors in their sample reported secondary traumatic stress symptoms related to the other spouse's trauma. A clear outcome was poor marital quality.

The greatest challenge in this kind of research is to separate the complex interplay of survivor reactions to traumatic experiences versus survivor reactions to marital discord. Goff and Smith's couple adaptation to traumatic stress model (2005) added another perspective to this inquiry by emphasizing the emotional impact of traumatic stress in terms of isolation, lack of support, and limited intimacy in the marriage. While the secondary traumatic response approach focuses on the symptomatic partner's behaviors causing a stress response in the other partner, this perspective focuses on the other partner's feelings of isolation (Goff & Smith, 2005). The problem, from the perspective of the caregiver, is not so much exposure to stress as it is coping with loneliness and unfulfilled emotional needs.

> ## DOMAIN 6
>
> ### <u>POSITIVE</u> AND *ADVERSE* LIFE EVENTS
> ### *RISK* AND <u>PROTECTIVE</u> FACTORS

In this box, positive factors are <u>underlined</u>; negative factors are *italicized*.

Positive and Adverse Life Events: Risk and Protective Factors   Domain 6 of the TTP model addresses the inevitability of adversity and the challenge of coping with life's vicissitudes. Positive events add a positive dimension to life for individuals and families and may foster growth on many levels for the system and its members. Adverse life events may have a negative impact on many dimensions of family and individual functioning. On the other hand, adversity also enables families to utilize their strengths and coping capabilities to effectively negotiate the challenges that they are facing. Handling these challenges well strengthens family resilience and individual coping, while handling them poorly affects the capacity of family members to cope effectively. Adversity challenges the resilience of a family and its members. Dramatic events are turning points in life. What role does the family play in determining how the members respond? The model developed by Walsh (2007) describes specific family-based processes that foster healthy adaptation and resilience in contrast to those processes that foster maladaptation.

Resilience is the overall domain addressed in this part of the model. How family members cope with positive and negative life events reveals the health or dysfunction of the family system. Masten's (2001) overview of resilience research concluded that resilience is not the result of extraordinary qualities in a human being, but rather that "resilience is common and that it usually arises from the normative functions of human adaptational systems, with the greatest threats to human development being those that compromise these protective systems" (p. 227). The study of resilience has led to the rejection of many deficit-focused models about children growing up under the threat of disadvantage and adversity. The most surprising conclusion emerging from studies of these children is the ordinariness of resilience. Masten described the underlying protective systems as brain development, cognitive development, caregiver–child relationships, regulation of emotion and behavior, and the motivation for learning and engaging in one's environment. She also defined those factors that support the processes underlying resilience as competent and caring adults in the family and community, cognitive and self-regulation skills, positive view of self, and motivation to be effective in the environment (p. 234). Risk and protective factors are embedded within family and individual development. They are the cause and the result of healthy and unhealthy patterns of behavior that have a long-lasting impact. Risk and protective factors are aspects of every domain in human development presented on the TTP model. They include biological realities, patterns of early nurture, qualities in parent–child relationships, interactional processes in the family of origin, and aspects of marital relationships.

To incorporate the concept of resilience into the model of coping and adaptation after extreme trauma, we began with a list of risk and protective factors with the intent to track their relationship to postwar adaptation. The four processes described by Masten (2001) that promote resilience refer to broad processes that cannot be easily broken down into specific behaviors. Therefore, much as the development of the quality of family dynamics paradigm provides specific qualities that facilitate the assessment of attachment, so, too, the delineation of risk and protective factors identifies specific life experiences that facilitate the assessment of resilience. The list of risk and protective factors assessed by the TTP model were derived from reviews of the resilience literature by Fonagy, Steele, Steele, Higgitt, and Target (1992) and by Greene and Conrad (2002c). These authors created lists of risk and protective factors that distinguish between children and adults who show resilience in response to adversity and those children and adults who do not. These factors are listed in Table 12.2.

The risk and protective factors listed here are predictive of the capacity for resilience. On the whole, they are the result of human development, from infancy through adulthood, as depicted on the TTP model. The list

Table 12.2 Risk and Protective Factors

Risk Factors	Protective Factors
	Individual Factors
Younger age	Higher intelligence
Lower SES	Capacity for developing intimate relationships
Lack of education	Achievement orientation
Low intelligence	Capacity to construct productive meanings and thus
Psychiatric history	enhance understanding the event
Childhood abuse	Ability to disengage from the home to engage with
Other previous trauma	the outside and then reengage
Other adverse childhood	Internally oriented: internal locus of control
experience	Absence of serious illness in adolescence
Family psychiatric history	Easy disposition
Trauma severity	Task-related self-efficacy
Lack of social support	High sense of self-worth
Life stress	Interpersonal awareness and empathy
	Capacity to plan
	Sense of humor
	Optimistic
	Family-Relational Factors
Lack of good fit with parents	Good fit with parents
Family avoids dealing with	Rituals in the family
problems	Family proactive and confronts problems directly
Role reversal	Absence of role reversal
Significant conflict in the home	Minimal conflict in the home during infancy
Divorce	Absence of divorce during adolescence
Lack of substantial	Substantial relationships with mother
relationship with mother	Selection of a nontroubled spouse
Early separations and losses	Absence of early separations and losses
Negative parenting	Competent parenting
Troubled relationship with	Good relationship with primary caretaker
primary caretaker	Social support from spouse, family, and other figure
Socially isolated	Network of informal friendships
Lack of friendships	
	Attributes
Low SES	Higher SES
Physical organic impairments	Absence of organic difficulties
	Younger at the time of trauma
	Community Factors
Not involved with the	Support from school
community	Support through religious affiliation

includes a few factors related to temperament, biology, and culture, while the vast majority are psychosocial in nature. Many of the risk factors are stated as the negative of protective factors.

DOMAIN 7

SURVIVOR—IDENTITY FORMATION

Personality and Skills	Cognitive Schema	Affective Functioning
Character traits	Meaning systems	Range of emotional
Coping styles	Beliefs and faith	experiencing
Skills and education	Roles in family	Affect regulation
	and in society	Self-reflection
		and self-awareness

Survivor Identity Formation   Identity formation, Domain 7 in the TTP model, focuses on those attributes that develop throughout childhood and mature in adulthood. A person's identity is the culmination of the first six domains of psychosocial development depicted on the TTP model and the combined influences of social interactions, academic training, accumulated knowledge, religious practice, cultural norms, and influential events. It includes descriptions of character traits, coping styles, belief systems, faith experience, emotional functioning, and whether or not the person is self-aware and reflects on internal experience. Under identity formation, there are three categories of human functioning that are interrelated within the person. Although this domain is focused on the individual, everything that describes identity, other than biologically based limitations, develops within the context of the family. The family and the individual assimilate the influences listed above as the child's identity is forming. The child may take on parts of a family's identity and in other ways depart from the family style in order to adopt alternative ways of functioning, based on internal motivation and sociocultural influences. When we describe individuals, we refer to the qualities contained in this domain of the TTP model. People refer to themselves with descriptors from this domain. In terms of identity, this domain reflects the outcomes of earlier development.

The first category, labeled "personality and skills," includes three aspects of human functioning: character traits, coping styles, and achievement. Character traits refer to descriptions of behavioral, cognitive, emotional, and social functioning. The gestalt of these qualities is referred to as personality. For the individual, these qualities reflect the subjective experience of "self," the sense that "this is who I am." Specific character traits function as "coping styles," or in other words, how the person manages responsibilities and responds to stressors are listed in this category. Also in this category are skill attainment and educational achievement, which are the outcomes of the psychosocial development of competence and mastery. They are, to some extent, dependent on a person's ability to complete goals, handle responsibility, sustain motivation, and experience confidence. This list is a combination of character traits and coping styles that help an individual learn skills and attain knowledge.

The second category, "cognitive schema," includes meaning making, belief systems, faith, and one's philosophy about the purpose of life, one's role in the family, and one's role in society. Cognitive schema includes the thoughts that are part of meaning making, beliefs, faith, and philosophy, as well as the feelings that are associated with the thoughts. It is a mistake to see meaning, belief, faith, and philosophy merely as cognitions. They are thoughts that are closely tied to emotion, which is why they are so important in a person's life. Together, thoughts and feelings motivate action, which is the definition of a *cognitive schema* (Dattilo, 2005) When feelings and thoughts motivate action, this is called an *emotional schema* (Greenberg, 2002). Beliefs sustain people emotionally and give them a reason to live. As part of identity formation, beliefs are consolidated and affirmed. They become guideposts in deciding what path to take in life and what choices to make.

The third category, "affective functioning," is at the core of human functioning. The quality of a person's emotional experiencing is directly related to his or her mental health and well-being. The capacity to be open to emotional experiencing and to be able to regulate emotions so that they are neither extreme nor out of control is essential to psychological health and the negotiation of healthy relationships (Fosha, 2000; Greenberg, 2002; Johnson, 2002, 2004; Mccullough-Vaillant, 1997; Rogers, 1961). Emotion researchers advocate that emotions are ubiquitous in day-to-day life, and that they influence everything from physical functioning to interpersonal relationships all the time (Algoe & Fredrickson, 2010). Also included in this category is the capacity for self-awareness, which involves knowing one's own emotions and being aware of how one explains experience to oneself. This capacity also includes being aware of others and intuiting how their emotions influence what they do. The capacity for self- and other awareness is called the self-reflective function (Fonagy et. al., 1992) and is, likewise, related to mental health and resilience.

Domain 7, identity formation, is the profile of the individual. The categories listed in this domain contain most of the ways in which people describe themselves and the ways others come to know them. The profile of the individual is the outcome of earlier stages of human development and includes cognitive, affective, social, and behavioral dimensions. Each category exists on a continuum from qualitatively better to qualitatively inferior ways to function. To understand the contributing factors that determine how individuals cope with trauma, it is important to know about their personality traits, cognitive schema, and affective experiencing.

From this baseline of functioning, it is possible to study how the positive and negative aspects of functioning contribute to a person's ability to cope with trauma. It is also possible to study why some individuals are more vulnerable to particular traumatic sequelae and why some individuals have a greater capacity to cope and adapt.

DOMAIN 8

SURVIVOR—COUNTRY OF ORIGIN
RACIAL, ETHNIC, AND CULTURAL BACKGROUND;
GENDER AND SOCIOECONOMIC STATUS

Racial, Ethnic, and Cultural Background   Racial, ethnic, and cultural background, in addition to gender and socioeconomic status (SES), influence human development and contribute to characteristics in the individual that have an impact on adaptation to adversity and trauma. These influences are active throughout a person's life. Domain 8 in the TTP model points to the importance of including these factors in the study of how human beings cope and adapt to trauma and adversity.

The long-term impact of ethnic persecution and attempted genocide is important to understand since these practices continue around the world today. Isserman (2005) conducted an extensive investigation of tolerance and intolerance in Holocaust survivors, utilizing the TTP sample of life histories. She included a broad range of demographic variables contained in this domain. A review of her primary findings is contained in Chapter 6. Goldenberg (2008) examined how being an adolescent during the war affected coping and adaptation after the war. She selected the life histories of teenagers from the TTP sample and examined their coping strategies related to the psychological characteristics of their life stage. She included various demographic factors in her study and found gender to be an important intervening variable. Her findings are summarized in Chapter 4.

The Impact of the Trauma on the Survivor   We now focus on the continuation of the TTP model as it tracks the traumatic aftereffects on survivors, the processes of adaptation, and the impact on the second generation. Again, the TTP model presents a broad range of negative sequelae experienced and adaptive processes utilized by survivors of extreme trauma.

DOMAIN 9

SEVERITY OF THE TRAUMA

Severity of the Trauma Research has shown that the severity of a particular traumatic experience does not necessarily determine the severity of the aftereffects except when the trauma involves physical violence and threat to life (van der Kolk, McFarlane, & Weisaeth, 1996). This raises questions about those Holocaust survivors who were in life-threatening circumstances and who experienced physical assault and yet did not experience severe posttraumatic symptoms. One would expect that survivors of death camps would have had the most difficult postwar adaptation since they experienced the worst trauma. Yet, studies of Holocaust survivors have shown a range of responses, including successful coping even in survivors of the death camps who lost entire families.

The TTP investigated the question of whether the severity of experience was related to severity of response. We charted all survivors in our sample, comparing war experience to other factors related to coping and adaptation. Consistent with other Holocaust researchers, we did not find objective measures of the severity of trauma reflected the subjective experience of the survivors. Instead, we found that when survivors were asked to describe the experiences that were most unbearable for them to endure, the attribution of severity was personal for each survivor and was related to the intensity of pain that each one felt about that particular memory, and not to the objective severity of the event.

DOMAIN 10

POSTTRAUMA IMPACT

Physiological vulnerability: Physical injuries
Hypervigilance: Mistrust, suspicion, lack of safety
Vulnerability: Anxiety, fearfulness, impending danger
Emotional reactivity: Emotions that come on suddenly and are
not modulated by thought or circumstance
Identity and role disruption: Who am I now?
Shattered beliefs about self and the world
Explanatory style: Pessimistic and negative attributions
Crisis of faith in G-d
Unresolved mourning
PTSD (posttraumatic stress disorder): Intrusion, avoidance,
arousal, dissociation
Vulnerability to psychiatric disorder
Relationship alienation, isolation, and loneliness

Posttrauma Impact   Posttrauma impact, Domain 10 in the TTP model, lists potential negative responses to extreme trauma. This list was not taken from existing paradigms of posttrauma responses but instead was developed by the TTP based on the experiences reported by Holocaust survivors in our sample and by other survivors of trauma reported in the clinical literature. It includes the symptoms of PTSD (American Psychiatric Association [APA], 1987), as well as many of the negative sequelae that Herman (1992a, 1992b) proposed in her conceptualization of complex trauma and that van der Kolk et al. (2005) presented in their formulation of DESNOS, disorders of extreme stress not otherwise specified.

Briere and Spinazzola (2009) conducted a review of research on post-traumatic symptoms and developed categories that included the broad range of traumatic aftereffects observed in the traumatic stress literature. A comparison of their categories of negative sequelae (p. 106) and the list of negative sequelae from the TTP domain on posttrauma impact corroborates the comprehensiveness of the TTP model.

> Symptoms associated with trauma exposure:
>> Post-traumatic stress disorder
>> Cognitive disturbance, such as low self-esteem, self-blame, hopelessness, preoccupation with danger
>> Mood disturbance, such as anxiety, depression, anger, aggression, panic, and phobias
>> Identity disturbance
>> Difficulties in affect regulation
>> Long-term interpersonal difficulties
>> Dissociation
> Not included on the TTP model are
>> Somatization
>> Substance abuse
>> Tension reduction activities, such as compulsive sexual behavior, binge-purge eating, impulsive aggression, suicidality, and self-mutilation.

The last three categories on this list, which are not included on the TTP model, are more common posttraumatic responses in adults victimized by child abuse; these symptoms are not commonly reported by Holocaust survivors. Not included on Briere and Spinazzola's (2009) list are two types of posttrauma responses that are listed on the TTP model:

> Crisis of faith in God
> Vulnerability to psychiatric disorder

The TTP model includes a broad range of responses for the category regarding posttrauma impact to ensure that the assessment of survivors and their family members based on this model will be all inclusive. This inclusivity is crucial in the attempt to understand the differences among survivors' responses to their devastating experiences.

DOMAIN 11

POSTTRAUMA ADAPTATION
BALANCE BETWEEN "SELF" AND "OTHER"
DETERMINES QUALITY OF RELATIONAL
FUNCTIONING IN THE NUCLEAR FAMILY

Establishing connection in significant relationships
Being aware of feelings and able to modulate their expression
Cognitive functioning
Reaffirmation of identity
Memories are available and neither obsessive nor blocked
Integrating the story of one's experience
Explanatory style: Optimistic and realistic attributions
Reconstruction of belief systems
Acceptance of life's realities and finding meaning
Opportunity to utilize potential, talent, and skills
"Self-reflective function"

Posttrauma Adaptation   Domain 11, on posttrauma adaptation, lists the psychological processes that promote recovery after devastating experiences. Since negative reactions to extreme trauma affect the realms of somatic, cognitive, emotional, spiritual, and relational functioning, it follows that recovery would have to repair these realms of experience. Presumably, those survivors who do not experience these negative reactions have the psychological tools to effectively cope with the trauma because of early secure attachment, positive parent–child relationships, adaptive family-of-origin processes, protective factors, healthy personality traits, positive belief systems, and open emotional experiencing. Even survivors who experienced problematic early nurture or adverse circumstances that disrupted family functioning could have had the determination to choose a healthier alternative and then worked hard to achieve it. This choice could have kept them on a healthy track even when traumatic events disrupted their lives.

A discussion of the key factors in this domain covers a broad range of human functioning. As we go through the processes of adaptation, it is important to keep in mind the overarching question that guided this inquiry: Why did some survivors cope well while others did not? What enabled some survivors to naturally engage in these adaptive strategies without suffering the extremes of posttrauma symptoms? Each factor discussed in this domain is a piece of the puzzle of human adaptation.

The subheading under posttrauma adaptation, "balance between self and other," is the synthesis of our overall observation that the well-being of the survivor after the Holocaust and the basis for how intergenerational transmission works lies in the balance between "self" and "other." This balance depends on how well the survivor utilizes the self-reflective function to understand his or her internal experience and how well the survivor can empathically understand the internal experience of significant others. It determines the quality of relational functioning in the nuclear family that the survivor establishes after the war. The survivor contributes to the positive functioning of the nuclear family by being other oriented and ensuring that loved ones are taken care of. This choice to focus on the other, in spite of one's own suffering, builds the foundation for psychological health in the next generation. The challenge for the survivor is to establish a secure bond and parent well in spite of personal anxieties, nightmares, and sadness. The extent to which a survivor can be aware of personal needs and yet focus on the needs of his or her child will determine the foundation for the child's physical and mental health.

Evidence for the positive role of self-reflection and emotional awareness in coping and adaptation is provided by the work of Courtois and Ford (2009), who integrated theory, research, and clinical practice in the study of symptoms related to complex trauma. They proposed a three-stage process that promotes recovery: Phase I is safety and stabilization, Phase II is memory reconstruction, and Phase III is the integration of learning into more adaptive living. The process of moving through these stages is based on self-reflection, and they distinguished between the "survival mode," which is the person functioning under duress and preoccupied with survival, and the "learning mode," which is the normal process of being open to oneself and making choices that promote well-being. Helping a survivor to get to the point at which he or she can be in the learning mode—aware of him- or herself without fearing the intrusion of painful memory—is an important step in the process of recovery. The goal is to enable the survivor to make choices that improve the quality of life instead of relying on automatic defenses that keep painful memories out of awareness.

Awareness of emotions and being able to regulate them is a key factor in psychological well-being and one that is often impaired after extreme trauma when the psychological tendency is to shut down emotional awareness as a form of self-protection. On the other hand, the impact of trauma can cause extreme emotionality, which causes suffering on many levels when the person cannot regulate emotional expression. Focused self-awareness can help the survivor learn to regulate emotions. Thirty years of research involved in the study of emotion has provided strong support for the predominance of emotion in day-to-day life (Keltner & Lerner, 2010). Traumatic stress studies have revealed that positive emotions enable survivors to respond with resilience. Those individuals who naturally experience positive emotions experience fewer traumatic symptoms, less anxiety, and fewer health problems. Positive emotions have been found to enhance immune system functions, to help bolster strong relationships that provide support during stressful times, and to increase creative, adaptive, and insightful thinking. Self-awareness is an important path to accessing positive emotions and enabling their healing qualities.

The negative impact of extreme trauma on cognitive functioning can lead to distorted thoughts about self-worth, blame, hopelessness, and the prevalence of danger. We know that cognitive functioning is affected by extreme trauma, and that working on one's explanatory style to be more realistic and optimistic helps alleviate, to some extent, the deleterious effect of negative thinking. The reworking of explanatory style fosters a more balanced view of life circumstances and a more compassionate view of self (Buchanan & Seligman, 1995). The reconstruction of belief systems and the acceptance of life's realities are aspects of cognitive adaptation that incorporate not only thoughts, but also the emotions that are elicited when life has meaning and important values guide decision making and personal choices (Janoff-Bulman, 1992; Wilson, 2006).

The disruption of relationships caused by extreme trauma requires remediation as part of recovery. Connection to others within caring relationships is essential to positive mental health under all circumstances and at all stages in a person's life (Bloom, 1997). Establishing loving relationships posttrauma is the primary path toward overcoming the past, being able to live in the present, and planning for the future (Johnson, 2002). Rebuilding families restores for survivors the sense of connection to their murdered parents and siblings by providing the opportunity to fulfill their legacy. It also provides the sense of continuity into the future (Figley, 1989). For many survivors, the wish that sustained them during the war and after liberation was having a family and raising children. Devotion to family motivated survivors to persevere in their move to a new country, their search for a new home, and their immersion in work to provide support. The ability to establish emotionally attuned, affirming family relationships after the war depended on the survivor's experience of positive relationships before the war. Finding a relationship is easy. Establishing a positive relationship based on connection and mutuality is difficult to attain if relationships were never positive in the survivor's life prewar.

Accessing memories of the traumatic war years and memories of life before the war is an important reparative process. Memories need to be accessible to the conscious mind so that they are not blocked or caught in obsessive rumination. The fluidity of this process is an important part of restoring normal functioning (Solomon & Siegel, 2003), as is the integration of one's war experiences into the totality of one's life story. Access to memory and the integration of a life story are important to the repair of the mind/body connection, which requires being open to a full recognition of one's most painful experiences (Foa et al., 2004). According to Solomon and Siegel (2003), the willingness to let go of self-protection in order to confront one's traumatic experiences helps the brain reconstruct neuronal synapses that allow for choice of response. For Holocaust survivors it is difficult to be completely open to the trauma of the war because of the emotional tidal wave that may accompany such an open confrontation with the enormity of the suffering and the scope of the losses. Therefore, many survivors are emotionally reserved as they tell their stories and remain reserved for their entire lives. This is an important protective mechanism. Many survivors took a long time to ready themselves for the telling of their stories, some only doing so for the first time through the TTP life history or Spielberg's Shoah Foundation interview. In spite of the need for some measure of self-protection from the pain and perhaps due to this healthy adaptive mechanism, many survivors have been resilient and rebuilt fulfilling lives marked by the successful launching of the next generation. Inherent in this resilience is access to historical memory, while living in the present with the full awareness of the needs of others.

Meaning making is a major topic in the resilience literature. It is a significant aspect of human development, mental health, posttrauma recovery, and posttraumatic growth. Frankl (1963) wrote that meaning making is the fundamental drive within the human being. Armour (2003) stated that the meaning constructed by individuals experiencing trauma is dependent on what is important to the survivor, and that survivors intently pursue what matters to them as a form of coping. Intentional acts related to what is important become symbolic of what is most meaningful. After traumatic events have passed, meaning making helps to reorient the survivor by affirming values and prioritizing what is truly important and worth living for. Greene et al. (2010) reported that Holocaust survivors rebuilt their lives based on the reconstruction of meaning that included awareness of priorities, dedication to family, and education of children, as well as living the legacy of a beloved parent, having children and grandchildren, helping others, valuing self-sacrifice, being a good person, living life on a higher standard, fighting injustice, and defying the Nazis with each act of living.

Goldenberg's analysis of the TTP life histories revealed a similar list of meanings that helped the survivors rebuild their lives (Chapter 5). These include continuing the chain of the Jewish people, raising families, bearing witness and telling the story, living as a form of revenge, helping others, building the state of Israel, and remembering what is truly important in life. In addition, Goldenberg found that a large number of survivors did not offer a statement about meaning making in their lives. They could talk about how they survived but could not express why. This is not a surprising finding when one acknowledges the enormity of the suffering and losses endured during the Holocaust. Devastating losses, including identity, home, and country—and basic trust in humanity—is a difficult vacuum to fill. Yet, even these survivors rebuilt their lives, had children, and moved on. The absence of an overarching meaning system did not stop them from fulfilling their responsibilities and from experiencing satisfaction from their families and life choices. Therefore, meaning making in the recovery process functions differently for survivors of extreme trauma and needs to be understood from the survivor's perspective.

Faith and religious practice are also important for establishing meaning in life. The trauma and resilience literature focus on the importance of faith as a sustaining element to get through trauma and adversity and as a restorative healing element after a traumatic experience (Pargament, 1997; Paragament, Koenig & Perez, 2000). The findings of the TTP revealed a more complex picture of the role of faith and religious practice in the lives of survivors (see Chapter 7). For many survivors in our sample, faith was, indeed, sustaining, but others experienced the rejection of faith as supportive of their survival. For most, faith and religious practice was affirmed but was experienced differently than in pre-war life.

DOMAIN 12

**CHARACTERISTICS OF COPING
DESCRIBED IN LIFE HISTORIES**

Temperament: Personality characteristics
External attributes
Positive beliefs about self
Pretrauma challenges
Faith and general beliefs
Focused endurance
Active and instrumental coping
Social connection: Relationship orientation
Family connection
Defense mechanisms

Characteristics of Coping   Domain 12 in the TTP model is a list of characteristics of coping. From the rich source of information provided by the life histories of 95 survivors in the TTP sample, we were able to assess the coping strategies of each survivor based on self-descriptions of their life before, during, and after the war. The synopsis of the analysis process provided a description of how the survivors characteristically coped throughout their lives. A review of these summary paragraphs for the survivors in the sample yielded 93 adjectives. Members of the TTP research team categorized these 93 adjectives by grouping them together according to common meanings. This parallels the Q Sort technique in quantitative methodology. Each researcher labeled the clusters of adjectives with a word or phrase that encapsulated the quality common to the category. The final label for each category was determined by consensus among the researchers. This domain of the model presents the results of this investigation and lists the 10 characteristics of coping that describe the survivors in the TTP sample. The 93 adjectives comprising the 10 categories are listed in Appendix 2 and help to illuminate the full meaning of each category.

The development of characteristics of coping provided an opportunity to examine the relationship between coping strategies and the division of families into positive, negative, mixed, and mediating groups (see Chapters 8 and 9). The 10 coping strategies as defined do not have a positive or negative valence. If the strategy was described as successful for the individual, then it was incorporated into the ten categories listed above. The question arose regarding whether the survivors who were members of positive families utilized different coping strategies than those survivors who were members of negative families. In other words, is there a mental health component to the utilization of certain coping strategies? Charting survivor use of coping strategies by type of family did not reveal a relationship between these two constructs. What emerged was a pattern of strategies utilized by survivors in the three family groups.

Survivors in the positive, negative, and mixed family groups tended to use active adaptive coping most frequently and positive beliefs about self second most frequently. These two strategies may interact with each other, so that being active is bolstered by positive views about self, and having positive views about self may enable someone to be active. Survival during the Holocaust was arbitrary in most circumstances, but having an active adaptive orientation and a positive belief about oneself helped survivors cope and act when possible. It was also observed that mediating families tended to utilize a different pattern of coping strategies. Survivors in these families tended to rely most heavily on positive beliefs about self, with family connection and defense mechanisms tied for the second-most-utilized strategies. Active adaptive coping was utilized next in the hierarchy. The presence of family bonds placed high on the list of coping strategies and may be related to what becomes the ultimate priority for the mediating survivor: the well-being of the children. Family connection appears on the list of coping strategies utilized by survivors in the positive families, but does not appear on the list of coping strategies utilized by survivors in negative and mixed families. We can speculate that survivors in positive families have a stronger orientation to family as a basis for coping.

Part 2: Intergenerational Transmission

In addition to the study of survivor differences, the TTP is committed to the study of intergenerational transmission. Along with a better understanding of coping and adaptation in Holocaust survivors, it has been part of our mission to study the impact of the Holocaust on the children of survivors (Table 12.3). This is the direct study of intergenerational transmission by investigating real families.

The second part of the TTP focuses on the children of survivors. Like Part 1 of the model, it tracks the development of the child from birth to adulthood with the same domains that track the development of the survivor. When the two parts of the model are continuous, they portray intergenerational transmission from survivor to child on all the domains discussed in the prior section. The study of intergenerational transmission involves tracking the pattern of influence from the developmental history of the survivor parent, through the trauma endured during the Holocaust, through the developmental history of the child to present-day functioning. The child model parallels the survivor model except that it does not contain the domains that assess posttrauma impact, posttrauma adaptation, and characteristics of coping. All the other domains are the same except for Walsh's (2007) model, which is repeated twice on the child model, one time as an assessment of interpersonal processes in the family of origin, which includes the survivor parent, and the second time as an assessment of interpersonal processes in the nuclear family, which explores the influences on the next generation.

Understanding how Holocaust survivors coped with the enormity of their traumatic experiences in the Holocaust and adapted to their new lives is important to know as part of the broader field of traumatic stress studies. It has implications for understanding trauma and its impact on survivor families in addition to implications for the treatment of survivor families who have endured other traumatic events. Our society has no shortage of traumatized populations, both in the United States and around the world. In addition, it is important to recognize that our interest in trauma must extend beyond the focus on just the survivor and must include the understanding of how survivors influence the well-being of spouses and children. Awareness of this has increased in the United States, with the mental health establishment challenged to treat not only the traumatized soldier returning from war but also the family members who are vulnerable to secondary traumatization in the home environment.

Table 12.3 Child of Survivors' Foundation of Psychosocial Development

IMPACT OF THE PARENTAL TRAUMA ON THE CHILD: POSTWAR, POSTTRAUMA

Domain 1

Child Biology: Genetic Predisposition, Temperament, Potential, Intelligences

Domain 2

Child of Survivor(s)—Foundation of the Individual Self

Interpersonal Neurobiology

Early nurture: Attachment to caregiver

Compensatory attention: Affection from other adults

Domain 3

Child of Survivor(s)—Foundation of the Relational self

Indicative of Attachment Relationship With Parents (Caregivers)

Quality of Family Dynamics Paradigm, Family of Origin

Closeness—*Distance*

Empathy—*Self-centeredness*

Validation—*Criticism*

Open communication—*Closed communication*

Expressive of positive emotions—*Expressive of negative emotions*

Domain 4

Child of Survivor(s)

Family-of-Origin Interactional Processes Related to <u>Positive Adaptation</u> and *Maladaptation*[a] (Survivors' Nuclear Family)

Belief Systems

<u>Make meaning of adversity</u> vs. *Senseless loss, failure, blame, shame, despair*

<u>Positive outlook</u> vs. *Powerless, helpless, overwhelmed*

<u>Transcendence and spirituality</u> vs. *Spiritual distress, injustice, disconnected, punishment*

Organizational Patterns

<u>Economic and institutional resources</u> vs. *Resources depleted or unavailable*

<u>Family and community connectedness</u> vs. *Vital bonds lost, exploitation and social isolation*

<u>Flexibility</u> vs. *Rigid, autocratic, unstable, enmeshed, conflicted*

Communication and Problem Solving

<u>Clarity of communication</u> vs. *ambiguous information, secrecy, distortion, denial*

<u>Collaborative problem solving</u> vs. *Blocked problem solving, no planning, overwhelmed*

<u>Open emotional expression</u> vs. *Blocked emotional sharing, gender constraints, no respite*

(Continued)

Table 12.3 (Continued) Child of Survivors' Foundation of Psychosocial Development

Domain 5
Quality of Child of Survivors' Parents' Marriage
Good, Moderately Distressed, Highly Distressed, Divorced

Domain 6
<u>**Positive**</u> and *Adverse* **Life Events**
Risk and <u>Protective</u> **Factors**

Domain 7
Child of Survivor: Identity Formation

Personality and Skills	Cognitive Schema	Affective Functioning
Character traits	Meaning systems	Range of emotional experiencing
Coping styles	Beliefs and faith	Affect regulation
Skills and education	Roles in family and in society	Self-reflection and self-awareness

Domain 4
Child of Survivor(s) and Spouse
Nuclear Family Interactional Processes Related to <u>Positive Adaptation</u> **and** *Maladaptation*[a]

Belief Systems

<u>Make meaning of adversity</u> vs. *Senseless loss, failure, blame, shame, despair*

<u>Positive outlook</u> vs. *Powerless, helpless, overwhelmed*

<u>Transcendence and spirituality</u> vs. *Spiritual distress, injustice, disconnected, punishment*

Organizational Patterns

<u>Economic and institutional resources</u> vs. *Resources depleted or unavailable*

<u>Family and community connectedness</u> vs. *Vital bonds lost, exploitation and social isolation*

<u>Flexibility</u> vs. *Rigid, autocratic, unstable, enmeshed, conflicted*

Communication and Problem Solving

<u>Clarity of communication</u> vs. *Ambiguous information, secrecy, distortion, denial*

<u>Collaborative problem solving</u> vs. *Blocked problem solving, no planning, overwhelmed*

<u>Open emotional expression</u> vs. *Blocked emotional sharing, gender constraints, no respite*

Domain 8
Child of Survivor(s)—Country of Citizenship
Racial, Ethnic, and Cultural Background; Gender and SES

Note: Positive factors are <u>underlined</u>; negative factors are *italicized*.

[a] Used with permission. Walsh, F. (2007). Traumatic loss and major disasters: Strengthening family and community resilience. *Family Process, 46,* 212. John Wiley & Sons Ltd. © 2010.

In our view, it is incumbent on the field of trauma studies to understand the impact of parental trauma on the next generation because their well-being is also our concern. There are many children of traumatized parents who will require our therapeutic services because the negative impact of trauma interferes with good parenting. Assistance to traumatized parents about coping with their own needs while focusing on the needs of their child can stop the long reach of trauma by helping parents nurture psychological health and resilience in their children in spite of their own suffering. A template for coping and adaptation not only enables mental health professionals to better help victims of trauma become successful survivors but also provides a template for raising healthy children who will be better able to cope effectively with the normal vicissitudes of life and the eventuality of catastrophic events.

Section 2

The Study of a Life

The TTP grew out of our interest in an integrated framework for understanding coping. The model was developed over time as our work progressed and the field of traumatic studies evolved as described in the review of literature. It was initially developed as a conceptual tool, a way of thinking about trauma and recovery. It was a means of putting concepts together that had always been treated separately in the literature. With the consolidation of the model over 2010–2011, we see that it provides coherence to the exploration of how pretrauma factors affect posttrauma adaptation. Advances in the field of trauma studies and the integration of systems theory and developmental psychopathology point to the need for a broad lens when studying posttrauma recovery. The new brain science affirms this expanded view based on the study of brain development and how early nurture affects later functioning. In fact, one needs a life perspective to integrate the extensive number of psychosocial factors that have been associated with successful adaptation.

Please note in the case studies that follow, positive factors are underlined; negative factors are italicized.

Case Studies

Two parent-child case studies will be presented as an exploration of how an integrated model can help researchers and clinicians put together the multifaceted story of a person's life by tracking the contributions from both the family of origin and the nuclear family. These case studies begin with synopses of the analysis process that examined the life histories. By means of the NVIVO qualitative research computer program, it is possible to organize the information from the synopses into categories determined by the researcher. The NVIVO coding was organized according to the domains on the TTP model. Therefore, the narrative text from the synopses was moved into categories reflecting the developmental framework of coping and adaptation. The next step in the examination of these parent-child dyads was to enter the information organized by the NVIVO coding system into the TTP model. You will see an outline of the TTP model and how information is organized on it when you read the two case studies.

This procedure is labor intensive, but the advantage, other than organizing a large amount of narrative data, is that it forces the researcher to gather the evidence for every factor on the model without assumptions and biases. It places everything under scrutiny and therefore does not obscure information that may be important but does not stand out under normal review. As a first attempt, this process has been very informative. Over time, it will need to be refined so that it can serve as a more effective tool for clinical practice and research inquiries. Two case studies are presented here of parent-child dyads—one from the positive family group and the other from the negative family group. The comparisons both within a case study that focuses on intergenerational transmission and across case studies that focus on family and individual differences are informative for clinicians and researchers alike. For therapists, the incorporation of so many facets of a person's life in one document provides the opportunity for a broader understanding of the multiple influences that contribute to a person's current reality. It also allows for a profile of a person to emerge that highlights significant life experiences. Both of these perspectives, the broader perspective and the distillation of key experiences, help the therapist guide the therapeutic process toward the exploration of significant life events that, in fact, contribute to the post-traumatic stress even though the person is unaware of the connection. With this knowledge, the therapist can effectively guide the therapy to incorporate the discussion of other significant life experiences, not just the trauma.

Bonnie: Survivor, Positive Family

DEMOGRAPHIC PROFILE

Born in Poland in 1930, Bonnie was 9 years old when the war broke out. She was born to an upper-class family. Her father was a health care professional. Her mother was a housewife. She had one younger brother. Her mother's extended family lived in the area. Her father's family was from a small town nearby. She attended Polish school and had a Hebrew tutor. She attended some night school postwar. She was married in 1952 in

Germany to another survivor. She started a nursery school 26 years ago. She is active in her synagogue and other Jewish organizations. She also belongs to New Americans. She has one son who is a professional, married with two children. She and her husband live in a working-class, non-Jewish suburb of Philadelphia.

FIRST IMPRESSION FROM INTERVIEW

Bonnie has blocked much of her traumatic memory, and it is coming back to her little by little. The team was struck by her strong coping skills for someone who had been through so much trauma at such a young age. She has a positive and forgiving attitude toward those who have hurt her in the past. She has an expressive, inviting, warm, and gracious manner. She is also positive and nonjudgmental, very perceptive in her descriptions of family relationships and very sensitive to her son's feelings. She understands herself and her motivations very well and is flexible, and strong. The team found her inspirational.

OUTLINE: TRANSCENDING TRAUMA MODEL[1]

SURVIVOR—FOUNDATION OF PSYCHO-SOCIAL DEVELOPMENT PRE AND POSTTRAUMA

↓ Biology: Temperament
   Intelligent, easy disposition, her "attractiveness" to adults helped her survive the camps
↓ Foundation of the individual self: Early nurture
   Very close to mother who cared for her and her brother
   Father worked but affectionate when he was around
   Very close to Christian housekeeper who cared for the family, taught her about tolerance of others
↓ Foundation of the relational self: Quality of family relationships
   Closeness: Very close to mother and with father when he was available
   Empathy: Mother
   Validation: Mother and father
   Open communication: Mother
   Expressive of positive emotions: Mother and father
↓ Interactional processes in the family
   Beliefs
      During the war, their home was converted to a Jewish library, and her mother took care of the children, which helped her to keep on going.
      Mother encouraged the two children to make the best out of the situation and that soon things would be back to normal.
      Mother was religious and had a strong faith in God; this gave Bonnie strong faith, and she felt that she was an angel.
   Organizational patterns
      Mother came from economic comfort, and father made a good living—a comfortable life with help in the home.
      Very close with maternal parents, many family gatherings.

[1.] Positive factors are underlined; negative factors are *italicized*.

Mother devoted to the children.
　Left with son during deportation to concentration camps so that he
　　would not suffer alone.
　Very attentive to the daughter's suffering when she was a victim of
　　experiments
Communication
　Discussed everything with mother
　Parents did not seem to have major disagreements; only tension was about
　　religion.
　Traditional roles: Decisions made by father, but parents seemed to agree
　　about most things.
　Very emotionally expressive toward children.
　She was very expressive with her mother about all of her feelings, which
　　sometimes got her into trouble.
↓ Quality of parents' marriage
　Very good marriage: Compatible backgrounds and compatible goals
　Limited tension about religion
↓ Risk and protective factors
　Risk factors
　　Age at time of trauma: 9 years old
　　Went through the worst of the war experiences, including experimentation;
　　　older women took care of her at critical times
　Protective factors
　　Individual
　　　Higher intelligence
　　　Achievement orientation
　　　Capacity to develop close relationships
　　　Absence of illness
　　　Easy disposition
　　　Interpersonal awareness and empathy for her mother's pain in watch-
　　　　ing her suffer the experiments
　　　Hopeful: Mother's message
　　Family
　　　Good fit with parents
　　　Rituals in the family: Many gatherings and religious practice
　　　Absence of role reversals
　　　Minimal conflict in the home
　　　Absence of divorce
　　　Substantial relationship with mother
　　　Selection of a nontroubled spouse
　　　Absence of early separation and losses before the war
　　　Competent parenting
　　　Good relationship with housekeep/babysitter
　　　Extended family relationships supportive
　　Attributes
　　　High SES
　　　Absence of organic difficulties

Community
    Family connected to religious community
↓ Identity formation
Personality traits

From analysis	Self-descriptions
Forgiving attitude	"Boy" in the family
Expressive	*Rebellious*
Warm	Good student
Inviting	Conscientious
Gracious	*Stubborn*
Positive	Proud
Nonjudgmental	*Bullheaded*
Perceptive	Very sensitive
Sensitive	*Mean to brother; lifelong guilt*

        Understands herself
        Flexible, strong
        Friendly
        Open
        Engaging
        Open minded
        Introspective
        Empathic
        Accepting
        Altruistic
        Realistic
        Makes the best out of situations
        Appreciative
        Hopeful

Coping styles
    Engaging personality that attracted people to her
    Will to survive
    Endurance
    Ability to accept help: Relationship orientation
    Mother modeled coping: Desire to be reunited with family
    Repression of traumatic memories from childhood war experiences
↓ Severity of the trauma

As soon as the Germans occupied Poland, her mother told her husband (Bonnie's father) to get out right away because she thought he would be persecuted, and what would happen to a mother and children? He was in hiding during the war. Mother started to run away, but she wanted to return home. Her mother forged her age from 9 to 12 so that she could get a yellow star and go to work. They took her brother, who was 5, on the transport, and her mother volunteered to go with him. Bonnie never saw them again. She started working in a factory making uniforms for German soldiers. Bonnie did not know how to make buttonholes for the uniforms, and a lot of women tried to protect her by putting out more work to cover for her. "I was very lucky this way. I don't know who the people were, but they all tried to help me." In 1942, she was sent to the Plaszow camp. She had to work in a stone quarry, carrying crushed stone. She says there were harsh conditions. She stayed in Plaszow until 1944 and then was taken to Auschwitz for 5 months. The Russians were coming, and she was taken to Bergen-Belsen and stayed there for 3 months until liberation.

Some soldiers were going to rape Bonnie, but an older woman said to them, "No, she's just a child. You don't want her." So they took out another (older) girl and raped her, instead. On the train from Auschwitz to Bergen-Belsen, there was a woman who helped Bonnie by taking food in her own mouth, gumming it to make the bread softer, and then placing it in Bonnie's mouth, like a mother bird would do.

"I was working at the stone quarry, and it was very cold, and I think at that time I must have been very weak, and I just fell. At that time the man, his name was Amon Goeth. He always rode on a white horse with hunting, dogs. He passed by on his horse, and he noticed I fell, and he had like a lasso. He grabbed it and threw the lasso over my waist, and then he started to drag me to a certain point which was like a hill. They called this where they did all the executions over there. You needed to take your own shovel, take the clothes, dig your own grave, and then they were shooting you. And I knew at that time that something is going to happen. And at that time, we dug our grave. There were people already shot, and I didn't know. I was hit here, and I fell in the grave and then on top of me were already other people who were shot. And I heard the siren. At that time, the Russians were very close to the camp, and they were bombing the camp. And suddenly it became very quiet. I crawled out of the grave. I was bleeding very, very hard. I was smart at that time. I grabbed, I don't know whose uniform, because people were already in the grave, and usually they threw them in the fire right away, but they didn't have time. And crawled to the dispensary. The doctor saw me and said, 'Child, by tomorrow morning nobody will be left in this dispensary because everybody will be shot.' They helped me. They bandaged my leg, and they took me back to my barracks, and they put me, there was a crawl space in the ceiling. They put me over there with a piece of bread and water. I don't know the time, how much I was there, until I heard voices, because they had roll calls every day."

One of the most difficult experiences she endured was the medical experiments. "I was among the children what they selected to do experiments on. And I know that my mother was beside herself. She did not know what to do to pull me out of those experiments, and at that time I remember so clearly she was only worried—now I am laughing—if I am a virgin. That's what she was worrying about. And I was in the experiments for over 3 months, because they found out my blood type was AB positive, and apparently AB-positive blood type was considered statistically not too many Jewish people have this blood type. It is more common—what did they tell me—by Aryan or something like that. And that's why I suffered so much is because of this blood type. Then after three and a half months they changed to a different group of children. They were terrible, all of those experiments. I don't even want to go through the details. But this was when my mother was still there [in the ghetto], and she suffered because of it terribly. That's when I could see in my mother that she was so helpless, and she couldn't do anything about it." When asked if she talked to her mother about it, she responded, "No. Each time I came she was crying, and crying, and crying, but we never sat down and talked. She wouldn't be able to talk, and I was too upset to talk. We never talk about it. And years after I never talked about it, either. I think much harder on my mother because at that time my mother was still with me ... because I didn't even know what is going to happen. I knew I was getting injections. I knew I was getting examined different ways, and each time I was crying my mother was hysterical when I was coming back."

↓ Posttrauma impact
Nightmares about her brother turn to images of her son: Linked to guilt about being mean to her brother at times.
Overprotective of son: Anxious about illness and everyone's well-being—but this did not control her behavior—she didn't want son to suffer her anxieties.
Lost her faith in God: Faith became emptiness.
Sought some traditional expression but with ambivalence.
Repressed traumatic memories about the worst of the camp experiences.

↓ Posttrauma adaptation
Devoted to husband and son: Loving and attentive to their needs; appreciative to have these relationships; feared that experiments damaged her so that she couldn't have children; grateful to have her son.
Modulated in her emotional expression: Rarely does anxiety take over her functioning; she is usually in control.
Works in a responsible role: Her cognitive functioning is good; she started her own school.
Focused on mothering until she was ready to go back to work.
Movie triggered her repressed memories; had a hard time but she came through it okay.
She is hopeful and realistic.
Faith never returned, but she has a strong Jewish identity and supports Israel.
Believes in making the best out of life and appreciating what one has.
Sensitive to people's pain so she can be an accepting friend.
Except for the repressed memory, she has been open to her experiences.
Aware of self and sensitive to others.

↓ Characteristics of coping
From analysis: "An engaging personality that attracted people to help her many times during the war, a will to survive to be reunited with her family, and an ability to accept help from non Jews learned probably from her Polish nursemaid."
Temperament and personality: Adults attracted to her and helped her.
Social connection: Ability to accept help.
Family connection: Parental models for coping/mother; desire to be reunited.
Defense mechanisms: Repression of traumatic memories in the camps.

↓ Impact on the next generation

Kenneth: Child of Survivors, Positive Family

DEMOGRAPHIC PROFILE

Born in 1954. Married since 1981, and they have two children. He has a professional career, as does his wife. They do well financially. They are community conscious, and he sits on a number of organizational boards and belongs to a number of professional organizations. He is not involved in any Holocaust-related activities.

FIRST IMPRESSIONS FROM INTERVIEW

Kenneth is a very serious person. He is humorless throughout the interview. He appreciates how fortunate he is. He has tremendous respect, awe, and empathy for his parents. Analytical and insightful.

OUTLINE: TRANSCENDING TRAUMA MODEL[2]

CHILD OF SURVIVOR—FOUNDATION OF PSYCHO-SOCIAL DEVELOPMENT

↓ Biology: Temperament
Intelligent, easy disposition: Never needed to be disciplined

↓ Foundation of the individual self: Early nurture
Very close to both parents; when younger closer to mother; adolescent and as an adult he is closer to father

↓ Foundation of the relational self: Quality of family relationships
Closeness: Both mother and father
Empathy: Both mother and father
Validation: Both mother and father
Open communication: Both mother and father
Expressive of positive emotion: Both mother and father

↓ Interactional processes family of origin: Adaptation and maladaptation
Beliefs
Very appreciative to be alive, to have a family, and to have a son
Working hard keeps the family going
Hopeful and realistic
Neither parent returned to a religious life, and they did not give their son a Jewish education, although son picked up that they wanted something Jewish in their lives.
Emphasized positive identity and Israel
Believed in being good people
Close, loving family relationships
Organizational patterns
Managed to rebuild life and make a comfortable living
In the beginning of the marriage, mother was more dependent; later in the marriage, she wanted to be more independent, and he adapted to her.
Close to the few remaining family members

[2.] Positive factors are underlined; negative factors are *italicized*.

Wonderful friends
Focus was on work
Communication and problem solving
Communication was always open.
Decision making included son, which he says made him stronger and more independent.
Answered questions about the war but would not initiate storytelling.
Open emotional communication and physical affection expressed in the family.
Anxiety never confronted negatively; attempts made to alleviate the anxiety
If son was upset, they modified their behavior to improve communication.
↓ Quality of parents' marriage
Started out friends and then got married; always grateful to have each other.
Son reports that marriage is even better than it was.
She thinks that being survivors helped them be sensitive to each other.
↓ Risk and protective factors
Risk factors
None
Protective factors
Individual
Higher intelligence
Capacity for developing intimate relationships
Achievement orientation
Capacity to construct meaning
Internally oriented
Absence of serious illness
Easy disposition
Task-related self-efficacy
Self worth
Interpersonal awareness and empathy
Capacity to plan
Family
Good fit with parents
Family confronts problems proactively
Absence of role reversals
Minimal conflict
Absence of divorce
Substantial relationship with mother
Selection of a nontroubled spouse
Absence of early separations and loss
Competent parenting
Good relationship with primary caretaker
Social support from spouse and friends
Network of relationships
Attributes
Higher SES
Absence of organic problems

Community
    Community involvement
↓ Identity formation
  Personality traits

From Analysis	**From Interview**
Serious	*Felt different – Only child of survivors in the*
Appreciative	*neighborhood*
Empathic	*Only Jew in school*
In awe of parents	Comfortable with self
Analytical	Self-directed
Insightful	Self-motivated

      Workaholic like his father
      Friendly
      Warm
      Open
      Engaging
      Open minded
      Introspective
      Flexible
      Accepting
      Trusting
      Altruistic
      Optimistic

Coping styles
  Active coping
  Family oriented/relationship oriented
  Positive view of self
Skill and school
  Good student
  Successful professional
Cognitive schema
  Education very important.
  Family is most important.
  Translated his childhood experience of Judaism being lived ambivalently by
     joining a synagogue and giving his children a Jewish education.
  Father always conveyed optimism that things would work out; this gave him
     strength.
  Tried to live up to parents' expectations.
  Being a child of survivors has had a huge impact on him.
  He is a better person for being a child of survivors.
  Aware of what is important in life.
  Inevitability of difficulties in life.
  Importance of facing problems directly.
  Optimistic.
  Trusting.

Affective functioning
 Family was very expressive.
 He is serious and perhaps not very expressive, but feels deeply.
 Aware of self and aware of others.
 Completely understands mother's need to be overprotective.
↓ Interactional processes nuclear family: Adaptation and maladaptation
Beliefs
 Important to have children.
 Has faith that things will work out well from his father.
 They are more clear about their Jewish identity and tradition than parents.
 Children go to Jewish afternoon school.
Organizational patterns
 He always made decisions with his parents, and wife always experienced
  decisions being made for her, so he makes the decisions, and she is
  the disciplinarian.
 He does not like imposing things on children, so she handles discipline.
 He is teaching the children how to make decisions.
Communication and problem solving
 Open between parents and children
 Tries to teach children decision making and coping mechanisms
 Open to emotional expression and spending a lot of time with the children
 Children encouraged to express themselves

↓ Ethnic and cultural background
 Dual-career couple
 Shared responsibilities
↓ Impact on the next generation
 Kenneth's children

Chava: Survivor, Negative Family

DEMOGRAPHIC PROFILE

Born in Austria in 1922. Her family was upper-middle class. She grew up with household servants. Her father had a successful business. The family had no religious affiliation. She has three siblings. She went to private schools and was tutored in Jewish studies. She finished high school in the United States. Married in 1952 and has one daughter. Chava worked for 16 years until she had her child. Conservative affiliation. Her husband is a professional.

FIRST IMPRESSIONS FROM INTERVIEW

She had a presence, but also an aloofness. Strong, determined, confident, and opinionated. Self-sufficient. Her voice showed emotion, and she cried during the interview. The team notes her husband was with her for support. Intelligent, intellectually insightful, "classy," and regal. She stayed with the script she wanted to tell; would not answer some of the interviewer's questions.

OUTLINE: TRANSCENDING TRAUMA MODEL[3]

SURVIVOR—FOUNDATION OF PSYCHO-SOCIAL DEVELOPMENT PRE AND POSTTRAUMA

↓ Biology: Temperament

Intelligence, beauty, social ease, *anxiety/control*

↓ Foundation of the individual self: Early nurture

Both parents were mostly distant; she learned early not to depend on her parents and to depend on herself; she did not complain about this situation; mention made of a housekeeper with no reference to the relationship with her.

↓ Foundation of the relational self: Quality of family dynamics

Distant: Both parents distant, mother narcissistic, and father doted on mother

Self-centeredness: Parents not actively demanding but more focused on themselves

Closed communication: Not much communication with parents

Expressive of negative emotions: More the absence of positive emotions

↓ Interactional processes in the family: Adaptation and maladaptation

Beliefs

> Strong will to live.
>
> Father found meaning in religious practice after the war in the United States. Chava began to say the Shema as a source of emotional support, sent her child to a Jewish day school—even though she was not religious.
>
> After coming to United States, she wanted to live life to the fullest.
>
> Believed that God helped her survive, *but at the same time she experienced fear and anxiety about something bad happening.*
>
> Not religious in Europe; children went to Catholic school and received Jewish education after school.

Organizational patterns

> Family was high SES—high society in Austria—connected to the community through their social status; used money to leave Europe in the beginning of the war.
>
> There were regular gatherings with mother's family; uncle gave her family his family's visa to leave Europe.
>
> Father also successful in the United States.
>
> Family encountered humiliation and brief incarceration at the beginning of the war, which was difficult, but they were able to leave quickly.
>
> *Family in the United States was very mean to them; they quickly established themselves.*
>
> *Mother had trouble adjusting to new status, which was no longer privileged; children were expected to help her.*

Communication and problem solving

> Very little said about communication and problem solving; traditional family and father may have made all the decisions.
>
> *Very little mention of emotional communication; again for her there was no one to talk to; emotional expression was blocked.*

---

3. Positive factors are underlined; negative factors are *italicized*.

Very independent when they came to United States; <u>she got a job very young because she was smart and talented; uncle believed in her; she felt proud of herself.</u>

Very little processing of war experience; brother's strange lifestyle was attributed to incarceration in a camp at the beginning of the war.

↓ Quality of parents' marriage

<u>Marriage good from parents' perspective; negative interactions were infrequent; father doted on mother.</u>

There was very little relationship with children.

↓ Risk and protective factors

Protective factors

    Individual

        <u>Intelligent</u>

        <u>Capacity for social relationships; very popular in school; had "close" friends</u>

        <u>Felt that God saved her</u>

        <u>Meaning was to have a child</u>

        <u>Ability to handle outside world; successful in work</u>

        <u>Very responsible; gets things done</u>

        <u>Absence of serious illness</u>

        <u>Self-efficacy</u>

        <u>Higher sense of self-worth</u>

        <u>Capable of planning</u>

        <u>Enjoys a full life</u>

    Family

        <u>Family left Europe together and stayed together.</u>

        <u>Minimal conflict in the family,</u> *but the emotional bonds were not strong with parents, not quite "good enough."*

        <u>Father was a planner.</u>

        <u>Absence of divorce.</u>

        Relationship with mother was not substantial.

        <u>Selected a good spouse who was refined and accommodated her.</u>

        <u>Absence of early separation and losses.</u>

        Parenting was not negative, but it was distant.

        <u>Very popular as a kid; talented singer;</u> *friendships in adulthood are tentative; friends not good enough.*

    School and community

        <u>She says that school was the strongest support in her life.</u>

        <u>No mention of community involvement in Europe or the United States.</u>

↓ Identity formation

Personality traits

From Analysis	**From Interview**
<u>Enjoyed life</u>	<u>Present but aloof</u>
Underlying anxiety expressed as control	<u>Strong</u>
Angry and controlling with daughter	<u>Determined</u>
Emotional withdrawal as punishment	<u>Confident</u>
Underlying narcissism: always right	*Opinionated*

Friendly
Warm
Open
Not introspective
Rigid
Self-centered
Critical
Suspicious
Realistic
Positive perception of self

Coping styles
  Strong
  Courageous
  Responsible
  Self-controlled
  Takes initiative
Skill and school
  Excellent student
  Did well on her job
Cognitive schema
  Meaning in life was having a child
  Respect for parents is primary
  Accepted being on her own as a kid
  No particular faith system
  Believed she survived for a reason
  Does not know what is in store for her and anxious about the future
  Anxiety causes plans to always be tentative
  Holocaust could happen again
  Friendships are conditional
  Status oriented
  Punished husband and daughter with the silent treatment
Affective functioning
  Not introspective
  Not empathic with daughter; narcissistic about what she considered to be right
  Anger was not loud, but controlling
  Silent treatment
  Emotions were unregulated
  No interpersonal cues
  No self-awareness; no attempt at self-awareness (even after daughter's suicide attempt)
↓ Ethnic and cultural background
  Family of origin: Upper class.
  Social context was Austrian high society.
  Mother home: Father the breadwinner.

Self-sufficient
Gets emotional
Classy
Regal
Tomboy
Responsible
Respectful of parents
Never contradicted parents
Worrier
Neat
Courageous
Took risks
Loyal

↓ Severity of the trauma: War experiences before emigrating

In March 1938, the Germans entered Austria. She and her family were taken out of their apartment and put into a Jewish ghetto. Her father and brother were taken away to Dachau for 2 months. They got affidavits to go to the United States and arrived there in 1942, living with an aunt, who treated them poorly. They then found a sponsor who helped them.

"So you know, the Kristallnacht. That was in 1939, I think. Or '38. Well, anyway, that night they took my father and my brother. I remember I had washed my hair that evening, and my hair was wet. But I followed them. I followed the truck, to see where they were taking them. And they took them to a Cassan in Vienna.

"We were shocked. And my father, I remember my father said, 'This is the end of the Jews in Vienna.' And my father, when it happened, he started, 'We have to get away. We have to get out.' We stayed there for 2 years because you couldn't get out. They took away the store; they took away the money. My father had to stand on line with a basket of like, you put laundry, a laundry basket, with silver. This all had to be given to Hitler. Jewelry also. And then you got a receipt for it, that you gave that to the Fuhrer. Not that you didn't want to give. You gave that to the Fuhrer. They didn't take anything from you. You gave it.

"'You Jew,' and a star of David. And they gave the Jews a toothbrush and a bucket and water to clean this. And my mother, I see my mother, on her fours, you know, washing the floor. And they … they did such cruel things." "Yes, I was frightened. But I didn't cry. I was just stunned. I couldn't believe. I had so many friends, Gentile girls. They didn't know me. You know, they didn't, I couldn't believe it. It was unbelievable. It was unbelievable from one day to the next.

"My father was taken, too, to do things. To work. Clean the streets. It was a very demeaning thing to go through."

↓ Posttrauma impact

Mistrusts people but does not overtly reject them
Constantly anxious and fearful about something going wrong
Very angry, but takes no responsibility for this emotional state
Anxieties cause her to have extreme negative emotions
Lack of self-awareness and unable to modulate emotions

↓ Posttrauma adaptation (maladaptation)

No balance between self and other: Self is first.
Many social relationships, but shallow.
Always thinking, worrying, and being judgmental.
<u>Came as a teenager and adjusted well to United States.</u>
Memories are available *but do not seem to be integrated; very sparse information.*
<u>Believes God saved her</u> *and fears that something will happen.*
Grateful for surviving but unclear about why she survived.
No capacity for self-reflective function.
Expresses sympathy for people who suffered in the war; little sympathy in the present.

↓ Characteristics of coping

From analysis: Strong, courageous, responsible, self-confident, takes initiative, self-assertive, sees the importance of the family remaining together. Does not 'look Jewish.

Personality characteristics: <u>Responsible, risk taking, and loyal</u>
<u>Positive beliefs about self</u>
<u>Focused endurance: Does what needs to be done</u>
<u>Social connection: Many friends</u> *but not close*
<u>Family connection: Respect for parents, ongoing loyalty</u>; *very negative relation-ship with daughter and controlling*
Defense mechanisms: *Compartmentalization, perhaps allows for the lack of awareness*
↓ Impact on the next generation

Karen: Child of Survivor, Negative Family

DEMOGRAPHIC PROFILE:

Born in 1956. Married, with three children. She is a health care professional. Her husband is also a health care professional. Middle class, no particular political affiliation. Very concerned about Israel; belongs to a Conservative synagogue.

FIRST IMPRESSIONS FROM INTERVIEW

Sweet, gracious, refined, kind, caring. There was some self-doubt expressed in the interview. Friendly. Her grammar was almost "immigrant-like," almost a direct echo of her mother's interview. She came across as a dominated personality. The team notes that she is a woman who struggles with the issue of separation-individuation. She wants to be her own person, but she wants to be somebody that her parents approve of. There is a very big sense of responsibility and respect toward her parents. Yet, because her mother was so critical, it is painful at times for her to do that. Compassion for her mother is a salient theme of the interview.

OUTLINE: TRANSCENDING TRAUMA MODEL[4]

CHILD OF SURVIVOR—FOUNDATION OF PSYCHO-SOCIAL DEVELOPMENT

↓ Biology: Temperament
<u>Intelligent, talented singer, easy disposition</u>
↓ Foundation of the individual self: Early nurture
<u>Very much wanted and most likely cared for well in infancy in terms of basic needs</u>. *Unclear whether or not mother could reflect back her emotional needs.*
↓ Foundation of the relational self: Quality of family relationships
<u>Validation: Father validated her and praised her when not in mother's presence.</u>
<u>Expressive of positive emotion (also away from mother) very loving in private.</u>
Distance: Father out working; mother angry, controlling, and often responding with the silent treatment.
Self-centered: Mother's parenting based completely on what mother thought was right; no room for child's needs.

---

4. Positive factors are <u>underlined</u>; negative factors are *italicized*.

Criticism: Mother was mixed; mostly complained about her <u>but sometimes complimented her</u>.

Closed communication: No discussion of child's perspective; open about the war with negative impact.

Expressive of negative emotion: Frequent and very destructive, tendency to induce guilt; daughter made a suicide attempt after a scene with the mother that manipulated guilt and did not give her a way to do anything right.

↓ Interactional processes family of origin: Adaptation and maladaptation

Beliefs

Perspective was not negative, but there was very little said about meaning of survival.

<u>Mother felt that God saved her for a reason, which was not clear to her.</u>

<u>Family lived well and enjoyed life.</u>

<u>No spiritual distress,</u> *but very little spiritual connection;* <u>positive Jewish identity, daughter sent to Jewish day school</u>.

Organizational patterns

<u>Comfortable economic status; involved in cultural activities.</u>

<u>Family connections complicated, but mother was the main support for her mother before she died and for her brother, who had psychological problems.</u>

No mention of community involvement.

Mother was rigid, uncompromising with daughter, self-centered with no sense of the child; strict, punitive, guilt inducing, controlling, and jealous.

Communication and problem solving

<u>Communication about war was open; mother wanted all children to know about it;</u> *may have been burdensome to the daughter.*

No collaborative problem solving with daughter; all rules were determined by the mother, and decisions were made by her.

Expression of negative emotions that were often unregulated.

Silent treatment was mode of control and punishment.

↓ Quality of parents' marriage

Marriage could have looked good on the outside, but mother was demanding with father and would punish him with the silent treatment. Father was very cautious with the mother in order not to start fights. Curtailed his relationship with his daughter in order not to start conflict. Distressed marriage.

↓ Risk and protective factors

Risk factors

Suicide attempt as a teenager due to conflict with mother

Opposite experience of protective factors:

Not a good fit with mother

Conflicted relationship with mother

Controlling parenting

Friendships limited due to social incompatibility due to mother's rules

Problems with mother were not confronted; father avoided conflict

External locus of control: Based on pleasing mother

Low sense of worth: Poor self-esteem

Social lack of conformity led to feeling isolated socially

Felt unattractive

Lack of personal awareness until suicide attempt and subsequent therapy

Escaped into sleep to cope with conflict with mother and sense of social misfit

Emotional burden of mother's war experiences and sense of obligation for her suffering

Protective factors

  Individual

    <u>Therapy</u>

    <u>Higher intelligence</u>

    <u>Achievement orientation</u>

    <u>Absence of serious illness</u>

    <u>Easy disposition: Enabled accommodation to mother</u>

    <u>Ability to build a strong relationship with cousin; became her second home</u>

    <u>Very talented singer and star in the school plays; felt appreciated</u>

  Family

    <u>Father praised her</u>

    <u>Absence of divorce</u>

    <u>Absence of early separations</u>

    <u>Good relationships with father even if hidden</u>

    <u>Did marry a caring partner who is supportive; his family also supportive</u>

    <u>Relationship with cousin</u>

Attributes

  <u>High SES</u>

  <u>Absence of organic difficulties</u>

Community

  <u>Loved children and became a nurse</u>

  <u>Excellent voice and star in school plays</u>

↓ Identity formation

  Personality traits

From Analysis	**From Interview**
Some depression	*Angry*
Some anxiety	*Depressed*
Anger	*Napper*
Escaped by sleeping	*Not in style; did not fit in*
Low self-esteem	*Unattractive*
<u>Talented singer and actress; felt appreciated</u>	<u>More mature</u>
<u>Loves working with children</u>	<u>Appreciated for her talent</u>
Anxious dependency	<u>Loves children</u>
<u>Friendly</u>	*Stressed about mother's war experience*
<u>Warm</u>	*Anxious; when will other shoe fall*
<u>Open</u>	*Pessimistic*
<u>Engaging</u>	*Sense she will not be old*

<u>Therapy helped her gain insight and sense of self</u>
Not generally introspective
Pessimistic
<u>Seeks help</u>
<u>Accepts help</u>
<u>Aware of what is important</u>
Coping styles
<u>Social connection to cousin</u>
<u>Talented singer</u>
<u>Loves children</u>
<u>Sleep as a defense</u>
<u>Endurance</u>
<u>Father's overwhelming praise</u>
Skill and school
<u>Star in school plays</u>
<u>Works with children</u>
Cognitive schema
Not much mention of meaning systems, faith, values, and goals
Important to be respectful of parents; seeking mother's approval and empathic
about her war experiences, but not expressed as a family value
<u>Caring for children professionally and having her own children is very fulfill-</u>
<u>ing for her and reflects what she loves</u>
Affective functioning
Lived in reaction to her mother's control and emotional punishment
Depressed and anxious, which she dealt with by sleeping
Calls herself angry
<u>Could experience positive feelings when singing, when being with her cousin</u>
<u>and her family, and when hearing her father's praise whenever possible</u>
↓ Interactional processes nuclear family: Adaptation and maladaptation
Beliefs
<u>Working hard to be optimistic</u>
<u>Works hard to be her own person</u>
Organizational patterns
<u>Economic comfort</u>
<u>Joint responsible decision making</u>
<u>Both parents working hard to establish better relationships with children who</u>
<u>are difficult; help each other see the good qualities and how the child tries</u>
Each parent has particular problems with a particular child; sometimes
causes conflict between them
Communication and problem solving
<u>Therapy</u>
<u>Effective communication around financial issues, children, and in-laws</u>
<u>Attempt to work together and they see each other as supportive</u>
<u>Very open to discussing anything that needs attention in the marriage and</u>
<u>family</u>
<u>Working on better communication with children; harder if child interaction</u>
<u>is negative</u>

↓ Ethnic and cultural background
  Dual-career couple
  Shared responsibilities
  He provides emotional support around self-esteem and problems with her mother
  Close with husband's family, *which is tempered by her mother's jealousy*
↓ Impact on the next generation
  Karen's children

References

Ainsworth, M. D. S., Blehar, M. C., Waters, E., & Wall, S. (1978). *Patterns of attachment: Psychological study of the strange situation.* Hillsdale, NJ: Erlbaum.

Aldwin, C. M. (2009). *Stress, coping and development: An integrative perspective* (2nd ed.). New York: Guilford Press.

Algoe, S. B., & Fredrickson, B. L. (2010). Emotional fitness and the movement of affective science from lab to field. *American Psychologist, 66,* 35–42.

Allen, J. G. (2005). *Coping with trauma: Hope through understanding* (2nd ed.) Arlington, VA: American Psychiatric.

American Psychiatric Association. (1987). *Diagnostic and statistical manual of mental disorders* (3rd ed., rev.). Washington, DC: Author.

Armour, R. E. (2003). Making meaning in the aftermath of homicide. *Death Studies, 27,* 519–540.

Bloom, S. (1997). *Creating sanctuary.* New York: Routledge.

Bowlby, J. (1988). *A secure base: Clinical applications of attachment theory.* London: Routledge.

Bretherton, I. (1992). The origins of attachment theory: John Bowlby and Mary Ainsworth. *Developmental Psychology, 28,* 759–775.

Briere, J., & Spinazzola, J. (2009). Assessment of the sequelae of complex trauma: Evidence based measures. In C. A. Courtois & J. D. Ford (Eds.), *Treating complex traumatic disorder: An evidence-based guide* (pp. 104–123). New York: Guildford Press.

Brom, D., Pat-Horenczyk, R., & Ford, J. (2009). *Treating traumatized children: Risk, resilience and recovery.* New York: Routledge.

Buchanan, G. M., & Seligman, M. E. P. (1995). *Explanatory style.* Hillsdale, NJ: Erlbaum.

Calhoun, L. G., & Tedeshi, R. G. (Eds.). (2006). *Handbook of posttraumatic growth: Research and practice.* Mahwah, NJ: Erlbaum.

Cassidy, J., & Shaver, P. R. (Eds.). (1999). *Handbook of attachment: Theory, research and clinical applications.* New York: Guildford Press.

Cowan, C. P., & Cowan, P. A. (2000). *When partners become parents: The big life change for couples.* Mahwah, NJ: Erlbaum.

Cowan, P. A., & Cowan, C. P. (2002). Interventions as tests of family systems theories: Marital and family relationships in children's development, and psychopathology. *Development and Psychopathology, 14,* 731–760.

Cowan, P. A., & Cowan, P. A. (2005). Two central roles for couple relationships: Breaking negative intergenerational patterns and enhancing children's adaptation. *Sexual and Relationship Therapy, 20,* 275–288.

Courtois, C. A., & Ford, J. D. (Eds.). (2009). *Treating complex traumatic stress disorders: An evidence-based guide.* New York: Guilford Press.

Cummings, E. M., & Merrilees, C. E. (2010). Identifying the dynamic processes underlying links between marital conflict and child adjustment. In M. S. Schulz, M. K. Pruett, P. K. Kerig, & R. D. Parke (Eds.), *Strengthening couple relationships: For optimal child development* (pp. 11–23). Washington, DC: APA.

Danieli, Y. (1985). The treatment and prevention of long-term effects and intergenerational transmission of victimization: A lesson from Holocaust survivors and their children. In C. R. Figley (Ed.), *Trauma and its wake* (pp. 295–313). New York: Brunner-Mazel.

Dattilo, F. M. (2005). The structuring of family schemas: A cognitive-behavioral perspective. *Journal of Marital and Family Therapy, 31,* 15–30.

Figley, C. R. (1989). *Helping traumatized families.* San Francisco: Jossey-Bass.

Figley, C. R. (Ed.). (1998). *Burnout in families: Systemic costs of caring.* Boca Raton, FL: CRC Press.

Foa, E. B., Keane, T. M.. Friedman, M. J., & Cohen, J. A. (2004). *Effective treatments for PTSD* (2nd ed.). *Practice Guidelines from the International Society for Traumatic Stress Studies.* New York: Guilford Press.

Fonagy, P., Steele, M., Morgan, G., Steele, H., & Higgit, A. C. (1991). The capacity for understanding mental states: The reflective self in parent and child and its significance for security of attachment. *Mental Health Journal, 13,* 200–216.

Fonagy, P., Steele, M., Steele, H., Higgitt, A., & Target, M. (1992). The Emanuel Miller Memorial Lecture 1992: The theory and practice of resilience. *Journal of Child Psychology and Psychiatry, 35,* 231–257.

Ford, J. D. (2009). Neurological and developmental research: Clinical applications. In C. A. Courtois & J. D. Ford (Eds.), *Treating complex traumatic stress disorders: An evidence-based guide* (pp. 31–58). New York: Guilford Press.

Fosha, D. (2000). *The transforming power of affect: A model for accelerated change.* New York: Basic Books.

Frankl, V. (1963). *Man's search for meaning.* Boston: Beacon Press.

Garmezy, N. (1983). Stressors in childhood. In N. Garmezy & M. Rutter (Eds.). *Stress, coping and development in children* (pp. 43–84). New York: McGraw Hill.

Gewirtz, A., Forgatch, M., & Wieling, E. (2008). Parenting practices as potential mechanisms for child adjustment following mass trauma. *Journal of Marital and Family Therapy, 34,* 177–192.

Gilbert, K. (1998). Understanding the secondary traumatic stress in spouses. In C. R. Figley (Ed.), *Burnout in families: Systemic costs of caring* (pp. 47–74). Boca Raton, FL: CRC Press.

Glicksman, A., Van Haitzma, K., Mumberg, M. H., Gagnon, M., & Brom, D. (2003). Caring for Holocaust survivors: Rethinking the paradigms. *Journal of Jewish Communal Service, 79,* 148–153.

Goff, B. S., & Smith, D. B. (2005). Systemic traumatic stress: The couple adaptation to traumatic stress model. *Journal of Marital and Family Therapy, 31,* 145–157.

Goldenberg, J. (2008). *"The feelings of my family are with me": The posttraumatic coping of adolescent survivors of the Holocaust.* Unpublished doctoral dissertation, Bryn Mawr College, Bryn Mawr, PA.

Greenberg, L. (2002). *Emotion-focused therapy: Coaching clients to work through their feelings.* Washington, DC: American Psychological Association.

Greene, R. R. (2002a). Holocaust survivors: A study in resilience. *Journal of Gerontological Social Work, 37,* 3–18.

Greene, R. R. (Ed.). (2002b). *Resiliency.* Washington DC: National Association of Social Workers.

Greene, R. R. (2006). *Social work practice: A risk and resilience perspective.* Belmont, CA: Thomson Brooks/Cole.

Greene, R. R. (2010a). Holocaust survivors: Resilience revisited. *Journal of Human Behavior in the Social Environment, 20,* 411–422.

Greene, R. R. (2010b). Family dynamics, the Nazi Holocaust, and mental health treatment: A shift in paradigm. *Journal of Human Behavior in the Social Environment, 20,* 469–488.

Greene, R. R. (2010c). A Holocaust survivorship model: Survivors' reflections. *Journal of Human Behavior in the Social Environment, 20,* 569–579.

Greene, R. R., Armour, M., Hantman, S., Graham, S. A., & Sharabi, A. (2010d). Conceptualizing a Holocaust survivorship model. *Journal of Human Behavior in the Social Environment, 20,* 423–439.

Greene, R. R., & Conrad, A. P. (2002c). Basic assumptions and terms. In R. R. Greene (Ed.), *Resiliency* (pp. 29–62). Washington, DC: National Association of Social Workers.

Harel, Z., Kahana B., & Kahana, E. (1988). Psychological well-being among Holocaust survivors in Israel. *Journal of Traumatic Stress Studies, 1* (4), 413–428.

Hazan, C., & Zeifman, D. (1999). Pair bonds as attachments: Evaluating the evidence. In J. Cassidy and P. R. Shaver (Eds.), *Handbook of attachment: Theory, research and clinical applications* (pp. 336–354). New York: Guilford Press.

Herman, J. L. (1992a). Complex PTSD: A syndrome in survivors of prolonged and repeated trauma. *Journal of Traumatic Stress, 5,* 377–391.

Herman, J. L. (1992b). *Trauma and recovery.* New York: Basic Books.

Hesse, E. (1999). The Adult Attachment Interview: Historical and current perspectives. In J. Cassidy and P. R. Shaver (Eds.), *Handbook of attachment: Theory, research and clinical applications* (pp. 395–433). New York: Guildford Press.

Hoyle, R. H. (Ed.). (1995). *Structural equation modeling.* Thousand Oaks, CA: Sage.

Isserman, N. (2005). *"I harbor no hate": The study of political tolerance and intolerance.* Unpublished doctoral dissertation, City University of New York, New York City.

Janoff-Bulman, R. (1992). *Shattered assumptions.* New York: Free Press.

Johnson, S. M. (2002). *Focused couple therapy with trauma survivors: Strengthening attachment bonds.* New York: Guilford.

Johnson, S. M. (2004). *Practice of emotionally focused couple therapy.* New York: Guilford Press.

Kaffman, A., & Meaney, M. J. (2007). Neurodevelopmental sequelae of postnatal maternal care in rodents: Clinical and research implications of molecular insights. *Journal of Child Psychology and Psychiatry, 48,* 224–244.

Kagan, J. (2010). *The temperamental thread: How genes, culture, time and luck make us who we are.* New York: Dana Press.

Kagan, J., & Snidman, N. (2004). *The long shadow of temperament.* Cambridge, MA: Harvard University Press.

Keltner, D., & Lerner, J. S. (2010). Emotion. In S. Gilbert & G. Lindsey (Eds.), *Handbook of social psychology* (5th ed, pp. 317–352). New York: McGraw Hill.

Krell, R. (1998, November). *Working with Holocaust survivors and the second generation.* Keynote address, AMCHA conference. Jerusalem, Israel.

Laub, D. (2005). From speechlessness to narrative: The cases of Holocaust historians and of psychiatrically hospitalized survivors. *Literature and Medicine, 24,* 253–265.

Layne, C. M., Beck, C. J., Rimmasch, H., Southwick, J. S., Moreno, M. A., & Hobfall, S. E. (2009). Promoting "resilient" posttraumatic adjustment in childhood and beyond: "unpacking" life events, adjustment trajectories, resources, and interventions. In D. Brom, R. Pat-Horenczyk, & J. D. Ford (Eds.), *Treating traumatized children: Risk, resilience and recovery* (pp. 13–48). New York: Routledge.

Lev-Wiesel, R., & Amir, M. (2001). Secondary traumatic stress, psychological distress, sharing of traumatic reminisces and marital quality among spouses of Holocaust child survivors. *Journal of Marital and Family Therapy, 27,* 433–444.

Main, M. (1999). Attachment theory: Eighteen points with suggestions for future studies. In J. Cassidy & P. R. Shaver (Eds.), *Handbook of attachment* (pp. 845–887). New York: Guilford Press.

Main, M., & Goldwyn, R. (1990). Adult attachment rating and classification system. In M. Main (Ed.), *A typology of human attachment organization assessed in discourse, drawings and interviews.* New York: Cambridge University Press.

Masten, A. S. (2001). Ordinary magic: Resilience processes in development. *American Psychologist, 56,* 227–238.

Masten A. S. (2007). Resilience in developing systems: Progress and promise as the fourth wave rises. *Development and Psychopathology, 19,* 921–930.

McCann, I. L., & Pearlman, L. A. (1990). *Psychological trauma and the adult survivor: Theory, therapy and transformation.* New York: Brunner/Mazel.

McCullough-Vaillant, L. (1997). *Changing character: Short-term anxiety-regulating psychotherapy for restructuring defenses, affects and attachment.* New York: Basic Books.

Pargament, K. I. (1997). *The psychology of religion and coping.* New York: Guildford Press.

Pargament, K. I., Koenig, H. G., & Perez, L. M. (2000). The many methods of religious coping: Development and initial validation of the RCOPE. *Journal of Clinical Psychology, 56,* 519–543.

Parke, R. D., Schulz, M. S., Pruett, M. K., & Kerig, P. K. (2010). Tracing the development of the couples and family research tradition: The enduring contribution of Philip and Carolyn Pape Cowan. In M. S. Schulz, M. K. Pruett, P. K. Kerig, & R. D. Parke (Eds.), *Strengthening couple relationships: For optimal child development* (pp. 27–40). Washington, DC: APA.

Patterson, G. R. (2005). The next generation of PMTO models. *Behavior Therapist, 28,* 25–32.

Patterson, G. R., DeBaryshe, B. D., & Ramsey, E. (1989). A developmental perspective on antisocial behavior. *American Psychologist, 44,* 329–335.

Patterson, G. R., DeGarmo, D. S., & Forgatch, M. S. (2004). Systemic changes in families following prevention trials. *Journal of Abnormal Child Psychology, 32,* 621–633.

Rogers, C. R. (1961). *On becoming a person.* New York: Houghton Mifflin.

Rubin, L. (1996). *The transcendent child: Tales of triumph over the past.* New York: Basic Books.

Rutter, M. (1990). Psychosocial resilience and protective mechanisms. In J. Rolf, A. S. Masten, D. Cicchetti, K. H. Nuechterlein, & S. Weintraub (Eds.), *Risk and protective factors in the development of psychopathology* (pp. 181–214). New York: Cambridge University Press.

Schore, A. (1994). *Affect development and origin of the self: The neurobiology of emotional development.* Hillside, NJ: Erlbaum.

Schulz, M. S., Pruett, M. K., Kerig, P. K., & Parke, R. D. (2010). *Strengthening couples relationships for optimal child development: Lessons from research and intervention.* Washington DC: American Psychological Association.

Siegel, D. J. (1999). *The developing mind.* New York: Guilford Press.

Siegel, D. J., & Hartzell, M. (2003). *Parenting from the inside out.* New York: Tarcher Putnum.

Solomon, M. S., & Siegel, D. J. (2003). *Healing trauma: Attachment, mind, body and brain.* New York: Norton.

Suomi, S. (2000). A biobehavioral perspective on developmental psychopathology: Excessive aggression and serotonergic dysfunction in monkeys. In A. Sameroff, M. Lewis, & S. M. Miller (Eds.), *Handbook of developmental psychopathology* (2nd ed., pp. 237–256). Dordrecht, the Netherlands: Kluwer Academic.

Valent, P. (1998). *From survival to fulfillment: A framework for the life-trauma dialectic.* New York: Brunner-Mazel.

Valliant, G. (1977). *Human adaptation.* Boston: Little, Brown.

van der Kolk, B. A. (2005). Developmental trauma disorder: Toward a rationale diagnosis for children with complex trauma histories. *Psychiatric Annals, 35,* 401–408.

van der Kolk, B. A., McFarlane, A. C., & Weisaeth, L. (1996). *Traumatic stress: The effects of overwhelming experience on mind, body and society.* New York: Guilford Press.

van der Kolk, B. A., Roth, S. H., Pelcovitz, D., Sunday, S., & Spinazzola, J. (2005). Disorders of extreme stress. *Journal of Traumatic Stress, 18,* 389–399.

Walsh, F. (2003a). Family resilience: A framework for clinical practice. *Family Process, 42,* 1–18.

Walsh, F. (Ed.) (2003b). *Normal family processes* (3rd ed.). New York: Guilford Press.

Walsh, F. (2006). Strengthening family resilience (2nd ed.). New York: Guilford Press.

Walsh, F. (2007). Traumatic loss and major disasters: Strengthening family and community resilience. *Family Process, 46,* 207–227.

Werner, E. E., & Smith, R. S. (1977). *Kauai's children come of age.* Honolulu: University of Hawaii Press.

Werner, E. E., & Smith, R. S. (1982). *Vulnerable but invincible: A longitudinal study of resilient children and youth.* New York: McGraw Hill.

Werner, E. E., & Smith, R. S. (1992). *Overcoming the odds: High risk children from birth to adulthood.* Ithaca, NY: Cornell University Press.

Werner, E. E., & Smith, R. S. (2001). *Journeys from childhood to midlife: Risk, resilience, and recovery.* Ithaca, NY: Cornell University Press.

Wilson, J. P. (Ed.) (2006). *The posttraumatic self: Restoring meaning and wholeness to personality.* New York: Routledge.

Wilson, J. P., Harel, Z., & Kahana, B. (1988). *Human adaptation to extreme stress from the Holocaust to Vietnam.* New York: Plenum Press.

Winnicott, D. W. (1960). The theory of the parent-infant relationship. *International Journal of Psychoanalysis, 41,* 585–595.

Zeifman, D., & Hazan, C. (1997b). A process model of adult attachment formation. In S. Duck & W. Ickes (Eds.), *Handbook of personal relationships* (pp. 179–195). Chichester, UK: Wiley.

Appendix 1: Demographics of the TTP Dataset

The majority of the interviews of the Transcending Trauma Project (TTP) took place in the mid-1990s, and at least one family member in each Holocaust survivor family resided in Philadelphia. The total sample size consisted of 95 survivors, 100 children of survivors, 36 grandchildren of survivors, and 44 spouses who were neither survivors nor children of survivors.

Survivor's Gender, Country of Origin, and Nature of War Experiences

In the TTP database, the split between female and male survivor interviewees was 2 to 1; 64.2% were females, and 35.8% were males. The largest group of survivors—46%—was from Poland, followed by survivors from Germany (18.9%) and Czechoslovakia (10.5%). The rest of the survivors came from Hungary, Romania, Lithuania, the Ukraine, Israel, Austria, France, Belgium, and Holland. This distribution reflects the demographics of the survivors' country of origin in the 2000 National Jewish Population Survey (NJPS; Kotler-Berkowitz, Blass, & Neuman, 2004).

Comparison of the TTP Sample to a National Survey

The TTP demographics are similar to the data collected during the 2000–2001 National Jewish Population Survey. The NJPS 2000–2001 is a national survey representative of the U.S. Jewish population (Kotler-Berkowitz et al., 2004). While the methodology of the survey has been criticized, it is the only survey of its kind on Holocaust survivors in the

United States. Consequently, it is a reasonable basis of comparison to the TTP data. In the demographic categories of age, gender, education, marital status, and country of origin, the TTP data demographics are similar to the 2000 NJPS survey data demographics.

The survivors in our database had a variety of war experiences. Of the survivors, 47% had been in a concentration camp, 48% in a ghetto, and 45% in hiding. A small percentage of the survivors experienced the war in more than one setting; 22% were in camps and ghettos, 11% were in camps and hiding; 12% were in ghettos and hiding; and 13% experienced all three.

Religion

The majority of the survivors, almost 70%, came from traditionally religious homes. Most of the rest came from liberal (12%) or nonpracticing homes (8%). It is important to note, however, that coming from a traditional home does not correspond to current religious affiliation in the TTP sample.

In the TTP study, the religious affiliations of our respondents reflected that of the greater Philadelphia area in the 1990s. In Philadelphia, the largest movement at that time was the Conservative, and in the TTP 45% of the survivors interviewed were affiliated with a Conservative synagogue; 24% participated in more liberal branches of Judaism or none at all; 28% were Orthodox. The higher percentage of Orthodox survivors results from the fact that interviewees were identified through personal contacts of the researchers in the Orthodox community using the snowball method of acquiring respondents (see Chapter 3).

Marital Status and Children

The majority of the survivors were married at the time of the interview (68%). There were no survivors interviewed who had never been married. Of those interviewed, 18% of the survivors were widowed, while the rest were divorced, divorced and remarried, or separated. In addition, in our sample 6% of the survivors were childless. The majority of the rest had either one child (20%) or two children (38%). Only 15% of the sample had three or more children.

Education and Income

The educational levels were as follows: 25.5% had an eighth-grade or lower education. Only 29% had a college or postgraduate degree. These survivors were for the most part well off economically. Survivors in the sample who labeled themselves at the low-income or poverty level numbered 4%. The rest were low-middle income (2%), middle income (69%), and upper middle at 22%.

Children of Survivors: Gender, Age, and Country of Origin

The TTP database contains interviews with 100 children of survivors. The gender distribution was similar to that of the survivors: 59% were females, and 41% were males. At the time of the interviews in the 1990s, 79% of the children were in their 30s and 40s. Only 10% were over 50, and just over 10% were below the age of 30. The majority of the children, 76%, were born in the United States.

Marital Status, Children, and Socioeconomic Status

Unlike the survivors, all of whom had been married at one point in time, 16% of the children of survivors were still single at the time of the interview. However, 76% were married. Of the married children, 24% were childless at the time of the interview. This figure is reflective of the fact that several of the children in our sample had only recently married. The bulk (34%) of the children of survivors had two children. As with the survivors, the majority (86%) of the children identified themselves as middle class.

Religion

As is expected from demographic trends in the Jewish community *(Jewish Population Study of Greater Philadelphia*, 2009), the children of the survivors were more likely to be more liberal in their religious affiliations than their parents. This study, conducted in 2009, presents a demographic view of the Philadelphia Jewish community in 2009. While 45% of the survivors were Conservative Jews, only 35% of the children were. In our sample, 28% of the survivors were Orthodox, while only 16% of the children were. However, while 24% of the survivors were Reform, Reconstructionist, secular, or unaffiliated Jews, 38% of the children identified with this group; 11% did not identify their religious affiliation.

Grandchildren of Survivors: Gender, Age, and Country of Origin

Of the 36 grandchildren of survivors that we interviewed, 21 or 58% were female, and 15 or 42% were male. At the time of the interviews, mainly conducted in the 1990s, 47% of the grandchildren were between the ages of 9 and 17; 39% were between 18 and 21, and 14% were over 21. The oldest grandchild we interviewed was 27. Unlike the survivors and the children of the survivors, all 36 were born in the United States.

Marital Status, Children, and Socioeconomic Status

Reflecting the young age of most of the grandchildren in the sample, none was married, and none had had any children. In comparison to the survivors and even the children of survivors, the grandchildren reflected the rising economic and social status of Jews in the late 20th century in the United States. Ninety two percent identified as middle or upper-middle class, 8% as wealthy. No grandchild in the sample claimed to be poor or low income.

Religion

Almost half of the sample chose not to identify their religious affiliation. Of the remaining 58% that did, 28% of the grandchildren stated that they were Reform, Reconstructionist, secular, or unidentified Jews; 8% were Conservative, and 22% were Orthodox.

References

Kotler-Berkowitz, L., Blass, L., & Neuman, D. (2004). *Nazi victims residing in the United States*. United Jewish Communities Report Series on the National Jewish Population Survey 2000–01, report 2.

Appendix 2: Characteristics of Coping Based on Life Histories

1. Temperament and personality characteristics
   - Engaging
   - Dynamic/charismatic
   - Energetic
   - Anxious
   - Intelligent
2. Positive beliefs about self
   - Self-efficacy
   - Self-confidence
   - Self-respect
   - Integrity
   - Strong self-esteem
   - Self-reliant
   - Autonomy/independence
   - Courage
   - Responsibility
3. General beliefs/faith
   - Belief in G-d
   - Prayer
   - Rituals
   - Jewish identity, link in chain of history
   - Expresses emotion in prayer and song
   - Optimism
   - Value of life
   - Work ethic
   - Trust
   - Strong value system
   - Hopefulness
   - Altruism
   - Tolerance
4. Active, adaptive coping
   - Takes initiative
   - Acts quickly
   - Takes risks
   - Resourceful
   - Fits in (chameleon ability to assimilate)
   - Shows leadership
   - Activist/fighter
   - Decision maker
   - Planner
   - Problem solver
   - Anger
   - Observant
   - Work

5. Family connection
- Parental models for good coping
- Devotion to family
- Message from family
- Selflessness toward siblings
- Parents protected them
- Strong relationships with parents
- Importance of family staying together
- Strong family bonds
- Strong parental role models
- Loving security provided by family of origin
- Went through war with family

6. External attributes
- Non-Jewish appearance
- Health
- Youth
- Attractiveness
- Developmental age

7. Prewar experiences/influences
- Only child
- Poverty, lack of food
- Early loss of mother
- Knows more than one language
- Resourceful
- Self-reliant prewar
- Strong parental role models

8. Focused endurance
- Will to survive
- Fortitude

- Self-control
- Discipline
- Determination
- Driven

9. Social connection/relational skills
- Altruistic
- Empathic
- Sociable
- Ability to accept help
- Ability to create and hold onto relationships
- People skills
- Ability to reestablish relationships
- Engages people
- Loyal
- Seeks social support
- Connected with adults
- Tolerance

10. Defense mechanisms
- Dissociation
- Compartmentalization: ability to block feelings and still act
- Repression of traumatic memories
- Minimization
- Numbing: shutting down emotions
- Denial
- Avoidance (distancing: active avoidance of negative stimuli)
- Humor
- Sarcastic humor
- Tough exterior

Index

2Gs, 4

A

Abandonment, by emotionally
  distressed parent, 194–195
Abuse survivors, 16, 55, 56, 58, 72, 74,
  79, 98–99, 161
  limitations of mediating
    parents for, 192
Acceptance, as dominant coping
  style, 182
Adaptability
  concentration camps as ultimate
    test of, 19
  and external attributions, 106
Adaptation, xii, 13, 15, 28, 40
  differential postwar, 11
  fostering by mediating parent, 175
  Karen's case study, 289
  to nuclear weapons exposure, 15
  posttrauma, 223
  systemic perspective, 235–237
Adaptive resilience, 27, 98, 101, 267
Adaptivity, 4
  post-Holocaust, 4
Adolescent survivors, 51
  experience of trauma, 29
  family messages and values, 57–58
  mastery experiences, 62–64
  men's narratives, 68–77
  prewar coping strategies, 51

and relationship to faith and ritual,
  137–138
  study methodology, 52–53
  women's narratives, 53–68
Adult Attachment Interview (AAI), 118
Adults, experience of trauma, 29
Adversarial growth, 22
Affection
  difficulty in communicating, 166
  in positive survivor families, 160
Affective functioning, 257–259, 258
  Chava's case study, 284
African National Congress (ANC), 140
Agency, 88, 92, 94, 96
  and ability to find meaning, 107
  as internal attribution, 87
Aktions, 94
Alcohol abuse, 105
Alcoholics Anonymous (AA), 100
Alicia's story, 81–82
Aloneness, comfort with, 62
Am Yisroel chai, 137
American Jews, sense of exclusion
    from, 214, 215
Anchor, loss of, 18
Angels, 93
Anger
  difficulty in expressing at survivor
    parents, 202, 229
  in father, 179, 180
  mediation of spouse's, 168
  in mother, 179